Crooked Cucumber

Also by David Chadwick
Thank You and OK!: An American Zen Failure in Japan

Crooked Cucumber

The Life and Zen Teaching
of Shunryu Suzuki

David Chadwick

Broadway Books • *New York*

BROADWAY

Broadway Books titles may be purchased for business or pro-
motional use or for special sales. For information, please write
to: Special Markets Department, Random House, Inc., 1540
Broadway, New York, NY 10036.

BROADWAY BOOKS and its logo, a letter B bisected on the diag-
onal, are trademarks of Broadway Books, a division of Random
House, Inc.

Library of Congress Cataloging-in-Publication Data
Chadwick, David, 1945–
Crooked cucumber: the life and Zen teaching of Shunryu
Suzuki / David Chadwick.
p.   cm.
ISBN 0–7679–0104–5
1. Suzuki, Shunryū, 1904–1971.   2. Priests, Zen—Japan—
Biography.   3. Priests, Zen—United States—Biography.
I. Title.
BQ988.U9C47   1999
294.3'927'092—dc21
[B]   98–46707
                                        CIP

Visit the Web site http://www.cuke.com

FIRST EDITION

Sequence of photos on page i: Shunryu Suzuki at Haneda
Airport, Tokyo, departing for America on May 21, 1959.

Designed by David Bullen
Line drawings by Frances Thompson

99   00   01   02   03   10   9   8   7   6   5   4   3   2   1

To Shogaku Shunryu Suzuki-roshi
and all sentient beings,
"wisdom seeking wisdom."

Contents

Do I contradict myself?
Very well then I contradict myself,
(I am large, I contain multitudes.)

WALT WHITMAN from *Song of Myself*

Introduction

The teaching must not be stock words or stale stories but must be always kept fresh. That is real teaching.

ONE NIGHT in February of 1968, I sat among fifty black-robed fellow students, mostly young Americans, at Zen Mountain Center, Tassajara Springs, ten miles inland from Big Sur, California, deep in the mountain wilderness. The kerosene lamplight illuminated our breath in the winter air of the unheated room.

Before us the founder of the first Zen Buddhist monastery in the Western Hemisphere, Shunryu Suzuki-roshi, had concluded a lecture from his seat on the altar platform. "Thank you very much," he said softly, with a genuine feeling of gratitude. He took a sip of water, cleared his throat, and looked around at his students. "Is there some question?" he asked, just loud enough to be heard above the sound of the creek gushing by in the darkness outside.

I bowed, hands together, and caught his eye.

"Hai?" he said, meaning yes.

"Suzuki-roshi, I've been listening to your lectures for years," I said, "and I really love them, and they're very inspiring, and I know that what you're talking about is actually very clear and simple. But I must admit I just don't understand. I love it, but I feel like I could listen to you for a thousand years and still not get it. Could you just please put it in a nutshell? Can you reduce Buddhism to one phrase?"

Everyone laughed. He laughed. What a ludicrous question. I don't think any of us expected him to answer it. He was not a man you could pin down, and he didn't like to give his students something definite to cling to. He had often said not to have "some idea" of what Buddhism was.

But Suzuki did answer. He looked at me and said, "Everything changes." Then he asked for another question.

SHUNRYU SUZUKI was a Japanese priest in the Soto school of Zen who came to San Francisco in 1959 to minister to a small Japanese-American congregation. He came with no plan, but with the confidence that some Westerners would embrace the essential practice of Buddhism as he had learned it from his teachers. He had a way with things – plants, rocks, robes, furniture, walking, sitting – that gave a hint of how to be comfortable in the world. He had a way with people that drew them to him, a way with words that made people listen, a genius that seemed to work especially in America and especially in English.

Zen Mind, Beginner's Mind, a skillfully edited compilation of his lectures published in 1970, has sold over a million copies in a dozen languages. It's a reflection of where Suzuki put his passion: in the ongoing practice of Zen with others. He did not wish to be remembered or to have anything named after him. He wanted to pass on what he had learned to others, and he hoped that they in turn would help to invigorate Buddhism in America and reinvigorate it in Japan.

BUDDHIST IDEAS had been infiltrating American thought since the days of the Transcendentalism of Emerson and Thoreau. At the World Parliament of Religions in Chicago in 1893, Soen Shaku turned heads when he made the first public presentation of Zen to the West. His disciple and translator, D. T. Suzuki, became a great bridge from the East, teaching at Harvard and Columbia, and publishing dozens of widely read books on Buddhism in English. When confused with D. T. Suzuki, Shunryu Suzuki would say, "No, he's the big Suzuki, I'm the little Suzuki."

The first small groups to study and meditate gathered with Shigetsu Sasaki on the East Coast and Nyogen Senzaki on the west. Books informed by Buddhism by Hermann Hesse, Ezra Pound, and the Beat writers were discussed in the coffeehouses of New York and San Francisco and by college kids in Ohio and Texas. Alan Watts, the brilliant communicator, further enthused and informed a generation that hungered for new directions.

Into this scene walked Shunryu Suzuki, who embodied and exemplified what had been for Westerners an almost entirely intellectual interest. He brought with him a focus on daily *zazen*, Zen meditation, and what he called "practice": zazen extending into all activity. He had a fresh approach to living and talking about life, enormous energy, formidable presence, an infectious sense of humor, and a dash of mischief.

From the time he was a new monk at age thirteen, Suzuki's master, Gyokujun So-on Suzuki, called him Crooked Cucumber. Crooked cucumbers were useless: farmers would compost them; children would use them for batting practice. So-on told Suzuki he felt sorry for him, because he would never have any good disciples. For a long time it looked as though So-on was right. Then Crooked Cucumber fulfilled a lifelong dream. He came to America, where he had many students and died in the full bloom of what he had come to do. His twelve and a half years here profoundly changed his life and the lives of many others.

ON A MILD Tuesday afternoon in August of 1993 I had an appointment with Shunryu Suzuki's widow of almost twenty-two years, Mitsu Suzuki. Walking up the central steps to the second floor of the San Francisco Zen Center's three-story redbrick building, I passed the founder's alcove, dedicated to Shunryu Suzuki. It is dominated by an almost life-size statue of him carved by an old Japanese sculptor out of a blond cypress stump from the Bolinas Lagoon. "Hi Roshi, 'bye Roshi," I muttered, bowing quickly as I went by.

Mitsu Suzuki-sensei was the person on my mind. We had been close, but I hadn't seen her much in recent years. Soon she would move back across the Pacific for good. I was a little nervous. I needed to talk to her, and although there wouldn't be much time, I didn't want to rush. What I sought was her blessing.

"Come in, David," she said in her sweet, high voice from the kitchen door at the end of the hall. I stepped inside and there she was, looking strikingly young for the last year of her seventh decade. "No hugs," she said quickly, holding her hands out to ward me off, then rubbing her ribs. About fifteen years earlier I had been a bit too exuberant in expressing my affection, and my hug must have bruised some ribs. I bowed, tipping my body as Japanese do (without joining hands), and said something polite in Japanese.

She stood almost a foot below me. Her face was round and child-like as ever, her hair long, straight, and black, with just a bit of grey here and there. She wore homemade loose pants and a blouse printed with chrysanthemums, the same material on top and bottom, an earthy brown and soft blue. The tiny kitchen was filled with knickknacks as always, the wall covered with art, photos, a calendar. After some polite chitchat about family members and about a book I'd written, I brought up the purpose of my visit.

"Some publisher may be interested in . . . it has been suggested to me that I . . . might . . . um . . . write some on Suzuki-roshi. Collect the oral history – stories about Suzuki-roshi, people's memories."

"Oh, thank you for writing about Hojo-san," she said, with the pitch ascending on the *thank. Hojo-san* is what she always called her husband. *Hojo* is the abbot of a temple; *san* is a polite form of address.

"So you really think it's okay for me to do a book on Suzuki-roshi?"

"Oh, yes, yes," she said emphatically. "Tell many funny stories."

"Umm . . . funny stories, yes . . . but not just funny. Serious and sad ones too, everything, right?"

"Yes, but people like the funny stories. Mainly you should tell funny stories. That will be good. Hojo-san liked funny stories. Everyone will be very happy to read them."

"There may be some people who don't think I should do the book."

She sat back down across the table from me and looked directly at me. "When I speak now, it is Suzuki-roshi's voice coming through my mouth and he says, 'Please write a book about me and thank you very much for writing a book about me.' Those are his words. I speak for him."

It was time to go. She offered me a green metallic frog that fit in the palm of my hand. "Here, take this," she said. "It belonged to Hojo-san. He would be happy for you to have it. He loved frogs very much," she said, drawing out the first syllable of *very*. "I'm giving everything away. When I go back to Japan I go like the cicada. It leaves its shell behind. I will do that too."

"I want to come visit you there and ask you about Hojo-san."

"No, no, no," she said adamantly. "No more English. I will leave my poor English behind me."

"Then I will speak in my poor Japanese," I said, in my poor Japanese.

"Okay, please come visit then. But keep your voice small when you do. Your voice is too big."

"Okay," I said in a tiny voice and passed her at the door, assuring her as she instinctively cringed that I wasn't going to hug her.

"Remember," she said, "tell many funny stories." Then, "Why would anyone not want you to do a book on Hojo-san?"

"Various reasons. You know he didn't want anything like that. It would be impossible not to misrepresent him. And you know what

Noiri-roshi said over twenty years ago?" Noiri was a colleague of Suzuki's, a strict and traditional priest, now old and revered.

"No, what did Noiri-san say?"

"That Suzuki-roshi was one of the greatest Japanese of this century and that no one should write about him who doesn't know all of his *samadhis* [deep states of meditation]."

"Good!" she said clapping, with delight in her voice. "There's your first funny story!"

Part One

Japan

1904–1959

Chapter One

Childhood

1904–1916

*Our mind should be free from traces of the past,
just like the flowers of spring.*

HIGH WINDS blew across the green hillside, driving rain
into the storm doors of Shoganji, an obscure Japanese country
temple, when on May 18, 1904, Yone Suzuki gave birth to a baby
boy. Her husband, Sogaku, the priest of the temple, gave his first-
born son the name Shunryu, using the written characters for Excellent and Emerging, a rather formal Buddhist name full of high
expectations.

It was the year of the dragon, the thirty-seventh year of the reign
of Emperor Meiji. Fierce battles were being fought on the plains of
Manchuria between Imperial Japan and Czarist Russia, and Sogaku
was preparing the main hall of Shoganji for yet another young soldier's funeral, as Shunryu had his first taste of life in a small *tatami*
room.

Cherry trees interspersed with shrub bamboo lined the steep

road up to Shoganji, a small four-hundred-year-old temple on a hill above the village of Tsuchisawa, on the edge of the city of Hiratsuka in Kanagawa Prefecture. From the temple *ohaka* – a peaceful sanctuary where the ashes of local families and prior abbots were interred below weather-worn stone markers – there was a commanding view of Sagami Bay, which opens into the Pacific with Tokyo Bay to the northeast. Kamakura, the ancient political and Buddhist center, lay at the edge of the green and blue vista. Shoganji's handsome grass thatch roof could be seen from afar, surrounded by forested mountainsides, just beyond the smoke of Yokohama's burgeoning industries.

AS A CHILD, Shunryu Suzuki was called Toshitaka – Toshi for short. Toshitaka is the old Japanese way of pronouncing the characters that make up Shunryu, with a softer and more casual feeling. Toshi grew up playing around the temple with his older half brother from his mother's first marriage, Yoshinami Shima. When he was three his sister Tori was born, and at six he acquired another sister, Aiko. Toshi was small yet strong, eager to learn, impatient to do things before he was old enough, sensitive, and kind but prone to quick bursts of anger. And he couldn't keep track of anything. Schoolwork and books, caps and coins – whatever it was, he'd leave it at home or at school, wherever he wasn't.

Toshi began his six years of compulsory education in April 1910, when he was almost six. It was at school that he became aware that his family was uncommonly poor. Most people wore *zori*, straw sandals with a dividing cord between the first two toes. When the cord broke on one, children would throw away both. Toshi would take the good ones home and make new pairs. Unwilling to spend money on a set of hair clippers, his father would shave Toshi's head like his own. All the boys at school had short-clipped hair, but not shaved heads.

Lean and proper, approaching fifty, Butsumon Sogaku Suzuki was old to be having his first son. Priests of the Soto school of Zen had only begun taking wives a few decades earlier, encouraged strongly by a government bent on diminishing the power of the

Buddhist clergy. The practice was easing in, though it was not yet permitted by the Soto school. At first families had to live outside the temples apart from the priests, but by 1904 it was beginning to be acceptable for families to live in. There were no family quarters at Shoganji; they slept in the buddha hall, the room used for daily services, and shared their home every day with neighbors and temple members.

Shoganji didn't have a large or a wealthy *danka*, the community of supporting members, nor did it have extensive temple lands that would bring in a sizable rice tax. Sogaku and Yone had to augment the temple income with outside work and practice meticulous thrift.

Yone was short and plain, with the tough look of a hard worker, and a softness that had withstood the rigors of a difficult life. She taught teenage girls at a vocational high school how to make clothing. She knew a good deal about sewing and would study till late at night from books to make herself a better teacher. As her reputation grew, she began sewing classes at the temple, eventually acquiring many students. Yone was the stricter of the parents. Her children were taught to be proper and respectful and to do well at school so as to make a good impression on temple guests and not to bring shame to the family.

People came to Shoganji for seasonal Buddhist holidays, for funerals, advice, or neighborly greetings. If Sogaku had guests, Yone would serve them tea and rice cakes. If he was out, she'd sit with them herself. This was in addition to tending to the children, cooking, cleaning, doing laundry, and other labor-intensive, pre-electric tasks.

SOGAKU MADE candles for the temple from an iron mold. He would pour extras, and when he had a good load he would walk five miles to Ohisa City to sell them. On the way back he would pick up discarded vegetables from the roadside, storing them in a bag he carried. It wasn't just because he was poor that Sogaku did this. It was his way. His son would talk about it half a century later.

There was a creek in front of my father's temple, and many rotten old veg-etables would float down from higher up the mountain. Farmers and other people would throw them away. They were vegetable-like things, not ex-actly vegetables! [laughing] They might have been good for compost, not for eating. But as soon as he'd find them he'd cook them up and say, "Every-thing has buddha nature. You should not throw anything away!" Wher-ever he went, he talked about how valuable food is and how you shouldn't throw it away.

Sogaku also raised pigs to supplement the family income, a rather shocking thing for a priest to do, but Japanese Buddhism in general and Soto Zen in particular have not been known for strict vegetarianism. In a 1971 talk, Shunryu Suzuki remembered the pigs.

Buddha is always helping you. But usually we refuse Buddha's offer. For in-stance, sometimes you ask for something special. This means that you are refusing to accept the treasures you already have. You are like a pig. When I was young, as my father was very poor, he raised many pigs. I noticed that when I gave the pigs a bucket of food, they would eat it after I went away. As long as I was there, they wouldn't eat it, expecting me to give them more food. I had to be very careful. If I moved too quickly they would kick the bucket over. I think that is what you are doing. Just to cause your-self more problems, you seek for something. But there is no need for you to seek for anything. You have plenty, and you have just enough problems. This is a mysterious thing, you know, the mystery of life. We have just enough problems, not too many or too few.

BORN IN Kakegawa near Hamamatsu in Shizuoka prefecture, So-gaku was from a poor farming family that for generations had also made bamboo stretchers for dyeing cloth. Despite being the eldest son, he left home as a young teenager to be ordained as a Buddhist monk and to become the disciple of a Soto Zen priest named Gya-kushitsu Sojun. Sogaku left the responsibility of providing for the family to his younger brother. Not that he was leaving home for an easier or more prestigious life. He must have been dedicated and determined, because by the time he was ordained, the Meiji Era (1868–1912) had begun, the old order was out, and Buddhism was no longer in favor with the planners of Japan's future.

Yone Shima, daughter of a priest from Hamamatsu, had been divorced by her first husband for being too independent. She married Sogaku Suzuki just after the turn of the century. When they met, Sogaku was living not far to the north in the town of Mori, in a fine old temple named Zoun-in, where he had been abbot since April 1891.

Not long after the wedding he got into a squabble with some of the temple elders over a matter concerning temple lands. A layman who helped conduct the affairs of the temple had sold off a tract of land without consulting with Sogaku or the temple elders. There was disharmony. Sogaku was embarrassed. Feeling compelled to take responsibility for the discord, he resigned and moved with his wife back to a lesser temple where he'd been before. That temple was Shoganji, and that is where he and his family would live in a sort of exile for twenty-six years.

BEFORE TOSHI was born, Sogaku had planted plum trees on the temple grounds. The boys, Yoshinami and Toshi, would help care for the vegetable gardens, prune the ornamental trees, and tend to the plants around the temple. They would sweep the leaves from the walks around the temple and clear the pathways of the mortuary ohaka, full of memorial stones standing behind offerings of flowers, burnt-down incense sticks, and cups of evaporating sake.

Toshi especially liked to help his father move stones into place around the temple and in the rock garden. He was friend to stones, rivulets, plants, beetles, worms, and butterflies. He'd sit beyond the oak trees on the low stone fence around the ohaka at dusk waiting for foxes, *tanuki* (Japanese raccoons), deer, and rodents. Massaging his mother's back in the evening, he told her and his siblings of his plans to build a zoo next to the temple; he wanted a train from the town below to run up to it, so that many people could come to visit the animals.

In spring when the rice fields were flooded and the frogs' ubiquitous croaking filled the air, children would dally and play on their way home from school. Some of the boys liked to catch frogs, insert straws into their anuses, and blow them up till they popped. When he first saw this Toshi flew into a rage, but that didn't help – the other boys were all bigger than he. So he devised a scheme. As soon as school was out Toshi would be off and running ahead with a long stick, knocking at the banks of the rice paddies, yelling and trying to scare his amphibious friends into hiding.

"TADAIMA KAERIMASHITA!" I'm back now! Sogaku would put his bag down, tip his body forward politely, and call this out when he returned home in the evening. "O kaeri nasai!" Welcome home! everyone within earshot would call back. His wife and children would come to the entryway. Sometimes he brought sweets, which Toshi was particularly fond of, and occasionally there was a special surprise, like ribbons for the girls.

Every little treat the children got, every piece of clothing they had to wear, they cherished. They appreciated it when, after a heavy winter snow, their father went down to school to walk them home. They loved it on a hot summer afternoon when he filled the outdoor iron bathtub with cold water for them to play in. And sometimes he would have a special gift for Toshi.

The skirtlike garment of the samurai is called a *hakama*. Boys wore hakama for special ceremonies at school. Toshi's mother hadn't found time to make him one, so he felt left out on ceremonial days. In December of 1912 there was to be a very important ceremony which marked the most significant historical event of Toshi's life up to that point. Emperor Meiji had died, and there would be a ceremony at Toshi's school to welcome in the new emperor and his era, Taisho, Great Righteousness.

The day before the ceremony Sogaku came home with a new hakama for his son. Excited, Toshi put it on, just as he'd seen his friends do. Sogaku insisted he'd done it incorrectly and retied the sash in a formal and old-fashioned way. None of the boys did it that way. Next morning, as soon as he passed through the temple gate, Toshi stopped and rearranged his hakama. Then he heard something behind him. Turning, he saw his father furiously running toward him waving a stick. Toshi ran away as fast as he could.

TOSHI GREW up in an atmosphere rich in ceremony, custom, and lore that defined the rules of life. Buddhist temples, Shinto shrines, schools, and families preserved and passed on stabilizing rituals that punctuated the year. Shoganji was alive with activity during the week of the Obon ceremony in late summer, when the spirits of the departed are said to return to earth. New Year was a special delight to Shunryu; he spoke of it with great fondness in his later years.

On New Year's Eve temple members and neighbors would come to strike the large bell. Sogaku would greet them, reciting with a robust voice a poem he had written for the occasion in classical Chinese style. And they'd make glutinous rice *mochi*. Children and parents took their turns with mallets, pounding the mochi in a hollowed tree stump till late at night. The next day the children put mochi rice balls on tree branches, and at the main altar Sogaku and Yone offered mochi balls stacked in pyramids on red and black lacquer trays. Inside, the oil lamps and a wood fire in the kitchen made the air taste smoky.

The children helped in the rite of renewal by collecting old decorations, small shrines, offerings, paper lanterns, and unneeded temple records. With their parents they took these old things to the neighborhood Shinto shrine on January first; there everything was piled high and mixed with what others had brought from their homes. Then on the night of the fourteenth they went to the shrine for a bonfire – burning last year's memories away and baking rice balls near the flames.

At bedtime, Yone enriched the celebrations by telling the children folktales and Buddhist legends from Japan, China, and India.

As the time of the New Year's bonfire approached she'd have their wide-eyed attention as she told of the deity who came to check up on everyone. He looked over the records of the past year, intending to turn his wrath on those who had broken the rules. But he could find no proof of any wrongdoing – the old had been burned away, and the people couldn't be punished for what they'd done.

"Oh, I'm sorry," Yone would say to the wrathful deity. "We burned it all so you can't check up on us. We'll try to be good this year. We'll be very careful! Come back next year!"

SNUGGLED UP in the evening with his brother and sisters, Toshi often asked his mother to repeat a story about a famous mythical Japanese warrior, a story he would pass on to his students, his dharma children, sixty years later.

People may say that the Japanese are very tough, but that is just one side of the Japanese personality. The other side is softness. Because of their Buddhist background they have been trained that way for a long time. The Japanese people are very kind. My mother used to sing a song that describes a hero called Momo Taro, the Peach Boy. An old couple lived near the riverside. One day the old woman picked up a peach from the stream, and out of the peach came Momo Taro. He was very strong but kind and gentle – the ideal Japanese folk hero. Without a soft mind you cannot be really strong.

My life at school was not so happy, so I preferred staying in the classroom rather than playing in the schoolyard.

SOGAKU KNEW that Toshi was having a hard time at school. The other boys slapped him on top of his bald head whenever his father shaved it, and they made jokes about his being the son of a priest. So Sogaku sat him down and told him about the Haibutsu Kishaku – the persecution of Buddhism during the Meiji Restoration. Haibutsu Kishaku means "throwing out Buddha, breaking Shakyamuni" (Buddha's given name).

In 1858, about the time Sogaku was born, Japanese crowds were overwhelmed by the sight of Commodore Perry's "black ships" in Tokyo Bay. Within a few years the ruling elite had made radical changes in policy. They decided to make Japan into a modern industrial nation-state along the lines of a European constitutional monarchy. A new all-Japanese state religion was needed. Shinto, their omnipresent, mythical, ancient animism, was the only candidate. Thus a nouveau Shintoism was created, with the emperor at the human apex of creation, regarded far more seriously as a living god than ever before. Buddhist influence was largely squeezed out. In addition to being the titular heads of Shinto, the emperors had been Buddhist for thirteen hundred years. Now the emperor was elevated to a position that was far higher and exclusively Shinto. Buddhist temples and Shinto shrines had had a close relationship for most of that period, but suddenly Buddhism was represented as foreign and contemptible, and there was a period of heavy persecution. It was an attack on the heart of Japanese culture.

Buddhist priests, however, weren't totally innocent victims. Buddhist temples had been an integral part of the shogunate government apparatus, involved with the education of the samurai and nobles. The priests had been the census takers. If anyone wanted to know about a family's background, to learn, for instance, if they were *eta* (untouchables), their records could be checked at the Buddhist temple. So Buddhism was associated with the old order. The leaders of the Meiji Restoration declared that the old class system – in fact, a castelike system – would be eliminated, to be replaced by social equality. The result was not equality but a shift in power, and Buddhist priests and temples bore the brunt of this shift. In ancient India, Buddha had rejected the caste system, and now ironically Buddhism would suffer because it had supported a caste system in Japan. Temples lost land to shrines, and during the worst year,

1868, thugs roamed around burning temples and killing priests. To this day, decapitated stone buddhas populate cemeteries as relics of the violent anti-Buddhist rages of that year. Soto Zen, one of the largest sects, although associated more with farmers than aristocrats, didn't escape this purge.

Buddhism in Japan had been subject to the designs of political leaders for centuries. Priests had been living luxurious lives in the Edo (Tokugawa) Era (1600–1867). Buddhism needed a housecleaning, and the Meiji Era provided a harsh one. It produced strong, noble Buddhist priests; because there was no status in the position, they had to be firmly committed and ready to endure suffering. The tremors of the Haibutsu Kishaku were still being felt during Toshi's boyhood. His father's historical explanation of the disrespect for Buddhism helped him to understand why he was treated badly by some of his friends.

One of the stories his father told was about a temple near his own former temple in Mori. It had a large Shinto shrine on its grounds. The Buddhist gate was burned along with the ancient guardian deity statues, and the title to the land was given to the shrine. The caretaker-priest of the shrine, who had been caretaker of both the temple and the shrine, was ordered by the government to make a bathhouse where the temple had been. He did so, and the governor came to take a bath. As he departed, the priest said to him, "Isn't it refreshing to bathe in a Buddhist-Shinto bathhouse? Buddha is so kind to make this unusual bath for you. I am amazed at his mercy." This frightened the governor, and when he went blind a week later everyone said it was because he had treated Buddhists so severely. He went to the Buddhist temple of Aburayama, known for its healing hot springs, and bathed in the waters and prayed for forgiveness and the return of his sight.

My father told me this kind of story once in a while. Being young, I was very much impressed. I couldn't have a normal life, since my friends sometimes made fun of me. Some laypeople made fun of monks and young trainees, and I saw them as my enemies. There were so many people who

did not respect Buddhism. The government's policy was to weaken Bud-
dhism and promote Shinto as a national religion. I think that is when I
made up my mind to be a priest. But not the usual kind of priest. I wanted
to be an unusual priest who could tell people what Buddhism is and what
the truth is. I wanted to be good enough to give lectures. So I determined to
be a good priest.

AT ELEMENTARY school Toshi had a teacher he greatly admired,
who encouraged him to be strong and to rise above sentimental-
ism. Toshi had doubts about being ordained by his father, who had
no monks in training anymore. His father, though very dear to
him, seemed a little weak. He often complained about losing his
temple, saying he never should have left. And he was too attached
to his son. Toshi just couldn't see him as a teacher.

My father took care of me too well, so here in my heart I always felt some
family feeling, too much emotion, too much love. My teacher at grammar
school warned me about this kind of thing. He always said, "You should
be tough."

Shunryu was always at the top of his class. His teacher told him
that he should grow up to be a great man and that the way to be a
great man was not to avoid difficulties but to use them to develop
one's greatness.

He said there were no great people in that area because the local people
wouldn't go to Tokyo and study hard, didn't have the courage to leave. He
said if we wanted to be successful, we had to get out of Kanagawa prefec-
ture. So I determined to get out.

TOSHI HAD made the first two critical decisions of his life by age
eleven: to become a monk and to leave Kanagawa. "My ambition at
that time was directed toward a narrow idea of attainment, but I

made up my mind to leave my home and to practice under a strict teacher." He had been impressed by a popular Buddhist belief that by being ordained one saves one's ancestors for nine generations back. But where should he go? With whom should he study? It was March 1916 and he had just graduated from elementary school.

This was the time when a boy's career was often decided, when he became an apprentice in a trade, began military school or some other training, or started working with his father in the fields. Very few went on to higher education, especially in that region. While it was normal for Toshi to follow in his father's profession, it was un-usual that he decided to go far away before his parents were ready to let him go, not even choosing to start with his father and move on later.

While Toshi was considering these matters, Shoganji had a visi-tor, a priest who came several times a year to pay his respects to his master, Sogaku. Gyokujun So-on Suzuki, Sogaku's adopted son, had just become the abbot of Zoun-in, Sogaku's former temple. He was like an imposing uncle to Toshi – tall, tough, exuding confi-dence. Toshi was enamored with him.

I knew him pretty well and liked him so much. When I asked him to take me to his temple, he was amazed but said it would be fine with him. I asked my father if I could go to Shizuoka Prefecture with him. He agreed, so I went to my master's temple when I was thirteen.

Toshi was actually eleven, almost twelve, at the time. He calcu-lated thirteen by the prewar counting method, wherein a person was one at birth and two on the following New Year's Day.

Although Toshi felt he was making these decisions on his own, discussions had been going on behind the scenes for quite some time. His intentions and those of his parents were in accord except for the timing. They thought he was too young to go and suggested he wait till the next year. But Toshi wanted to go right away. He pointed out that his father, Sogaku himself, had chosen to begin apprenticeship with his master at a young age. Toshi wanted to do the same.

It all happened so quickly that, to his sisters and half brother, it seemed he was being whisked away from the family. Sogaku and Yone did not want to spend the rest of their lives at Shoganji. It was right that So-on, as the first disciple, would inherit Zoun-in from Sogaku. If Toshi did well with him, he could inherit Zoun-in from So-on, and then Sogaku and Yone could retire there. If Toshi's father ordained him and became his principal master before he left, then So-on would become his second teacher and Toshi wouldn't be in line to get Zoun-in. Sogaku was too old to train Toshi anyway, and many believed that a father could not properly train his son. As the proverb went, "If you love your child, send him on a journey." So Toshi went off with his first master, Gyokujun So-on, at the age of eleven.

Chapter Two

Master and Disciple

1916–1923

*W*hen my master and I were walking in the rain, he would say,
"Do not walk so fast, the rain is everywhere."

SO-ON STEPPED off the train at the village of Mori. Behind him followed a new disciple, his young and very small devotee
Toshitaka Suzuki. They walked through the countryside and up a
hill to the temple. Carrying his belongings, Toshi climbed a steep
flight of stone steps to enter the grounds through a high old thatch-
roofed temple gate. Although he was moving only from one temple to another, he was also entering into a new setting that would
totally change his life. He showed up in the middle of the hundred-
day practice period. Eight students had joined So-on for this training, including some monks and some young trainees. Toshi was the
youngest. There were no small children or women in the temple.
While not huge, Zoun-in was much larger and more impressive

than Shoganji. There were many more rooms with tatami and wood floors, a spacious main hall with a fine central altar holding a Buddha statue and side altars for other revered figures, a founder's hall in back, and beautiful grounds, not extensive but with well-tended gardens. Toshi was taken to the room where the students slept. He put his belongings in a dark wood cabinet under which a futon was stored.

He had never before lived with such a demanding schedule. Everyone rose at four in the morning and sat zazen, Zen meditation. Then there was a service where they chanted sutras, followed by a thorough temple cleaning, which the students carried out vigorously. They dusted, swept, and wiped the woodwork down with damp cloths. They ran down the wood floors bent over, pushing the towels before them. Even in the cold morning they wore only kimonos and thin underwear – no warm layers of monk's robes. After a breakfast of white rice with raw egg, miso soup, fish, and pickles, some of the younger boys who were permanent residents went off to school. For Toshi there was work all day and then more zazen in the evening. He had to learn how to sit in the lotus posture with legs crossed, instead of the traditional *seiza,* sitting in a kneeling position with bottom on heels. He was told nothing about zazen except just to sit and not to move.

Toshi did not become homesick, because the activity at Zoun-in was so invigorating, and because he was in love with So-on. Buddhism was not what motivated him; he had only vague, simplistic ideas of what it was. It was So-on who inspired him. Toshi focused on So-on, throwing himself into serving his new master, much as So-on had served Sogaku twenty-five years before.

WHEN SOGAKU became the abbot of Zoun-in in 1891, he asked the temple elders for a young boy to be his student, and he received a fourteen-year-old orphan. Sogaku adopted the boy and ordained him, giving him the Buddhist name Gyokujun So-on and his own family name, Suzuki. Sogaku sent So-on to school, and before the turn of the century he entered the Soto Zen college in Tokyo.

After three years there, So-on went to the famous training temple of Shuzenji, on the Izu Peninsula south of Tokyo. There he studied with the great Oka Sotan, who had been the head of the Soto Zen college when So-on had attended. Oka was a recognized scholar and author of several books on Buddhism. He emphasized the practice of zazen and the careful study of Buddhist teachings, especially the precepts, the guidelines of conduct. Continuing the work of his master, Nishiari Bokusan, Oka was a leader in the resurgence of interest in studying the lengthy *Shobogenzo* (Treasury of the True Dharma Eye). This book is the masterwork of Eihei Dogen, the thirteenth-century monk and founder of Japanese Soto Zen, whose voluminous, profound writings are now generally considered a pinnacle of Zen philosophical expression. Following tradition, Gyokujun So-on received dharma transmission – authorization to teach – from his first teacher, the priest who ordained him, Sogaku Suzuki, and took his place in that lineage, but his understanding of Buddhism had matured under Oka Sotan. So-on flourished at Shuzenji and went on to become the chief administrator of the temple.

In 1916 So-on left Shuzenji to become the abbot of Zoun-in, the temple of his early training. Thus, although Sogaku had departed from Zoun-in thirteen years prior to that time, he had managed to keep it within his lineage through his disciple So-on, who had gained a reputation as a good administrator. It was not long after So-on assumed the abbotship of Zoun-in that his master's son, Toshitaka Suzuki, arrived at Zoun-in to begin his new life.

SO-ON CARRIED himself with a fierce authority. His presence was everywhere. When he couldn't be seen he was felt. So-on was the man who stood commandingly where Sogaku wished to be – in Zoun-in.

Big and strong, So-on had long practiced *kyudo,* the way of archery. One day when a guest at the temple asked So-on about an exceedingly tall bow that hung on the wall, he called his disciples and announced there would be a kyudo demonstration. He took the long, thick bow, taller than he was, and had Toshi set up a straw target. After placing an arrow in the bow with the same attention he devoted to offering a stick of incense at the altar, he pulled the string back slowly and deeply and let the arrow fly. Turning to the boys, he asked them to try to pull back the bowstring. One by one they tried but couldn't budge it, even though some of them were older teenagers, not weaklings at all. The guest then tried and couldn't bend the bow either. The demonstration was over.

So-on related to Toshi gruffly, mainly ignoring him, but also giving him some slack because he was so young. If Toshi didn't rise with the wake-up bell, nothing was said to him. He tried, but it was hard. Many mornings he'd go back to sleep, and his eyes would next open when he heard the sounds of the *Heart Sutra* coming from the buddha hall – "Kanjizai bosatsu gyo jin hannya haramita . . . ." At Shoganji he'd heard his father chant that alone in the mornings and with others in ceremonies.

Not long after Toshi's arrival, the aging Oka Sotan came with his close disciple of many years, Keiza. They were referred to reverently by So-on as Oka-roshi and Keiza-roshi, *roshi* being a term of respect for older priests. Seeing his master with them, observing the strictness with which they all conducted themselves, Toshi felt he was in the midst of the greatness he had heard of. His task in life was to be like them.

"I was lucky to be there and was encouraged by them, but the difficult thing was to get up in the morning as they did." This was the first lesson Toshi learned at his new temple. It took time, and nobody would help him, but eventually he discovered that he could do it if he jumped out of bed before he had a thought. Once he knew how, he never stopped. It became a lifelong practice and teaching of his: "When the bell rings, get up!"

Karma can change into a vow.

ON MAY 18, 1917, his thirteenth birthday, Toshi was ordained as a novice monk. He received the precepts, took the vows,
and formally became a disciple of Gyokujun So-on. He also received a set of black robes to go over his Japanese kimono: a *koromo*, the Chinese outer robe with long sleeves; an *okesa*, a large rec-
tangular cloth with finely sewn sections in seven rows resembling
rice fields, which is the sacred robe of the monk; and a *rakusu*, a
miniature and less formal okesa with straps, which is worn on the
chest and over the shoulders like a bib. He was given the Buddhist
name of Shogaku Shunryu. Shogaku, Auspicious Peak, was combined with his birth name, Shunryu, Excellent Emergence. He was
called Shunryu-san by his fellow students. So-on had taken to calling him Crooked Cucumber, a private nickname for his absent-
minded, idealistic, quirky little disciple.

Life with So-on was harsh. Even in the winter they weren't
allowed to wear *tabi,* the socks worn with zori, on the cold wood
floors where young Shunryu would often work all day. Some of the
boys would walk on tiptoe when So-on wasn't looking, so as to reduce the amount of skin that came in contact with the freezing
floor. So-on suspected that the only reason the boy was at Zoun-in
was to inherit the temple from him and to return it to his family. He
was obligated to his master Sogaku to train the little fellow, but if
the basis of his being there was such an ambition, then he wouldn't
be a good priest.

In addition, So-on still had some feelings about Sogaku, who had
been a severe and unsentimental master himself. So-on taunted
Shunryu about his father, whom Shunryu loved and felt loyal to,
and who had mellowed since the time of So-on's apprenticeship.
There was nothing Toshi could do but listen to So-on. He told the
boy how Sogaku had often hit him on the head when he was young
(a common disciplinary practice of the time) and claimed that it
had made him dim-witted. So-on said that once when he got into
mischief, Sogaku had hung him upside down on the temple gate.

SO-ON SENT Shunryu to the village upper-elementary school but did not provide him with proper clothes. His kimonos were old and tattered. A woman who lived near the temple took pity on the boy and made some new kimonos out of scraps, but they had a different pattern on each sleeve. He was so embarrassed at his appearance that he'd wear his coat even during physical education, saying he was sick. In winter he was never warm enough. Though his family at Kanagawa had been poor, and he didn't have as much as the other boys, at least his mother had always sewn him good kimonos, so he never had to suffer this sort of indignity. Zoun-in wasn't that poor a temple, so there was no reason for this except to test his endurance.

We say, "Only to sit on a cushion is not Zen." The Zen master's everyday life, character, and spirit is Zen. My own master said, "I will not accept any monastery where there is lazy training, where the rooms are full of dust." He was very strict. To sleep when we sleep, to scrub the floor and keep it clean, that is our Zen. So practice is first. And as a result of practice, there is teaching.

Instead of complaining and asking to be taken back home, Shunryu tried to show his sincerity through his actions. Taking to heart So-on's admonitions on daily practice, Shunryu applied himself with energy in each activity, especially cleaning. He vowed to clean the blackened kitchen pans and surfaces. All the boys worked in the kitchen, and some of them were lazy cleaners. So-on said that Dogen, in his instructions to the cook, had emphasized the importance of finding liberation in kitchen work. So Shunryu threw himself into scrubbing off the layers of soot that came from smoky, open-fire cooking.

Then I felt some joy in cleaning the smut off the pans. In this way each of us must have some vow; then we will find joyful mind and big mind and kind mind. When we clean because of our vow, we will find that we are kind to everyone, instead of angry. That is bodhisattva mind.

After a while little Shunryu's conscientious effort softened big So-on a bit. While continuing to be tough, imperious, and critical of Shunryu and his father, So-on began to take the boy seriously and to respect his motives.

The honeymoon phase was over. Now So-on wanted more from Shunryu than puppy love. He wanted him to listen to the intent of his teaching, get beyond his limiting idealism, meet him on the dharma (teaching) ground.

So-on told a story about the Chinese ancestor Yakusan, who emphasized to his disciples that he was not a philosopher or a scholar but a teacher of Zen. "Do not acknowledge me," he kept saying to his disciples. His point was the opposite of what he was saying: acknowledge me! His disciples didn't accept him or relate to him as a Zen teacher, but always expected him to be something else, to fulfill some other role.

It is the character or personality, the crosscurrent of teacher and disciple, that makes transmission and real lineage Zen possible. The relationship between the teacher and disciples is quite important for us. I didn't know it at the time, but the first problem given me by my master was this story about Yakusan. I could not acknowledge my master for a long time. It is quite difficult to believe in your teacher.

*O*ur *practice should be based on the idea of selflessness. Selflessness is very difficult to understand. If you try to be selfless, that is already a selfish idea. Selflessness will be there when you do not try anything. When you are practicing with a good teacher, you will naturally be not so selfish.*

THE BOYS were cleaning out the temple pond, scraping the mud from the bottom. So-on was working at the edge. Shunryu reached down and caught a little goldfish and noticed that there was a tiny worm attached to it. He had learned about this worm in school. He held the fish up, pointed to the worm, and proudly said for all to hear, "This is Mijinko!"

"Shut up!" So-on barked at him.

Shunryu didn't understand why So-on had shouted at him, but much later he told the story to show how So-on was always watching, ready to pounce on any sign of selfishness.

To encourage a student by setting a good example is one sort of mercy. To shout at me when I was proudly showing off was another sort of mercy, another kindness.

SO-ON DID not have any particular teaching or system, and his students were often in the dark about what they should be doing or how they should be doing it. Suzuki said that So-on was usually silent, so much so that his disciples had to learn most things on their own, just watching what he did. But they weren't necessarily supposed to be doing exactly what he did, so they'd get nervous and feel lost. Suzuki said they actually developed a liking for the sound of So-on's scolding voice, because then they knew what to do. How to clean a pond with concentration and selflessness was one thing, but So-on was also mute when it came to more complicated subjects such as how to conduct a memorial service.

The boys often went out with So-on to perform services in the homes of danka. The details of what they chanted and how they went about it were always changing. And the nuances of how to strike the bells and *mokugyo,* the wooden fish drum, how and when to bow, and so forth were so various and subtle that they could never do it quite right. Right in front of a family seated solemnly before them, So-on would look over at Shunryu hitting a bell and would suddenly growl, "What are you doing?" Then he'd take the striker out of Shunryu's hand and show him how it was done. It was embarrassing, but at least in that way he'd been shown something. Later Suzuki said that through this sort of study he learned how to apply himself to new problems without preparation, developing confidence in his ability to meet situations as they arose.

Returning from such a memorial service one summer evening, having been well fed and carrying gifts of food, the boys walked with So-on on a path in the twilight. So-on had taken the tabi off his feet at the door and slipped them into the sleeve of his robe, but the boys still had their tabi on. When they reached a wooded area he told them to go first since they were wearing tabi, and it was the time of year when the *mamushi*, poisonous snakes, would be out. Mamushi are not large snakes, and tabi offer a certain amount of protection. So the boys said, "Hai!" and went ahead feeling like brave monks.

When they got to the temple So-on said, "Why don't you boys sit down?" They knew something was up but had no idea what. "I knew you boys were not so alert," he told them, "but I didn't know you were that dull. When I am not wearing tabi, why do you wear them? You should have noticed." Then the boys were deeply ashamed. They were not supposed to be dressed more formally than their teacher. This subtle and indirect way of communicating is what Suzuki-roshi later called "learning to listen to the other side of the words."

So-on KEPT cakes and other goodies on hand to serve to guests who dropped by the temple. The boys, usually hungry, were always pilfering these treats. He kept hiding them in new places, but his young disciples would find them. Once he put a jar of sugar high on a shelf in the kitchen. They saw it and figured out what it was. They brought a table over and put a short ladder on top of that. One of them got on the ladder and another climbed on top of him and grabbed the pot, but before he could get down they lost their balance and came crashing to the floor, breaking the pot. That got them a tongue-lashing.

They'd find a cake and take off little slices so that he wouldn't notice; later they'd go back and cut the corners off; finally they'd realize that they were going to get caught anyway, so they'd divide it up and eat it all. He wouldn't get angry at them for this sort of mischief, but if he thought someone had taken something to eat all by himself, he'd get very angry.

Once So-on put a large persimmon in the rice so it would ripen there. When he came to get it, it was gone. He asked who had eaten it. Shunryu said he didn't know. So-on found out who ate it and gave the thief hell – not because he took the persimmon, but because he hadn't shared it. Shunryu regretted that he hadn't taken the blame.

SUZUKI'S FAVORITE story about his novice days with So-on was a cautionary tale, not of selfishness but of discrimination, and of pickles gone bad. At Zoun-in pickles were made to eat year-round but especially in the winter, when there were few fresh vegetables. There were pickles made from cucumbers, carrots, eggplants, cabbage, and daikon, the giant white radishes. A batch of *takuan*, daikon pickles, had been undersalted and had gone bad. So-on was told about it. He was just like Sogaku when it came to food. He wouldn't throw it out. "Serve it anyway!" he ordered. So for meal after meal decomposing daikon were served, and the pickles were getting worse with the passage of time. One night when they could take it no more, after they were sure So-on was asleep, Shunryu and a couple of cohorts took the pickles out to the garden and buried them.

The boys were pleased with themselves, thinking they had gotten away with their prank. But a few days later when they sat down for breakfast at the low wooden table, So-on brought in a special dish – the rotten pickles back from the dead! So-on ate the pickles with them. Shunryu gathered his courage and took the first bite, then the next. He found that he could do it if he didn't think about it. He said it was his first experience of nondiscriminating consciousness.

If we have surrendered to our master, we employ all our effort to control our mind so that we may exist under all conditions, extraordinary and ordinary.

The pickle saga wasn't quite over, though. The boys decided to boil them to see if that helped. It did; they were much easier to eat. So-on said, "What is this? You boys must have cooked something extraordinary!" And then they all ate the cooked rotten pickles together. He never asked his students to do anything he couldn't do himself.

Sometimes it is better for your teacher to be mean, so you don't attach to him.

WHEN SHUNRYU arrived at Zoun-in there were eight boys studying with So-on. After the first year there were only four, and midway through the second year they too had gone. So-on was not just hard on Shunryu; one by one the boys had been driven away by his imperious manner and the privations they had to endure with him. Now it was just Shunryu and So-on. He had a lot of responsibility for a fourteen-year-old. There was schoolwork, cooking, cleaning, memorial services in homes, assisting with ceremonies at the temple, and serving So-on and his guests. Shunryu was lonely without his friends, but he was getting lots of personal attention. That often didn't work out the way he wanted it to. For instance, he had some resistance to making full bows, down on the knees with forehead descending to touch the bowing cloth and hands extended palms up. So-on noticed Shunryu's resistance and told him that from that day, instead of bowing three times to Buddha at the end of the services, they would bow nine times.

Sometimes being alone with So-on did work out to Shunryu's liking. He got to work more in the gardens and to move stones with So-on, who was a rather accomplished stonemason. On a trip to Shuzenji a monk had shown Shunryu the bell tower, the stone base of which So-on had built when he was young. The monk said that a master stonemason had inspected it and commented that it was built by an amateur. He knew, because it was too precise.

A HARD PART of being alone with So-on was that now Shunryu had to carry everything when they went places. One day there was a service in the next valley, a few miles away, and So-on sent Shunryu ahead with a small trunk and a bag of scrolls. So-on went down to the village to get a *jinrikisha,* the two-wheeled taxi of the time that was pulled by a man on foot. Shunryu stopped to rest his feet on the way and went down to a riverbank to catch frogs and let them go. Enjoying himself, he forgot the time till he saw So-on crossing a bridge on a jinrikisha. Shunryu hid till So-on had passed, then took the shortcut over the hill. He arrived huffing and puffing just before his master. After a ceremony and a short sermon, they ate a big meal, and So-on headed home. Shunryu received an offering envelope from the family. The scrolls were to stay there so he thought his trip back would be lighter, but the wife gave him a box with melons and a pumpkin. Then she said, "As it's so hot, how about this watermelon?" So he thanked her and trudged back to Zoun-in loaded down with gifts. Day after day it was like that.

"I saw you under the bridge playing," So-on said, wagging a finger at Shunryu. "You crooked cucumber. You're sticking with it but I feel sorry for you. You're such a dimwit."

Shunryu wanted to leave So-on just as the other boys had. But he couldn't go back home now. Actually, his parents would have loved for him to come back, but he didn't see that as an option. He had visited his family a couple of times since his ordination, and his father had been proud to see his son greet him so properly and formally with his hakama skirt tied correctly. There had been no complaints from Shunryu's lips or talk of his return.

My master always called me "You crooked cucumber!" I understand pretty well that I am not so sharp. I was the last disciple, but I became the first one, because all the good cucumbers ran away. Maybe they were too smart. Anyway, I was not smart enough to run away, so I was caught. For study-

ing Buddhism my dullness was an advantage. A smart person doesn't always have the advantage, and a dull person is sometimes good because he is dull. Actually there is no dull person or smart person. They are the same.

"DON'T COMMIT adultery, Crooked Cucumber!" Shunryu had been admiring an old tea bowl, and that is how So-on told him not to be so attached to fine things. He used that metaphor a lot with the boy, who had good taste in antiques and craftsmanship. Shunryu found it funny, because there were no women living in the temple, but that wasn't the point. It was not that Shunryu shouldn't appreciate beauty, just that he shouldn't be caught by it. The irony about So-on's choice of words was that there was a woman in So-on's life. She wasn't living in the temple, but she visited a lot. And she was married.

Her name was Yoshi Marushichi. The daughter of a family in Mori that sold tofu, she had married a local rice merchant whose family was associated with Zoun-in. She was smart and attractive, with a reputation for flattering others to get her way. So-on was much more interesting and manly than her husband, who was older and in poor health. So-on was forty-one at the time and she twenty-eight. Shunryu knew her pretty well. She'd been spending more and more time at the temple, and she'd caught on to So-on's habit of kicking the boy around. People said they treated Shunryu like a stepson. They used him to relay messages back and forth. It wasn't really his calling. He'd get to the rice shop and realize he'd left the letter back on his desk, and several times he lost letters. Yoshi got very angry with him about that, and So-on had a fit. This might have been the reason that everyone knew about their relationship, though any type of secret would have been hard to keep in such a small community. No one did anything to stop their trysts, but there was general disapproval. It was a contributing factor to So-on's loss of students.

One day So-on sent Shunryu to the rice shop with a gift for

Yoshi, and she sent him back with a covered wooden tub of a special, high-quality rice cooked with edible mountain orchids. Shunryu had to smell the delectable fragrance all the way to the temple but had been instructed not to taste it. He didn't like being their go-between, but he accepted the situation and continued serving his master. As things began to get uncomfortable around Mori, a new development relieved the situation.

IN 1918 SO-ON was asked by his superiors in the Soto sect to become the abbot of a temple named Rinso-in on the outskirts of Yaizu, a coastal town about fifty miles northeast of Mori toward Tokyo. He would be responsible for both temples, but a junior priest could handle most of his duties at Zoun-in. He wasn't being sent to Rinso-in just to get him out of Mori. Rinso-in was a moderately important temple that needed rejuvenation. It had seniority over two hundred branch temples in the area and had around five hundred danka families. In the Meiji Era it had gone downhill and never really recovered, but before that time it had been a bustling training temple. It was spacious and had a *zendo* (zazen hall), a bell tower, and much surrounding land that brought in revenue through rice payments from the tenant farmers.

The prior abbot had not managed the temple properly and had resorted to selling temple possessions to make ends meet. It had become dilapidated: the thatch roof had to be replaced, all sorts of structural work needed to be done, and foxes and badgers had taken to living in some of the back rooms, where the shoji screens had not been repaired for years. Many members had switched to other temples. Rinso-in needed to be pulled back together in every way, a job that would take years. So-on had a reputation with the Soto elders as a man who could do that. And the assignment would also get him out of Mori.

Shunryu would go with him. It was almost time for him to leave Mori's upper-elementary school. The plan was for him to attend the best middle school in the prefectural capital of Shizuoka, just a short train ride north. But he failed the entrance exam, a great embarrassment, so So-on told him to take a year off from school. He could study for the next test while at Rinso-in.

With Shunryu's help So-on started getting Rinso-in back into decent physical shape and improving Rinso-in's relationship with its branch temples. Members started returning, and the temple came back to life socially and spiritually. So-on made sure the farmers on temple land paid the proper share of their rice crop to the temple, going so far as to glower over them as they divided it up, grunting if he didn't feel the temple had gotten its due. He was known for his large stature, his air of importance, and his strict manner. The residents of Takakusa village, immediately below Rinso-in, were grateful for the restoration of prestige to their neighborhood and paid So-on the respect due to such a priest.

Families started to send their boys to So-on for training, so Shunryu was no longer alone with his master. So-on's nephew, Soko, had come and taken his uncle as his master. There was a new disciple named Kendo Okamoto, to whom Shunryu became close. Two of Yoshi's nephews began to study with So-on too, which indicated that her family didn't mind their relationship. Shunryu was now the senior *unsui* ("cloud water," or novice).

So-on was well educated and perhaps felt bad about Shunryu's school situation, for he started giving occasional classes to the boys in Japanese history and the Chinese classics. He taught them to read and write old Chinese. This helped prepare them to study Buddhist texts, Chinese poetry, and calligraphy with other teachers who would come to the temple.

Every morning they'd sweep the temple road down past the farmhouses till it looked as if it had been paved. They collected firewood from the woods above and helped So-on to plant more trees there. In spring they picked the top tender tea leaves from the rows of dark green tea hedges on the mountainside. They swept and wiped the temple clean daily and tended the gardens and ohaka, where the ashes of priests and danka were enshrined.

ONE DAY Shunryu's father showed up at Rinso-in and had tea with So-on. He asked for Shunryu to come home to visit his ailing mother. She missed him terribly, and Sogaku was afraid she would not get better if she didn't see her youngest boy. Sogaku missed him too, though he didn't express it so dramatically. But when Shunryu arrived home with his father, Yone immediately got well, and it was clear that the "illness" was just a ruse to get him there.

Shunryu's parents asked if he wanted to live at home again. Having heard many things through the clerical grapevine, they were upset about So-on's treatment of their son, uncomfortable about the affair with Yoshi, and dismayed that Shunryu had failed his middle-school entrance exams. Sogaku had not had such opportunities and wanted his son to have a good education. The school at Mori had been inadequate, as its students generally didn't go on to higher education.

Shunryu wished to stay with his master, and it was hard to argue with him, since he had become such a fine young monk. His manner did not attest to abuse, and his parents still believed that he could best train away from home in order to one day take over Zoun-in. They were torn between feelings for their boy Shunryu and the monk Shunryu. He decided for them. After staying a few days he bid his parents farewell and returned to Rinso-in.

SO-ON ARRANGED for his students to study with another teacher for a while, a Rinzai Zen teacher. Before they left, So-on had some words of advice: Don't forget beginner's mind; don't stick to any particular style of practice. When you go to a Soto temple, practice the Soto way; when you go to a Rinzai temple, practice the Rinzai way. Always be a new student.

They studied a completely different type of Zen, which emphasized attainment of *satori,* sudden enlightenment, through assiduous concentration on meditation teachings called *koans,* which pose such questions as "What was your original face before your parents were born?" The boys were excited by the challenge. They were to concentrate on their koans in zazen and throughout the day. They weren't to talk about them though. Shunryu endured the rigorous Rinzai training but had trouble with his koan. Every morning and evening during zazen, he'd take his turn to visit the teacher, bowing before him, reciting the verse of his koan, and presenting his answer. One day one boy passed, then another, and finally all but Shunryu had passed their koans. He became distraught. On the day they were to leave he had still not passed his koan, and there were to be no more interviews, just a closing ceremony for their period of instruction. Just before the ceremony Shunryu went running into the master's room and yelled out one last attempt to answer his koan to his master's satisfaction.

"Okay! Okay! You pass!" the master said. Shunryu was happy, but later he felt that he didn't really understand the koan and believed the master had just passed him to be nice. This left him with an unsatisfied feeling about koan practice, although he continued to read and reflect on them all his life.

YOSHI MARUSHICHI's husband had died. Leaving her teenage son in care of the family, she moved into Rinso-in. She did so formally but at the same time rather secretly – formally in that she took a new name, Shuko, which sounded like a nun's name, and was adopted as a Buddhist practitioner into the home of a Yaizu family that would be responsible for her while she lived at Rinso-in; secretly in that she stayed in the temple as much as possible and did not socialize on the outside. So-on made their living quarters off-limits to the monks; they ate their meals together and sat around the warm hibachi in the evenings separate from his disciples. Even though she wasn't particularly friendly, her presence did improve the atmosphere of the temple, and So-on himself became softer. The food improved, too.

Everyone knew about Yoshi. They didn't know if she was a nun or cook or So-on's mistress. What they did know was that So-on was a man of character who did things in the proper way, and Yoshi's residence at the temple had occurred discreetly, in a recognized and traditional way. She was known as the Daikoku-sama of Rinso-in.

Daikoku-sama is one of the seven gods of good fortune. He is not enshrined on the Buddhist or Shinto altars in homes or temples; his altars are in kitchens or entryways. According to legend, he stays at home when the other five good-luck gods go to Izumo in October for the gathering of the gods. Daikoku represents bounty and is pictured sitting on bales of rice. In the Edo Era, Buddhist priests did not marry, but temples were busy places, and the priests in many cases were somewhat worldly. Women began living in the temples, to work and, at times, to love. They did not show their faces because they weren't supposed to be there to begin with. These women were often called Daikoku-sama.

I don't trust anything but my feet and my black cushion. My feet are always my friends. When I am really standing on my feet I am not lost.

SHUNRYU SAT nodding in the train. It was 1921. He was sixteen and wore a dark blue school uniform. Beside him was a backpack. He was dreaming of one good woman. So-on had at times spoken of "one good woman," an old woman in whose home he did services once a year. She worked hard at home doing chores all day for her son and his family, and as soon as the chanting started she would fall asleep. Even though she was nodding while So-on was chanting, she never missed hitting the bell at the right time. He said she never missed because she didn't stick to her personal problems. She looked sleepy but was alert. There were a lot of stories like this in the monasteries, and they inspired Shunryu. He himself had learned how to get up on time without an alarm clock, and that had been a revelation to him. It made him trust his body and mind to take care of him. When the train stopped at the station, he woke up and got off.

IN 1919, WHEN Shunryu was fifteen, Sogaku and Yone killed the deal with So-on and took their son back to Shoganji from Rinso-in. This time Shunryu had agreed, as had So-on. In the minds of Shunryu's parents, maybe he'd get Zoun-in down the road and maybe he wouldn't, but it wasn't worth sacrificing him for it. Yone had been complaining about her son's mistreatment for some time. Sogaku hadn't been so vocal, but as far as he was concerned, So-on had been treating Shunryu as though he were a nuisance. Three years was enough.

Shunryu had passed the entrance examinations for middle school at Kaisei Chugaku, a first-rate institution. He commuted there by train. He'd have to redo most of the courses he'd taken in Mori, with classmates three years younger than he. This wasn't unheard of at the time. In the countryside, anything past elementary school was higher education, and the few youngsters who went on, did so as they could.

When not in class at Kaisei, Shunryu helped his father with temple duties, performed services in people's homes, and gave his father the envelopes of money he received. He got special treatment at home and accepted it. He had gotten used to that as a monk and as a male. His mother would make him special meals, different from what his sisters got.

For the first time he had friends who weren't monks and who did the normal things that boys do. When it got hot he could be found with a schoolmate cooling off in the temple pond. He joined a boating club. One day a boy he knew drowned when his boat turned over. It took Shunryu a while to get over it; he couldn't swim either.

Friends would come by the temple and they'd exchange plants. Once he brought home a tree so big he needed help to carry it. After school on snowy winter days, still carrying his school bag, he'd brush the snow off the branches and leaves of the flora around the temple before going inside.

Even into his late teens Shunryu's faults remained. Despite his kind nature he had a short temper, though fortunately his bursts of anger would rise and fall quickly. He was a fairly quiet person until he got into an argument, and then he could be explosive.

Shunryu had a compulsive weakness for sugar, an expensive item that laypeople often gave to the temple as an offering. Shunryu regularly raided the big pot where it was kept, and when he got to the bottom he'd add water and drink the rinse. After his mother put a stop to that, he hid a can of sugar by his desk so he could make hot sugar-water.

But Shunryu's most notorious weakness was absentmindedness. He'd lose everything but his books and his mind. Everybody loses umbrellas, but Shunryu lost them in record numbers, mainly on trains. Once his mother stayed up all night making him a coat. She watched him walk off, with his gaitered legs and new coat, down the hill toward Hiratsuka, where he got the train for Kaisei. He came home that evening without the coat.

My habit is absentmindedness. I am naturally very forgetful. I worked on it pretty hard but could not do anything about it. I started to work on it when I went to my master at twelve. Even then I was very forgetful. But by working on it steadily, I found I could get rid of my selfish way of doing things. If the purpose of practice and training is just to correct your weak points, I think it is almost impossible to change your habits. Even so, it is necessary to work on them, because as you do so, your character will be trained and your ego will be reduced.

WHEN THE six-week summer vacation arrived, to his parents' surprise Shunryu was off on a train to Yaizu to be back with So-on. He would continue to go there whenever he could to help out at Rinso-in and at Zoun-in, sometimes missing school. Shunryu had no intention of quitting his study with So-on, but he was getting a new perspective by living away from intense temple practice; the absence helped him realize how wonderful it was. So-on used to emphasize Dogen's teaching of beginner's mind, and this is when Shunryu first experienced it, because he was losing it. During this period he experienced a sort of temptation, a clinging to purity and an attachment to Zen. He was becoming aware of Buddhism in a new, self-conscious way.

When we were little boys, we were all innocent buddhas, even when we were sixteen or seventeen years old. But Zen can be dangerous to innocent minds. Such minds may easily see Zen as something good or special by which they can gain something. This attitude can lead to trouble. An innocent young person can become careless of his buddha nature and instead attach to an idea of innocence, creating problems for himself. We need beginner's mind, not innocent mind. As long as we have beginner's mind, we have Buddhism. If we know our unchanging original nature, we can believe in the innocence of beginner's mind. At the same time, we should beware of slipping into hell through attachment to this or any idea.

So-on had his own ways of dealing with Shunryu and his fellow monks thinking they were special. Every now and then he'd tell them, "You stinky boys, wash your underwear!"

AT SCHOOL Shunryu's favorite subject was English. He excelled at it. He'd always been interested in foreign things, true to his crooked nickname. The cucumber is *kyuri* in Japanese, the barbarian gourd. He did so well in English that a doctor named Yoshikawa in Mori asked him to tutor his sons in English. Shunryu had known the Yoshikawas since his early days at Zoun-in. He used to patrol the doctor's private forest and come back to report that all was okay, a pleasant task. Dr. Yoshikawa became Shunryu's sponsor, giving him spending money and friendly advice. When Shunryu got pleurisy the doctor kept him in his home till he was well. Dr. Yoshikawa didn't want Shunryu staying with So-on at Rinso-in when Shunryu was sick, because he'd end up obediently serving So-on and neglecting himself. Shunryu would come home feverish and coughing and report that he'd been up late the night before tending So-on's smoky hibachi while his master played *go*, an ancient board game played on a grid with black and white stones.

ONE EARLY autumn day when he was seventeen, Shunryu left Zoun-in in the morning and walked to the station in Mori to get the train to Rinso-in. After just missing it, he decided to keep walking. He walked all the way, about forty miles, arriving that night. Shunryu's youth was full of walking. In that respect he had more in common with his ancestors than with modern people. Walking made him the man he became, as did his parents, teachers, and karma. Yet he saw the prior generations as the strong walkers.

Before his father's time, only nobles, ranking samurai, and important civil servants could ride on horses or be carried on palanquins. Everyone else walked; it was not only how they got to town and around town, it was also how they got from town to town. Shunryu grew up hearing walking lore. He heard of old women who walked to Tokyo to pray for the emperor and of monks who walked fifty miles to chant sutras on mountaintops. He liked the story of Buddha's disciple Mokuren, who was not only a scholar but a yogic walker who appeared in so many places it seemed that he must have flown through the sky.

Shunryu liked to tell a walking story about his father. One Saturday while Shunryu was at Rinso-in, one of the most dramatic and tragic events in modern Japanese history occurred. The first day of September is a traditional day of bad omens, and on Saturday, September 1, 1923, the great Kanto earthquake devastated Tokyo and Yokohama. It was a hot, windy day. Well over half of the buildings in those cities were completely destroyed by the quake and by the blazes that followed. A hundred thousand people died. The quake was strong in Hiratsuka. Sogaku was in the tub when it struck, and the water sloshed back and forth. An unusual butterfly danced around him. He became convinced that it was a sign that Shunryu had died. Soon word spread to the temple of the severity of the quake. The sky was filling with smoke.

The Suzuki family was distraught. That morning Shunryu was to have left Rinso-in to return home. They calculated that he might well have been on a train in the Hakone tunnel when the quake struck. The damaged tunnel had been closed. Fears raced through their minds. Communication and transportation were either cut off or restricted to emergency use. The family waited for Shunryu to arrive. They sent a letter and waited days for an answer. Finally Sogaku headed out on foot. Yone wanted to go with him, but she was not in good enough condition. He crossed the mountain Hakone-san, all the way to Yaizu and Rinso-in, where he found Shunryu, who was fine. He spent a day with his son, then walked the seventy-five miles back to tell the family the good news.

Chapter Three

Higher
Education

1924–1930

*E*ven a mistaken approach is not a waste of time.

IN APRIL 1924 Shunryu Suzuki was almost twenty. Having skipped his last year at Kaisei, he was now a junior at the Soto preparatory school in Tokyo, living in the dorm and studying hard. In terms of age, he was still way behind because of all the time he'd spent serving So-on and helping with the two temples. But that was not considered a handicap. This school was attached to the Soto college, where Soto Zen monks from all over Japan came to get the degrees now required by the government.

Shoganji wasn't far away. One Sunday on the way back to school after visiting home, Shunryu got off the train in Yokohama to see a section of the bustling port city that was said to have a few fine shops selling antique ceramics. Dressed in his quasimilitary-style school uniform he ambled about, following his fancy and eating an occasional sweet. One shop led to another and one street to the next; by and by he found himself among storefronts exhibiting all kinds of imports: clothes, shoes, jewelry, records, and books. He looked long at a magazine that had photographs of San Francisco and carefully made out the captions below. He wandered on past sidewalk tables full of Japanese items bound for export: cups, paintings, umbrellas, toys, and tables, and all of it junk – tasteless, gaudy junk. He felt a profound embarrassment that this was what Japan was offering to the world. It wasn't really Japanese; it was superficial, pseudo-Japanese.

Shunryu thought about what he considered really Japanese: handmade crafts, furniture, scrolls, and ceramics that embodied the culture and traditions and would add to the harmony of the house they went to. Then he had a little epiphany: if only he could go abroad and bring to foreign people not the worst of Japan but the best – something truly Japanese that could be applied to another culture. The best way to do this would be to completely understand Zen first and then bring Zen to others. Maybe, he thought, maybe I could do that.

IN EARLY July Shunryu was hanging out on a sweltering, muggy Sunday afternoon with his friends Kundo and Araki, playing go, sweating and fanning himself. He was a man now, over twenty, the age of majority in Japan. But they were still kids in school, with less responsibility than they had had before they arrived. Now they had only to concentrate on their studies. Shunryu suggested that he go liberate a melon from the cold-storage room in the basement off the kitchen. His fellow monks heartily agreed.

Shunryu switched on the light for the basement, then for the storage room. He went in, closing the door behind him. Beneath the low ceiling were shelves filled with tubs of tofu, barrels of pickles, boxes of vegetables, fish, meat, and fruit. He picked a nice ripe melon by the wall at the end. Then he froze: footsteps were coming down the stairs. There was no place to hide. A voice called out. Silence. Then a click and another click, and Shunryu was holding a melon in total darkness. He waited a moment, then started walking back toward the door. Suddenly there was a piercing pain above his left eye. He jerked and screamed, dropped the melon, quickly got his balance and reached up. He felt sharp, cold steel and blood. He had snared himself on a hook hanging from the ceiling. He couldn't extricate himself, and every move he made worsened the situation. Finally his breathing slowed down and he stood there in pain like a statue, unable to budge, blood dripping down his uniform. He waited for over an hour till he heard someone coming down the steps again and called out for help.

No one was angry at him for his escapade. Like him, they were worried that he'd blinded his left eye. He hadn't. The hook had gone in through the eyelid and out over the eyebrow. He lay in his bed that evening, stitched up and bandaged like a pirate, and reflected on the events of the day. He ached, but something wonderful had happened. All that he would say later in his life is that he had had an important awakening experience. He wanted to return to the clear, inexpressible, and timeless calm he had felt as he stood there, dripping blood. At the time he thought it was the great enlightenment. He would learn later that it was just a little one, and he would find that he could not re-create it: that was then and this is now. For the rest of his life he would have a nifty little arch above his left eye.

FROM MID-NOVEMBER 1925 to mid-February 1926 Shunryu was in training at Kenko-in in Shizuoka City. So-on had sent him to be initiated as head monk under the guidance of Dojun Kato-roshi. Kenko-in offered the formal hundred-day practice period that is the heart of Zen training. One of the milestones of the training is the head monk ceremony. It wasn't like being head monk at one of the major training centers, where there would be many monks and teachers. At Kenko-in there were only Kato-roshi and a few novices, and Shunryu had to continue going to school during the day.

Many monks merely went through the motions of the cere-

mony for a few days at their home temple, an abbreviated formality
to move a son closer to inheriting his father's temple. But Shunryu
was head monk for the full one hundred days. Nine older priests
came to the culminating ceremony, some arriving a few days early
to participate in the practice and help build momentum for his rite
of passage. Sogaku and So-on, with a few of his disciples, were
among them.

On February 18, the day of the ceremony, Shunryu walked before them all, head bowed and arms raised, holding a staff. He recited a traditional poem, saying he felt unworthy to be there.
"Dragons and elephants," he concluded, "give me your questions!"
He thumped the staff on a block of wood. It was time to be grilled
by his peers and elders in the traditional dharma-combat ceremony.
The answers were classical, memorized by the head monk for his
ceremony. But the timing, the delivery, how he held himself, the
quality of his voice – all would add up to what sort of ceremony
this would be. It was his day. He set the tone.

Afterward there were high-sounding congratulatory statements.
No longer considered a novice, Shunryu was welcomed into the society of priests as their new young friend.

We have to study with our warm heart, not just with our brain.

IN APRIL of 1926, at the age of twenty-one, Shunryu
Suzuki had graduated from prep school and moved up to the Soto
college, which had just been renamed Komazawa Daigakurin, and
was now a university offering a wide range of study. Mainly he was
studying, but he commuted regularly to spend time with So-on in
Yaizu, and he could not ignore the vast and fascinating world that
was springing up around him in Tokyo.

Shunryu watched movies with his friends, played tennis and go,
and went rowing in the bay. He studied Chinese astrology but finally

gave it up, deciding it was unnecessary to know so much about one-self. Even if it were true, he felt it was not a Buddhist practice. He went to the coffee shops and attended school in an atmosphere of "dangerous ideas." He was in Tokyo at just the right time to have his curiosity and humanity fertilized.

Tokyo in the twenties was an uneasy mix of the traditional, the foreign, and the experimental – the scene of a tug-of-war between old and new, with each side pulling hard since Japan's sudden emergence from isolation. Businessmen wearing Western suits and women in dresses mixed with those in traditional costume. Foreign tourists were no longer a complete oddity. There were trolleys, taxis, and private cars among the jinrikishas, coffeehouses, and *pachinko* game parlors next to the noodle shops. Art and literature were breaking into new territory. Occasionally one would see a *moga* and *mobo* (modern girl and boy) in their ostentatious London and New York clothes. Some older folks called it the era of *ero guro nansensu* (eroticism, grotesquery, and nonsense), but to the intellectual elite it was a new age cracking out of the shell of the repressive past.

The emperor was an invalid and mentally feeble, but his son, Crown Prince Hirohito, who had been regent since 1921, was perceived as one of the new liberal breed. He had gone to England and France and been photographed in stylish English clothes and a tweed cap. He was a marine biologist and, with his friend the Prince of Wales, had helped to introduce golf to Japan.

Traditionalists feared the "dangerous ideas" that had crept in from the West: internationalism, socialism, communal living, pacifism, democracy, anarchy, even women's rights. It wasn't quite legal to have organizations promoting radical causes, and the police discouraged them as they could, but there wasn't popular support for too much control. Fifty years prior, Tokyo had been Edo, the capital of a feudal, closed Japan. Now it was the hub of the industrial giant of the East, and there were possibly more college students there than in any city on earth.

Japan was now a global power that had successfully prevailed against China and Russia in previous decades, had forged a dominant role among the imperialist nations in China, had made virtual colonies of Korea and Formosa, and had supported its Western allies in defeating the kaiser in World War I. Japanese nationalism had mellowed; there was less support for Japan's aggressive foreign interventions, which had been a little too successful in the eyes of the West.

Some Japanese hadn't forgotten the humiliation of the Triple Intervention of 1895, when Japan was forced by the West to return possessions and concessions won from China, and Emperor Meiji had urged the nation to "endure the unendurable" and do as they were told. The ultranationalists and reactionaries in the military continued to wield strong influence; there was now compulsory military training in the schools. But the prime minister and cabinet had the upper hand and were holding the right-wingers in check. Even in the face of insulting racist policies abroad, such as America's ban on Asian immigration and the League of Nations' refusal to acknowledge the principle of racial equality, there was pride in Japan's international role. The national self-confidence that was lost when Commodore Perry's ships caused Japan to come out of its cocoon had been largely regained.

THIS WAS an exciting time for Japan not only socially, but in terms of Buddhism as well. Most Japanese Buddhist priests saw Buddhism only in reference to their own culture and the past, but Shunryu was being reminded at the university that Buddhism was a universal religion that had already adapted to many different Asian cultures and subcultures, that it was not the sole property of priests but could be understood by laypeople as well.

A number of professors at Komazawa were taking a new look at the teaching of their sect and how it might be presented to a wider audience. The president of Komazawa, Nukariya Kaiten, had just published a book on Buddhism for laypeople which created some controversy because of its simple explanation of Soto Zen and its popular appeal. Nukariya had been to Europe and America and had also written the first popular book on Zen in English, *The Religion of the Samurai*. Also at Komazawa, Shunryu met a professor of Pali named Shundo Tachibana, who published *The Ethics of Buddhism* in English that year. The first book on Dogen's thought for the general public, *Dogen Shamon* (Dogen the Monk) by Watsuji Tetsuro, was also published in 1926 in Japan. It was hard enough to bring actual Zen practice to Japanese; Shunryu could not imagine how one could communicate the subtleties of Buddhism to Americans and Europeans. But he was listening.

When you can laugh at yourself, there is enlightenment.

IN HIS college dorm Shunryu awoke before the sun was up, quietly slipped on some loose work clothes, and tiptoed out of the sleeping quarters in the dark. He entered the latrine, which was lined on one side with squat toilets and a long urinal and on the other with a continuous sink with faucets every couple of feet. He crossed the room to a cabinet, took out bucket and rags, and there under the dim light of a kerosene lamp he began to clean. The room was always a stinking mess, not like those in the temples he'd lived in. Public toilets in Japan at that time were notorious for being undertended.

As a freshman at Komazawa University, Shunryu had taken it upon himself to do this onerous task before his classmates arose. As head monk at Kenko-in, one of his responsibilities had been to clean the toilets and sinks, and he was determined that in the midst of his studies and activities in Tokyo he would not forget that he was a monk. "I wanted to practice true practice, and I wanted to know what the way-seeking mind is in its true sense. I thought that to do something good might be the way-seeking mind."

It was especially important to him not to be seen. He was convinced that if others knew what he was up to, he would no longer be involved in pure practice. He'd listen for sounds of stirring and stick his head out in the hall periodically to see if a light was on. He particularly didn't want to be found out by Nukariya-sensei, the president of the school and his most important role model during this period. Nukariya stayed in a private room in the dorm during the week to be near his students, only seeing his family on Saturday evening and Sunday. He had impeccable humility and dignity. Visitors would often think he was a janitor. His presence had further inspired Shunryu to take on this lowly duty. But if his light was on, Shunryu would get flustered and make an escape.

At first he felt good about what he was doing, but more and more he analyzed the purity of his intention. He obsessed: Why am I doing this? Do I really like doing it without being noticed? Do I actually wish to be found out?

I was mixed up, and my mind was always wandering, trying to get things straight. I was not so sure of the purity of my way-seeking mind. Should I continue or not? I didn't want to have this type of silly problem, but my nature was pretty stubborn, and I didn't want to give up on something so easily.

One day in a psychology lecture the professor started talking about the impossibility of repeating experience. "You might think you can do so," his professor said, "but that's just thinking, and thinking about an experience and the experience itself are not the same." He added that it was impossible to catch the mind of the past, to know what we have done, or even to know the mind that is acting right now.

So I was enlightened, you know! [laughing] Okay! I understood that what it is not possible to think about, forget about. No wonder it was so difficult to understand my mind. I had this kind of realization. Since then I have given up trying to be sure of my way-seeking mind. I have done things just because they were good, without analyzing them. Whether or not people saw me was not my problem anymore.

Shunryu kept up his early morning cleaning of the lavatory with a more lighthearted approach. And he continued learning about the way-seeking mind from his college teachers. His years of Zen practice had opened his ears. It was necessary, he realized, to have what Dogen called "enlightenment after enlightenment with no trace of enlightenment."

Zen is the teaching of accepting "things-as-it-is" and of raising things as they go. [Suzuki often used a singular verb with a plural subject on purpose.] This is the fundamental purpose of our practice, but it is difficult to see things-as-it-is. I don't mean that there is a distortion of sight, but that as soon as you see something, you already start to intellectualize it. As soon as you intellectualize something, it is no longer what you saw.

IN EDUCATION class, a professor said something that further inspired Shunryu to drop his hindsight and foresight and live directly in each moment. He couldn't believe what the professor had said, but he checked his notes against those of a fellow student, and they were the same. "Formal education is to explain what is and what it means. Actual education is to let it be, whatever it is, without explanation." He couldn't accept that at first, but he came to see the connection – that one had to begin practice without knowing the way-seeking mind and for "a long, long time go round and round in the same area until you get tired of trying to understand."

To do something without thinking is the most important point in understanding ourselves. When you want to see, or be sure of your mind, you cannot catch it. But when you just do something, and when your mind is just acting as it is, that is how you catch your mind in the true sense.

ON AUGUST 21, 1926, in a private ceremony at Rinso-in, Shunryu Suzuki received *shiho,* dharma transmission, from So-on. He was twenty-two. In shiho the disciple receives his master's robe and his place in the lineage. It symbolizes the passing of Buddha's mind from generation to generation. Buddha meets buddha. Shunryu knew that it was just a formality and that he had a long way to go to understand the teaching of Buddha. So-on wanted Shunryu and his family to be responsible for Zoun-in, and the ceremony authorized the transfer.

Though Shunryu could now wear the brown robes instead of the monk's black, he would not yet change colors. That would be presumptuous. And though he was now his own man, he was still called Crooked Cucumber by So-on, who would continue to be in charge of his life for many years to come.

This was a big event for Sogaku as well. He retired as abbot of Shoganji, leaving it to a priest from Shizuoka, and finally moved with his wife, Yone, and daughter Aiko back to Zoun-in to be *inkyo,* retired master. So-on was still the abbot of Zoun-in in name, but Shunryu's family resided there and was in charge.

FALL ARRIVED and Shunryu's fortunes took a change for the worse. He had always had a weak constitution and was especially susceptible to respiratory illness. He'd been coughing constantly for weeks and had missed a lot of classes. Dr. Yoshikawa, his patron, was now living with his family in their Tokyo home. He visited Shunryu in the dorm and immediately had him hospitalized. He had tuberculosis, a mild case, but any case of TB was taken very seriously. It was career-threatening and life-threatening. He needed total rest and hospital care. Fortunately, the disease did not progress, and after a while Shunryu was well enough to leave. He moved out of the dorm and into Dr. Yoshikawa's house, remaining there after he had recovered, until the doctor said he could start attending classes again.

In 1926 Shunryu had completed his head monk training, entered the university, received transmission from So-on, and developed tuberculosis. One last important event in his life and in the lives of all Japanese would transpire at the end of that year. On December 25 the invalid emperor died, and his son Hirohito became the new emperor. The imperial year was no longer Taisho 12, but Showa 1, a year that would last for ten days and usher in a new era of hope: Showa, "enlightened peace."

Whatever the teaching may be, the teaching confronts each in accordance with the circumstances.

ON A HOT, muggy day in mid-July 1927, during summer vacation in his second year at college, Shunryu was on his way back to Dr. Yoshikawa's after doing some errands, when he realized he was not far from Miss Ransom's house. Nona Ransom, a striking forty-year-old woman from England, was his English teacher at Komazawa. His friend and fellow student Kundo, who lived with her, had pointed out the building to Shunryu and urged him to drop by sometime, saying she always had something cold for the intolerable afternoons. Shunryu wanted to get out of the heat, so he gathered his courage and went to Miss Ransom's. It was a formidable place, a traditional wooden house with white stucco between the beams and around the shoji, enclosed within a solid wall, and in a wealthy neighborhood in the Shibuya section of Tokyo.

He entered the gate and decided to go to the back door, having never before approached a foreigner's house. Japanese slide open the door and make themselves known with a formal greeting from the entryway. He knew the English didn't do that – they knock or ring something – so he just called out from the back door without opening it. In a moment she appeared and most graciously invited him in to a sitting room near the kitchen. It was a fine home on the inside as well. There were chairs and a high table, a Turkish rug in the hall, and it was neat and clean – more so than many Japanese homes and temples. She asked if he'd like something to drink. Shunryu said water would be fine. She went to the kitchen and came back with cold watermelon.

Shunryu had been Miss Ransom's best student right from the start of his classes with her, having studied English hard for some years, and he was eager to make the most of this precious chance to learn conversation with a native speaker. There was almost no emphasis on conversation in the study of any foreign language in Japan. The main point of such learning since the gates had opened was to read technical books in order to copy foreign technology. When the political winds blew to the right, any other interest was considered almost unpatriotic. Of course there was always the need for diplomats and translators, and there was that handful of students like Shunryu who had their own goals.

Over watermelon, Miss Ransom asked Shunryu if he might be available to assist her. She said she needed help with shopping and communicating with Japanese guests and private students. She didn't speak any Japanese and had great difficulty in communication. Shunryu tactfully pointed out that she already had Kundo and another boy living there, and they were both her English students. She said that the other boy would leave soon and that she'd like Shunryu to consider taking his place.

Shunryu started helping Miss Ransom right away. On the first of August he moved into the room with the other boys, and soon there were only Kundo and Shunryu. Dr. Yoshikawa was sorry to see him go but knew this was an important opportunity. He would continue his support, and Shunryu would likewise keep in touch and help his sons with their English studies. After a while Kundo moved out too, leaving Shunryu alone with Miss Ransom. This meant that he was busy indeed, with his schoolwork as well as her translating and various personal needs. It had soon become clear to him why the other boys didn't stay long. She was not an easy person to be with.

She was quite strict and stubborn and she tried to force her English ways on us and on Japanese people in general. And she always had some complaint. Mostly what I had to do was listen to her complaints about Japanese people – what happened at school, what happened in the car. She was always complaining about Japan. I was the only person who would listen. But I also complained a lot to her.

After his many years of study with So-on, Miss Ransom was really not so hard to take. Shunryu was enthusiastic; he and Miss Ransom were close and worked well together, despite their squabbles. At first he felt his English was not adequate, but his ability to communicate progressed rapidly, especially since there was so much talking going on, much more than he was used to in Japanese company. She had an active social life, so Shunryu not only got to translate but to speak English with other foreigners from England, America, Europe, and even China.

In that era, when a man and a woman went down the street together, it was almost always a husband with his wife walking behind him. Miss Ransom and Shunryu made a sight going down the street side by side, talking and even laughing at times. He was twenty-three that fall and she was forty. Shunryu, short among his countrymen, was four feet eleven. At almost six feet Miss Ransom was lean yet shapely, beautiful and stately, and her bowl-shaped grey hat made her seem even taller. Her nose was long and straight, her eyes round and wide, her eyebrows thick and expressive. They both walked erect, energetically, Shunryu in his uniform and she in her subdued dresses and heavy overcoat as winter set in. At first the neighbors said she had a new houseboy, but in time people said she had a live-in interpreter.

As they returned home, Shunryu would often be carrying her packages, just as he had done for So-on. In fact, Shunryu's relationship with Miss Ransom had a number of parallels to his early apprenticeship to So-on. They were both demanding, eccentric, ornery, and dignified; his life revolved around theirs; they had knowledge he wanted; and, despite their faults, he loved them. But there were differences. Miss Ransom treated Shunryu much more like an equal. She was direct and opinionated but let him speak his mind as well. She was still his teacher, landlady, and employer, and he treated her with a level of respect that satisfied her proper British standards. But he could never have talked back to So-on the way he did to her.

Shunryu was incurably curious, and Miss Ransom was quite forthcoming about her life. He learned a great deal more about her than he ever had about anyone else. She was the ninth child, born in Bedford, England, on October 5, 1887. Before coming to Japan she had spent three years in Tientsin in northern China, teaching at the grammar school for the British concession. She also tutored privately. Among her students were the children of the president of China, Li Yua Hung, and those of Shigeru Yoshida, the Japanese consul. It was through Yoshida that further doors began to open for Miss Ransom. When the former emperor of China, Pu Yi, and his wife, Wan Jung, fled the Japanese legation in Peking in 1925 and escaped to Tientsin, Yoshida arranged for Miss Ransom to be companion and English teacher to the former empress and subsequently to the former emperor as well.

Through Yoshida, Miss Ransom came to Japan in 1927 and moved into a house that his parents owned. There she taught at three colleges. She was also the "Teacher of the English Language and Foreign Etiquette under the Imperial Household." Among her students was Jiro Kano, the founder of modern judo and president of the school attended by members of the royal family.

One day Miss Ransom asked Shunryu to buy some large daffodil bulbs. When she saw what he got, she said, "These are too small, get me some big ones." So he looked all over the Shibuya section of Tokyo, going to several florists, and buying the biggest bulbs he could find. Still she wasn't satisfied. That got him angry. He came back later with a bag and told her, "I got some very big daffodil bulbs, here they are." Then he got scared and sneaked away. She was quite pleased until she opened the bag and smelled them. "These are onions!" He knew she detested onions. She started shouting and searching the large house for him. Then he burst out laughing in his hiding place, and she came at him with the onions held high. He ran up the stairs with her chasing after him, but he was faster and went to the roof and hid.

One kind word can turn over all of heaven and earth.

ON DAYS when Shunryu's classes were over early enough and Miss Ransom was not busy, they would have high tea in her sitting room. He learned about her youth and studies in England, Belgium, and France, of her graduate work in education at the Bedford Froebel Training College, where she became head of the Preparatory School, of her ten years as form mistress at the Edinburgh Institute in Scotland, and of her decision to go to China at the age of thirty-seven.

She was particularly fond of her memories of the young empress, Wan Jung, Beautiful Countenance, a lovely though tragic figure. She had married Pu Yi at fourteen, just one year older than his second wife, and when only sixteen she had latched onto Miss Ransom as a pillar of sanity in her bizarre and treacherous circumstances. A picture of the empress stood atop a chest in the corner of the sitting room.

Shunryu was curious about Miss Ransom's approach to Christianity, a subject which he knew little about. Christianity was said to be like Amida Buddhism, more faith oriented – relying on "other power" as opposed to the "self power" of Zen. Christians were generally respected in Japan as sincere and devoted to good works. Jesuits in Tokyo had founded the first university in Japan, and some of them had a keen interest in Rinzai Zen. Japanese Christians had known periods of persecution and favor, but they never made as much progress as Christians in China and Korea. Miss Ransom had no respect for Catholicism or Buddhism.

She had been born into a Quaker family. Theirs was a simple, straightforward approach to truth without many of the common forms of religion, since Quakers use no statues or images of God or Jesus and refuse to recognize any tie between state and religious authority, such as the taking of oaths.

Quakers are pacifists, and though Miss Ransom taught the children of generals, she was not fond of the militaristic trappings of governments in the East or West. She did not like the increasing role of the Japanese military that she had seen in northern China, where they had ostensibly come to guard the train lines. She especially resented suggestions by certain high officials that she might be able to use her sway with ex-emperor Pu Yi to Japan's benefit. But she said little about all this; she merely rose above it and set out to do what good she could.

AFTER HER years in China and Japan, Miss Ransom was convinced that Buddhism was a cult of idol worship, worthy of no more than a passing glance for the sake of a better understanding of history and culture. She visited sacred buildings and was quite taken by the architecture and art, the gardens and sculpture, but she shook her head when she saw believers bowing and making offerings before statues. It bothered her slightly that her houseboy was to be a priest of one of these temples. It created an uncomfortable gap between them. And then there was her statue of the Buddha.

In Japan, outdoor shoes customarily go on a wooden rack just inside the front door, before the step up into the house proper, where the indoor slippers are. Shoes or zori never touch the floors of the interior. The surface outside is dirty, outside shoes are dirty. Inside floors and slippers are clean. The two do not mix.

The statue was in the sitting room, a small attractive space with tatami floors and smooth clay walls between dark brown wooden posts. Extending half the length of the wall opposite the entrance was an alcove called the *tokonoma*. The statue sat in the tokonoma. The tokonoma is in some ways the center of a Japanese home; it is not an altar, but a nook on the floor for a flower arrangement in a treasured vase, possibly a special stone or an antique, and a hanging scroll. The tokonoma is the family's aesthetic altar to nature, art, and wisdom. Miss Ransom hung no scroll in her tokonoma, nor did she include any vase of flowers. Instead, on a stone pedestal, there was a beautiful foot-high carved Buddha statue. She made clear to Shunryu that this sitting Buddha figure was there solely for its aesthetic and sentimental values and not for any religious purposes. It had been a gift to her from Pu Yi.

Miss Ransom kept her shoes in the tokonoma as well – right next to the statue. Shunryu told himself that she was not a Buddhist and it didn't matter, but still it was hard for him to take. It embarrassed him when she'd come home from school and slip off her shoes and put them right next to the Buddha.

One morning, before he went to school, Shunryu quietly entered the sitting room where Miss Ransom sat drinking her black tea and cream. He had some tea too, hot green tea in a small Japanese cup. He held it carefully with both hands but did not sit down with Miss Ransom to drink it. Instead, he lifted it above his eyes and then placed it softly before the Buddha, bowed in *gassho* – a standing bow with palms together – and left the room as quietly as he'd entered. This is what he would later call the beginning of the cold war.

Weeks passed, and every morning Shunryu would offer tea and bow to the statue of Buddha. Miss Ransom at first just watched him, but increasingly she expressed amusement and began to tease him. He didn't try to explain himself, and she didn't ask him to. They were getting along fine in terms of shopping and meals, but the cold war persisted.

Miss Ransom would tell her guests about her houseboy's strange behavior toward the Buddha statue and the shoes next to it. The shoes were always straight, as they were in Japanese entryways, and he lined them up from the left so that they'd be as far from the Buddha as space would allow. "Shunryu's being a very naughty little boy," she said, pointing out a cup of tea before the statue. Her guests would join in the ridicule, not realizing how much he understood. Often he would find newly placed cigarette butts, burned matches, and used toothpicks lying in the Buddha's hands. He did not remove them but continued his practice of offering tea and, at times, incense.

Meanwhile, he also prepared for the hot war, the war of words, which he knew was to come. He pondered skillful means and took to studying English in his room with increased concentration. He sought help from a professor of Buddhism at Komazawa, with whom he worked out translations of basic technical terms. He made a list. In particular, he studied the vocabulary that might explain to a Westerner what Buddhism was and why Buddhists make offerings to statues.

For the first three hundred or so years, Buddhism had had no physical representation of Buddha. The Greek-influenced artisans who stayed behind at Gandhara in present-day Afghanistan after Alexander's push into India made some of the first known Buddhist icons with a human image. The idea caught on.

It might seem easier to explain Buddhism without having to justify any particular forms or practices. Dogen wrote that offering incense is a good practice but not necessary, that only zazen is necessary to follow the way. But instead of saying something like, "Oh it's just a piece of wood," as some early masters had said, Shunryu would not deny the statue, but included it as part of his practice and as a way to get through to Miss Ransom. He savored the opportunity to communicate but didn't make a move.

Miss Ransom and her friends continued to tease him; he ignored them. He knew that her curiosity was mounting and that eventually there would come a chance to explain what Buddhism is. One rainy morning in the sitting room, after several weeks of cold war, the moment he had waited for arrived. Shunryu and Miss Ransom had no classes or appointments and no desire to leave the comfortable protection of her roof and walls. As she sat sipping her tea, a silence came over her and she sighed, lost in thought.

"Tell me something please, Shunryu. Please tell me why on

earth you worship that Buddha statue. You seem like a reasonable young man and you are obviously sincere, but I just cannot understand what you find so compelling in this superstitious nonsense."

So he told her why he related to the statue with such respect, and he told her about Shakyamuni Buddha and buddhahood. He said that such a statue reminds us that the way is everywhere, and that we ourselves are buddha, so that when we offer incense to the statue we are recognizing our own true nature, the true nature of all that is. The nature of our existence is not something we can know or remember so easily. Buddha is not a god or a being who can be easily described. You can't put your finger on what buddha is, but Buddhism does have various teachings. There is, for instance, the teaching about the three bodies of buddha: the sublime, indescribable Dharmakaya Buddha, beyond any particular experience, the first principle of religion; the Sambhogakaya Buddha, the subtle body of rapture or grace, the fruit of practice; and the Nirmanakaya Buddha, the historical person who awakened under the bodhi tree. He was a person just like everyone else, who attained something wonderful that is possible for others to attain – women and men.

Maybe these aspects of buddha have something in common with the Christian concepts of Father, Son, and Holy Ghost, he explained. But to understand these bodies of buddha, or to deeply know ourselves, it isn't helpful to think about it too much. That's why Buddhists apply themselves wholeheartedly to experience direct insight of the truth through meditation and other mindful practices like chanting and offering incense or tea to a statue of a buddha.

Miss Ransom was amazed. It was not at all what she had expected. She thanked him for his explanation and praised his command of English. She said she'd had no idea that there was such profundity in Buddhism, such realization of the divinity of the individual. She was not only affected by Shunryu's explanation, but was also impressed with his composure in the delivery.

After that there was no more teasing. Miss Ransom became very quiet for a few days. Then one afternoon, Shunryu walked into the sitting room and saw that the shoes were gone from the tokonoma, and there was a fine arrangement of flowers by the wooden Buddha statue. She asked if he would tell her more about Buddhism and explain Buddhist practice. He showed her how he would clean the tokonoma, and together they went out and got some candles, incense, and an incense bowl, even a little bell, and they turned the tokonoma into an altar. He taught her how to sit zazen. She made the acquaintance of Buddhist professors at Komazawa who could speak some English and she set about studying Buddhism. Shunryu studied English all the harder and was pleased at what had happened. They were freely trading in the knowledge of their respective religious traditions. The wall between them had fallen, and she'd come walking through the opening.

This affair of the Buddha statue was momentous for Suzuki, literally changing the course of his life. He would later call it the turning point of his life. He had seen that Miss Ransom's total ignorance of Buddhism, her beginner's mind, was not an obstacle, but had made it possible for her to understand more clearly. He talked to Miss Ransom about his dream to go abroad, admitting that he had become fairly disgusted with the state of Buddhism and the attitude of many priests in Japan.

I felt very good. I developed some confidence in our teaching and in the thought that I could help Western people understand Buddhism. For Japanese people it is pretty difficult to study Buddhism in its true sense, because the tradition has been so often mistaken and misunderstood. It is difficult to change misunderstandings once we have them. But for people who don't know anything about Buddhism, it's like painting on white paper. It is much easier to give them the right understanding. I think that the experience I had with Miss Ransom resulted in my coming to America.

*M*oment *after moment, completely devote yourself
to listening to your inner voice.*

THERE WAS a Western-style rattan bed and chair at Zoun-in especially purchased for Miss Ransom's visits. Shunryu would take her to Rinso-in as well. The monks got to know the English lady, as did all the people in the villages of Mori below Zoun-in and Takakusa below Rinso-in. A foreigner in those parts was a distinct oddity. Their relationship was the first thing people would mention when Shunryu-san's name came up. The second was his absent-mindedness. Sometimes the two qualities came together. The first time Shunryu took Miss Ransom to Rinso-in he left her luggage at the Yaizu station and had to take the commercial horse-drawn buggy back five miles to get it. As Shunryu rode off, So-on called out to him as he had so often in the past, "Oh, this forgetful boy! What can we do about him?"

So-on knew just what to do about Shunryu. He gave him a lot more to keep track of by passing Zoun-in on to him, this time officially. On January 22, 1929, at the age of twenty-four, Shunryu was installed by So-on as the twenty-eighth abbot of Zoun-in in the Mountain Seat Ceremony. The evening before there was a ceremony in which So-on stepped down, and the next day Shunryu ascended the mountain seat and assumed the title of *jushoku,* abbot. Sogaku would continue to run the temple, now for his son rather than for So-on. Through years of effort, Shunryu had regained for his father his lost temple. It had been possible only because that wasn't Shunryu's main goal.

IN TOKYO, Shunryu continued to be immersed in his dual life as a college student and Miss Ransom's companion. Her interest in Buddhism continued, but not to the exclusion of her many other pursuits such as art, socializing, and arguing with Shunryu. Then one April day while the cherry trees were blooming, something happened to Shunryu that made him decide to move back into the dorm.

*This was brought home to me the day I went to the Turkish embassy on
some business for Miss Ransom. I was speaking in English with an assistant to the ambassador, and as I looked at him the thought came: Maybe
someday I shall be like you. This scared me. If I stay with Miss Ransom,
will I become an ambassador and not a priest?*

He went home and told Miss Ransom that it would be best for
his studies if he moved out for his last year at Komazawa University.
Miss Ransom sadly acquiesced. On May 30, 1929, Shunryu moved
into a Komazawa dorm.

ONE DAY Shunryu and several other monk students went to
the docks of Yokohama harbor to see off a priest named Daito
Suzuki, who was leaving for Los Angeles. There he would assist
Hosen Isobe-roshi, the founder of Zenshuji, a temple for Japanese-
Americans. Isobe had plans to start another temple in San Francisco, and Daito would eventually take charge of Zenshuji. Most
Japanese could not understand why anyone, especially a Buddhist
priest, would want to leave Japan, but Shunryu and his friends
greeted Daito with enthusiasm. To this little group of Komazawa
students, his departure was heroic. When the ship pulled out, the
young monks on the dock cheered, and tears streamed down Shunryu's face. Thirty years later Shunryu and Daito's paths would cross
again, and again memorably, though their roles at the time would
be quite different.

ON JANUARY 14, 1930, an important public ceremony for Shunryu
at Zoun-in, called *ten'e*, acknowledged Shunryu Suzuki's dharma
transmission from So-on. For Miss Ransom he defined it as "public
determination and consent from the Soto-shu to be a chief priest
and to teach Zen." A special brown robe was handed down to him
by So-on in the incense- and flower-filled main hall. Short recitations were interspersed with longer recitations chanted and mumbled by attending priests and punctuated by bells and drums.

This final ten'e ceremony gave Shunryu-san institutional credentials. The whole community turned out for this big occasion, as did Miss Ransom, Dr. Yoshikawa's family, friends from school, and various priests and teachers he'd studied with. The next day he left by train for the two head temples of the Soto school, Eiheiji and Sojiji, for ceremonies in which he was honorary abbot of each for a day. This was the last of the ceremonies between So-on and Shunryu. His father would continue to be acting abbot while Shunryu finished his studies. That could go on indefinitely as far as Shunryu was concerned; he had other things in mind. Sogaku was old but still in good health, and his dharma brothers and fellow disciples of So-on, Kendo and Soko, would occasionally come from Rinso-in to help him.

AT THE late age of twenty-five, on April 10, 1930, Shunryu graduated from Komazawa University, second in his class, in Buddhist and Zen philosophy, with a minor in English. His graduate thesis, written under his academic advisor and the school's president, Nukariya Kaiten, focused on the relationship between master and disciple, as discussed by Dogen in an essay of the *Shobogenzo* emphasizing submission to the master. (It is called the *Raihai tokozui,* a chapter in which Dogen also forcefully asserts the equality of women.) In his thesis Shunryu leaned toward Nukariya's "religious experience" point of view rather than Buddhism as philosophy. Another key professor whose instruction influenced Shunryu's thesis was Sokuo Eto, an eminent *Shobogenzo* scholar who emphasized an open-minded approach to study integrated with zazen and Buddhist practice. Eto had been a classmate of So-on's, and they had studied together with Oka Sotan. Like many of Shunryu's professors, he was also a priest with a temple back home, and, like Nukariya, he emphasized religion over philosophy, direct experience over systemization.

Not long after he graduated from college, Shunryu was honored with another credential that he greatly valued. On the recommendation of Shundo Tachibana, a dean of the school, he received government certification to be, as he translated it, "a Teacher of the

English Language and Ethical Conduct for High School Boys," a respected and almost professorial status, since high schools then were roughly equivalent to today's junior colleges.

Shunryu, now finished with his formal education, had moved his books and wardrobe from the Komazawa dorm to Zoun-in. But he did not want to settle down there. He had bigger ideas. When So-on came to Zoun-in, Shunryu asked if they could speak. He'd been building up his courage for this encounter. Shunryu described his experience with Miss Ransom and what it had meant to him. He described seeing Daito Suzuki off at Yokohama harbor. So-on listened silently. Then Shunryu got to the point. He suggested that he too go abroad to teach Buddhism. Anywhere, it didn't matter where – say, America.

"No!" So-on replied.

"How about Hawaii?"

"No!"

"Hokkaido?" The northern island of Japan was a kind of frontier, and there were a lot of foreigners in Sapporo who wouldn't know about Buddhism.

"No!"

Shunryu persevered for too long. So-on became infuriated. "Here!" he yelled, smashing his fist on the table. It was just one word, with some percussion, but his anger filled volumes.

He was so furious. I knew there must be some reason why. And I knew that he loved me very much, so I gave up my notion of going abroad. I completely gave up my idea of going to America.

Chapter Four

Great Root
Monasteries

1930–1932

One falling leaf is not just one leaf; it means the whole autumn.

SHUNRYU SUZUKI had thought that after Komazawa his training would be over and the world would be ready for him. He was, after all, an abbot with his own temple and had received transmission and recognition by the Soto organization. But So-on, the man of many growls and few words, hadn't mentioned that there was more training to look forward to – at Eiheiji in Fukui Prefecture, one of two *daihozan,* "great root monasteries" of the Soto school (along with Sojiji).

TO SHUNRYU, the giant cryptomeria trees outside the open shoji were shrinking and swaying. Sweat was running down his face. His crossed legs cramped as another wave of pain came over him in the *tangaryo,* the waiting room, the initiation, the place where he and the other fledgling Eiheiji students had to sit for a week or more from early morning till late at night to prove themselves worthy to enter the temple. The others were younger than he, but they would have the same Eiheiji age, determined by the day they entered the temple. He had arrived in early September 1930, at the age of twenty-six. At the end of the endless tangaryo initiation, Shunryu walked, bowing, past all the monks in his brief entering ceremony.

Tangaryo was uninterrupted sitting in the full-lotus posture – sitting for meals, sitting to listen to the near-constant chastisement of senior monks, sitting to receive the *kyosaku,* the long flat stick whacked against sleepy monks' shoulders, and sitting waiting for the next wave of pain to grip muscles and mind. He would have looked at his watch to time the intervals of pain, but they had taken his watch away. In the midst of the pain, the cryptomeria would shrink and sway – but no, it was his mind playing dizzying tricks. Those big trees don't move. It's the mind that moves.

EIHEIJI, TEMPLE of Eternal Peace, the treasure of the Soto school, the destination of pilgrims, spoken of in hushed tones, revered by the nation and generations of emperors, was founded by Dogen in the thirteenth century. Eiheiji with its spacious, artful buildings, endless tatami halls, massive pillars, covered walkways, and curved, tiled roofs – this living museum and priest's finishing school of a thousand rules was his new home. His father and mother could take care of Zoun-in indefinitely while Shunryu walked on Dogen's path in the deep forest monastery.

Over a hundred monks and more than thirty senior priests, some of the most venerable of the Soto school, walked the corridors in the early, early morning to zazen and services. The resplendent rooms were a feast for the senses – the sounds of the bells, gongs, clackers, and drums, the deep, the mid, the high, with the clearest and richest peals and booms; the overlapping echoes, the voices and overtones of so many devotees rhythmically reciting the teachings of the ancestors; the paintings on ceilings and scrolls, massive brass chandeliers, curtains, cords, and brocades. The old monks could recite even the longest ancient Chinese chants by heart, and most of them could make it up the ninety-five steps to Dogen's tomb.

CLEANING IS first, they said, then zazen. We must take care of our surroundings before we use them: polish the wood, polish your mind, wipe down the floors, cover the cosmos. He had to learn the steps, the Eiheiji way to do everything – how to sweep, how to walk, how to enter a room, how to use the study, how to greet a senior and later a junior. He learned precisely how to put on and put away his robes, how to roll up the futon on his tatami in the zendo, how to brush his teeth, how to clean the pots in the kitchen, how to eat in the zendo with *oryoki,* the wrapped bowls that were the forerunner of the tea ceremony. You had to walk and work slowly and silently; you shouldn't speak much and then it must be softly. In zazen, you didn't move, not for pain, not for the mosquito on your face. And when something was not done in the right way, there was always a senior to scold the offender. Shunryu felt their eyes on him when he walked in a room, checking him out from foot to head. It was not entirely new – he'd gotten the same from So-on – but it was no longer coming from one source. He was part of a larger team in a wider theater, getting the physical practice down with the precision of Noh or Kabuki performers. It was overwhelming, and after the initial nervousness and bungling, gradually it became harmonious and invigorating.

Upon waking Shunryu folded his futon and slid it under the cabinet at the end of his tatami. Then he put on his kimono and koromo and went quickly to take his place in a line of monks at the wooden sink and washed his face over an individual basin filled seventy percent with water. When finished he emptied the remainder toward his body, not away from it. All monks followed this practice Dogen had established at the Hanshaku-kyo, the Half-Dipper Bridge beyond the entrance gate, where he drew his water in a pail and returned what was left to the creek.

You may think it doesn't make sense to return the water to the river. This kind of practice is beyond our thinking. When we feel the beauty of the river we intuitively do it this way. That is our nature.

Morning began with zazen. The outer okesa robe was not worn but was kept in its case on the tatami. Zazen ended with a four-line verse proclaiming what a wondrous opportunity it was to wear the okesa, which was placed on the head for this chant. At the end of the chant the monks bowed and, still seated, donned the robe, which dates back to Buddha's day. Then they swung from side to side, turned around on their cushions, and stood in the aisle waiting for the final high bells to signal them to bow. Then, with hands clasped at the solar plexus, they walked slowly off to morning service and the recitation of sutras in magnificent, ancient rooms.

Life at Eiheiji was simple, with attention to minutiae. As the months passed, it became monotonous yet liberating – so far from the struggles and complexity of Zoun-in, Komazawa, and Tokyo. Once Shunryu and his new mates became accomplished at doing everything the same way, day after day, they'd look for a way to enjoy something new and get into mischief. For instance, they could go over the wall into the town below for *soba* noodles and sake. One night when almost everyone was asleep, Shunryu and a few friends considered sneaking some food from the kitchen. They weighed the risk of detection and decided to go for it. They went into the storeroom in the dark and selected a box. It was full of radishes. Eager for anything different, they scraped the dirt off with their fingernails and ate a few. Unable to eat many raw, they decided to cook them. They put the radishes in a bucket, took them outside, and built a fire. They tasted even more horrible after cooking, and they muffled their laughter as they gobbled them anyway. Soon the whole area was filled with the strong odor of cooked radishes, and they were caught and chastised. But even a scolding by groggy senior monks (who didn't find it funny) was something interesting to experience, and they savored the bitter taste.

WINTER AT Eiheiji was as cold as the summer was hot. It was deep snow country, and the buildings were closed up, dark, and candlelit. The only heat available was from the calories exerted shoveling snow off the paths and roofs, from heavier robes covering their chilled bodies, and from crowding round a hibachi in a common room. The thick cigarette smoke in the closed rooms was hard on Shunryu's weakened lungs, but he enjoyed the discussions. In dharma talks they had been told to practice with no purpose in mind – just sit, just sweep. But what was the goal of the practice? To attain buddhahood, to save all beings, or just to be yourself as you are?

The idea cannot be the reality, but is practice the bridge from idea to reality? We had this kind of discussion. But according to Dogen, practice is just practice-buddha, a bridge is just bridge-buddha, reality is just reality-buddha, an idea is just idea-buddha. There is no problem. When you say, "I am a human being," that is just another name for buddha – human being–buddha.

THE ABBOT of Eiheiji and archbishop of the Soto school was an old priest named Gempo Kitano-roshi. Shunryu regarded Kitano with great respect, for his sense of decorum and because he'd been abroad. Kitano had been the head of Soto Zen in Korea for a number of years and had been a founder of Zenshuji, the Zen temple in Los Angeles. One day in a dharma talk, Kitano spoke to the monks about smoking, which most of them did. He didn't tell them not to smoke, but described his own experience with tobacco. In his youth he had loved smoking. Once when he was out alone on *takuhatsu,* a begging trip, he was walking over the Hakone pass. At the top he stopped in the mist to sit on a rock. He lit a cigarette and found it immensely enjoyable to smoke and look down at the town below through the mist and the wisps of smoke. He particularly liked to smoke in damp weather and was so struck by the taste of the tobacco at that moment that he examined his desire directly and decided that it was a perfect moment for his last cigarette. And it was.

Though Kitano-zenji gave up smoking, he had the desire as long as he was alive, but he knew how to treat his desires. It is very foolish of you not to notice this point. I know it is difficult to quit smoking. I don't say you should give it up, but if you know this point, you will know how to treat yourself, even though it is difficult.

Kitano was older than Shunryu's father, but Sogaku said they'd been in school in Nagoya together and had trained together at one time. There was more than a hint of rivalry in Sogaku's tone when he spoke of the old man. Shunryu remembered how his father had complained about Kitano's becoming such an important priest while he, Sogaku, remained insignificant. Sogaku said it was because of Kitano's superior background and connections. In Kitano's presence, however, Shunryu knew there was much more to it than that.

As abbot of Eiheiji, Kitano was grandfather to all Soto Zen priests. He conducted himself with impeccable humility and grace. He was thin and not in good health, but Shunryu was mesmerized by the way he would lay out his bowing cloth and lower himself to place his forehead on it, and above all by the way he would rise up again. He was so frail that every time he bowed, Shunryu thought he wouldn't be able to get up, but he did, time after time. Eventually Shunryu realized that it was harder for him to watch Kitano bow than it was for Kitano to do so.

He looked almost like a sick person on the verge of dying. He stood up with joy, but actually it was a terrible effort for him. It was such very strong, fresh activity. It was not just formality; he was full of spirit.

He was the supreme example of heart and will. Some of the old priests were just strict and formal, and when they led a ceremony Shunryu would find himself getting bored, but when Kitano came out, there would be a special feeling in the room. He combined strictness with a deep gentleness.

Wherever you go, you will find your teacher.

"DON'T OPEN that side!" Shunryu stopped. He thought for a second, then slid the shoji door a few inches back to the center. He knew it was correct to open the right side. The elders were exacting about these things. But the command from inside was unmistakable, so Shunryu slid the left shoji open, stood up with the tray, entered, and served tea and snacks to the old priest and his guest. The next evening he returned to the same place, kneeled, and placed his fingers in the indentation on the frame of the left shoji and slid it open a bit to announce his presence. "Don't open that side!" came the voice from within. Shunryu was confused, but he obeyed and opened the right side.

It went on like this for some days, with Shunryu not knowing which side to open. He thought about it over and over. Such a tiny thing to agonize about, but it was through just this sort of detail that the mentor priests at Eiheiji regularly put pressure on their underlings. Shunryu couldn't just ask for an explanation; he had to figure it out for himself. Then one morning as he approached the door he stopped for a moment to listen to the conversation. One voice, the guest's, was coming from the right. Then he realized. Of course! He should open the right shoji unless there was a guest sitting there. How simple and obvious. Confidently he slid open the left side. From then on he knew which shoji to open by looking at the placement of slippers outside, listening to the voices within, and watching for shadows.

You may think our teaching is very strict. But our teaching is always near at hand – not easy, but not difficult to observe. At the same time, however, it is very strict and very delicate. Our mind should always be subtle enough to adjust our conduct to our surroundings.

The priest whom Shunryu had been chosen to serve was Ian Kishizawa-roshi, considered to be one of the greatest Soto masters of the day. So-on had arranged this connection. A disciple of the great root teacher Nishiari Bokusan, he had also studied under Nishiari's disciple, Oka Sotan, and had known So-on at Komazawa and at Shuzenji. He had also known Sogaku back in their younger days. He was sixty-five years old, thirty-nine years older than Shunryu and twelve years So-on's senior. He was strict and particular, but not mean like So-on. A highly respected Buddhist scholar, he had a cultured air about him. Like Oka he had continued the work Nishiari had started in Dogen scholarship and in 1919 had succeeded Oka and Kitano as the official Eiheiji lecturer on Dogen's *Shobogenzo*. Kishizawa saw great promise in Shunryu and kept a close eye on him. With Kishizawa, Shunryu found he had to be alert at all times – nothing was to be taken for granted.

KISHIZAWA HAD two rooms separated by shoji and Shunryu was to clean them during the morning break. There wasn't much time, so he worked as fast as he could. Kishizawa would come in and search for places Shunryu had missed, walking around with his hands behind his back. He inspected the corners, the frames of the shoji, and below the table for dust. "No good," he'd say. "Rather than clean two rooms, do one room well. Light one corner of the world."

Tasks at Eiheiji were done with great vigor, like wiping down the floors in the morning or bracing the temple for a storm. One day after a rain Shunryu enlisted the assistance of two other monks to help him return the rain doors to their cabinet at the end of the walkway. The heavy wooden doors protect the paper shoji from the rain and wind. The two monks were energetically pushing five of them at a time down to Shunryu, and he was stacking them in the box. They were opening the building back up to the light as quickly as they could and making a racket. Kishizawa came out and stopped them. He told Shunryu to do it by himself: one by one, don't hurry, show respect.

ON SHUNRYU's first day with Kishizawa he had served him green tea, pouring his cup three-fourths full and preparing it as he had learned to do. "Fill it up!" Kishizawa had told him. So Shunryu filled his cup to the top. When Kishizawa drank it he complained it was too weak and not hot enough. His every desire was out of the ordinary. So Shunryu made him very hot, bitter tea filled to the top, and Kishizawa was satisfied. Then Kishizawa had guests and Shunryu set out cups for them on the tray and poured exceedingly hot, bitter tea in each cup right up to the top as Kishizawa preferred. Kishizawa stopped him saying, "What are you doing? You can't serve tea like this." He should have known that when there were guests he was to revert to the usual style. A mechanical approach would not do; he had to constantly be alert.

Shunryu had to set out Kishizawa's robes for early morning zazen and have his tea ready. "You're late!" he was told. So he got up twenty minutes before the bell, got everything done ahead of time, and was scolded again. "Don't get up so early, you disturbed my sleep! That is selfish practice, you should get up when everyone else does."

I felt like I'd swallowed a straight stick. I couldn't even try to be a good student. I had no answer and couldn't move. "Umph!" was all I could say. I had to understand things better, without any rules or prejudice. That is what selflessness means.

Of all that Shunryu learned from Kishizawa during this time, nothing impressed him more than Kishizawa's continual practice of bowing. During morning service the names of the ancestors from Shakyamuni to the famous fourteenth-century master Keizan-zenji were recited by the monks as they spread their bowing cloths and bowed to the floor over and over. Afterward Kishizawa would go to his room and continue the service, reciting the names of the succession of teachers right up to his own. He would bow over and over as he chanted. Sometimes when Shunryu would come to Kishizawa's room he would just be bowing. His bowing cloth was frayed and darkened by skin oil where his forehead would touch it. Kishizawa said that Nishiari Bokusan had given him the practice of doing many prostrations to wear down his stubbornness, and he continued doing it daily out of respect for his master.

To bow is very important, one of the most important practices. By bowing
we can eliminate our self-centered ideas. My teacher had hard skin on his
forehead because he knew that he was a very obstinate, stubborn fellow, so
he bowed and bowed and bowed. And bowed because he always heard his
master's scolding voice. He joined the order when he was thirty-two. His
master always called him "You-lately-joined-fellow." If we join the order
when we are young it is easier to get rid of our selfishness. But when we
have a very stubborn, selfish idea, it is rather hard to get rid of it. So he
was always scolded because he joined the order so late. Actually his master
was not scolding him: he loved him very much, because of his stubborn
character.

We should be very careful of half-baked enlightenment,
and especially of taking pride in our enlightenment.

SESSHIN, LITERALLY a mind-gathering, is one or more
days of continuous zazen. It is an essential part of Zen training, and
some monks continue the practice of sesshin one or more times a
year in addition to daily sitting.

Starting December 1 Shunryu sat a seven-day sesshin, which
concluded on the morning of the eighth with a ceremony observing Buddha's enlightenment. According to tradition, this occurred
when Shakyamuni saw the morning star after having undergone a
similar concentrated period of cross-legged sitting and absorption.
It was in such undistracted sitting in China that Dogen had dropped
body and mind and later received the mind-seal from his teacher,
Nyojo. During that week at Eiheiji the operation of the temple was
reduced to a minimum, and most monks and a number of older
priests sat zazen from morning till night. It wasn't an ordeal like
tangaryo. There were the brief walking *kinhin* periods, bare-bones
services, and the customary ceremonial oryoki meals.

Shunryu had participated in other sesshins, but never one like this, so fully attended and orchestrated. On the third day he felt terrible pain in his legs, but by the fifth it was bearable. When it ended on the seventh he felt he could have continued the sesshin forever. Shortly afterward his first training period at Eiheiji was over, but Shunryu's time there had only begun.

IN THE spring Miss Ransom arrived to follow a modified program for lay practitioners. After initial resistance to her presence had subsided, she was accepted by the monks, who were impressed with her stamina and decorum. Shunryu was naturally put in charge of her, since no one else could speak English, and once again everyone was struck by the figures of the diminutive monk and his tall foreign lady friend. She brought photos from her visits to Korea, where she had stayed at temples with Shunryu's monk friend Sugioka, who had become her houseboy after Shunryu left. Shunryu showed her the trees he'd trimmed around the grounds and the gardens he'd worked in and brought her to tea with Kishizawa-roshi. In the summer Shunryu took off from Eiheiji and spent a month at Zoun-in. Miss Ransom joined him, staying mostly at a large nearby temple named Kasuisai. As always, wherever she went with Shunryu, it was usually everyone's first experience with a Westerner. And she made quite an impression.

"Don't do that! You shouldn't do that!" Miss Ransom said to Shunryu's sister Aiko as she brought in bowls and platters of food stacked precariously upon one another. They wouldn't carry dishes that way in England or at Eiheiji. She disapproved of serving sake at the dinner table, and she chided Sogaku for smoking, saying that good Christian ministers neither smoked nor drank. Aiko did not know what to make of this domineering woman, but she had gotten used to her visits. She wondered if all foreign women were as bold as this. Shunryu respected Miss Ransom's opinions on these matters but not her righteousness. He didn't get into an argument with her, however, for she would soon return to China, and this was no time for tempers to flare up.

When they parted, Shunryu gave Miss Ransom a scroll, and she gave him the old mah-jongg set with big tiles that they had so often played with in his college days. She said she would always keep what she had learned from him of Buddhism, and she admonished him to continue his study of English. He said that her bed with the long white silk futon and her rattan sofa would remain at his temple waiting for her return. He would miss her greatly.

After she went back to Tientsin she sent me a picture of the same Buddha who had caused trouble between us. She had enshrined the Buddha in the wall where there was an alcove, and she said she was offering incense every day.

HAVING COMPLETED two practice periods, each concluding with a seven-day sesshin, Shunryu told So-on he wished to continue at Eiheiji. Being there and attending to Kishizawa had opened his eyes wider. He realized he had a long way to go, and it seemed best to follow Dogen's way at the great temple he had founded. He told So-on that he would like to continue there, where he had found out what monk's practice is really all about. In particular he felt that his zazen had deepened. Though zazen had always been part of his practice, it hadn't been emphasized as at Eiheiji, where he sat first thing in the morning and last at night.

So-on let Shunryu have his say and then responded from an unexpected point of view. "Crooked Cucumber, you better be careful or you'll be a rotten crooked cucumber. One year is enough! I will not let you become a stinky Eiheiji student! Soon you should go to Sojiji," he said, referring to the other major Soto training temple. Once again Shunryu was crushed by So-on.

On the train back to Eiheiji, Shunryu replayed his master's words. He would have only two more months there, and those months would be on the relaxed summer schedule. Wistfully he remembered the year gone by as the train rolled toward mountainous Fukui. Being away had magnified how wonderful it was. There was something of the stink of pride at Eiheiji, but there was also something of incalculable value. Yet when he was there, Eiheiji wasn't special at all.

For us, monastic life was our usual life. People who came from the city were unusual people. We felt, "Oh, some unusual people have come." It is the people outside the monastery who have a deep feeling about it. Those who are practicing actually do not feel anything. I think that is true for everything.

Reaching the temple, Shunryu walked back up the steps through the giant two-tiered entrance gate. From a distance he heard the sound of monks chanting, the colossal mokugyo being thumped, and a deep resonating gong. He smelled the cryptomeria and was overcome with feeling. It was not just Eiheiji, it was himself he had come back to – with all beings, everything, beyond description. He broke down, and "tears flowed from my mouth, eyes, and nose."

Your real practice is something that you cannot compare to something else. It is greater than that, deeper than that. It is so great that you cannot compare it to your ordinary experience.

ON SEPTEMBER 17, 1931, Shunryu took the train from Eiheiji to Sojiji in Yokohama, where So-on had arranged for him to continue his training. He entered tangaryo the next day. Located near the hub of Japan's growing commercialism, the atmosphere at Sojiji was softer, less lofty and medieval than at Eiheiji. Whereas Dogen was said to be the father of all Soto monks, Sojiji had been founded by Keizan, who was considered their mother. It was he who had brought Soto Zen to the farmers and peasants. As a result, Soto Zen had gradually become one of the largest Buddhist sects in Japan.

While at Sojiji, Shunryu kept an eye on his temple. Commuting to Zoun-in, he oversaw the construction of two additions: the Kannon-do, or Kannon hall, in which Avalokiteshvara, the bodhisattva of compassion, was enshrined; and the *seppin,* a meeting room for guests and practitioners. There was a dedication ceremony for the additions in March of 1932. Shunryu's close attention to the well-being of his temple contrasted with his lack of desire to be tied down to the duties of a temple priest.

Soon after that So-on showed up at Sojiji. Shunryu told him that he was content with the practice and thought he could continue living there much more easily than at Eiheiji because of the proximity to Zoun-in. He'd been there half a year and was hoping to stay for a few more years. There was no thought of going abroad. He had a fully engaging life among likewise well-educated monks, some of whom shared his sincere devotion to realizing the heart of Buddhism.

After they'd been talking for ten minutes So-on said, "Maybe it is time for you to leave Sojiji."

Chapter Five

Temple Priest

1932–1939

*W*hen a tree stands up by itself, we call that tree a buddha.

ON THE first day of April 1932, Shunryu Suzuki reluctantly left Sojiji and moved into Zoun-in with his family. He was twenty-seven, finished with his formal training and, for the first time since childhood, not visiting but living at the country temple where he would be the priest. Shunryu's sisters Tori and Aiko had finished their schooling but were still living at home.

His mother had been sickly for years. So Shunryu's sister Aiko took care of him. She did so well that visitors to the temple would mistake her for Shunryu's wife. She would serve him and his guests, do his laundry, and prepare his clothes in the morning. She had to keep his robes in perfect shape because he was a careful dresser for a priest, though he never wore Western clothes or shoes. Like her mother before her, Aiko taught sewing to local girls and had become the family seamstress. Shunryu would often find her sitting on the tatami sewing his robes, with a cat on her lap. Over time her own kimono became tattered where the cat sharpened its claws.

At Eiheiji Shunryu had cultivated a refined but austere taste in robes. He didn't want to wear the more colorful robes for ceremonies, and he especially didn't want to wear a fancy *okesa,* the outer robe that drapes over the others. *Kesa* was originally a Sanskrit word meaning subdued color, and for his okesa he preferred black, indigo, and brown, as worn by the monks at Eiheiji. The kesa is the patchwork robe of ordination that dates back to India. Originally it was made from rags, to symbolize the voluntary poverty of the monk. Dogen was known for having twice refused to take a purple kesa from the emperor. People might expect something fancy, but Shunryu didn't want to feel like one of the actors from the city who came walking down the streets in their gorgeous costumes, hitting drums and bells to announce their performance.

The first funeral Shunryu did at Zoun-in was for a wealthy, venerable old man. In keeping with his philosophy, Shunryu wore a black robe with a brown okesa. He thought everything had gone just fine, but later he learned that the family was angry with him. "Why didn't you wear more beautiful robes as your master does?" asked the widow. He had brought attention to himself and insulted the family, they thought. He was dealing with laypeople regularly now and had a significant position in the community for such a young man. It was essential he conduct himself in a manner that fostered harmony. Eventually he realized that it was not good to upset people at such important times in their lives by stubbornly adhering to his own idea of right dress. It was the same as cherishing elegant robes, but in reverse.

I think we should not be attached to the material or to the look of robes. A gorgeous one is all right, a shabby one is all right. That is my attitude now, but at that time I was very concerned about what I wore.

SOGAKU CONTINUED to play a major role at Zoun-in. Shunryu was often away helping So-on at Rinso-in and had taken over So-on's positions in two large, well-known temples, Kasuisai and

Daito-in, where his responsibility was to give lectures to unsui and lead them in zazen. Shunryu brought to his duties a youthful enthusiasm and an almost zealous devotion to the teachings and practice he had learned at Eiheiji and Sojiji. Uchiyama-san, a priest who was to marry Aiko, thought Shunryu was a terribly sincere priest, since he led *zazenkai,* the lay sitting groups, and said in his soft-spoken way, "We must keep Dogen's practice and encourage it so it will prosper." Uchiyama said it was rare for a priest to talk like that. Shunryu's style of speech was largely inspired by his continuing association with Kishizawa.

My master Kishizawa-roshi used to say that we had to have a vow or aim to accomplish. The aim we have may not be perfect, but even so it is necessary for us to have it. It is like the precepts. Even though it is almost impossible to observe them, we must have them. Without an aim or the precepts we cannot be good Buddhists, we cannot actualize our way.

He had not wanted his relationship with Kishizawa to end when he left Eiheiji. Fortuitously, the great master's home temple had changed in recent years to Gyokuden-in, a small branch temple of Rinso-in located about three miles from Rinso-in. On May 1, 1932, Shunryu visited Kishizawa and, with So-on's blessing, requested permission to continue studying with him. Kishizawa accepted and Shunryu became his *zuishin* (follower), a name given to the relationship with one's second teacher. He would always be So-on's *deshi* (disciple), but he would later attribute most of his understanding of Buddhism to Kishizawa.

Kishizawa had become one of the best-known Buddhist lecturers in the land, and Shunryu went to hear his talks on Dogen's seminal work, the *Shobogenzo.* Shunryu visited Gyokuden-in for private instruction and to consult with Kishizawa when he had some crisis or turning point in his practice.

Kishizawa did not forsake the central practice of zazen. Most temple priests did not sit zazen after their training, except perhaps for a weekly or monthly zazenkai. Kishizawa admonished his student Shunryu through his example not to forsake formal practice. There was no zendo at Zoun-in, but zazen doesn't depend on having a zendo, just a body.

SEISON SUZUKI, a local potter in Mori, liked to tell a story about Shunryu, a little girl, and a train ticket. Shunryu had just arrived at the station in Mori on his bicycle when the girl's crying caught his attention. She said her mother had no money to buy her any candy.

"Don't cry," he said. "I'll buy you some candy." He let her choose what she wanted from the stall and paid for it. When he went to get his ticket he discovered he was short, so he talked to the stationmaster, who said he'd call up the station in Yaizu and arrange to have the ticket paid for later. When Shunryu reached Yaizu, an employee told him that the stationmaster was waiting for him in his office. He served Shunryu tea and they talked for a while; finally the stationmaster said he'd never made an arrangement like this before and Shunryu remembered he hadn't bought a ticket. He apologized and promised to pay the next day on his way back to Mori. When he returned the next day he met the stationmaster again, who was dumbfounded when Shunryu once more forgot about paying for the ticket. Finally with a little nudging he remembered and paid his debt. Soon people in Yaizu and Mori were laughing about Shunryu's shocking behavior. Seison the potter said to Shunryu, "How did you like the taste of ride-now-pay-later?"

SHUNRYU'S DHARMA brothers Kendo and Soko were in charge of Rinso-in most of the time, because So-on was leading a practice period at a temple in neighboring Shizuoka. Shunryu arrived at Rinso-in early one evening to find that Kendo and Soko had gone out to a movie. He knew that So-on wouldn't like that and that his dharma brothers would not want to get caught relaxing by their fierce master. He lined up his *geta*, wooden platform sandals, at the bottom of the steps in the entryway in the spot where So-on, and only So-on, left his. When Kendo and Soko got back they were filled with terror at the sight of the geta until they heard Shunryu laughing from behind the shoji.

Things are always changing, so nothing can be yours.

EVEN THOUGH Buddhist priests had been getting married since the previous century, it was still controversial. When Shunryu's parents were married, it was legal for priests to do so, but the prohibition against women being lodged in temples was still part of the Soto regulations when he was born at Shoganji. The teachers in Shunryu's dharma lineage didn't get married: neither Nishiari, Oka, nor Kishizawa. Though So-on had not officially married, Shunryu considered Yoshi to be So-on's wife. So to Shunryu, both his father and his master were married. As the Japanese say, "The child of a frog is a frog." And so, soon after he had settled down in Zoun-in, it was arranged for Shunryu to get married. The young woman selected shared Shunryu's interest in English and had even studied with Miss Ransom before her return to China. It seemed likely to be a good union.

Not long after they were married though, Shunryu's new wife was diagnosed with tuberculosis. She was hospitalized, and it was hoped that she would recover as he had six years earlier. With the passage of time, though, it became clear that she was not improving and would not be able to fulfill her duties as temple wife, nor could she receive proper care at Zoun-in. There was a stigma attached to having had tuberculosis, even if one recovered, because people were afraid they'd catch it. With much sadness Shunryu and his wife agreed to an annulment. She went back to the home of her parents, where she could be well looked after. He wanted to take care of her but was bound by duty – as a priest first, a family man last. He would seldom speak of this wife. Her name and the dates of the marriage are forgotten.

In November of 1933, after a number of months of deteriorating health, Shunryu's father, Sogaku, died in his sleep. He had been a good husband and father. He was proud of his son, who had made it possible for him to spend the last seven years of his long life back at Zoun-in. His body was laid out in the buddha hall. Shunryu and his mother greeted neighbors and danka as they arrived to pay their respects and offer incense. Tori and Aiko gave people cushions and took care of tea and food. At twenty-nine Shunryu became the head of the family and was now truly in charge of the temple.

IN LATE April 1934 So-on arrived at Eiheiji to assume the position of assistant director. He would be involved both with administration and with the training of monks. On his third day at Eiheiji, after lunch, he said, "I'm going to the toilet," then had a stroke and collapsed in the hall. From the Fukui hospital he was moved to Rinso-in for recovery, but his condition deteriorated. A week later, on May third, So-on passed away at the age of fifty-seven.

So-on had always walked with his head up and greeted people without looking at them, yet hundreds of laypeople and priests attended his funeral. His ashes were interred at both of the temples that he had run. Shunryu conducted the ashes ceremony at Zoun-in. So-on's new teardrop-shaped granite stone was placed next to Sogaku's in the abbots' line. During the ashes ceremony, chanting the *Heart Sutra*, Shunryu picked up some of So-on's bone bits with chopsticks and placed them in an opening at the base, then picked up a bamboo ladle and poured water over the stone. How many times he'd watched So-on do this – for eighteen years starting right here and ending right here. Shunryu had many memories of the man who, more than anyone, had molded his character. Never again would he be called Crooked Cucumber. He could not help noticing that he did not feel much at the passing of his master.

Yoshi did not attend the funeral. For a time she stayed at Rinso-in helping out and doing ikebana flower arranging. Once when Shunryu's mother visited, Yoshi went upstairs and hid. Then one day she had Soko deliver So-on's robes to Shunryu at Zoun-in. She moved out of Rinso-in and returned to her family in Mori.

The loss of Miss Ransom and his wife and the deaths of both his father and his master gave meaning to the age-old Buddhist teachings that everything changes and life is suffering. It was not just his own suffering and transience that he felt, but that of others as well, of all beings – there was no difference. Reflecting on his years with So-on and his time at Komazawa, Eiheiji, and Sojiji, Shunryu saw two big mistakes he had made. First, he wished he'd made a stronger effort. He could hear So-on's frequent admonitions to realize how precious the opportunity to practice was: "You should not waste your time!" At first he'd thought that meant he had to work all day and all night or, since he couldn't work all night, at least behave well all night. Later So-on had explained, "To understand Buddhism is not to waste your time. If you do not understand Buddhism, you are wasting your time." When he was a boy, it had seemed like some convenient logic and he had not felt encouraged, just confused. Now he was beginning to appreciate his master's words, if not his personality.

The other mistake he saw was his practice of "stepladder Zen," a systematic approach.

Actually, what we are talking about is that enlightenment and practice is one. But my practice was stepladder practice: "I understand this much now, and next year I will understand a little bit more, and a little bit more." That kind of practice doesn't make much sense. Maybe after you try stepladder practice, you will realize that it was a mistake.

He was beginning to see that he couldn't organize his practice, his life, the teachings he was receiving, and the lessons he was learning. He had to let go of all that and leave it to ripen on its own. He had to adjust minute by minute. He was getting a glimpse that the way is to have "a complete experience with full feeling in every moment," not to use each moment to think about the past or future, trying to make sense of it all. What he was coming to was not some mushy all-is-one-let-it-be approach. It included a view of oneness, but it also included the opposite – that each moment, each thing, is distinct and must be addressed mindfully, not with some vague idea of universal significance.

When he had first returned to Zoun-in to live, Shunryu discussed this point with So-on. He explained that he could accept that all things are one, but not that they are different. Yet in his studies he had learned that both were true. So-on had simply said, "Emptiness and existence – if you stick to either one you are not a Buddhist."

It is only because our life is so habitually and so firmly based on a mechanical understanding that we think that our everyday life is repetitious. But it is not so. No one can repeat the same thing. Whatever you do, it will be different from what you do in the next moment. That is why we should not waste our time.

Now that he had lost so much and been so changed, it was easier for Shunryu to give up his systems and beliefs and just be in the world, walking step by step with no person, thing, or idea that he could depend on permanently. He had his duties, his relationship with Kishizawa, his mother, his fellow monks, and some friends – especially Kendo and the potter Seison. But he wasn't so attached to anyone or so sad at his aloneness. His life would go on, and So-on's passing would lead to the next big step – and to a lot of trouble.

*B*ecause *things don't actually go as you expect, there is suffering.*

SO-ON'S SUDDEN death created a vacuum at Rinso-in. He had appeared to be grooming his nephew Soko to be abbot, possibly so that So-on could comfortably retire there, but surely also because Soko seemed to have So-on's administrative ability. So-on could have remained the abbot in absentia for years while at Eiheiji, without anyone worrying too much about who was running it in his stead. In that way he could have eased Soko into the position and slowly built consensus within the danka. But now the decision would be made by the board, which represented various factions in the membership.

An old priest named Ryoen Risan was trying to take over Rinso-in. He was a dharma brother of the former abbot, the one So-on had been asked to replace because the temple had been going down-hill. Ryoen had strong backing among the danka, especially among a clique of local priests. At first there was no one to oppose him, so he started handling some of Rinso-in's affairs.

There were many danka who did not like the idea of Ryoen getting the temple back for his lineage. Some of these backed Soko to be the abbot. But he was still in Komazawa, hadn't received transmission from So-on, and was quite young. Also, Yoshi didn't like him, and she had some influence. She wanted Shunryu.

Before I took over my master's temple, I didn't cause any trouble. I was just trying to study. But after I determined to take over my master's temple, I caused various problems for myself and for others. There was confusion in my life, a lot of confusion. I knew that if I didn't take over his temple, Rinso-in, I would have to remain at Zoun-in. That would be more calm, and I would be able to study more, but I determined to take it over, and there were two years of confusion and fighting.

Shunryu had mixed feelings about his own qualifications. On the one hand, there were many prominent older priests in the two hundred branch temples associated with Rinso-in. The abbot of Rinso-in wouldn't have any authority over them but would be required to serve a central function at occasional important ceremonies. At that time any slip in his demeanor would call into question his eligibility for the position. But he also felt, as So-on's number-one disciple, that he knew what So-on would want. He felt that Soko wasn't ready and would be used by others for their own ambitions, and that Ryoen and those whom he represented were definitely not good for Rinso-in. Shunryu did not want to see So-on's sixteen years of hard work go to waste. He was determined that Rinso-in not fall into the hands of greedy and ambitious priests. Keeping a low profile while strengthening his ties to important danka, especially Koga-san, the head of the temple board of directors, Shunryu patiently participated in ongoing discussions. He actually felt quite impatient and angry but kept these emotions in control.

Some saw him as the candidate who represented So-on's high standards. Others felt he was too young. He was thirty, and Rinso-in had an unbroken tradition of having abbots over fifty. Some felt he was not qualified. He was fine for a lesser temple like Zoun-in, a man of excellent character, good at leading services, but not the type to run a large temple like Rinso-in. He couldn't even keep track of his cap!

Months passed with small meetings and large meetings. Koga-san, previously a backer of Ryoen, now inclined toward Shunryu. Soko pulled out of the running, became a disciple of another master, and lent his support to Shunryu. Kishizawa had discreetly indicated that he, too, preferred Shunryu. While Koga-san was considering all this, Shunryu made an offer. Give him three years to prove himself, and if it didn't work out he'd resign. The usual trial period, if there was one at all, was ten years. Shunryu's suggestion reduced the weight of the decision. Finally, a venerable elder of the Soto school, Shunko Tettsu-roshi, put his stamp of approval on Shunryu's three-year trial. The board agreed.

This all took a good deal of time. While the slow beast of consensus had been crawling along, Shunryu was already living at Rinso-in and doing the job, commuting between there and Zoun-in. No sooner had he gotten approval than he gave the board and membership another major piece of news to consider. He was planning to get married.

NEAR ZOUN-IN was a temple named Bairin-in. The abbot there was an old friend of So-on's and had been a close advisor to Shunryu, especially in practical matters. Seison the potter and Shunryu had originally met at Bairin-in and now frequently visited and played go. One day the abbot told Shunryu that it was time for him to get married again and that he had someone in mind. Shunryu said he had confidence in being a priest but wasn't so sure about his ability to be a family man. But Shunryu agreed, she agreed, then they met. Chie Muramatsu was twenty-two and the daughter of a priest. Her father was the treasurer of Kasuisai, a large temple, where Shunryu had been instructing young monks since he'd taken over Zoun-in. Chie knew Shunryu had recovered from tuberculosis. He would always be grateful to her for marrying him in spite of this stigma.

Some of the danka at Rinso-in were not happy with the prospect of having a married priest. They had accepted Yoshi, the Daikoku-sama, as long as she was unofficial and kept a low profile. A wife would mean children, and there had never been a family at the temple. Many older people remembered the time when almost no priests had wives or families. One member suggested that Shunryu's family could live elsewhere. Another offered his house. Shunryu thought they were being extreme, especially as So-on had established a precedent by living with Yoshi there. But there was a difference between Yoshi's low-profile role and that of a wife. When Shunryu and Chie were married in February 1935, she moved into Zoun-in instead of Rinso-in. On November 11 of that year, the Year of the Boar, their first child was born, a girl named Yasuko.

GEN'ICHI AMANO, a prominent member of Rinso-in, was one of those rare laypeople who actually saw Buddhism as a way of liberation in addition to its role as caretaker of deceased ancestors. One day some representatives of the Rinso-in board asked him to be Shunryu's new *gishin* (parent of duty), a sort of godfather. Amano was reluctant to take on such responsibility, but when assured that it wouldn't cost anything, he agreed. From such dubious beginnings a lifelong relationship of trust and friendship began.

On April 23, 1936, Shunryu Suzuki ceremonially entered the home of Gen'ichi Amano, making it his home and Amano his godfather. From then on he would address Amano as father and would be considered a son of that house, while not erasing his birth-family history in any way. Then he formally entered Rinso-in and climbed the mountain seat, to take the position of chief priest as the thirty-sixth abbot. As part of the compromise, the much older Ryoen, who had been his rival for the job, was symbolically recorded as the thirty-fifth abbot; in the ceremony he stepped down from the mountain seat and turned the temple over to Shogaku Shunryu.

Now that Shunryu had two temples, he resigned from his considerable duties of guiding monks at Kasuisai and Daito-in. He had his hands full. The power struggle over Rinso-in had caused great dissension within the danka. It was an extraordinary time for Shunryu. Soon after he took over, eighty families changed to other temples. He did nothing to discourage them. At monthly meetings with the board and general membership, Shunryu was roundly criticized for not encouraging people to stay. He was accused of being irresponsible, of not asking for help in trying to keep these families in the fold. "If Rinso-in is such a poor example, how will we be able to restore harmony? This is your responsibility," he was told. Shunryu worked to control his impatience and temper. Rather than argue, he just asked them to let him do his job and not to criticize for three years, and so it was agreed.

FOUNDED IN 1493, Rinso-in had a long history. More important to Shunryu, it had a zendo, having been a training temple with a number of monks in residence in the Meiji Era. He wanted to return Rinso-in to those days of glory, to develop it as a temple where both monks and laypeople could practice. He had helped So-on get the temple in shape and complete the refurbishing of the living quarters, but there was still a lot to do.

During the first three years of Shunryu's leadership, the congregation, buildings, and gardens of Rinso-in were put in good order. Almost all the families who had left returned. Shunryu gained a reputation as a friendly, gentle priest of good character and traditional values. So-on had been respected, but people were afraid to go to the temple when he was there. That changed when Shunryu took over. Rinso-in became a kind of community center where various groups met to study Buddhism, practice the arts, discuss politics, solve neighborhood problems, and have small banquets and celebrations.

In 1939, when he had been abbot for three years, Shunryu paid a visit to board chair Koga's home. Over tea Shunryu said that according to their agreement his time was up, and he offered his resignation. "What agreement?" said Koga. "I don't know what you're talking about."

The only way you can endure your pain is to let it be painful.

YASUKO WAS nearly two and a half and her father was almost like a stranger – to her he didn't belong in Zoun-in, but at Rinso-in, where he lived. When he was at Zoun-in, he didn't hold her much, so that even if he called her she wouldn't come. She would tiptoe up behind him though, as he sat on his cushion reading, and try to snatch the newspaper away saying, "No, it's grandma's!"

Yone was like another parent to little Yasuko. The girl would watch with fascination as her grandmother applied acupuncture needles to her mother's back. She would sit playing by Yone as she mended the family clothing, while Chie made dinner. Monks, neighbors, workers, danka, and Shunryu came and went. The caretaker worked part-time. Kendo was supposed to cover for Shunryu, but he too was often away with other obligations; so the three Suzuki females were often the only ones at Zoun-in.

One late afternoon in April 1938 Yone had gone out to the fields to collect grass for her rabbits. By dark she had not come back, so Chie went to look for her. Time passed. Yasuko was feeling lonely by herself; she heard an owl hooting from the hill up behind the temple and got scared. Then she heard her mother's voice crying out from below. Yone's body was brought in and laid on the floor in front of the family altar. Yasuko tried and tried to awaken her grandmother, but she couldn't.

The word spread and people started to arrive. Someone had gone to town to get a message to Shunryu at Rinso-in. When he had not arrived after four hours, people got concerned. Finally he showed up after midnight. He'd fallen asleep on the train, passed Mori station, and gone way up into the mountains. The word would get around: he fell asleep on the day of his mother's death, on the way to join his family in crisis. His mind was in the clouds.

IN THE Year of the Rabbit, 1939, a son was born. At Shunryu's request, the abbot of Bairin-in gave him a name – Hoitsu, Embracing Oneness. Later that year Chie and the children moved from Zoun-in in Mori to Yaizu, where they stayed with the Kogas. Soon Shunryu's family was living with him at Rinso-in, but getting them into the temple had taken more time than prevailing in the struggle for the abbot's position. The only things they brought with them were Miss Ransom's futon, rattan sofa, and chair – brought in hope that she might come back from China for a visit. Shunryu passed Zoun-in on to Kendo Okamoto, who moved in with his family, though Shunryu retained some responsibility to keep it in his father's lineage. Kendo promised that the next abbot of Zoun-in would be Shunryu's disciple – maybe Kendo's own son Shoko.

SHUNRYU HAD no disciples, only monks sent to train with him by other priests, and a few lay students. They would sit in the buddha hall. The old zendo at Rinso-in was still just a room for storage, rats, and a ghost.

Shunryu didn't believe in the ghost, but the old caretaker of Rinso-in had scared him as a boy with the story of a shape-shifter fox from the mountains who sat zazen in the zendo to attain enlightenment and be reborn as a monk. When he takes the form of a ghost you can sometimes see a white flash go by, the caretaker had told him. The frequent scurrying sounds from that wing had given young Shunryu the chills. Now twenty years later the old caretaker still teased him about the ghost in the zendo.

One summer night the caretaker was sitting with some friends smoking and talking in the room directly opposite the zendo. The shoji windows and doors were open to cool things down. Mentioning to the old men that some funny things had been going on in the zendo, Shunryu said he was afraid the ghost of the fox had come back. Then he slipped back through the buddha hall, hung a paper lantern in the back of the zendo, and waved a white cloth from a bamboo pole so that it could barely be seen in the flickering light.

"Mmmm?" The caretaker squinted, looking toward the zendo. His eyes opened wide when he saw the wisp of white go by, and he froze with fear. Shunryu came back to find him still petrified. After that he didn't tease Shunryu anymore, because everyone was now teasing him. Shunryu was called the priest who scared away superstitions.

SHUNRYU WAS even more interested in dispelling another type of superstition – the ugly specter of Japanese ultranationalistic militarism that was bent on conquering Asia. It was based on theories such as that of the Showa Restoration, which aimed to restore the emperor to what they claimed was his rightful place over a Japan whose supremacy was guaranteed by the sun goddess, Amaterasu, from whom the Japanese had descended. The thirties have been called the dark valley of modern Japanese history. Throughout the decade hot-blooded zealots would move two steps forward for each step back, while the progressive factions that promoted democracy and openness in Japan and constructive engagement with an independent China continued to lose ground.

Chapter Six

Wartime

1940–1945

*W*e should know our tendencies.

IN 1940 Miss Ransom wrote to Shunryu Suzuki that she could no longer stay in Tientsin. The Japanese army had taken control, the British were not on good terms with the new administration, and she would return to England. After Japan had occupied Manchuria and set up a government in 1932 with Pu Yi as the puppet emperor, the army had set its sights on the rest of China and Southeast Asia. They had methodically swept to victory on many fronts, although America, England, and Holland had established a boycott to try to force Japan to back down. Japanese airplanes had been bombing cities, and a Japanese newspaper, the *Asahi Shinbun,* reported on a massacre of civilians in Nanking. The war in Europe was raging; there was talk that Japan might break its neutrality and align itself with Germany. The political parties were dead, and totalitarians had taken almost complete charge in Tokyo. In the schools, imperial myths and propaganda were taking the place of literature and history.

In this precarious political climate Shunryu felt compelled to help his society as best he could. Most people didn't want to think about what was happening, but he had a special rapport with young people, whose minds were more open.

Even before the war I had strong feelings against war. I organized young men in my area to have the right understanding of the situation in Japan at that time. We invited good people from the government to come and answer our questions. My focus was not so much on preventing war as on trying to counter one-sided views of Japan's situation, of ourselves, and of human nature. I didn't have any big purpose for my group; I just didn't want my friends to be involved in the kind of nationalism which I thought might destroy Japan completely. It's more dangerous than war.

Shunryu met primarily with educated young men of eighteen and nineteen, men who would enter the military when they were twenty. Teachers, artists, intellectuals, and others would also come by to talk discreetly and express their views. Sometimes Shunryu handed out papers he'd written, urging that Japan work with other nations toward amicably solving problems rather than acting rashly in a way that might bring on destruction. In his understated, low-key way he questioned some of the absurd yet popular assumptions and false accusations of the right, and he encouraged a balanced view. Liberal politicians and teachers were being purged and assassinated, but a priest could couch his views within Buddhism's traditional pacifism and dialectic. Shunryu was blessed with a lack of didacticism and ideology, which protected him from criticism by right-wingers. But not completely.

Some people in the town had been uncomfortable with the goings-on at the temple. Shunryu was occasionally criticized for misleading people, but his way of expressing himself was accepted by his superiors in the Soto organization, and they invited him to head a new organization to promote patriotic imperial Buddhism. He felt they wanted to use his skills to help organize civilians against America and England. He was put on the spot. Japan was supposed to be like one big family built around national identity and adherence to duty without regard for oneself. It would be unpatriotic to decline. Shunryu thought about how to deal with the offer and decided on a course of action. He accepted, his sponsors were happy, there was a celebratory dinner party, and the next day he resigned. The subtle distinction between refusing and resigning made all the difference. When he returned to Rinso-in, neither he nor the temple had lost face.

Japan had had a wartime economy for years, building a mighty military machine to carry out the improbable plan of establishing a new order in Asia. Some had hoped that reason might win out, that there could be a compromise with the West. One idea was to pull out of Southeast Asia and insist only on China as their natural sphere of influence. But then the fanatic minister of war, Tojo, became prime minister, the army seized power, and the dark valley turned pitch-black.

THERE WAS a service at Rinso-in one Monday morning with just his family in attendance, for Buddha's enlightenment day, the most important day in the Zen Buddhist year. There had been a big ceremony the day before and a banquet with hundreds in attendance, but Monday was the actual date. Six-year-old Yasuko offered aduki beans and sweet rice soup to Shakyamuni at the family altar and listened to her father and mother chant, the latter holding on to two-year-old Hoitsu. After the service, Shunryu told his family that a war with the Americans and the English had started.

It was December 8, 1941, still December 7 in the West. In the name of the emperor and with his full knowledge, the Japanese military had struck in Hawaii, Hong Kong, Malaysia, Singapore, and the Philippines on the morning of Buddha's enlightenment. What a day to have chosen to launch this insanity! There was nothing Shunryu could do now but recite a sutra.

*The way that helps will not be the same.
It changes according to the situation.*

Of the many young men who passed through Rinso-in during World War II, a few would have a lifelong relationship with Shunryu Suzuki. One of these was Yasuo Suetsune. Suetsune shyly stepped into the entryway at Rinso-in for the first time and called out, "Ojama shimasu," meaning excuse me for bothering you. Chie came out from the kitchen, greeted him as an honored guest, and took him to a room at the back of the hall where a group of people were sitting around a large low table. He sat down quietly and nodded as she served him a cup of tea. It was 1943 and he was seventeen years old, soon to be a new student living in the dorm at Shizuoka Preparatory School. He'd heard about Rinso-in and the priest Suzuki-san from students at his school. Some spoke highly of their experience at Rinso-in – and of the food. You could never get enough food in those days.

Suetsune listened. It was interesting, very interesting. People were talking freely with no set agenda. There was reference to the war without the parroting of slogans, and frank talk about alternatives and new directions – nothing seditious, but most unusual. A middle-aged monk in a grey robe sat next to him. Every once in a while the monk would add something to the conversation. People were friendly; there was occasional laughter and an informal feeling, but still an intensity and seriousness commensurate with the times. What struck him most was that there didn't seem to be anyone in charge.

When it broke up he was introduced to the group by an acquaintance. The monk welcomed him and said his name was Suzuki.

"Suzuki-san? This is your temple?" he asked.

"Yes."

Suetsune was shocked to find out that the inconspicuous monk was the abbot of that prestigious temple. He was acting just like one of the group. Japanese priests didn't do that; they were of high status, and regular people were below them. This was indeed a unique place. He asked if he could live at Rinso-in, and Shunryu straightaway accepted him. He wouldn't have to pay anything, but there was one condition: that he sit zazen in the morning with the others before going to school. He could stay with the other four boys in the wing on the opposite side of the buddha hall from the family quarters.

A T 4:40 A M Shunryu lifted a mallet and struck the *han,* a thick wooden board, calling the boys to get out of bed, wash their faces, and come to zazen. He sat with them at five, and after fifty minutes of zazen led them in a service that was over at six. There was a brief cleaning period, then breakfast, and the boys were off past the blooming camellias, walking an hour to the station. The train took thirty minutes to get to Shizuoka; then they had to walk another half hour to get to school. It was a lot of trouble, but well worth it to Suetsune.

As Suetsune's fellow student Kozuki said, Shunryu set an example by his own attitude and conduct. He never scolded them, but treated them with unusual respect, like friends. If they asked a question his answer would be brief, simple, and clear. There was a lot of talk. They were all starved for the chance to express themselves, and he was the quiet mediator of the ongoing salon in the evenings and on weekends, when others would come to share thoughts and feelings – and food.

W HEN S HUNRYU went to Gyokuden-in to see Kishizawa, he would often bring one of the boys along. His teacher would drop by Rinso-in at times and sit zazen in the buddha hall without announcing his arrival. Kishizawa came to Rinso-in on occasional Sunday afternoons and gave lectures to Shunryu's students on Dogen's *Shobogenzo, Shishobo,* and other texts. It was hard for the boys to understand all the specialized terminology, and eventually he stopped, saying they weren't going to be monks, so that was enough. After that they went as a group to hear his more simple lectures for laypeople. Kishizawa would scold Shunryu in front of the young men at times, and Shunryu would accept his teacher's words with no resistance. But he did not agree with the old man on everything. Kishizawa was lending Buddhism's support to the nation's war effort. He wrote a book on the precepts in which he expressed support for Japan's militarism. He told young men to fire their guns with the mind of Buddha, like the samurai of old, with no thought of life and death.

SINCE 1942 the informal fraternity of Shunryu's students had called themselves the Takakusayamakai – the High Grass Mountain Group, after the terraced and forested mountain that rose above Rinso-in, and Takakusa, the village below. That year a new and brilliant student, Nishinakama, had come to Rinso-in. Masao Nishinakama was supercharged, a born leader and organizer, yet he had a light, friendly nature. Nishinakama and Shunryu immediately became kindred spirits. Meeting Shunryu had given focus to Nishinakama's energy, and he in turn had given more direction to Shunryu's group. Nishinakama was a brilliant student, always top in his class, and Shunryu respected his scientific way of thinking and his dedication to truth. He was almost reckless in his drive to get to the bottom of things, and he got Shunryu to allow them to hold meetings that would go on for days. He was full of ideas and charisma, by far the most outspoken of the students. Perhaps he was protected by his father, a retired senior officer of the dreaded Tokko, the secret police, in Tokyo.

There were few people in Japan those days who thought the war was wrong, and few of those had figured out how to talk about it without going to jail or losing their positions. No one could voice strong doubts or criticize the state, but there was room for positive suggestions. Anything Shunryu had done that could be considered remotely antiwar he had done before the Pacific war started. Now in 1943 there was little he could do. He didn't oppose the war, didn't oppose the government, didn't advocate surrender, didn't say that Japan was wrong. He didn't want Japan to lose the war, he just wanted it to be over. He was torn between his belief in Buddhism and peace, and his devotion to duty and country. But if he was careful he could talk about how much more Japan could accomplish if there were peace. The official policy of the government was that the war was being fought for peace, so the students could talk about the root cause of war and risking their lives for peace. It would be difficult to say that the war should be ended right away, but so many had already died in the fighting, and people were living in such hardship, that it was a patriotic duty to suggest ways that Japan could become strong and healthy as a nation again. Shunryu never overtly invoked the precept against killing to advocate an end to the war on moral grounds.

WITH SO many males at war, it was unusual to see all those young men going in and out of Rinso-in. People noticed, but the boys seemed to be upstanding citizens. When their time came to enter the military they bid farewell to their comrades and went off. In 1941 all Japanese men had been required to take a physical exam, and all were subject to the draft, including Buddhist priests. If they refused, they would go to jail. After being drafted they would be treated as priests again only when they died or returned home. Men over forty or those who failed the physical would be sent to factories or left to work in the fields.

Shunryu had escaped the draft. Some said it was because he was too small or because of his persistent cough from having had tuberculosis, others thought it was because he had influential friends such as the eccentric Kozo Kato, a former member of the Diet's lower house. Shunryu himself thought he had escaped military duty because the authorities feared that his unusual ideas would hurt morale and decided to keep him marginalized in his temple, where he seemed to be doing no harm. "My name had a mark by it," he said.

Shinto was a central part of the establishment, and Shinto priests encouraged the martial spirit. Many Buddhist priests took on that role too, and they almost all performed funerals and memorial services for soldiers, prayed for the dead, and recited special chants called *eko,* which included new passages for the benefit of the emperor and winning the war. There were plenty of funerals at Rinso-in – often joint funerals for the ashes of soldiers sent back from the battlefields. No institution could escape the shadow of government authority or complicity in the course of events. Shunryu was grudgingly helping out a great deal more than he wanted to. To him there was no way out. All of Japan was part of the battlefield and, by necessity, everyone was contributing to the life and death struggle of the nation. There was a more radical alternative: Some communists were going to jail for not supporting the war effort, but no Buddhists took that strong a stand.

Soldiers and naval engineers took over the far wing of Rinso-in and eventually even part of the family quarters as their residence. A communications station was being built on the mountain and an airfield was under construction in the city. The military needed the spacious temple to house the overflow of personnel. Shunryu and Chie did not like having soldiers in the temple. They were coarse, arrogant, and rude, and they would not make themselves useful in any way. It was almost unbearable to have to listen to their merrymaking late into the night. While distressed at the attitude of these guests who had been forced on the temple, Shunryu and his students had to suffer it in silence. The soldiers would take food from the temple and make unreasonable demands on his and Chie's time. Officers would strike underlings – the army used a stick, the navy a strap. Their presence made Chie and Shunryu value the young men from the High Grass Mountain Group all the more. Some soldiers came to Shunryu for advice and sat zazen with him; he treated them with the same respect as he would a monk. He was ready to respect soldiers if they were sincere, but he found that most were not.

It was most painful when the authorities informed him that they would also house Korean laborers at Rinso-in. These were men who had been yanked from their homeland and who were now forced to work for their captors. The Koreans moved into the zendo, which Shunryu had been fixing up for his students to sit in.

And then there was the day they had to give the temple bells to the navy to be melted down for ship propellers. This was heartbreaking to Shunryu; he especially loved the big old bell. Its sound would carry far away into Yaizu and was part of the soul of Rinso-in. But all metal belonged to the war effort: families gave the metal in their homes, women gave their rings. So on the appointed day Shunryu helped the old men in the congregation gather the bells and gongs. They lowered the large bronze bell from its tower, decorated it, and tied it to timbers with rope. In front of the temple in fancy robes he conducted a service to send these sacred instruments to war. The men hoisted the timbers onto their shoulders and the procession went off to the docks to deliver Buddha's gift and their sacrifice at an official military reception. Shunryu refused to join them and went to his room to be alone.

On one side we are all fools, but when we realize this we are enlightened, and when we make efforts in the face of it, we are bodhisattvas.

BY EARLY 1945 Rinso-in was crowded. In addition to the Suzuki family, the students, soldiers, and Korean laborers, there were now more than sixty children living there, evacuated from Tokyo to escape the bombing and subsequent firestorms. Chie and Shunryu's sister Tori helped look after them. Tori and her family had also left Tokyo and moved in – all six of them. Aiko, now Aiko Uchiyama, was with her priest husband and children in a temple in Hamamatsu, having returned in 1942 after a three-year stay in Taiwan.

Fearing air raids, godfather Amano came at times in a horse-drawn carriage with his family, often spending the night outside in the valley below the temple, far away from any targets. Some cities, such as nearby Shimizu, had been shelled by ships. There was fear of that in Yaizu as well, but it never happened. There were many displaced people, and Shunryu and Chie tried to keep the temple open to them, while helping them find other places to stay. The Suzukis were crowded into a small room of the temple next to the kitchen. They now had a girl named Omi, born in 1942, and a boy named Otohiro, born in 1944.

Food had become scarce. The soldiers and Korean laborers cooked for themselves and were better supplied. Much of the nation's rice was going to the troops; the Suzukis and their guests subsisted by foraging in the woods and growing food in the temple garden. The garden had been inspired by the sweet potato crop at a nearby little Soto temple called Zuioji, run by the Sugiyamas. One day after returning from Zuioji, Shunryu went out and started removing stones from a plot below the temple. Soon the caretaker and some villagers were helping. They put in manure and built a fence to keep animals out. They had a good crop of sweet potatoes, pumpkins, cabbage, and a variety of other vegetables, though it was never enough.

Yasuko and some of the other children would go with Tori and Chie up into the mountains and return with chestnuts, acorns, and locusts. Anything edible was a treat; there was no concept of three meals a day. Most civilians were willing to eat less so that the soldiers in the field had more. In this way they were fighting the war too. In that spirit Chie would feed Shunryu's students before her own family.

The children saw every wild berry as a contribution to the war effort. They believed in the divinity of the emperor, saluted the soldiers, and thought the war was a righteous and winning cause against white devils. Even nine-year-old Yasuko thought that way, and it would have been futile for her parents to try to contradict the propaganda she absorbed at school.

Shunryu would go out with his begging bowl on takuhatsu, a practice that was no longer merely ceremonial. Without looking up from his conical begging hat, he would receive food and small change while chanting verses for the donors. On these walks he would stop to help workers dig ditches for refuge in air raids and would plant cucumbers and eggplant around the edges.

AS TIMES got harder, the ideas coming from some of the High Grass Mountain Group became more bold. During his stay at Rinso-in, Nishinakama had come up with the idea of starting a type of peace corps in the rural areas of China, as a model of how Japan could move from military to peaceful activity. Shunryu was enthusiastic. Nishinakama was well connected and, through his relationship with General Takagi, he had gone to China to check out the situation. He returned disillusioned and depressed, saying that conditions everywhere were chaotic and deteriorating. There he had learned that Japan was losing the war.

Nishinakama urged Shunryu to go to China and try to get Chiang Kai-shek to communicate directly with Emperor Hirohito. Nishinakama had told General Takagi in Tokyo about the High Grass Mountain Group and other salons he was involved with, and had suggested that groups like this could help develop young leaders. He asked the general to help him meet with Prince Takamatsu, who was said to be the highest-ranking person in Japan who wanted peace, and who later personally asked the emperor to surrender. These were the sorts of incredibly ambitious ideas that Shunryu was hearing. He admired the young men greatly for their sincerity, courage, and willingness to think beyond the war.

SHUNRYU'S WELL-PLACED friend Kozo Kato was encouraging him to go to Manchuria, which had now been occupied by Japan for over a decade. Free of fighting at this time, it was considered a new frontier. Kozo was in charge of emigration from Shizuoka Prefecture to three villages in Manchuria. Though a colonizer, he was a great admirer of the Chinese and Manchurians, and a student of their history and poetry.

In a world where wild propaganda was coming from everywhere, where most people kept their mouths shut and their eyes down, Kozo was a colorful, outspoken character. As a member of the dissolved lower house of the Diet, he had not been an enthusiast of the war, but he was loyal to his country and did his part to see that Japan was successful. He believed they were establishing a better society in Manchuria. Though he was tied to government, he claimed to be an anarchist and was sympathetic with the communists, whom he felt were in touch with the natural order.

Kozo had gotten into trouble for holding a community meeting in his nearby hometown of Shimada and announcing that Japan was losing the war. The secret police had abruptly dispersed the assembly, threatening to imprison anyone who stayed. Kozo was always being watched, and after that the surveillance was increased.

He was a friend to the downtrodden. Those who went to Manchuria were the poorest of farmers. He recruited wives for them. He also regularly visited a leper colony and wrote a book on the eta, the Japanese untouchables – a subject that was virtually taboo.

Kozo felt he could best contribute to Japan by helping to feed the population. There were almost unlimited possibilities in Manchuria for farming. He and his wife were heavily involved in the local Brown Rice Movement; they argued that eating white rice was a waste of nutrition and national resources. If everyone ate unhulled brown rice the nation could be better fed with much less. The Katos were influenced by *Food to Win the War With,* a book that advocated, among other things, eating more alkaline than acidic foods. Shunryu was familiar with such ideas from his master So-on.

In the area of Manchuria colonized from Shizuoka, there was a shortage of Buddhist temples and priests. Many people had died without having had Buddhist services. According to Kozo there were vast possibilities for Shunryu there. It was a much brighter place to be, without the food shortage or the gloom that was hanging over Japan. Kozo said that the Japanese had a much more positive relationship with the Manchurians than with the Chinese. The Japanese shared the view of many Manchurians that Manchuria should be separate from China. Kozo said there was a cooperative spirit among the farmers – Manchurians, Japanese, and Koreans – who could homestead there as well. Maybe it would become an independent nation after the war or be divided up into anarchist villages.

Kozo had urged Shunryu to go a number of times. Shunryu was interested in Kozo's offer, but he had too many responsibilities in Yaizu.

KUSUMI SHUNGO was an important administrator in Manchuria whom Shunryu had come to know through Kozo. Shungo leaned more toward an imperial form of government than Kozo, who was mainly concerned about the Japanese people. But neither Kozo nor Shunryu was anti-imperial; they were just not fond of the emperor's recent ridiculous role as demigod. The three of them agreed on many things. They talked about the Brown Rice Movement and how to end the war, and they shared a dislike for fanaticism and the demonization of foreigners. Shunryu said that if the Japanese based their actions on Buddhist principles, they wouldn't get sucked into such one-sided thinking – just as he had said publicly in prewar times. Kozo had brought Shungo to some of Shunryu's discussions before the war, when he was stressing the importance of accomplishing goals through peaceful means. They had also met at Gyokuden-in, where they went to hear Kishizawa lecture.

The three friends sat in Kozo's house one night drinking sake and talking quite freely. The windows were taped and covered. They were covered so the dim light wouldn't escape to help the bombers see the city, and taped so that if a bomb went off nearby the glass wouldn't shatter. Shungo joked that they'd better be careful what they said. Kozo showed them piles of communist magazines he had collected and laughed defiantly, saying that they had nothing to fear in his home because they were well protected by the secret police outside – his son Taro had been going out and playing with them for years.

To live in the realm of buddha nature means to die as a small being, moment after moment.

TARO KATO was going to Manchuria with his father. The boy had pestered and pestered him, and Kozo had finally given in, even though his son was only twelve years old and small for his age.

Like his father and his father's friends, Taro had a bent for big ideas. He attended an agricultural school and wanted to look into the possibility of establishing large-scale farming in Manchuria using modern techniques. The land was wide and open like Hokkaido. He had been studying hard to prepare for the trip. When he had first mentioned his ambition, Shunryu and Shungo were present, and all three men had taken him seriously. Now his father would let him risk his life venturing across the Japan Sea. But just as father and son were about to board the express train at Shizuoka station, there was an air raid, and Taro headed for the station basement. The train would not wait. Kozo called to the boy, "I'm going," and left him behind in Japan.

Taro showed up at Rinso-in and told Shunryu about his disappointment. His father had sent a message to Taro suggesting he get Shunryu to come over with him. "I'll do it!" Shunryu said and set about making arrangements. He contacted Soto headquarters, which immediately gave him an official appointment – not as a chaplain for the army but as a missionary priest. They hadn't sent anyone to Manchuria for over a year. Shunryu contacted the appropriate government department, but they didn't think it was a good idea. He continued with his plans anyway; Manchuria was called Outer Japan and no special papers were needed. Getting the tickets was harder, but with Kozo's connection, it proved to be no problem. Taro got them tickets as emigrants at half price.

Aside from Shunryu's time at Eiheiji in Fukui, neither he nor Taro had ever left the Kanto region of Japan where they lived. It was a perilous time for travel. Shunryu packed a few things and bid farewell to godfather Amano, his family, and a few students who were living there. It seemed like a rash, even an irresponsible thing to do. Above all, those close to him were worried they'd never see him again.

On May 14, 1945, Shunryu and Taro stood on the platform at the Shizuoka station. They were taking the train to Shimonoseki, where they would board a ferry to Pusan, Korea. Taro's mother was there to see them off, giving each a box lunch with brown rice balls and cucumbers. The train was at the station, but they waited to see what direction the bombers would take. The B-29s went east that day, so it was safe to board. They picked up their rucksacks and off they went.

THE CONDUCTOR on the train to Shimonoseki warned them that they'd have a hard time getting across the straits on the ferry. They were stuck at an inn for a few days, where they ate rice and beans. But they didn't have much money, so they went to the house of a college friend of Shunryu, who welcomed them and served them rice, fish, and seaweed – better food than they had at Rinso-in. They couldn't have managed it without him. During the days they searched the docks during constant bombing till finally they heard that a ferry would be leaving. It was early June. Ferries were prized targets for American submarines and planes, which were trying to cut off communication between Japan and the mainland.

But the ferry did make it to Pusan, where there was no bombing. They stayed overnight, even saw a movie, then took a night train to Manchuria. The train schedules were undependable, and they had to get their tickets one segment at a time, since they didn't have authorization for longer rides. Efficient and alert young Taro was the navigator; he bought the tickets, carried the maps and money, checked the timetables, and made sure they were at the right place at the right time with all their possessions and that they got off the train when they reached their station. Shunryu, in good hands, was free to look at the scenery and doze. And he didn't lose anything.

In Korea they could easily get by speaking Japanese. Once they arrived in Manchuria, Shunryu found that his English was useful. Taro knew some Chinese, the language of agricultural studies in Japan. When the train stopped, they would get off and barter with farmers for potatoes and pumpkins. After a few days and some lengthy delays, they arrived in Shinkyo, Manchukuo (as the Japanese called it), where Kozo was living. He was waiting at the station. He had been meeting every train for days and had been worried. Not everyone got to their destination in those times.

"I've been so worried about you two," he said as they approached him. "How did you make it?"

"By crawling out from under the debris of the firebombs in Fukuoka," said Shunryu.

SHUNRYU AND TARO had been riding in third class with the peasants and were covered with lice. In Japan lice were sometimes called Kannon-sama, the bodhisattva of compassion, and as they shook and picked the lice off their bodies they joked that it would be wrong to hurt Kannon-sama. While in Shinkyo they took desperately needed baths, then made further travel plans. Kozo could get them all tickets for the whole journey at once. After a few days they went to Harbin, the capital of Manchuria. In Harbin there was such a shortage of vehicles and fuel that the mayor had to commandeer a fire truck for their tour. They had a high time seeing the sights and meeting various dignitaries, completely unaware that hideous biological experiments were being conducted in that very city by Japanese army doctors on captive soldiers and civilians.

They visited three villages of immigrants from their home prefecture of Shizuoka. At one they stayed with a Shinto priest, who took Shunryu to the homes and farms of people who needed services performed. At another they stayed with a former Diet member. There were so many homes that needed memorial services that Shunryu would stand in front of them chanting, and people would come outside and give him envelopes with a few small bills of currency or offerings of food. They thanked him over and over, their bodies bowed in respect as he walked on.

Shunryu and the Katos went on to other cities and villages, passing wide expanses of land and mountain ranges. In each place they would see the sights and would meet with friends of Kozo and with local officials like the Manchurian mayors and their subordinates. Taro didn't join the meetings; he'd go out and play in the fields and look around. But he also had plenty of opportunities to examine agricultural practices. His dream of managing a large farm was closer to becoming a reality. All the Japanese immigrants paid attention to Shunryu in his brown priest's robes. People inquired about how things were back in Shizuoka. Was there enough food? How much had been destroyed? There was plenty of food in Manchuria, and banquets were held for the visitors. As Kozo had said, the mood among the Japanese there was upbeat compared to the mood in Japan. Many wanted Shunryu to stay.

"What do you think?" asked Kozo.

"I want to establish a branch temple of Rinso-in in Manchuria," Shunryu answered.

Kozo talked to various officials and merchants about finding Shunryu land for a temple. After some research he decided on a large tract of land bordering a train line about ninety miles northwest of Harbin. He went there with Shunryu, Taro, and an engineer from the Manchurian Development Agency. There were flatlands, hills, a river, and luxuriant forest growth as well. Shunryu fell in love with it right away; it was the ideal environment. From there he could take care of the needs of the Japanese from Shizuoka Prefecture and also build a training temple where he could practice and teach the way he had learned from his masters. The Japanese people he met in this area were not so narrowly programmed as those back in Japan. He could make a fresh start and the temple would be open to Manchurians as well as Japanese.

"There's one problem with this land though," Kozo told Shunryu. "It is remote, and tigers are known to frequent the area."

"Tigers will make it all the more interesting," said Shunryu. "If I'm not good enough to practice with the tigers, then I have no business being here."

The decision was made; they hurried back to Shinkyo, where Kozo could make arrangements without delay.

Weeks passed. July 1945 arrived, and everything changed. Okinawa had fallen. Germany had been out of the war since its surrender in April, and the Americans could now concentrate on the Pacific front. Japanese troops were returning from occupied places throughout Asia to defend the home islands from certain invasion. There were rumors that the Russians were about to break their neutrality; soon they might be coming down from the north. Suddenly Japanese were trying to get out of Manchuria as fast as they could, and the Manchurians were clearly elated to see them go. A thin facade crumbled – the pretense that anything other than force had made it possible for the Japanese to stay. Kozo was ordered by his superiors to return to Japan right away. He embraced his son, bowed to Shunryu, and flew off for Tokyo on a rattling airplane used by black marketeers. Now Shunryu and Taro had to get out as quickly as they could, forgetting the temple and the farm.

Of the three ferries that had been running sporadically between Korea and Japan, only one had not been sunk. Every day Shunryu and Taro would go to the train station, only to be told that the boat wasn't coming in from Pusan. Finally one day tickets were available, and the two left on the 3:15 PM train.

At the station in Harbin they were told that the ferry from Pusan had been damaged. Shunryu said that there would be a way, and they should just continue. They made it to the coast and found a steamboat carrying a cargo of chickens to Korea. Soon he and Taro were steaming south. On the boat were many Koreans in a jubilant mood. They had taken all the good seats and now were pushing the Japanese around, shouting, "You're going to lose the war!"

The steamboat ride ended in northern Korea, and they went to the train station. A sign read, "We will not sell tickets. There is no boat to Japan."

Shunryu said not to worry, that they could not depend on signs. "To me the sign reads, 'We will sell tickets. There is a boat to Japan.'" He felt they should just take the train and something would happen. They asked for tickets to Japan, and when told that none were available, Shunryu asked for tickets going south along the coast: "That's where the boats are." At each station they would get out, go to the docks, and talk to the workers about how dangerous it was to go to Japan, about the condition of ships, and about where one might be leaving from. Keep going south, they were told. Eventually, at a small station the conductor announced that all who wanted to go to Japan should get off and go to Sanroshin.

When they reached Sanroshin they were told to go to nearby Fort Mason at the harbor.

No one knew if a boat would come. There was talk of all the ships that had been sunk. America was in total control of the seas. Finally one day a huge navy troopship came into the harbor escorted by two cruisers. Shunryu looked at it, and like the sound of a bell ringing in his head came the certainty that this would be their last chance for a long time. Shunryu and Taro watched as troops boarded. Many were wounded and carried on stretchers. A crowd of Japanese civilians was desperately trying to get on board.

"We will be on this ship, just wait here for a while," Shunryu told Taro and walked off. He came back with permission from the captain to board.

When darkness fell they steamed out of the harbor. At three in the morning they anchored far from shore. Watching the skies and listening to the waves, Shunryu was reminded of Dogen's perilous journey to China and back in the thirteenth century and felt confident that, as Dogen survived to bring Nyojo's teaching to Japan, so would he survive to sow his dharma seeds.

Morning approached. They learned that Hakata harbor was considered too dangerous to enter. The ship had anchored outside Onishi, a port that was too small for it to enter. Launches were sent at dawn to take them to the mainland. Shunryu and Taro boarded a civilian express train that stopped at Shizuoka. The mood in the station was different from anything they'd felt before – angry and frightened. People were breaking windows to get into the train. They were attacked by airplanes three times on the way back, but the train kept going.

On the night of July 15, having been away for two months, they arrived at Shizuoka station during an air raid. They both went to Rinso-in, where everyone was overjoyed to see them back safely. In Japan it is customary for a traveler to bring gifts home from a trip, and Shunryu surprised his children with a box of Korean hardtack. He and Taro scrubbed themselves down, then took long baths in hot, clean water.

Kozo showed up the next day. "It's a miracle! You've come back!" he exclaimed, crying and hugging his son and Shunryu. "How did you make it?"

Shunryu and Taro looked at each other. "We don't know," Shunryu said.

As long as you depend on something special, something it is assumed you should depend on, you are not strong enough to go on by yourself. You cannot find your way. So first of all, know yourself and be strong enough to live without any sign, without any information – that is the most important point. There is truth, you say, but there can be various truths. The question is not which way you should go. If you only try to go in one direction, or if you always depend on signs, you will not find your own way. The best thing is to have eyes to read various signs. I had this kind of experience when I was in Manchuria.

When you are fooled by something else, the damage will not be so big. But when you are fooled by yourself, it is fatal. No more medicine.

AMERICA HAD dropped bombs of incredible might on Hiroshima and Nagasaki. Shunryu Suzuki couldn't believe what he'd heard – that anything could be that powerful, that a whole city could be destroyed by a single bomb. Some Japanese were still under a spell, believing that victory was ordained. Others said they wouldn't live long anyway if there was an invasion, so maybe the best way to go would be under these giant bombs. Shunryu said the fanaticism and bombs were what should be feared, not the Americans. The ultimate foolishness would be to not surrender. If we don't, he thought, everything will be over for Japan. This blind sacrifice of yourselves for Japan, he said, will only have been a sacrifice for the mistaken ideas of certain leaders.

Through some miracle Nishinakama and other former students from the High Grass Mountain Group were working in the General Planning Office in Tokyo. Shunryu had gotten the hint through them that there were other good people in the capital pressing for peace, such as General Yonai and Kintaro Suzuki, the new prime minister. Gempo-roshi from Mishima near Yaizu, whom Shunryu knew, had been advising the prime minister and the royal family. He had suggested that Japan was an *ozeki*, a sumo wrestler of the second-highest rank, who could lose with grace.

Avoiding annihilation was not an easy task. Now it was mainly a matter of convincing the top army staff. The Russians had declared war on Japan and were on their way. On August 13 there was another massive air attack on Tokyo by fifteen hundred planes. On the fourteenth the Americans returned to deluge the city with leaflets. It was said they wanted unconditional surrender, with no guarantees that the emperor could retain his position or even his life. Could there be peace with no guarantees at all? Would there be an invasion? Once a decision was made, everyone would go with it.

Then on Wednesday, August 15, the unprecedented word had gone out by radio, newspaper, and sound truck that the emperor's voice, the "jewel sound," would be broadcast at noon and heard for the first time by the public.

As noon approached all the radios in Japan were on. An announcer said in hushed and reverential tones that what was about to be broadcast was a recording that the emperor had made for all to hear. Only later did people learn of the intrigue, heroism, and sacrifice of life that had transpired at the Imperial Palace the night before to protect that recording so it could be broadcast.

Shunryu and Chie kneeled formally in seiza with Omi and Otohiro on her lap and Hoitsu and Yasuko at their sides. Tori and her family were there. The children from Tokyo had moved on; there were no students around. The shoji to the family area were open and a number of soldiers and navy men sat in the large open *genkan* (entryway) and wide hall. Some of them were smoking and even chatting with each other, showing, as usual, no respect for anything or anyone. The Koreans in the zendo listened on their own radio; it would be very hard for them or any person not well educated to understand all the special words the emperor would use, but they would get the essence. All Japan was still and waiting. The most unifying and heart-tearing event in the history of Japan was about to take place. The recording began with formalities and moved slowly to the subject.

"The war situation has developed not necessarily to Japan's advantage," were the first words, hinting with colossal understatement at the intent of the message. "The enemy has begun to employ a new and most cruel bomb, whose power to do damage is indeed incalculable, taking the toll of many innocent lives." The emperor said that Japan had accepted the Potsdam Treaty. "Should we continue to fight, it would not only result in the ultimate collapse and obliteration of the Japanese nation, but also it could lead to the total extinction of human civilization." The emotional core of the emperor's pronouncement sank into the hearts of the nation. "We are keenly aware of the inmost feelings of all of you, Our subjects. However, it is according to the dictate of time and fate that We have resolved to pave the way for a grand peace for all the generations to come, by enduring the unendurable and suffering what is insufferable."

As the last words of the emperor's voice echoed through the halls of Rinso-in, Shunryu and his family wept openly. So many feelings, so much loss. Tori's husband and Chie's brother had died, as well as some of Shunryu's students and the sons of friends and danka. And now the empire was dead, Japan crushed and charred. The children cried for Japan's loss and because everyone else was in tears. So much struggling and suffering and madness, and now it was over. Cheers were coming from the Koreans in the zendo. Most of the soldiers were crying too, but there were some snickers and cynical comments from a couple of them.

Shunryu looked at them and saw not the slightest sincerity or caring, only a despicable insensitivity from these representatives of the forces that had, in their ignorance, brought Japan to the brink of total insanity and destruction. He stood wet-faced, breathing heavily, glaring at them. Then he erupted. Screaming out the years of frustration and inner turmoil, he snatched up a large, full sake bottle and heaved it into a solid wall. He began to grab anything within reach to fling through shoji and down the hall – plates, books, and cups. The children cried piteously. The soldiers were mute. Shunryu spent his wrath and walked outside.

The hot sun burned in the cloudless sky, and while Shunryu stared at the pond, from the zendo came the sound of Koreans jubilantly singing folk songs from home.

IN SHIMADA, at his aunt's house after the emperor's speech, Taro Kato had watched his father go berserk, swinging a sword in the air, yelling that all he had done for the emperor was for naught. His brother-in-law handed him a large bottle of sake and put his arms around him saying this was no time for swinging swords, that he should go home and drink and sleep.

He would need the rest. The people he had sent to Manchuria had been coming back since July, and the trickle was turning into a flood. It was the beginning of harvest time, and they had just walked away from their homes, fields, animals, and possessions. Kozo's home was right in front of Shimada station, and the displaced had nowhere to go but into his house, carrying burlap bags and angry disappointment.

In Yaizu many people were panicking, burning records in homes, businesses, and at city hall; there was even an attempt to torch the building itself. The Americans were coming, and people feared that anything they had done might be used against them. Lists would be compiled, and the soldiers would go from home to home executing them. Of the survivors, men would become slaves and women would be raped. In Okinawa hundreds of women had jumped off cliffs rather than face the invaders.

The Americans had been called beasts and demons for so long that ordinary people were in terror. In meetings, on the streets, and in the temple, Shunryu urged them to be calm and not to worry.

He had always said it wasn't only foreigners who could be devils; those among us who need to call them that may be the devils, the enemy. He encouraged people not to worry about the Americans. "They are people just like us, and they will understand us."

I didn't really know anything about America or other countries, but I had confidence in human nature and that human nature is the same wherever we go. I'd always expressed these sorts of views in my lectures or when students came. I had been criticized, but I hadn't been acting officially. It was just my opinion.

In the playground of a local elementary school sat a large inscribed memorial stone, the *chukonhi,* a monument for the spirits of fallen soldiers. People wanted it to be destroyed or buried.

Shunryu intervened. "Why do that? Isn't it natural to have a memorial for those who have sacrificed their lives for their country? There is nothing wrong with it. They'll understand."

But the locals feared they'd be punished, whereas if they destroyed it the Americans would be pleased.

"Carry it to my temple then," Shunryu said to them. "I will protect it as long as I'm alive, and I will take all the responsibility for any damage done by the Americans to this memorial."

So the chukonhi was moved to a spot in front of Rinso-in, and Shunryu held a service there for the war dead and enshrined it. Then everyone waited for the Americans.

Chapter Seven

The Occupation

1945–1952

*When you look at human life carefully, you will find out
how important it is to become a trustworthy person.*

THE AMERICAN soldiers came and proved not to be devils. The Japanese forces were allowed to disarm themselves, and the
Japanese civil authorities were given the power to administer the nation under the watchful eye of GHQ, General Headquarters, the
American army of occupation.

But there was a new war: the enemy now was starvation. Food
was scarcer than ever, and the harvest had been poor. Temple life
was just as hard as in the days of Haibutsu Kishaku, the nineteenth-
century persecution of the Buddhists, except now everyone suffered.

One morning a neighbor came to Rinso-in to help out in the
kitchen. Shunryu brought in some vegetables from the garden, and
there was seaweed and miso for soup, but when the woman opened

the large temple rice box she gasped. It was empty. Her family didn't have much either, but she ran down the hill, took half of what they had, and gave it to the temple. Soon all the neighbors and members of Rinso-in heard that the temple was in need, and the rice box filled up.

The homeless, the jobless, and the hungry were wandering the roads, and some found their way to Rinso-in. Shunryu would see them coming and tell Chie, "Look after them." She would share what they had – cooked rice, sweet potatoes, pumpkins, cucumbers – and admonish them to go find work and take care of themselves. Just as Chie was giving it away, some old woman with a bag of rice would come down the mountainside to make an offering to the temple. The temple rice box had a life of its own.

AS HE WALKED to Rinso-in, Taro Kato collected locusts and strung them together with needle and thread. At Rinso-in he cooked them with soy sauce. He had been living in the temple quite a bit since his Manchurian dream had been crushed. He had held on to hope for a while, and had even sent his belongings ahead. He figured they had reached Hiroshima when the bomb dropped. His parents, seeing him dejected and directionless, had sent him to be with Shunryu.

Taro suggested that his father could easily get Shunryu a government job, which would provide money to buy food and to pay off some of the temple's debts. But Shunryu would not consider such a thing. A number of priests were working to support their temples and families, going off in Western suits and shined shoes, but not he. He was testing Dogen's teaching. Dogen had said that when we are supported firmly from within, external support follows. Every morning in Soto temples a priest chanted a brief dedication that included the line, "May the two wheels of the temple gate turn smoothly forever." The two wheels of the temple are the dharma wheel and the economic wheel. Dogen said that the former turned the latter, so if the temple went broke or the people starved, it would likely be because their dharma was weak.

Ever since I first knew the world of Dogen-zenji, I tested my belief that if I observed the Buddhist way faithfully, I would be supported. This was true during and especially after the war, when there was not enough to eat.

Japan and Dogen's hypothesis got a nudge of support from America when shiploads of food started to arrive at the docks, feeding the faithless and faithful alike. Among the foodstuffs were powdered milk, which was a curious drink, and hard dried fruit. Chie encouraged her children to eat this strange food by telling them things like, "Prunes make you beautiful."

Chie was nursing the last of their children, a son named Otohiro, and she nursed a neighbor's baby as well. It was Yasuko's job to go get the other baby several times a day from the milkless mother and bring it home. People would tell her on the way what a wonderful, generous woman her mother was.

So the early days of the occupation passed, and the nation was grateful to the victors for their magnanimity. People weren't being rounded up and shot, they had their emperor and their own government, there were shiploads of food, and, in general, the militarists had been exposed for their great lies and barbarism. Indeed, the whole world had been turned upside down: everything was the opposite of what they'd been taught for decades.

In Tokyo at least five members of the High Grass Mountain Group were now working with the new government. Masao Nishinakama was involved in negotiations with the Americans and was said to have pushed successfully to see that Japan was not required to pay reparations to countries it had occupied and fought with. Others, including Masao's little brother Shigeo, were involved in economic planning and national policy making.

SHUNRYU WAS deeply committed to the reinvigoration of a wounded Japan, not only through Buddhism but also by general education. He still had the certificate he had received from Komazawa University to teach English and to be an ethical guide to youth. But there was a purge going on, and he felt in some danger of losing his certification and being ostracized from any public duty beyond his immediate priestly tasks. This purge was far reaching; all leaders, teachers, and priests were being examined by GHQ and the new Japanese authorities to determine if they had actively supported the war, nationalism, and fascism through speaking or writing. On October 30, 1945, they issued an Order of Investigation, Expulsion or Approval for Teachers and Educators, and on January 4, 1946, Notification on the Expulsion of Unfavorable Individuals from the Public Occupations.

Priests were needed to be teachers, as there was a shortage of college graduates after the war, but they had to pass this scrutiny, and GHQ deemed them guilty unless proven innocent. The Shinto priests were obvious targets, and most of them were excluded, but Buddhist priests were suspect as well. Some had been enthusiastic supporters of the military, some had become officers, and others had gone on lecture tours promoting militaristic imperial Buddhism. All religious institutions, including Christian ones, had supported the military. The official policy of both Soto and Rinzai Zen had been to subordinate Buddhism to the war effort.

Shunryu knew he had several possible strikes against him. One was that his temple had housed military personnel and Korean slave labor. Another was that before the Pacific war he had, for one day, headed that new organization to promote public support for government policies. The third strike was his trip to occupied Manchuria, which could be seen as participation in Japan's imperialism. In his favor, there was sympathy now for those who spoke and taught English. He hadn't worn the military-style uniform of the day. There were the meetings he'd held. And he had saved a stack of papers at Rinso-in that documented his lack of support for the madness.

Suetsune-san of the High Grass Mountain Group showed up at Rinso-in one day to find Shunryu laboring over a questionnaire from GHQ. Suetsune's English was good, and they stayed up all night working on it. On another occasion Shunryu had to go see Japanese authorities in Shizuoka; he brought his papers to that meeting as well.

The purge did not turn into a mindless witch-hunt; reason seemed to be prevailing. All Japanese had cooperated with the war effort whether they wanted to or not. Practically every noncombatant, including women, had gone to evening meetings where they'd practiced lunging with pointed bamboo spears, preparing to kill the paratroopers as they landed and charge the invaders on the beaches. Officers at GHQ knew the situation was complex, and they left most of the nuts and bolts of the purge to the Japanese authorities. They were just looking for those who had been vocal and committed, and Shunryu definitely did not fit that description. But more than eighty-three thousand people were subject to the purge through the summer of 1952.

I was not purged after the world war. I had no record of supporting the military. And I had many printed documents expressing my feelings, many papers suggesting what our policies should be, what kind of danger the nation was in. Most of this may be difficult for Americans to understand. I didn't say anything about war. I said that if we neglected to understand Japan's situation clearly, if we based our understanding merely on what was broadcast or printed, then we would lose the real picture of Japan.

I cared more about the fundamental way of thinking that causes war. That is why I didn't like the nationalists in Japan. Their view was very one-sided and unrealistic. They brought accusations against others without knowing what they were doing. They created tremendous problems. So I put the emphasis on studying what was actually happening in the country, in the army, and in the political world.

Wherever you go, if you have a flexible attitude you can help people quite easily.

ON DECEMBER 31, 1945, the temple was buzzing with enthusiastic preparation for the New Year. Tori's family was back in Tokyo. Chie's mother, Kinu Muramatsu, had moved in, and she, her daughter, and a group of danka wives were making the best meal they could come up with. In the buddha hall, cards were passed out for people to chant a chapter of the *Prajna Paramita Sutra*. All night mochi was pounded, sake was sipped, and songs were sung. All week long they had cleaned the temple and thrown away what was worn out and not of use – Miss Ransom's chair, which the children had jumped on till it was beyond repair, old newspapers, magazines, and some offensive wartime books.

It was a time to pay debts, and with the help of the danka the family paid off what they could. They decorated and made offerings at the altar. This was New Year celebrated as it hadn't been for a long time. People were still depressed from the war, but Shunryu felt this week of rejuvenation would help lift them up together.

We fool ourselves in some way and enjoy the last day of the year. This is based on the Buddhist way of understanding life. Moment after moment we should renew our life, we should not stick to old ideas of what life is, or what our way of life is. Especially at the end of the year we should completely renew our feelings and completely clean even our cars. If we always stick to old ideas and always repeat the same thing over and over again, then we are confined in our old way of life. Some excitement or some occasion is necessary to encourage us along.

IN 1946 Shunryu established the Takakusa-juku, a study group for young men and women in their late teens and early twenties. It was considered to be part of the New Life after the War Movement. Local townsfolk and families from Shizuoka and Tokyo also sent their youth to Rinso-in. They sat zazen and chanted, Shunryu gave talks, and there were discussions. Taro Kato attended. Shunryu didn't have to censor himself anymore, but he was still not an absolutist. "This may be right, but this may also be wrong," he would say. A neighbor, twelve-year-old Masao Yamamura, too young to attend, would hide outside the shoji and listen to the exciting new ideas being discussed. He heard Shunryu say passionately that the war had been a big mistake and that people should open their eyes to the world.

Now what Shunryu said was in harmony with the mood of the nation and even with GHQ. MacArthur himself said that war could only be eliminated with a spiritual awakening. Many Japanese felt a deep shame for the course their people had followed and vowed that their nation would never again resort to force except in self-defense. Indeed, it would be written into their new constitution. Shunryu noticed that since they had lost the war the Japanese people had dropped a great deal of their national arrogance and had more of a sense of the contradictions within their own culture. Many felt they had lost their way, but to Shunryu the new humility and insecurity were better. Now they were more skeptical and sensed, at least theoretically, the emptiness of all existence. They saw that their traditions were always changing and not set in stone.

Sometimes people were sleeping, exposing their bellies to the sun. So I helped by covering them so the sun wouldn't burn them, and they were very happy to see me. If you have that kind of feeling, you can help people quite easily. Without anything, with an empty hand you can help them.

Shunryu thought that the best way he could alleviate the pain in people's minds would be to promote Buddha's dharma and Kishizawa's teaching. In March of 1947 he organized a lay ordination at Rinso-in for four hundred people, mostly women, in which they received precepts and Buddhist names, and rededicated themselves to following Buddhist principles. It was presided over by Kishizawa, who gave lectures, and people came from all over Japan to hear him. The ceremony took one week – a sort of modified sesshin. There wasn't enough rice, so barley was mixed with it. Sugiyama, the abbot from nearby Zuioji who had been helping out at Rinso-in since 1937, was in charge of the cooking. He and Chie worked together and got along well; he had been her father's attendant when she was a young girl. It was said he purposely burned the rice so there would be something for the kitchen workers to eat – the charred grains on the bottom. Otherwise there might have been nothing left for them.

At the ceremony was a disciple of Kishizawa's named Kojun Noiri. He was ten years younger than Shunryu and admired him greatly. In the most important part of the closing ceremony on the last day, Kishizawa stopped the proceedings and, in front of all present, criticized Shunryu for offering incense at the wrong point in the proceedings. It was clear to Noiri that Kishizawa was speaking to everyone through scolding Shunryu; he wanted to do it in the most dramatic way possible. To Noiri, Shunryu gracefully accepted his position as representative of the whole group and, without any sign of anger or embarrassment, bowed respectfully to his teacher. He said that this illustrated that Shunryu and Kishizawa had the proper student-teacher relationship, that Shunryu had been strong enough to take on this role and had confirmed Kishizawa's confidence in him.

Noiri described another large lay ordination led by Kishizawa at Jokoji, a prominent temple in Shizuoka Prefecture. Since Jokoji was a branch temple of Rinso-in, Shunryu had to step forward at one point in the ceremony as a leader among many older and more experienced priests. Noiri was struck by Shunryu's bearing, by the way he carried himself, moved, and handled his bowing cloth. His tempo was just right. Noiri felt that that kind of perfection could not have been achieved in one lifetime. Other priests did not necessarily notice these things about Shunryu.

Noiri saw a profound stillness in Shunryu. He had strongly felt this stillness once at Yaizu station where they had passed each other. Shunryu just greeted Noiri and went on. As he watched Shunryu

go up the stairs to the platform, Noiri had the undeniable experience of his calmness and humility.

In that brief greeting, Noiri felt contact, an active presence. Noiri
had just published a book about some of Dogen's writings and was
dashing past Shunryu. The contrast was striking. In Shunryu's
greeting, he perceived a kind of *gokurosama,* an appreciation for his
work, not congratulating but encouraging him. As Noiri watched
Shunryu walk slowly up the stairs he was left with a wonderful
image.

SO-ON HAD done the major restoration work on the Rinso-in
zendo long ago, and now it was finally finished, appointed with
new shoji, tatami that smelled of the fields, and a statue of Man-
jushri, the bodhisattva of wisdom. On June 3, 1947, there was a
well-attended opening ceremony for this new zendo, a ceremony
that affected the status of the temple. Now the Soto organization
recognized Rinso-in as a temple with a self-supporting zendo. It
was Shunryu's decision not to have a zendo supported by the Soto
organization, since such support would include financial and other
obligations on Rinso-in's part.

Shunryu had two monks living with him at the time. Now they,
his lay students, and the monthly zazenkai had a room just for
zazen. Shunryu wanted Rinso-in's zendo to be well used, but his enthusiasm for zazen did not receive any sustained response. He
would rather have had lots of people at zazen and very few show
up at the opening. He could accept the decline of prestige of the
priesthood, but the lack of interest in actual Buddhist practice was
discouraging.

AFTER THE war the position of priests in society changed radically.
The temples were forced by the government to sell off land for
practically nothing, especially land that others were working. Rinso-
in was no longer a landlord to the farmers below, though it kept the
forest land on the mountain. This meant that the temple had to depend on its membership for support to a far greater extent. With

civilian control of the army came greater lay control of the temples.

Shunryu had been a benevolent landlord, with a friendlier relationship with the farmers than untrusting So-on had had. He was sorry to see the land go but continued to believe in Dogen's teaching that a priest need only follow Buddha's way in order to be supported. Buddhism represented one of the last vestiges of feudalism, and the GHQ and new government had put an end to that. As a result, temples became corporations. The farmers who had had almost nothing were able to buy land cheaply. It was said that the head of the ogre had been cut off.

There is no fixed moral code or standard,
but you find yours when you try to teach others.

MITSU MATSUNO was head of a residential kindergarten for the children of war widows in Shizuoka, the capital of the prefecture about thirty miles from Yaizu. On one side of the school was a dorm for the children and on the other side were their mothers. Mitsu lived with her twelve-year-old daughter, Harumi, in a room on the children's side. She was an intelligent, energetic woman with a round face and fair complexion. On a simmering summer day in 1949 she was returning to work when she unexpectedly discovered an old friend sitting on the hallway floor, eating a box lunch with a handsome monk in his mid-forties. "What brings you here, Tsuneko-san?" she asked.

"I've come to introduce you to this monk."

"And is this esteemed monk looking for a wife?" she teased, without the sort of respect women customarily showed to priests.

"No, no, Hojo-san has a fine wife," Tsuneko managed to say as she bent over laughing.

"Is that so?" Mitsu continued. "Then what is it you want of me?"

"He has opened a kindergarten and hasn't found a head teacher to manage it. My father recommended you, so we came here. I'm sorry we didn't let you know beforehand."

"I risked my life to get the children here into bomb shelters time after time during the war. The whole city burned down but we lived. After all I've done to keep it open in these difficult times, you want me to leave? I can't do that. I've resolved to spend the rest of my life here."

Shunryu had expedited the reopening of a Buddhist kindergarten in Yaizu that had been closed during the last year of the war and used by the army. It had been empty for three years, and neighbors were growing potatoes in the playground. Originally Shunryu had asked the Yaizu Buddhist Council to get the kindergarten reopened. They agreed it was a good idea and asked him to please take care of it. Called Tokiwa Kindergarten, it was the oldest such school in the prefecture. The priest who had founded it in 1924, Aoshima Zen'an, was now eighty and the abbot of a small neighboring branch temple of Rinso-in. Shunryu had known his kindergarten and sympathized with Zen'an's philosophy of Buddhist education; his emphasis wasn't on curriculum as much as on attitude – strict yet gentle.

Before Japan was defeated in the war and completely surrendered, the Japanese people thought that their moral code was absolutely right and straightforward and that if they just observed it they would not make any mistakes. Unfortunately, that moral code had been set up at the beginning of the Meiji Era. After losing the war they lost confidence in their morality and didn't know what to do. But morality should not be so difficult to find. I said to them, "You have children. If you think of how to raise them, you will naturally know your moral code."

Shunryu encouraged Zen'an to get the school going again and agreed to become involved, as Zen'an was too old to do the legwork. All over Japan priests were opening preschools, and Shunryu was glad to take part in this trend. It was another way to help reinvigorate his community, which was still weary and recuperating from the war.

Zen'an advised Shunryu about education and about getting the school reopened. Shunryu visited other Buddhist kindergartens, subscribed to a magazine on Buddhist education, gathered support from businessmen including godfather Amano, formed a board, and sought out teachers from among the daughters of the danka of Rinso-in and his young women students. He saw to the restoration of the building, dealt with the local government, got it licensed, and put the word out. It opened on May 5, Children's Day, 1949, with all classes full and Zen'an as principal.

Soon after it opened Zen'an died, and Shunryu needed to find a qualified principal. Shunryu's well-connected friend Isobe in Shizuoka told him about Mitsu, and got his daughter Tsuneko to make the connection. But Mitsu turned him down. Shunryu was struck with her straightforwardness and decided not to give up on her.

MITSU SAW Shunryu walking up to her school on the sidewalk, clattering in his wooden geta with white socks, shading himself from the sun with a black bamboo monk's hat and a monk's large black lacquered paper umbrella. That funny priest is back, she thought, looking at him. After Shunryu greeted her, she said, "I hate the idea of moving second only to dying."

A few days later he came again and she told him not to wear that strange flapping hat because it looked like a witch's hat and scared the children. He returned next time without the hat and she said she was too busy to see him. He kept coming every few days.

One day she told Shunryu, "I think you don't know that I'm a Christian. It would be inappropriate for me to run a Buddhist school."

"That's better than having no religion at all," he answered firmly.

"Go find a good Buddhist principal," she said.

On another visit she said, "I don't know anyone in Yaizu, but I think it is an ugly city full of fishermen – it even smells like fish. I've never wanted to go back there."

"My temple has no fishermen. The members there all smell like farmers, bureaucrats, and businessmen."

Every few days he'd show up and each time she'd rebuke him in one way or another. He even sent Chie over with fruit wrapped in colorful cloth. After a couple of months and a lot of train trips, Shunryu said to Mitsu, "There are some people I'd like you to meet in Yaizu, that city you detest so much. Why don't you just come once to visit?"

Shunryu met Mitsu at her school the next day and escorted her to a large home where a doctor named Ozawa lived with his family. He and his wife greeted Mitsu and served tea. Mitsu found them to be sophisticated and gracious. They were intellectuals; his wife taught *koto* (a stringed instrument), which Mitsu too had studied. It worried her: they would be hard to turn down. The doctor implored her to come take over the school.

She explained her responsibilities in Shizuoka. "Isobe will take care of that," the doctor said, referring to the man who had originally recommended her to Shunryu. "He has clout at the prefectural office."

She protested that she was unqualified to run this historically prominent school.

He gave her a piercing glance and said, "You don't have to be so brilliant. All you'd have to do is show up and stand there."

Mitsu felt as if a bolt of lightning had struck her, simultaneously burning away her feelings of conceit and unworthiness. "Then I only need to be there, standing and doing nothing? That's all?"

"Yes, that's right. Just stand there and do nothing."

"I'll do it then," she said.

Mitsu found a replacement for her former position, went right to work as the acting principal at Tokiwa, and moved into Rinso-in with her daughter Harumi. She started to attend temple services and soon found out that Shunryu was well thought of by his congregation. She admired Chie and got along with Chie's mother, Kinu, called Obaa-san, grandmother. She took Obaa-san on as a sort of new mother, as hers had died when she was eleven and her mother-in-law had died just after the war. After a month she and her daughter moved in with the family of a master plasterer who was a friend of Shunryu's. On January 1, 1950, she was installed in her new position at the Tokiwa Kindergarten, and she did a great deal more than just stand there.

MITSU WAS born to Kaemon and Toki Sakai in Shizuoka on April 23, 1914. She was so vocal that people joked she had been born of her mother's mouth. She loved storytelling and drama. Her father worked at city hall and her family was Buddhist, members of Jodo Shin-shu, the True Pure Land sect, which emphasized faith and gratitude. She went to a Methodist school and converted. She felt that she had been hardened by the early loss of her mother and that Christianity would help her to develop a warmer personality. In 1936 she married a navy pilot, Masaharu Matsuno, a kind man who had the sort of character she wished she had. After only nine months of marriage, he had to go to fight in China in a war that neither had anticipated.

He flew fifty-eight bombing missions to Nanking. She wrote him letters saying, "Please remember people in China are no different from me. They are families waiting for the safe return of their husbands, fathers, brothers, and sons who have gone to war. So please don't drop bombs on towns. Please try to drop them on places like rice fields only to startle the snails." Masaharu died there, leaving her with a daughter he'd never met. Mitsu called her Harumi, a combination of their two names.

EVERY MORNING except Sunday, Shunryu pedaled down the road on his bicycle to the Tokiwa Kindergarten, not far from the center of town. He would lead the teachers in a circumambulation of the building and then go to the playroom, where a Buddha statue was enshrined at an altar. There he would offer incense and lead the teachers, each holding a text, in a recitation of the *Shushogi* (The Meaning of Practice and Enlightenment), a modern compilation from Dogen's writings. After that he would say a few words of encouragement. Then the children would arrive, Chie bringing Otohiro, who was now five.

One day when he was eleven, Shunryu's son Hoitsu went to a ceremony at the school and heard his father speak.

All beings have buddha nature and all life is precious. We are nurturing Buddha's children and we should do so with Buddha's compassionate mind. We shouldn't see some as sharp and others as dull. By treating all children without discrimination, we enable them to see all beings as equal. We should perceive things with our fundamental eye, not only with the consciousness that makes the distinctions of daily life. That is the eye of wisdom – to appreciate things and people "as they are" and live our lives fully in the universe that is "as it is."

On her first day at work, Shunryu asked Mitsu to attend Kishizawa's lectures as part of her job. That she was Christian didn't matter, he said, she had a religious mind, which his teaching would penetrate. Kishizawa was teaching at a university in Kobe, but he still returned to his temple to give talks once a month. When he gave a dharma talk on Dogen's *Shobogenzo* at his temple, monks would come from all over. At his talks for laypeople nearly everyone would be in their sixties or seventies. Mitsu was just thirty-five. She would sit in the front row and listen carefully. His talks were often on the *Shushogi,* which she wanted to understand because they chanted it at school. She couldn't understand much, but Shunryu told her not to worry: "Just sit there with your ears on your head."

One day she said to Kishizawa, "I feel refreshed when I walk out through the temple gate after your lecture, but when I return I feel muddy all over again. Isn't it bad to repeat this pattern?"

Kishizawa answered, "After walking in the fog my robe doesn't dry easily. After getting caught in a shower it does. Either is fine. I'm still walking in fog. That's all for my talk today."

MITSU JOINED the zazenkai of the kindergarten teachers. One day after zazen and Shunryu's brief talk, she asked a bold question. "Hojo-san, I know I shouldn't ask this, but could you please tell me what is gained from zazen? I don't want to do it for no reason."

A practical question called for a practical answer: "The practice of zazen makes you capable of dealing with a situation in the best way, on the spot."

Another time Mitsu told Shunryu that she was having trouble understanding Kishizawa's lectures and asked if he could tell her in a few words what Buddhism was all about.

"Mmmmm," he murmured breathing out slowly. "Accept what is as it is and help it to be its best."

Mitsu applied that attitude with the teachers in the kindergarten, praising rather than criticizing them. Soon she noticed that they were treating her like family. She now considered herself a Buddhist, but didn't mention it to Shunryu.

In reflecting on our problems, we should include ourselves.

A DEALER in garden stones was working in the creek to the west of the Rinso-in buddha hall, digging out stones. Shunryu was trading them for a pile of quarried rock, which he was arranging into a wall on the bank. Chie came out and told Shunryu he should slow down, get some rest. He waved her off. "Please be careful," she said. This was nothing compared to the job they'd done bringing in the jumbo stone above the pond in back. That had taken a week to get in place. Everyone in the village had thought he was somewhat crazy. It weighed tons, and Chie was sure he was going to kill himself getting it in. He seemed to be more concerned about the frogs than himself and spent a good deal of time making sure there weren't any in the way. They had used bars, timbers, a winch, muscle, sweat, heavy breathing, and the skilled application of leverage to get it just where he wanted it. Now Shunryu was getting the sharp mountain rocks placed just right to build a wall to stop the bank from eroding.

Yasuko watched him in awe while he worked. There was such a contrast between Shunryu in robes and Shunryu in work clothes.

In his face too, there was the soft aspect and the tough aspect. He seemed to get bigger and more masculine when wrestling a rock into place. Sometimes he seemed gentle and feminine – like when he spoke to visitors. He was thin, the height of a woman. He wore size twenty-three tabi – not a man's size – and he liked sweet potato, which to her was a woman's food. But there was the fierce man too, the one who could move big stones and big people.

Suddenly he let out a yell.

The stone dealer drove Shunryu to the hospital, his hand wrapped in a bloody headband. He'd caught a finger between two rocks, and a sharp edge had cut him right to the bone. It was the fourth finger on his right hand. The doctors sewed it up. No sooner had they returned than Shunryu was back down in the creek working with the stones, his arm in a sling, with Chie scolding him and telling him to come inside. The finger was never the same again. When the muscles and tendons healed, they were shortened, and his finger was permanently bent. From then on he had a distinctive bent-finger gassho.

ONE DAY at Yaizu station in 1951 Shunryu ran into Gido Yamada while waiting for the noon express. Gido was in his sixties and had a little temple near Rinso-in, but spent most of his time at the Soto headquarters, where he was head of the international section – Soto Zen abroad. Shunryu decided to stay on and ride to Tokyo with his friend. He was always interested in hearing how things were going in Brazil and America. When they reached Tokyo, Shunryu realized to his dismay that he'd forgotten that he was on his way to perform a memorial service in Shizuoka. He phoned the family, apologized profusely to all who had gathered, and said he'd call for another priest to go over immediately. One was already on the way, he was told. It was not the first time he had missed a ceremony, and it was mortifying.

Godfather Amano was amused at Shunryu's absentmindedness. Shunryu would forget his watch at Amano's hotel, come back to get it, and leave without taking his umbrella. Seison the potter would keep quiet when he noticed that Shunryu had forgotten his wallet. Seison would let him walk all the way to Mori station to find out. To Chie it was more distressing. She would greet a deliveryman at the entryway and unexpectedly receive Shunryu's bag, which he always carried with him. He might not even have noticed that he didn't have it anymore. When they went out together she would carry his wallet, and when he went alone she would tie it to a string. She had him write his name on his watch. She had to cover for his absentmindedness and impracticality with money as well. He would buy a bell for the temple without regard for how much money was available. He would also lose money. People said that Shunryu could be the way he was because of her support.

Emotional difficulty is as hard as splitting a lotus in two. Even though you split it in two, long strings will follow and you cannot get rid of them. The strings are still there. But intellectual difficulty is as easy as breaking a stone in two. Nothing is left.

HIS FORGETFULNESS bothered Shunryu almost as much as it did Chie, and he didn't want to pass it on to his children. One cold morning not long after the war was over, his sisters had gone off to school when Hoitsu, now a first-grader, came back. When Shunryu asked what he was doing, he said he'd forgotten a book. Shunryu became furious and picked Hoitsu up, took him outside, and threw him into the little pond by the kitchen. Chie dragged the boy out. He was sobbing and sopping as she sat him before Shunryu. Hoitsu cried, shivered, apologized, and said, "I won't forget anything ever again for the rest of my life." At least he would never forget that experience.

Again, Shunryu's two-headed nemesis – forgetfulness and anger – had arisen. Once he got aggravated with Hoitsu over what he saw as a lazy attitude toward his third-grade homework. He gave Hoitsu a bowl and some chopsticks, put him out, and told him to go away and not come back. Hoitsu cried and said he was sorry and walked around the temple for hours, but the doors were closed and there was no response. Finally when it was quite late his mother brought her boy in and asked Shunryu to forgive him.

JAPANESE BUDDHISM was infused with two traditions from China – Taoism and Confucianism. Like Buddhism, neither of them relied on the concepts of soul or god. The Tao was the soft way, the natural way, like water seeking the lowest level. Confucianism was the way of ethics, hierarchy, and obedience to a patriarchal social order. Only with his family did Shunryu seem to express this Confucian heritage. He wasn't as tolerant with his own children as he was with the children at school, whom he didn't scold at all. At home he occasionally spanked Hoitsu, almost never on the head as they had done in his father's time, but often enough so the boy knew it was an option.

Once when the old priest Zen'an and Shunryu were talking about the kindergarten, Hoitsu heard Zen'an chastising Shunryu about something he had said. After Zen'an left Hoitsu said, "That man yelled at you. I wish he would die!" Hoitsu's backside would never fully recover from the spanking that followed. Hoitsu would run from his father at times, frightened by the fierce look in his eyes. He was glad to see visitors, because his father didn't scold the children when guests were around.

Shunryu scolded Yasuko a lot too, more than the others, because she was the oldest. The danka and neighbors would tell her what a quiet, soft, and kind person her father was. Yasuko wondered why he behaved so differently at home and suspected it was because of his strict temple training. Maybe he thought that was how a good father should be in order not to spoil the children; or maybe it was the dark side of So-on's heritage.

Shunryu's children saw him as esteemed, distant, and preoccupied, and this was even harder on them than his temper. Sitting in the warmth of the hibachi in the evening, he wouldn't say anything or pay any attention to them, but seemed to be looking far away. He walked slowly, lost in thought. Yasuko wished he were more of a father and not so much a public man, but she supposed that was what religious people were like. He just wasn't a family man. She wished he was more like her friends' fathers, and that he would hold her and play with her – at least a little. One day when she was eleven he took her to Shizuoka, and she found it difficult to walk by his side, because she wasn't used to being with him. Embarrassed because he seemed so superior to her, she moved to the other side of the street.

Shunryu would speak sharply to Chie, but she didn't return the sharpness. They had an old-fashioned relationship with defined roles and status. Men were considered higher than women through-out the nation, and since they were a temple family those customs were even stronger. He slept alone, while Chie would fall asleep with the children. Following the old custom, he walked ahead of her on the street. Chie did not complain; it was her way too, and they were a well-oiled team that had endured a lot together. He re-spected her and she respected him, as did her mother, who ad-dressed him with the formal title Hojo-sama. Obaa-san would tell the children that their father was a priest to be revered, and that he was more strict with himself than with anyone else. They called him Oto-sama, unlike their friends, who addressed their fathers in more familiar ways, such as Otosan or even Tosan or Tochan.

CHIE PAID close attention to her children. She didn't get angry much, but she nagged and was always telling them to do things. She was self-sacrificing, constantly working, in a hurry to do things for her family and others, and sometimes she would be in a bad mood, but the children were comfortable with her – especially at bedtime. Then she would relax and be affectionate. With her two youngest, sweet Otohiro and sensitive Omi, snuggled up to her, and Hoitsu and Yasuko on their own futons, she would start a story. Often she would get sleepy and slur her words. Then Yasuko would continue for her mother, till everyone had nodded off but her. Yasuko got so good at this that she gained a reputation at school as a good storyteller.

At last Yasuko would go to sleep, and eventually Shunryu's light would click off in his study. Kinu would be asleep in her room across the wide tatami hall, and maybe a few monks and lay students would be in the far wing beyond the buddha hall. It was time for the darkened temple to dream, floating above the turmoil of human interaction.

Chapter Eight

Family
and Death

1952−1956

Most problems we create because we don't know ourselves.

TWO SMALL creeks plunge down the steep mountain past either side of Rinso-in and converge in front of the temple at a point watched over by a row of old, merciful Jizo statues decked in faded red bibs. The rainy season was three months off, but in late March of 1952 the rocky creek beds were swelling with gushing spring runoff from the wooded and tea-hedged slopes above. Around the stones and water, small yellow butterflies danced.

The gardens and woods surrounding Rinso-in were lush, overflowing with diverse shades of green and laced with the wide stretching webs of large orange and black spiders. In the back pond around a large mossy stone, frogs croaked beneath the lilies. Fat hornets buzzed around the dark wooden posts and beams of the sprawling old building. Under the extensive overhang of the straw thatch roof, swallows swooped in and out, building nests. In front, under an eave, slept the family dog, an old mongrel.

In the mud of drained rice fields below, women and men stooped, planting the year's rice crop. The nights were still cold, but the days were becoming warm. At times the smell of the morning's catch would blow in from the fishing boats docked by the bay. Yaizu was buzzing. The streets were full of women going shopping, men doing business, and children out of school on spring vacation. It was a good season in a good year. The occupation was finally over, the wounds of the war were almost forgotten, and Japan was beginning to feel good about itself again, as it enjoyed money, food, progress, and modernization. Cars and bicycles covered the streets. Everyone was working. The plum trees were in bloom.

BEFORE SUNRISE Shunryu had risen, sat zazen, and performed the morning service in the buddha hall. A monk named Otsubo joined him. Otsubo was thumping the mokugyo while they recited the *Heart Sutra*. Shunryu's chanting was soft, almost muffled. The choppy old Sino-Japanese words moved in a steady rhythm in contrast to Otsubo's erratic voice, which rose and fell in intensity and pitch. Shunryu stopped the service repeatedly to correct Otsubo's handling of the wooden drum – through lack of talent or stubbornness he could not seem to get it right. After service, which concluded amidst the statues and memorial plaques of the dark founder's hall behind the main altar, Otsubo swept the front courtyard, and Shunryu swept his way down the hard-packed dirt road to the farmhouses, as he did every day. Then he returned, bamboo twig broom in hand.

Otsubo was about thirty. He was there not because of any strong tie to Shunryu or Rinso-in, but because he had nowhere else to go. If he'd come on his own, the customary one night's hospitality for a traveling monk would have fulfilled Shunryu's obligation, but he had been sent by Kishizawa, who had no work for him at Gyokuden-in. And he was just too eccentric and uncontrollable to function smoothly with Kishizawa's disciplined monks. Shunryu's accepting nature would work better for the out-of-step Otsubo. Even Shunryu had at first suggested that Otsubo go elsewhere, but he couldn't deny Kishizawa's second request and reluctantly took on the strange monk. Everyone would have been happier without him; something about his presence was unsettling.

At seven in the morning, smoke poured out the opened shoji doorway from the unvented wood-burning stove in the kitchen and hovered over the red and gold carp in the kitchen pond. Chie and Kinu Obaa-san put the breakfast out: steaming hot white rice with raw egg, scallions, and seaweed, a four-inch sardine for each person, a gob of *natto* (a sticky, fermented soybean paste), miso soup with a cube of tofu, and green tea. It was more than they'd had for days at a time during the war and the years of scarcity that followed.

The women sat at the large, low table with the children: Yasuko, seventeen and in her next to last year of high school; Hoitsu, twelve and taller than his father; Omi, ten, the quiet, artistic girl; Otohiro, seven and just starting school. The monk Otsubo was uncomfortable with others and ate by himself on the steps leading down to the bath area. Everyone gave him plenty of space.

Shunryu also ate alone, at his own table a short distance from the family. It was an old patriarchal custom. Everyone was quiet. Periodically Chie would pour tea for him and offer more rice. Shunryu responded with monosyllables or short gestures. After breakfast every day he said, "Ohayo gozaimasu" and his family responded to his "good morning" in kind, their bodies bent in respect. He would wash his own bowls – no one else could touch them. Then he went to his room to get ready for the day. Chie put his cloth-wrapped box lunch into his bicycle basket. He was off down the hill with the equivalent of "Be back later," Chie calling back a response and tilting her body in farewell. These would be the last words they would ever speak to each other.

The children soon went out with lunches prepared by Obaa-san, their grandmother. As there was no school, the girls went to the shopping street to do errands and meet friends, a thirty-minute walk. Hoitsu and his little brother went down to the flats by the river with other neighborhood boys to fly kites and throw rocks in the water. They didn't get out to play much. Even today their father might have wanted them to stay home and study, but he was too busy to keep up with them, and he would be in town till late afternoon. The children would be gone most of the day as well. They didn't like to be around the temple when Otsubo was there.

Otsubo hadn't gone into town to work as he sometimes did. The day before he had helped do a memorial service for a family at Zuioji, Sugiyama's temple. It had not been clear when Otsubo had first arrived that he could handle that sort of responsibility. Sugiyama, who had assisted at Rinso-in since 1937, said that the first time Otsubo had shown up at his temple, he heard someone calling from outside. When he went out, Otsubo was on the ground rubbing his head into the dirt saying, "Please be good to me."

If he wasn't doing something weird, he'd find small ways to express his contrarian nature. At Sugiyama's father's funeral Shunryu admonished Otsubo for pouring his miso soup over his rice. Combining dishes was not proper form, which is especially important to priests. Still, Shunryu was generally tolerant of Otsubo's oddities. He allowed the strange monk to wear the civilian uniform from the war days. It made him look like a soldier. Otsubo had been in the army during the war, and people thought that was what had made him so peculiar. He was considered to be a war burn-out, a shell-shocked monk.

Nobody wanted him at Rinso-in. The family resented having his dark cloud floating around the place. Chie had spoken to Shunryu about him a number of times. She said he gave her the chills. He especially frightened the children, who were afraid of his crazy eyes and had told their father so. He said that was no way to talk about another person, and finally he just told them to shut up. He spoke more politely to Obaa-san when she mentioned her uneasiness with Otsubo. It couldn't be helped, he told her. Fine for him to say:

he was gone most the time, and they were stuck with Otsubo. Chie might be in charge of day-to-day life at Rinso-in, but Shunryu had the final say.

Otsubo had first come to Rinso-in in the fall but hadn't stayed long. He'd gotten into an argument with Chie and walked off. After a couple of fruitless months searching for a temple that would keep him, he returned. Shunryu took him back in without a word. Otsubo tended to hang out in back behind the racks with the laundry drying poles, where he would cut up firewood for cooking and the evening bath. He wasn't much help inside the temple, but maybe that was for the best. He would go into the woods, bring back branches, and cut them up with a hatchet, or sit on his heels, smoking cigarettes and tossing the butts into the creek. One thing that particularly infuriated Chie was his habit of teasing the dog by blowing cigarette smoke in its face.

It was a quiet day at Rinso-in, Thursday, March 27, 1952. No visits or business were planned. No one there but Chie, her mother, and Otsubo. Even the old caretaker had gone up into the mountains looking for mushrooms. Chie and Obaa-san kept working. Food had to be prepared, tatami swept, bedding aired and whacked, deliverymen met, flowers picked and arranged at altars. Chie took care in selecting flowers from the surrounding gardens and hillsides, lush in the early days of spring. Like Yoshi before her, she specialized in ikebana flower arranging, and her aesthetic sensibility was evident at each altar and entryway.

A little before three o'clock, Chie heard the dog barking in the genkan. She was as sensitive to his sounds as she was to the cries of her children and could tell that the dog was in distress. She went down to see what it was – probably Otsubo torturing him again. So inexcusable.

Our human destiny is to have suffering.

THE TANAKAS, the couple whose memorial service Otsubo had assisted with the day before, were walking up the road with gifts in hand for him and the Suzukis. They were more than a little unsettled to meet Otsubo moaning and staggering down the road like a drunk, blood splattered on his face and shirt, and more blood streaming down from his neck. He mumbled something about going to the police station. Then they heard pitiful cries for help coming from the temple. It was Obaa-san calling.

They ran into the genkan and saw a terrible sight. Chie lay against the wall by the wood stove, her whole body covered in blood. Obaa-san was putting a thin towel over her daughter's head, futilely trying to stop the bleeding. Next to her the dog's limp body lay in a pool of blood, and not far away lay a bloody hatchet. Mr. Tanaka ran to the phone and called for a doctor. Neighbors rushed up to see what was happening.

A priest named Sone had taken the train from Shizuoka and was early for a weekly English class with Shunryu. He flew off on a bicycle to Zuioji to tell the Sugiyamas to come right away. Down in the village the word was quickly spreading. But still no doctor had arrived.

Hoitsu and Otohiro were playing by the river and had seen Sugiyama riding over the bridge on his bicycle as if in a great hurry. The boys knew he could only have been going to Rinso-in, so they followed out of curiosity. They came up the road through the village, passed the bell tower into the courtyard filled with neighbors, and went inside to witness the horrible sight. They watched as their mother was carried outside.

Yasuko and her little sister, Omi, were walking up the road when a neighbor ran to them and said, "Something horrible has happened to your mother! Go quickly!" The girls ran to find their mother lying unconscious with Obaa-san tending to her. Blood was everywhere. They stood with their brothers, helpless and overwhelmed.

In town, Shunryu was stopped by a merchant who had heard rumors flying. He raced back on his bicycle to Rinso-in to find a police car in the driveway. Then he saw his wife, groaned loudly, and kneeled down before her.

Soon he and Obaa-san were in a police car following the ambulance to the hospital. Otsubo had struck Chie seven times in the face and head with the hatchet. There was nothing the doctors could do, and gradually her vital signs faded. Shunryu and Obaa-san were with Chie when she died at eight that evening.

A grieving and shattered Shunryu returned home and gathered his numb children together in the family room. He spoke as he had never spoken to them before, with humility, softness, and overflowing sadness. He told them that their mother was dead, that she had died at the hands of Otsubo. Then he said, "Please do not hate this man who has killed your mother. Rather you should hate me, because I didn't listen to her or to Obaa-san or to you when you all warned me about him." And he added, "From now on let us be together."

He continued to confess responsibility for his wife's death to everyone he spoke to. "It was my fault," he said to Amano, his godfather and confidant. "I was too stubborn. I wouldn't bend. I was so wrong."

Suetsune-san arrived at Rinso-in to pay his respects. He started crying as soon as he saw his teacher. "She took such good care of me when I lived here. She fed me when food was scarce and washed my clothes when there was so much to do." Shunryu nodded, in tears. "It was my fault. I asked her to do what she could not do; I made her try to do the impossible."

Obaa-san silently acknowledged Shunryu's confessions and sincere apologies. She did not alter her respectful way of relating to him. Her sadness was great, but she had a strong inner core and would endure this tragedy for the sake of the family. Her first child had drowned in a river when still small, a son had died as a soldier in the war, and now Chie, the last, had been murdered at the age of thirty-nine by a monk. Her strength flowed out to the whole family as Kinu Obaa-san stepped with composure into the position of nurturer of the temple's interior, encouraging Shunryu to continue his outside duties. To dwell on her daughter's death in bitterness was not her way and would dishonor her daughter's life.

Hoitsu had taken to heart his father's admonition not to hate Otsubo. Father is right, he thought. But neither could he hate his father. Hoitsu rather saw the tragedy as the family's fate, something beyond his understanding.

His older sister, Yasuko, did not adjust with such philosophical detachment. At first she had been too confused to speak or to think. When she finally realized what had happened, she saw her mother's murder as her father's fault. The fact that he took the blame did not bring her mother back, and she could not forgive him. He had become warmer, but when she had a bad dream and called out for her mother, he scolded her harshly, with the same tough attitude he had always shown. He was making an effort, but Obaa-san was the one who could come closest to filling the vacuum created by Chie's death. Yasuko's position as the oldest child was now all the more important. She determined to be strong for her younger brothers and sister. She cried least of all.

Little Otohiro didn't think about blame or cause – he just wanted his mother, and he wept and clung to Obaa-san. Omi, the third child, the most vulnerable and dreamy, became even more quiet and withdrew into herself.

In an outpouring of sympathy, people came to the temple to console the family and to thank them for Chie's good deeds. For years they would continue to remind the children of how much their mother was loved in the community, how much she had contributed, and how much she would be missed. She had always kept food in the basket of her bicycle to hand out to the hungry; she had served her husband and guests in sickness as in health. Her life had been a full and useful one.

Otsubo was tried for the murder of Chie Suzuki, acquitted by reason of insanity, and sent to a mental institution.

The night of Chie's death, Shunryu put his futon in the room in which his children slept. They all huddled together in silent anguish. He would continue to sleep in the same room with them for some time. And even though the children would still be raised by Obaa-san, he was less distant. He would hold Otohiro more, and listen more attentively to what they had to say. Shunryu's life had been deeply changed, his heart softened, and his ears opened. He would always harbor a deep pain, unexpressed in words.

Our way has no end and no beginning, and from this way we cannot escape.

HOITSU'S PARENTS had always told him, "Study! Study!" But he wanted to play. He would sneak away from his schoolwork to join the farmers' children in the fields below. He wanted to be a farmer, not a priest, but he assumed he had no choice.

In the summers Hoitsu was sent to Rinso-in's parent temple, Sekiun-in, for a few weeks to practice like a monk. He also went to Sekiun-in in the winter for sesshin. The master there was kind to him and didn't hit him with the stick. He liked it better there than at home, except when they shaved his head – that embarrassed him. At home he would just get a close-cropped haircut like the other boys.

At home his father would call, "Hoitsu, get up!" early each morning. He would hold on to the covers, but Shunryu would pull them off from the bottom. Sometimes his father would drag him off to zazen, and afterward Hoitsu would have to read the chants while still rubbing sleep from his eyes. He didn't at all like the idea of becoming a priest.

Then one day he was bicycling home from town with his father, and Shunryu said, "You don't have to be a priest you know."

"What? I don't?"

"No. It's all right if you study hard and become something else, but study hard."

When the words sank in, Hoitsu understood that Shunryu's plans were not built around having his son succeed him. So now what was he going to be? Memories of his dying mother colored his every thought about the future. There were some simple books on Buddhism in the temple, and he would look at their covers now and then. Finally he read one, then another, and thought about his life.

Now and then Shunryu took Hoitsu to hear Kishizawa lecture. Hoitsu was twelve years old and didn't understand what was being said, but he knew he was hearing a great teacher, just as Shunryu had known when he heard Oka Sotan as a boy. Something began to rub off. One day Kishizawa spent some time with Hoitsu, showing him a seashell. Shunryu and Noiri stood off to the side and left them alone. When it was time to leave, Kishizawa said, "Would you like to have that seashell?" Hoitsu said yes, took it home, and hung it in a special spot.

Only when you give up everything can you see a true teacher. Even the name of Buddhism is already a dirty spot on our practice. It is not teaching. The character and effort of our teachers is our teaching.

Kishizawa was a lover of books. He read and wrote many books, and when he traveled and met other Buddhists he would ask them to show him some text he might not have seen before. Kishizawa's only regret toward the end of his life was that he had supported Japan's militarism before and during the war. Ian Kishizawa died in 1955. He had helped Shunryu refine his speech and thinking and deepen his precepts and zazen – bounteous gifts to share with all people, not just with priests. It is said that Zen is the way beyond words and letters. Shunryu would always hold even that to be a half-truth after his experience with Kishizawa.

Sincere practice means to have sincere concern for people.
Our practice is based on our humanity.

IN MARCH of 1954, a fishing boat from Yaizu returned
with a crew of critically ill fishermen who had been contaminated
with a heavy dose of radioactive fallout from an American hydro-
gen bomb test on the Bikini atoll, and one of the men had died. Before the crew realized what the problem was, their fish had entered
the marketplace. Tons and tons of fish had to be discarded. A general panic seized Japan, and rumors spread that all ocean life had
been contaminated. Anti-American rhetoric ran high – this was
seen as the third atomic bomb, even worse in a way than the first
two, because they had been at war then. The Americans were not
apologizing or admitting any wrongdoing. At that time Shunryu
became involved in some meetings with Americans and locals. His
voice was small, but when he had the chance to talk he encouraged
people to calm down. He tried to counter the hysteria and self-
righteousness he saw erupting everywhere. To him most of the
rhetoric was just a confused political game.

Some saw him as always taking the American side, but when a
march was called to protest American nuclear testing, he decided
to go. People around the temple told him not to, warning that he
would be discredited by being associated with communists. The
Japanese Communist Party, a relatively tame organization with
members in the Diet, made a big issue of the Bikini incident. Shunryu said he was happy to walk with anyone who opposed nuclear
weapons; it didn't have anything to do with political beliefs. It was
just a chance to make a small statement for peace. He wasn't an
outspoken leader but walked unobtrusively with others, doing
what he thought was right.

Masaji Yamada, one of the senior danka of Rinso-in who lived
just below the temple, had watched Shunryu carefully through the
years. He was from the oldest and most conservative family in the
village. Masaji didn't criticize Shunryu for going on the march.

"Everyone knows he is a pacifist," he said, "and especially pro-American at that, but he does not force his views on others. Like So-on, Shunryu-san is a priest as a priest should be. He recites the sutras well and isn't preachy."

JUST BELOW Rinso-in at a bend in the creek, right at the spot where Shunryu would stop sweeping the dirt road every morning, a danka family named Yamamura lived in a pristine thatch-roofed farmhouse. Young Masao Yamamura was often out in front of his home, and Shunryu would come over to say hello. It was 1956; Masao was twenty-two.

The young man treasured the opportunity to talk to Shunryu. As a boy he had looked forward to the day when he would be old enough to join Shunryu's post-war program for youth, but that program had ended in 1951. Nevertheless, he felt he was learning a lot from Shunryu in these occasional morning talks. To Masao there was no one else like him.

It was from Shunryu that Masao first heard the word "internationalism." Shunryu told his young friend that the Japanese must learn from their mistakes in the thirties and forties and must help the world get beyond the Cold War. Shunryu didn't say a lot at one time, but he chose his words carefully, and in time they added up.

"We must educate ourselves about the ways and languages of other peoples," Shunryu said one day. "We must think globally and not be limited by national boundaries, in order to achieve world peace."

At times he'd mention his old yearning. "I want to leap the border."

"Why is that?"

"I want to do more with my life than what I'm doing, more than look after the danka here."

"Where would you go?"

"Abroad, maybe to America."

"What do you want to do there?"

"Teach Buddhism, for world peace. If I could do that, my life would be fulfilled."

Masao knew that Shunryu was expressing ideas that he didn't necessarily tell to his family or fellow priests; most people's worldviews were narrow. They, as well as the danka, had faith in him and he in them, but they didn't necessarily know his dreams.

A person who falls on the earth, stumbling on a stone, will stand up by means of the same earth they fell on. You complain because you think earth is the problem, having caused your fall. Without the earth, you wouldn't fall, but you wouldn't stand up either. Falling and standing up are both great aids given to you by the earth. Because of mother earth you can continue your practice. You are practicing in the zendo of the great earth, which is the problem. Problems are actually your zendo.

AT SEISON the potter's home Shunryu liked to take off his outer robe, lie down on the tatami, even drink some sake, though he had to be careful, because it didn't take much to put him to sleep. He was known as a weak drinker, when he drank at all. If Seison wasn't there Shunryu would just say to his son, "Excuse me, I feel like I'm at my parents' home," then grab a pillow and fall asleep in his white kimono. There weren't many customers coming in. When Shunryu saw a piece of pottery he really liked, he'd take out his wallet and leave all the money he had for Seison, saving only what he needed for train fare. He never had much money, so he usually paid less than the cup or bowl was worth. Once when Seison's son pointed out that Shunryu had underpaid for a plate, Seison sternly told him not to regard Shunryu as an ordinary person.

"How nice it would be if all customers were like him," Seison said. "I wouldn't have to be in the awkward position of having to tell them the price. But don't confuse him with laypeople."

Seison was ten years older than Shunryu, and Shunryu treated him like a senior monk. After the war when Shunryu had not attended Seison's pottery class because he didn't have any money, Seison had scolded him, saying, "This isn't just something you buy for your own pleasure." So Shunryu kept coming, whether he had money or not, and considered Seison one of his teachers.

When Seison showed Shunryu a beautiful large pot that bore his characteristic splash of crimson, he told Shunryu he wasn't going to sell it. "Good," said Shunryu, "I'll take it," and he did. Later when Seison and his son were visiting Rinso-in, he brought a wooden storage box he had made for the pot. Shunryu asked Seison if he would give the pot a name and write it in sumi on the box. "Pot stolen by a monk," Seison wrote, to Shunryu's delight.

The ashes of Seison's oldest son, who had been killed in the war, were finally received from abroad. Shunryu came the day before the funeral in his work clothes to help with preparations. The next day he wore his most beautiful robes to conduct the ceremony. It was one service that meant a great deal to Shunryu, but that wasn't true of them all.

As HAD been his fate since he was thirteen, Shunryu had to do endless memorial services in people's homes. He would stay afterward to eat fancy meals and accept the family's contributions tucked into white envelopes tied with black ribbon. In the evenings he would sometimes end up in noodle shops and bars with his friends. Shunryu was well respected and popular in Yaizu, but his life consisted of either priestly duties or socializing with friends. It was not the life he had dreamed of as an idealistic young man.

On most days Shunryu would do the morning service and then set off to town on his bicycle. Unless there was a funeral or meeting to attend, he would frequently not return till after dinner or even after bedtime. He had some responsibilities at nearby training temples, but all he did was help out with ceremonies or with the training of boys who were eager to do what was expected so they could take over their fathers' temples and leave the rigors of practice behind as soon as possible. Inevitably he would get involved with the problems that go with such positions – temple politics. He was disgusted not only with the current state of Zen as he saw it, but also with his own situation. He had some good friends among the temple priests and in the hierarchy, but there was nothing he could put his heart into.

The children still didn't see him much, although he ate breakfast with his sons and Obaa-san and wasn't as distant and strict as he had been before his wife's murder. Hoitsu had been ordained as a monk and would soon go to Komazawa University. Otohiro was still in elementary school. Yasuko was at college in Tokyo.

Omi no longer lived at home. About three years after her mother died she had started to act strangely. She would laugh at inappropriate times or wander away from home and have to be found and brought back. She couldn't apply herself in school and got caught shoplifting. Finally her behavior became so unsettling that Shunryu consulted the family physician. Dr. Ozawa recommended that Omi go away for treatment; he thought her family could no longer take care of her. By 1957 she had been in an institution for several years. Now and then Shunryu or her siblings would visit her.

Now Shunryu had two kindergartens to tend to, and Mitsu was principal of both. In April of 1954 he had opened a branch of the Tokiwa Kindergarten near the train station. In a brand-new building with living quarters for Mitsu, a second kindergarten had been created by popular request. He would see Mitsu in the mornings when he went to greet the kindergartens' teachers.

After stopping at the kindergartens, Shunryu would visit with friends. If there were no other obligations, he would go to Amano's hotel to socialize, drink tea, and maybe play go. He would go to Zoun-in, his old temple, and visit with Kendo and his son Shoko, who had reluctantly decided to become a monk. Before leaving Mori he would always drop by Seison's home-studio. Some of

Shunryu's friends, like Amano, threw business parties at Rinso-in, which were attended by geisha. Shunryu attended and enjoyed himself but ultimately didn't want that kind of life.

In many ways Shunryu had a full and useful life, but it wasn't fulfilling enough for him. He could not be satisfied unless he was practicing and teaching the way of the many great teachers he had met and studied with. He had to pay his debt of gratitude to them, pass on the torch he had received, and engage with people in a deeper way. He started to get irritated at the way people would say "Hi Hojo-san!" when he rode by on his bicycle. It made him feel marginalized and meaningless, exchanging greetings with no real relationship. Just as when he lived with Miss Ransom, he again saw himself drifting off course. He had become the temple priest he didn't want to be – busy with many responsibilities yet coasting along, with life going by, stuck in Yaizu.

The idea of going abroad was always in my heart, even though I'd given up. I thought I'd given up, but I hadn't.

Chapter Nine

An Opening

1 9 5 6 – 1 9 5 9

In your life, if you come to a great difficulty, like a big mountain in Nepal that looks like it has no passageway, you know there is a way to get through.

FROM TIME to time Shunryu saw his friend Gido from Soto headquarters. In 1956 Gido asked offhandedly if Shunryu might like to go to San Francisco for a year or so to be an assistant to Hodo Tobase, the priest there. He didn't expect a senior priest like Shunryu to be interested in the assignment, but considering Shunryu's long-term study of English and interest in America, it was natural for Gido to bring it up. He couldn't find a priest who would go; there was no money or status in it. Shunryu said he wouldn't mind being an assistant and being poor, but that he couldn't consider going anywhere till he had finished the ambitious restoration work that So-on had started in 1918.

In September 1958 Gido was at Rinso-in telling Shunryu about his continuing difficulty in filling the vacancy in America. Tobase, still nominally in charge, had come back six months before, leaving a semiretired nun and a part-time monk who was working on his doctoral thesis in charge of the San Francisco temple. Gido wanted an assistant to Tobase who could go right away. He had even appointed a couple of priests, who had refused to go. There were problems in San Francisco, and headquarters didn't want Tobase to go back, though they were still pretending he would. So whoever took the position would end up being the de facto abbot of the temple.

"Why don't you go?" Gido asked Shunryu, half-joking, "It's sort of a mess there, but maybe you could help."

"Since I didn't cause their problems, they would understand if I failed to make things better," Shunryu said. He would have more freedom there – he was sure of it.

A month later Gido stopped by Rinso-in again. The bright leaves of fall were covering the hillsides and roadways. It was a comfortable, breezy day. "How is it going in America?" Shunryu asked him over tea. "Surely you've found someone by now."

"No," said Gido. "I get letters every few weeks from Komiya-san, the head of the board there, asking me to send someone. I feel so bad. He's been writing for years."

"I'll do it," Shunryu said.

"Yes, you know English. You would be perfect. Too bad you can't get away. I would miss you though."

"I'll do it," said Shunryu, and this time Gido heard him.

He was truly amazed. "You mean really do it? You're joking, right?"

"No, I'm serious. I've thought about it a lot these last few weeks. I can do it. If Rinso-in and my family will let me go, I can leave in six months."

"WOULD IT be all right with you if I went to America?" Shunryu was on the train with Hoitsu, who was in his second year at Komazawa University. Shunryu was going to Tokyo to meet with Gido, but first he wanted to spend some time with his oldest boy.

He said it would be for three years. Hoitsu would be at Eiheiji by the time he came back.

Hoitsu knew he couldn't influence his father's decision, but he appreciated being asked anyway. He wasn't completely surprised. But what about his obligations to the danka?

"Who will take care of Rinso-in?"

"Our friends have offered their support."

"What about your other obligations at other temples and at the kindergartens?"

"I'm fifty-four, a year short of retirement age. Someone else should have the chance."

Hoitsu thought his father should wait until his son was through with his college and monastic training and was ready to succeed him. He should run the temple until Hoitsu was installed as abbot. Only then would he have fulfilled his responsibility. Three years was a long time. But if that was what Shunryu wanted, Hoitsu knew he couldn't be stopped.

"If you need to go, please go."

"Study English," Shunryu said. "Maybe you could come help me."

SHUNRYU HAD already talked with Yasuko. She was living at Rinso-in and teaching at the original kindergarten. She told her father that she knew this was his lifelong desire, and of course she would support his decision, but before he went she wanted to get married. He agreed. She had someone in mind. Shunryu said he would ask Amano to arrange a meeting to see if she and her prospective husband could come to an agreement.

Otohiro, in junior high school, was being raised mostly by Obaa-san. Still, he was not happy about the idea of his father leaving, and he was afraid to go with him. He didn't know what to do. He would prefer that his father got stung again by a *suzumebachi,* a giant sparrow-bee. When that had happened, Shunryu had been in bed for a week. They had never before spent so much time together. Obaa-san told Shunryu that if he had to go, please go, but take Otohiro.

She didn't think the boy should be left with her alone, with no father at all. It was too much responsibility. Shunryu said Yasuko would help, that he couldn't take Otohiro right away, but maybe later – when his wife came.

"Wife?" Obaa-san was taken by surprise.

Shunryu explained that he had to find a woman to marry. The temple in America had requested that a married priest be sent, and Gido had told them that's what they were getting. Shunryu had applied for a visa as a married man, so now he needed to get married. He asked Obaa-san for a suggestion as to who his bride should be.

"You can only marry Mitsu," she said.

"Oh, of course," he answered.

It wasn't the first time her name had come up. A year after his wife died, some of the danka had suggested he find a new wife, and Kinu Obaa-san had said then that it could only be Mitsu. Rumors spread, but the couple kept putting off the decision, until finally they dropped the matter, each saying it was because of the other's stubbornness.

Of course. Mitsu.

They had been a team for years, and there was affection between them. She was tough enough to stand up to him, and he could accept her independence. Their eccentricities seemed to match well, and it was thought that neither of them should be with an ordinary person. It wouldn't be fair. They were perfect for each other.

Obaa-san talked with Mitsu, who accepted without hesitation. She said there was no thought about whether she wanted to or not, that Obaa-san had asked her and she would do it. On the other hand, Mitsu was a strong-willed woman who wasn't easy to push around. And Shunryu, though even smaller than she, was a handsome man.

AMANO HAD his hands full. The danka were divided. Some supported Shunryu's plan to go to America and understood how important it was to him. Others didn't mind as long as there were priests to conduct the ceremonies. But most were against it, and some were absolutely opposed. Why did he want to go there and abandon us? There were those who said he was leaving because of shame over his wife's murder, which was known throughout Japan via the Zen grapevine. There was gossip in Yaizu that he was escaping criticism from the danka for being away and socializing too much. But the real problem was that the danka did not want Shunryu to leave because he was popular, and it was also a matter of principle. "This is where he should be! This is his duty!" members said in meetings. Some thought he should just go for one year. Amano said that three years would go by quickly, and there were good priests who would cover his duties.

Kozo, the irascible old anarchist, predicted that Shunryu wouldn't return. "What do you think about that?" he said. "My friend Hojo-san is going to become American soil!"

There was another problem. Just as Shunryu had sprung on them that he was marrying Chie right after they had accepted him as abbot back in 1936, Amano told the board that Shunryu wanted to get married again. A number of danka strongly objected to Shunryu's marrying Mitsu. But after another round of discussions, Amano persuaded them to go along with Shunryu's request.

In early December Yasuko got married. A week later Shunryu and Mitsu were married in a private ceremony. They had a small party in the evening to celebrate. Yasuko's husband moved into the temple with her. They agreed to stay till Shunryu came back. Obaasan would need her help.

Mitsu continued to live at the school. She and Shunryu maintained their normal work schedules except for necessary preparations. She wouldn't go with him right away. He wanted to get situated first and prepare for her and Otohiro. He really wasn't thinking much about them. He assumed it would work out. There was a lot to do, and the day of departure was only months away.

*D*o not say too late.

SHUNRYU HAD been gradually restoring Rinso-in for decades, but without a major effort it would have taken forever. After Gido's offer of the post in America, Shunryu sought more contributions, and with help from Amano, the board allocated enough money for the completion of the work.

I restored many buildings as they were in ancient times. That was the difficult part. It cost more money to do it that way and didn't look good to some people, so no one agreed with me. It seemed crazy, but I felt I had to do it. It took many years to rebuild Rinso-in. I worked on it the whole time I was there, constantly studying the architecture of the time when it was built, and making an effort to get it all done.

The grass thatch roof he had insisted on, redone at great expense, had not proved durable. Every year it got more expensive to maintain. They would redo one side every five years or so, storing thatch for the next time in the rafters. But now Shunryu gave in to modern convention, agreeing on tile. The main building was over three hundred years old. Most of the large beams could stay, but there was a lot of repair and replacement left to do, as well as detail work. Shunryu insisted on the most traditional and expensive temple carpentry techniques and materials, even though many danka wanted a more contemporary look. Members and neighbors joined in the big push to complete the job, and often Shunryu was up there with them, doing the hard work.

The purpose of restoring a building is not just to have a facility. The most important thing is to continue the practice and to have a successor who will share our responsibility. The point is where you don't expect it to be.

In the spring of 1958 the work on the main building – the founders', ancestors', and sutra halls – and the bell tower was finally completed. Ceremonies were held in March and May to commemorate the restoration, a job Shunryu had been involved with for forty years, a task he felt So-on had left for him to finish. So-on had restored only the family quarters and the zendo, the two wings off the buddha hall. "I could do the whole thing if I wanted to," So-on had told Shunryu, "but I must leave something for my disciples to do." Shunryu hadn't understood him at the time. Why not fix it all up now? he had wondered. Later he realized it was part of what So-on had transmitted to him.

When I made up my mind to go to America, I said to one of the members of my temple that if I could have gone ten years earlier, I might have been able to do many things. Maybe it was too late. I had forgotten almost all my English, and I regretted that I probably wouldn't be able to accomplish much. But then I thought, ten years before I didn't have so much understanding of Buddhism. So maybe it was a good thing for me to stay in Japan, finishing the work my master left for me.

IT WAS May 18, 1959, Shunryu's fifty-fifth birthday and his forty-second year of priesthood. With Hoitsu at his side Shunryu offered incense to his father, Sogaku, and his master, So-on, at the ohaka behind Zoun-in – the temple where he and So-on had lived so intensely, so intimately. How about me going to America? he had asked his teacher. So-on was adamant. No!

Twenty-nine years had passed. Now the answer was yes. How right So-on had been. How much Shunryu had learned. So-on had made him who he was, had guided him. Now he appreciated it. So-on had died, leaving those decaying beams still there, and Shunryu felt it was no accident. As he recited the *Heart Sutra,* his heart filled with gratitude. His appreciation for So-on had continually deepened over the decades. "When I offer incense to my father, I feel sad," he later said, "but when I offer incense to my master, tears stream down my cheeks."

Shunryu and Hoitsu visited the ashes site of the one Shunryu called So-on's wife, Yoshi Marushichi. They cleaned the area and made an offering. She'd been gone for six years now. While she was alive Shunryu had taken Hoitsu and the other children to visit her whenever they went to Zoun-in. She had lived to an old age and eventually was nearly blind. They always left her gifts of fruit and candy.

MEANWHILE, MITSU had become ill. Her energy was low and she had a bad cough. She had been to several doctors, but they didn't know what it was. She didn't want Shunryu to go to America until she was better or at least until they knew what was wrong with her. She thought she might die. Shunryu visited her frequently but wouldn't postpone his trip. Her medical problem was chronic, and she still didn't know what it was. At the going-away banquet for Shunryu she kept her complaints to herself.

Shunryu's sisters and half-brother, Shima, came to the banquet, as did Dr. Ozawa's family, and Seison's family. The Amanos and Katos were there. Taro, his guide and companion in Manchuria, was now twenty-six. "Here's to another adventure!" he toasted Shunryu.

Many of Shunryu's fellow priests came to say farewell: Gido, who had found his priest for America; Kishizawa's heirs Noiri and Niwa; his helper, Sugiyama from Zuioji; Kendo Okamoto from Zoun-in; and others, none of whom would want to trade places with him. Members of the High Grass Mountain Group came to Rinso-in to wish Shunryu a successful journey. They felt Shunryu's excitement and were proud of their old teacher, who had been such a guiding light and good friend in the days of the country's madness.

"We were the wild ones!" said Suetsune in a toast. Later he reminded Shunryu that he was ready to help with any books he might write. Suetsune was in publishing, and Shunryu had suggested in a letter that he might want his friend's assistance in that regard some day. Sadly, the most vibrant of them all, Masao Nishinakama, was not there. After the war he continued his search for truth, but turned more toward philosophy than Buddhist practice. He committed suicide in 1955 after a long period of mental anguish. On the way to the airport the next day, Shunryu visited with Masao's brother, Shigeo Nishinakama.

As THE WESTERN sky turned pink in Yaizu on May 21, Shunryu stood by his pond in the chilly morning. He had concluded his last morning service at Rinso-in. Carp swam in murky water as tadpoles darted about. Goodbye to the big living stone, now covered with moss. Goodbye to the frogs. As the rays of the sun struck the bamboo on the hill, the air heated quickly, and the stalks expanded, emitting sharp, pinging noises of different pitches, a strange little song of farewell in the still morning.

The cars were leaving for the train station. Shunryu brought only a few bags. The rest had been sent ahead by boat. He was wearing his priest's traveling robes with a rakusu hanging around his neck, zori, and white tabi socks.

"Shouldn't you wear shoes and a suit to go to America?" asked Yasuko's husband half in jest.

"Gido-san tells me the other priests have gone with new suits and shiny shoes. I will go in an old robe with a shiny head."

He bid farewell to Obaa-san and thanked her for her help. They stood with each other a moment. "Be careful," she said, and tilted her upper body in respect as they drove off to the station.

That night at Haneda airport, Yasuko and her husband, Hoitsu; Otohiro; Mitsu and her daughter Harumi; Godfather Amano; and members of the High Grass Mountain Group all bid farewell to Shunryu Suzuki.

"Study hard. Behave yourself, and listen to Obaa-san – she's a great woman," Shunryu said to Otohiro at the gate.

The call came for the passengers to board the plane. Shunryu and his family and friends bowed and waved and called out Goodbye! Take care! Shunryu kept turning around and looking up through the glass as he walked down the hallway bowing, waving, and smiling broadly. Everyone continued to bow and wave in return.

Holding in one hand a large, flat package wrapped in brown paper, a gift from the old temple for the new one, and waving a bouquet of flowers held high in the other, Suzuki laughed and clowned as he approached the airplane parked on the tarmac. A happy man, dancing and laughing, was off to America.

Part Two

America

1959–1971

Chapter Ten

A New Leaf

1959

*W*_{hen} *I came to America, I was determined to turn over a new leaf.*

MAY 23, 1959, the day of Shunryu Suzuki's arrival in America, a dozen elderly, conservatively dressed Japanese-Americans waited at the gate of the San Francisco airport. They represented the sixty or so families that were members of Sokoji, the only Soto Zen temple in the Bay Area and one of a few in the United States. With the group was a young man named Wako Kazumitsu Kato, who had been filling in as their part-time temple priest. Kato wondered what sort of person this Suzuki would be and why he came to America as his age.

Then there he was. Bodies tilted forward in formal bows and polite, enthusiastic greetings. He was friendly yet obviously a traditional priest, nothing Western about him. He was not intimidating, neither fat nor thin, not much taller than a child – short even for an elderly Japanese. And there was a glow of anticipation about him.

NO ONE WAS more pleased than Kato that Suzuki had finally arrived. Kato was twenty-eight and had been in charge of Sokoji for a year and a half by default, since Hodo Tobase had gone back to Japan. Kato had arrived in 1952 at the age of twenty-two to be Tobase's assistant. He had gone to San Francisco State University to study English so he could communicate better with the younger members of the congregation, then had fallen in love with the Western academic scene and had never stopped studying. After the spirited and stubborn Tobase had left, Kato had spent as much time as possible at Sokoji, but now he found himself overextended. He was busy finishing his Ph.D. in comparative philosophy. Because the congregation couldn't afford to pay him anything, at times he had to do menial labor to support himself and his family. Yet the duties at Sokoji could not be ignored, and Kato had been taking care of Sunday services, funerals, and everything else for a long time. He respected the older Japanese-Americans, but to him the situation was an artifact of the past, lifeless and stale. Being at Sokoji was too much like being back in Japan – stuck with obligations that didn't interest him. He preferred being with his friends – poets and artists – and in the stimulating atmosphere of the university.

Kato drove Suzuki from the airport north toward San Francisco. The wealth of this country was apparent in everything he saw – warehouses, new suburban neighborhoods, distribution centers lined with trucks, and the foundations of Candlestick Park stadium rising on landfill that once was marshland. Then the handsome, low, white skyline of the city came into view, along with glimpses of the bay bordered by shipyards and piers, and on the water sailboats and cargo ships.

Most of the cars were large, and there were so many of them, of such varied colors and makes. There were hardly any bicycles. In San Francisco the streets were wide, lined with large Victorian houses. Everywhere were billboards and store signs in English to decipher.

As Kato drove on, a fog crept over the city from the ocean and obscured the sunlight. On the sidewalks were whites, Asians, Hispanics, and blacks. Soon they were passing more Asians on the sidewalks, storefront signs in Japanese, bonsai on fire escapes. They came to a stop before a deeply inset arched doorway.

Suzuki got out and looked up at the curious building – wooden, time-weathered, three stories high, with a mock-Moorish tower on each side and a wide balcony in the middle with fancy columns. The facade was full of Romanesque decorative detail. It was an old synagogue, Kato explained, something of a landmark to students of architecture. There were three arched doorways, the central one the largest. The paint had dulled and lost its intended Venetian marble effect. It looked a bit shabby, though it must have been impressive in its day. A wooden plaque read: Sokoji, Soto Zen Mission, 1881 Bush Street. Entering through the small, high-ceilinged lobby, they went up a stairway with a mahogany railing, from which one could look down on a dark, funky hallway, empty except for a plain wooden bench.

Kato knew that the old building with faded plaster walls bore no resemblance to any temple Suzuki had ever seen, and he sympathized with Suzuki's obvious shock. There were no tatami, no shoji, no Japanese woodwork, and no sign of a garden. Kato and some of the members had cleaned it up in preparation for Suzuki's arrival, but he still was not proud of its appearance. At the top of the stairs they walked through double doors into a large room filled with about seventy middle-aged and older Japanese-Americans sitting on high-backed pews, waiting to greet the new priest.

Suzuki followed Kato along the worn wood floor under cylindrical paper lanterns. They stepped onto a wide platform cluttered with flower arrangements, cushions, and ritual instruments. Suzuki followed slowly behind Kato and stood at a wide altar before a two-foot-high statue of Kannon flanked by pyramids of fruit, vases of flowers, and three lit candles. Then Kato kneeled before the wide bronze bell and watched for the cue of two hands joining to bow in gassho. Suzuki paused. The room was hushed. He stood as unhurried as the flowers around him. He raised his hands. The deep, rich sound of the bell echoed through the high-ceilinged room.

After three prostrations he and all present chanted the *Heart Sutra*. Then Suzuki turned and bowed again in gassho, palms together, to those assembled – expressing his sincerity, warmth, and also his authority through the expression on his face, the way he wore his robes, how he used his hands. He said he was grateful to have arrived safely in America and thanked them for coming to greet him. These older Japanese, still close to the culture of their homeland, bowed solemnly in return.

Suzuki had just flown for the first time, crossing the widest expanse of water on earth. He had left one set of obligations for another, gone from the known to the unknown, to this musty old building and this expectant crowd. The limbo between the old life and the new, the unique meditation of the flight and arrival, was over. Life had shifted, and Suzuki assumed his new role without the slightest hesitation or resistance. He settled comfortably into the shrine room in the midst of his congregation, like a vase that was made for its altar.

AFTER LUNCH with the temple elders and a tour of Japantown, Kato, carrying two bags of gifts from local stores, accompanied Suzuki to his office adjoining the shrine room. Then he took him up a narrow flight of stairs to two clean, characterless rooms above the office. One was for storage and the other was a small bedroom holding a single bed and desk. Neither room had a window to the outside. No one had lived up there for decades. Back in the office Kato noticed a small potted orchid sitting on the desk. "Where did that come from?" he asked. "I sneaked it in through customs," Suzuki said. It was his first act of mischief in the United States.

Later, Suzuki walked around his new temple, turning lights on and off, peeking into back rooms full of cardboard boxes, folding chairs, and tables, inspecting the cavernous auditorium with rows of pews, a stage, a large organ in back, and balconies along both sides. There was no plumbing in his private area, so he brushed his teeth in the rest room next to the office, took his customary evening bath in the deep old basement tub, and climbed back up the three flights to sleep on his first night in America.

THE FOLLOWING morning, Kato arrived in a coat and tie, carrying his priest robes in a bag. His wife followed holding a package of rice balls wrapped in a silk cloth for the new priest, their young daughter at her side.

They found Suzuki in the shrine room upstairs. He had rearranged the flowers and was cleaning the memorial plaques in a dark wooden recess, reaching in and wiping the surfaces with a damp cloth. The whole place looked and smelled as if he'd been cleaning for hours. Kato was pleased to see this early sign of industriousness. Suzuki's predecessor, Tobase, had many fine qualities, but keeping the temple clean wasn't one of them.

Kato introduced Suzuki to his wife, Emi; their three-year-old daughter, Kazumi, hid behind her mother's dress and peeked out at the new priest. Then she reached into a paper bag, pulled out an apple, and handed it to Suzuki. He accepted it with delight, and she retreated once more.

People began to arrive. By quarter to ten, many were sitting in the pews. Men were smoking and talking in the hallway and in the office, standing by the desk and sitting on the green vinyl couch. Suzuki was upstairs getting ready for his first Sunday service, changing into his more formal brown robes. Looking down from his quarters through a sliding window onto the shrine room below, he recognized a few people already.

A short time later Suzuki stood facing his new congregation. Kato had explained to him that the custom in America was for ministers to give a sermon at the conclusion of Sunday services. He cleared his throat, placed his hands together with his short carved staff held between his palms, and bowed. "Ohayo gozaimasu" (good morning), he said in his gentle yet penetrating voice. "Ohayo gozaimasu," they responded. Then he gave his first lecture in America, in Japanese.

When Shakyamuni Buddha first started to teach twenty-five hundred years ago in India, he lived in the forest and would at times give talks to all who came: monks, nuns, laymen, and laywomen. Many, many people came to hear him, since he was so great and his talks were so wonderful and liberating. When he stepped up on his dais, a monk would hit a tree stump with a mallet and his disciple Ananda would say, "We are now going to hear Buddha's talk, so please listen carefully." And Buddha would deliver his lecture. When he was finished the monk would pound the stump again, and Ananda would say, "The Buddha's gracious talk is finished."

Kato looked at the spotless surface of the bell stand in front of him. Suzuki spoke so slowly. The members of the congregation sat impassively. A few looked at their watches. Children squirmed in the pews. From the kitchen behind the altar came occasional sounds of food preparation – the clinking of pots and lids, women's voices, a chair being moved, footsteps. Suzuki continued.

One day the people came, Buddha arrived, and a monk hit the tree stump and Ananda said, "We are now going to hear Buddha's talk, so please listen carefully." But that day the Buddha just sat, and didn't say a word. Then he stood up.

Kato listened to Suzuki's delivery. He did not speak in the usual theatrical style of lecturing priests, with dramatic rising and falling pitches. Suzuki wasn't trying to impress them with his knowledge and use of esoteric terms. He spoke simply, directly, almost informally.

Ananda said, "Excuse me, oh honorable one, but are you not giving a talk today?" "Oh, but I just did," Buddha answered, and he descended his dais and walked away.

Suzuki stood silently for a moment. Then with stick in hand he put his palms together, gasshoed, and thanked the congregation.

Kato smiled. A good story and a very short story. Now there

would be more time for refreshments and socializing. How ordinary their new priest was, Kato thought, yet what a gracious style he had. He was off to a good start.

You may say that things happen just by chance, but I don't feel that way.

AFTER A FEW days at Sokoji, Suzuki received his first Western visitor. Lou McNeil was an Irish-American in her early twenties and a student of opera. Except for a few exchanges on the trip, Suzuki hadn't used his English in a long time, but he made himself understood and caught the gist of what his guest was saying. Her husband wished to go to Japan to study with a Zen master; she asked Suzuki what he thought about that. She was concerned for him and for their marriage. Suzuki said that he did zazen at 5:45 in the morning and suggested that it might be good for her husband to try Zen in San Francisco first.

Bill McNeil arrived a few days later. A handsome man about five foot eight, with buttery blond hair combed over his ears, he was alert and spirited yet awkward in the unfamiliar surroundings of the shrine room. His wife had made a few comments about Suzuki without letting on that she'd met him. Bill had eagerly taken the bait. He asked Suzuki if this was a Zen temple and if he was a Zen master. There was that term again. He told Suzuki about his plans to go to Japan. He'd read some books about Zen and enlightenment, and now he wanted to go meet the real thing. But was this the real thing right in front of him? Suzuki told him what he'd told Lou – that it might be good to have some experience with Zen practice in America first. He got a cushion from the altar, placed it in the aisle, and showed Bill how to sit. He corrected his posture, pushing the small of his back in, pulling his shoulders back and his chin in. He pushed his knees down gently, showing him how to put his hands together with the left palm on the right palm and the thumbs touching just enough to hold a piece of paper between them. He told him to keep his eyes half open, and to place his attention on the in and out of his breath. He advised him in the future to wear looser pants, so his legs would cross more easily.

This was not at all what Bill had expected. The books on Zen were full of stories of dramatic interchanges between monks. But there was something about this priest that made him want to return. Beneath the charm, Bill sensed authority and humility. Early the next morning and each morning thereafter, Bill McNeil showed up and joined Suzuki for zazen.

IN 1959 the Cold War was as icy as ever. The Eisenhower era had a lame-duck year and a half to go before the Kennedy era would begin. Japan was still poor, and America was enjoying seemingly endless affluence. American Christianity and Judaism were generally supportive of society and its materialism. Only a few voices were pointing out the dangers of nuclear weapons, the narcotic effect of pop culture, and the soullessness of assembly-line products, but there was a concentration of these voices in the San Francisco Bay Area.

SUZUKI HAD arrived at the height of what Kato called the "Alan Watts Zen boom." His early students came to him from the loose subculture of artists, nonconformists, and beatniks in the Bay Area, where interest in Asian thought was high. They heard about Suzuki at the American Academy of Asian Studies (the Academy), at the San Francisco Art Institute, where Bill McNeil studied, and in the coffeehouses of North Beach and Berkeley.

Kato had been associated with the Academy from the mid-fifties, ever since the former director, Alan Watts, had asked him to join the faculty. The staff included distinguished teachers from India, China, Cambodia, Thailand, Japan, and Tibet, who imparted first-hand instruction in Hinduism, Buddhism, Taoism, Sanskrit and other languages, and the arts and histories of Asia.

D. T. Suzuki lectured at the Academy when traveling between Japan and the East Coast. The highly respected avant-garde *sumi* artist and printmaker Saburo Hasegawa taught calligraphy and tea ceremony there and had been a sort of informal resident therapist, encouraging Watts to slow down and smell the powdered green tea, which he called "the froth of jade." Tobase, Suzuki's predecessor at Sokoji, had taught calligraphy at the Academy and at Sokoji as well, and was well loved by his students.

It was at the American Academy of Asian Studies, earlier in the decade, that the poet Gary Snyder and the whole student body had been captivated by Ruth Fuller Sasaki's formal exposition of the Rinzai Zen method of working with koans. The matriarch of American Zen, she had married Shigetsu Sasaki, her Zen teacher and the teacher of the First Zen Institute in New York City. After his death she had moved to Kyoto to study and help foreigners who wanted to study Zen. She subsequently helped Snyder get a grant to go to Japan to study Rinzai Zen and work with her translation team.

The three-story Victorian East-West House was near Sokoji on California Street. An early attempt at communal living organized by poets, artists, and students of Asian studies, it was set up after Alan Watts was asked to leave the Academy because of philosophical conflicts with the administration, and because they objected to his libertine lifestyle. The East-West House was so popular that in 1958 the Hyphen House was started a few blocks away, a big grey building informally named for the hyphen between East and West. Many of the best-known characters from the San Francisco Beat scene lived in or visited these houses, including the poets Gary Snyder, Joanne Kyger, Lew Welch, Lawrence Ferlinghetti, and Philip Whalen.

Whalen was about to publish his first book of poetry. He'd caught the Zen bug and was aware of Suzuki, having seen him walk by on the street wearing his priest's cap. He later met him at a wedding Suzuki performed. Whalen thought he was a delightful person, but was on his way to Japan to study the real thing, Rinzai Zen.

Everyone seemed to be going to Japan or wishing they could. Watts criticized the old-fashioned Japanese monastic way as "square Zen." He also put down "Beat Zen" and made a case for what he dubbed "Zen Zen." Whalen called Beat Zen a hallucination but wondered if there could be any Zen Zen without checking out the "squares" in Japan. Just before he left for Japan he ran into McNeil with his wife and two children. McNeil said he'd see Whalen over there before long, but he loved studying with Suzuki and was going to continue that for a while until Suzuki thought he was ready to go.

There was definitely a buzz about the new priest at Sokoji. A few of the hip crowd, like McNeil and Joanne Kyger, had joined the morning zazen. But it seemed awfully early in the morning to most of them.

Suzuki was surprised by all this interest in Zen. He had never experienced anything like it in Japan. He enjoyed the lively, hip, intellectual milieu, but he didn't venture out much into its world; he just tended to his temple. When people asked about Zen he always said, "I sit at 5:45 in the morning. Please join me." It was his calling card. There didn't seem to be any hook. But to the few who were joining in and getting to know him, Suzuki himself was the hook.

Seeking for something in the dark is not like usual activity, which is based on an idea of gaining something.

KATO INVITED Suzuki to join his class on Buddhism at the Academy. It was located in a fine old rambling mansion in the fashionable Pacific Heights section of San Francisco. Twelve students sat at a round oak table. Among them were three women in their forties: Betty Warren, Della Goertz, and Jean Ross. Kato introduced the class to "Reverend Suzuki." Suzuki was reserved and they were shy with him, as he was surely a Zen master and therefore enlightened – something they'd all been reading a lot about in the books of Alan Watts and D. T. Suzuki. A Zen master was said to be someone who had had satori – a flash of insight that changed one's life forever. There didn't seem to be any satori that night, but there was a lot of smiling between Kato's students and Suzuki, who was comfortable being quiet and listening. In the latter part of the class Kato asked Suzuki if he'd like to say something.

"Let's do zazen," he replied.

The little zazen that had been taught by Japanese priests in America had been done in chairs, but Suzuki suggested they get down on the floor and face the wall. It was awkward, because there were no cushions. Suzuki's English was a bit garbled, but soon he had everyone sitting on the floor, where they remained for twenty minutes.

Before they parted Suzuki told them he sat zazen for forty minutes every morning except for days with the numbers four or nine in the dates (the traditional days for an abbreviated schedule and doing personal chores in Zen monasteries). "Please come join me if you wish."

BETTY WARREN and Della Goertz were both native Californians who came to the Bay Area in the thirties to go to college and become teachers. After taking a college semantics class with the noted linguist S. I. Hayakawa, Della saw things in a new light, took some comparative religion classes, and began studying at the Academy in the early fifties. After hearing Alan Watts on KPFA radio, Betty decided to take a course on Zen Buddhism at the Academy. Betty, Della, and Jean Ross met each other in Kato's class, and for many years their spiritual paths would run parallel.

The three women decided to continue their Buddhist study with Suzuki at Sokoji. Jean would join them after a trip to Europe. All three felt an attraction to Suzuki as a teacher. Della said that as soon as she met him she wanted to be with him – regardless of what he was teaching. Betty agreed. "There was something about his bearing, a look in his eye that made me feel that whatever he said was something I could trust. He was a rare person."

BETTY PICKED up Della on her way in from Sausalito and the two joined the few others at Sokoji. After zazen they were invited to tea with Suzuki at a long wooden table in the kitchen, just behind the shrine room altar. Bill and Lou McNeil were also there. Lou had started sitting with Suzuki, too. The first day she came, her husband was surprised to find out that she and Suzuki already knew each other. "We tricked you," Suzuki told him. An architect named Bob Hense had been sitting every morning with Bill. Hense was friendly, short, and prematurely balding, and had a lot of nervous energy. Like Bill, he'd originally come to Sokoji to ask about studying Zen in a monastery in Japan, and he was sitting with Suzuki in preparation for that. Like Bill McNeil, he had become enamored with the man, his simple lifestyle, and the experience of sitting zazen with him.

Day after day these few returned in the dark mornings, and soon a few more regulars joined them for zazen. Traffic sounds and softly flashing headlights came and went in waves with the timed signal lights, merging with the flickering candlelight and wisps of incense smoke in the shrine room. The room slowly glowed brighter as the sun rose on the bay. Sometimes before or after they sat, Suzuki would offer a few words on zazen: just sit, follow your breath, count your breaths, or keep yourself centered on your *hara* (the lower abdomen).

At first there was no proper place to sit on the floor, so with some effort they joined the heavy pews together in pairs and placed them lengthwise along the walls, running from the altar, two sets on each side. Facing each other, the pews formed a sort of boat, wide enough for people to sit cross-legged, two or three to a boat. The fledgling meditators climbed over the armrests and plopped themselves on cushions they had brought from sofas and chairs at home. They faced the walls, with Suzuki watching from his place on the altar platform. In the dimly lit room the pew-vessels floated on a dark ocean, with torsos and heads sticking up and occasionally bobbing with sleepiness – strange cargo on a shadowy voyage.

Zazen was physically difficult, and toward the end of the period most people's legs were in pain. But day after day the stillness of Suzuki's sitting filled the room with confidence and encouraged the others to persist.

It is important to work for future generations, for our descendants. We must be proud to do something, even though people do not usually know its value.

DAIJU HOSEN Isobe had come to San Francisco from Los Angeles in 1933. On Buddha's Enlightenment Day, December 8, 1934, he founded Sokoji. The name he gave the abandoned synagogue had a simple meaning: *Soko* stood for San Francisco and the *ji* meant temple. Daito Suzuki, whom Shunryu Suzuki had seen off as a young man in Japan, moved from Zenshuji in L.A. to become the third head priest of Sokoji, again on December 8, Buddha's Enlightenment Day, 1941 – the day after Pearl Harbor. He was abbot-in-absentia through the years of the Japanese internment and continued after the war, until 1948. Through great effort he and others had managed to keep the temple in the hands of the congregation. A Hindu temple had helped them by taking over the deed during the war, although a Christian group used it as a church. In 1948 Daito returned to L.A., where he became the abbot of Zenshuji and Soto Zen bishop of North America until he died on July 9, 1959. At that time Suzuki was asked by his friend Gido at Soto headquarters in Japan to become the bishop and to move the North American Soto headquarters to San Francisco. He refused.

Suzuki flew to L.A. to conduct Daito's funeral. A young Soto Zen priest named Taizan Maezumi joined him. Maezumi had been an assistant priest at Zenshuji, the Soto temple in L.A., since the early fifties. He had recently been studying at San Francisco State. In L.A.

Maezumi had sat zazen with Nyogen Senzaki, the pioneering Rinzai Zen priest who had taught Zen to Westerners for decades, and Maezumi said he too hoped to start a zazen group in America.

This was the first funeral Suzuki had performed in America. Daito would become American soil. In 1929, when Suzuki and a group of fellow college student–monks had seen Daito off at the docks in Yokohama, Suzuki had cheered him, wet-eyed, as the boat pulled away. How he had wished back then that he could be the one starting a new life in America. Now, thirty years later, he was.

Buddhism has many annual layers, like a big tree. It is our tradition to respect those efforts that our ancestors have made for more than twenty-five hundred years. When this temple was founded, there were not many priests in America, and the founder worked so hard to collect donations to buy this building. He was able to raise only part of the cost, and the Japanese members year after year paid on the mortgage. Even in detention camps during the war, they collected money for the mortgage. This was an important effort, but it is nothing compared to the effort and devotion of our ancestors in India, China, and Japan in preserving and developing Buddhism. We should continue these efforts generation after generation forever.

When I came to American I had no idea, no particular plan.

GRADUALLY, AND with the help of others, Suzuki started to introduce certain traditional elements of Japanese form and practice to his San Francisco zendo.

George Hagiwara was among the few members of the congregation who were friendly with the zazen students. When he greeted them at the temple on Sundays or weekday afternoons, he always smiled and made them feel welcome. The Hagiwara family had founded and been caretakers of the famous Japanese Tea Garden in Golden Gate Park and had lived in the house there till World War II. Though he had lost a fortune during the war, he still was better off than most of the Japanese-American members, who were recovering from the terrible losses suffered during internment.

Having heard from Suzuki how cumbersome it was to sit zazen on the pews, Hagiwara talked to other members and took up a collection. They ordered tatami mats from Japan to go around the edge of the room and also bought grass goza mats to bow on and black cloth to make round zafu cushions. In six weeks the new materials arrived.

On Saturdays Betty and Della stayed for breakfast and afterward sewed and stuffed kapok into the zafus. Bill McNeil and some of the other men cleaned the floor and moved the pews back in from the balcony for the Japanese congregation's service on Sunday. Thus started the tradition of an extended Saturday morning schedule that included a work period.

The shrine room took on a radically different look and from then on was called the zendo. Suzuki guarded the appearance of the newly appointed zendo and kept a watchful eye out to see that people fluffed their zafus back into a round shape after zazen and placed them in the center of the tatami, lining them all up straight. Betty's first reaction to the zafu was that it felt as hard as the tatami underneath. "Next," she said, "Sensei's going to give us a nice rock and tell us that's what they sit on at Eiheiji in Japan."

ANOTHER INGREDIENT that Suzuki carefully introduced at this time was sutra chanting. After the first month he started reciting the *Heart Sutra* each morning after zazen, accompanying himself by thumping on the mokugyo and ringing the low and high bowl-shaped bells, while the others stood and listened. Then one morning he passed out cards to the seven people present with the romanized sutra printed on them. They chanted the *Heart Sutra* three times as Suzuki hit the bells and drums. He made no comment on their efforts, which sounded like an orchestra tuning up. Soon they were developing their own style of chanting. Suzuki put up a sign on the altar that read, "Chant the sutra with your ears."

An element in the zendo environment that attracted particular attention was the *kyosaku,* which came to be called "the stick." The kyosaku is an integral part of Japanese Zen, used primarily to awaken a practitioner who has become drowsy while sitting on the cushion. His stick was about two feet long and an inch and a half wide, oval at the handle end and flat at the other. During the zazen period Suzuki would walk around the zendo with the stick held vertically in front of him. When students appeared to be sleepy or unfocused, Suzuki would stand behind them and rest the flat end of the stick on their right shoulder. They would put their palms together in gassho and bend over to the left. He'd hit each student twice on the muscles between the shoulder blade and the backbone, then repeat the procedure on the left shoulder. It made a penetrating sound that caused the others in the room to open their closed eyes and straighten their backs. But it was more invigorating than painful and frightened only newcomers. There is no record of Dogen's having used the stick, but Dogen's master Nyojo, in China, would hit his monks on their shoulders with his sandal if they were nodding.

Now that the pews were out of the room during the week, Suzuki would walk around during zazen. He would adjust their posture, especially if they were new to the zendo, and would occasionally whisper advice like, "Please keep the eyes half open." He emphasized other details, like how to hold the hands together in the proper position, or mudra: an oval shape held at the lower abdomen, but not resting on the feet, thumbs together at the navel with a tissue paper's breadth between them. He tended to pay more attention to students on their first day, usually touching them in some way, as if to say hello – straightening posture or even briefly massaging someone nervous or stiff. But mostly he left his students alone, and there was stillness. People came and sat with Suzuki and each other in candlelight and silence, chanted a sutra, maybe stayed for tea afterward, and then went on about their lives. Those who continued day after day, week after week, began to feel a change in themselves. Suzuki did, too. He was no longer frustrated with how his life was going.

You should forget what I say, but be sure you know the real meaning of the words.

KATO HELPED translate at times, but Suzuki didn't want more assistance than absolutely necessary. His English was taking off. At adult school, which he attended every day, he'd done so well on tests that his English teacher had accused him of cheating.

Suzuki bravely began giving talks in English on Wednesday nights. They were brief – fifteen to thirty minutes. He spent hours preparing for them, but many listeners, especially those hearing him for the first time, had trouble understanding his English and went away scratching their heads.

After one of his talks when he and Kato were alone together in the office, Suzuki took off his okesa, folded and draped it over a chair, then sighed and said to Kato, "Such a chore. I have to think of what to say."

"Yes, in English as well as Japanese," Kato said, looking at the Japanese-English dictionary on his desk – the cover worn and the corners curled up.

But Suzuki's efforts were appreciated. Della understood him right away. To her he was clearly saying what she already believed: we have what we seek, and the way to find it is just to be ourselves.

Betty noticed how much he contradicted himself, coming back around to the opposite of what he'd just said in the same lecture, sometimes even in the same sentence. He just didn't think in a way she was used to. "One week he says we have to put our entire effort into it," she said to Della, "and the next week he says there's no use trying, give up and the answer will come. No use trying, and you've got to do your damnedest!"

Even though you expect some answer, you know, sometimes my answer will go in another direction. Even though my answer is something you didn't expect, you should be able to follow the direction. You shouldn't be lost. Of course, sometimes your teacher will give you some answer you do expect. A teacher will always try to put you in confusion. Back and forth in this way, we will help each other.

To Kato, Suzuki's progress had been astounding: "Amazingly, with his sort of calm, slow pace," he said to Hagiwara one day, "Suzuki-sensei has communicated with his students within a short time. To many he is a fascinating person when he speaks English. His character communicates to them as well; nothing excites or angers him. He is a kind and gentle priest, yet with backbone. He actually has stern zazen in the zendo, but after zazen he is a warm person."

Kato liked to hear Suzuki's English-language version of classic Zen stories – some about the great old masters of China, others about the life of Dogen. In one story Suzuki told during a Wednesday evening lecture, Dogen met an old monk in China who was drying mushrooms by a monastery wall on a hot summer day. "Why are you out here in the heat? Why not go in and rest until the sun is lower in the sky?" Dogen asked. "This is what I'm doing now," answered the monk. "It's my job and no one else's job. Why would I try to be somewhere else?"

"The time is now," Suzuki said after he told the story. "What we are doing is now. There is no other time. This is reality. I am here now. You are here now. That incident with the old monk taught Dogen what a Buddhist life is, what reality is. It is not for another time or another place or another person."

A single piece of thread is not useful until we make a beautiful cloth with it. So each single school of Buddhism is meaningful as part of the overall religious life.

ONE MORNING after breakfast in the fall of 1959, a Japanese Rinzai Zen priest in robes showed up unexpectedly at Sokoji. His name was Soen Nakagawa. He had heard that Shunryu Suzuki was sitting zazen with Westerners, and for that reason he had come by to pay his respects. Kato, who answered the door, led him upstairs. Nakagawa offered incense at the altar and the three of them chanted the *Heart Sutra*. Kato and Suzuki had heard of Nakagawa and were impressed that this priest from the Rinzai sect would visit them. Kato did not like the Japanese sectarian tradition in which priests from different sects avoided fraternizing, but he was used to it. These two, however, were quite open with each other. They had in common that they wished to transmit their way to Westerners.

Nakagawa had also sat zazen with Westerners in America and in Japan, where he had become involved with the Soto Zen maverick Sogaku Harada and Harada's heir, Hakuun Yasutani, who used koans extensively with their Japanese and Western students. Nakagawa had several times gone to L.A. to visit and sit zazen with Nyogen Senzaki. Senzaki had taught his low-key, anti-institutional brand of Rinzai Zen for decades – first in his Bush Street San Francisco apartment and then in L.A. Suzuki knew of Senzaki, respected him for having concentrated on teaching laypeople, and admired Senzaki's concept of the floating zendo: he had no temple.

They presented a nice contrast – Suzuki, the short, slight, modest one, and Nakagawa, taller, thicker, more assertive, and animated. Suzuki chanted quietly, Nakagawa strongly. After the service Kato blew out the candle and tended to the altar. At that moment he feared the harmony between the priests was over.

Nakagawa asked to see a sutra book that was on the altar. He looked at it, then suddenly exploded, stamping his foot on the floor and shouting, "This is not Zen!" He tore the book in two and threw it on the floor. Kato froze with shock.

Suzuki calmly squatted down and picked up the pieces. "Oh, that's a sutra book that was donated to the temple on the occasion of a memorial service for an old woman from a different sect not represented in this area," he said. "We accept everything here. We chant everything. We eat everything." For a moment Nakagawa still looked angry, but Suzuki put him at ease. "Let's go have some tea."

Buddhism is not any special teaching. It's our human way.

IN SEPTEMBER Jean Ross returned from Europe. Her classmates from the Academy, Betty and Della, were already pillars of the zendo, and from then on Jean joined them three times a week, when she wasn't working as a nurse. She took the bus over from Berkeley for the Wednesday night sitting and lecture, spent the night, and stayed for Thursday morning zazen. She came back for the Saturday sitting, breakfast, and work period, and for the Sunday lecture that preceded Suzuki's lecture to the Japanese congregation.

Jean was from a middle-class Detroit family with strong ties to the Methodist Church. At fifteen she became curious about Asia and started reading all the books she could find on China and Japan. In college she pursued Christian studies and started to read about Buddhism. She fit right in with Suzuki temperamentally: she was independent and sharp-eyed, with no time for nonsense. She was heavy and had a hard time sitting on a cushion on the floor, but she could accept the difficult regimen when it came from Suzuki. Jean had a constancy and determination that impressed Suzuki. "The harder it is for you to sit, the deeper your realization," he always said.

Della was accustomed to coming by in the afternoons when her kindergarten class was over to see if she could be of use. She drove

Suzuki to visit Alan Watts and to the homes of Japanese-Americans so he could perform memorial services for their departed ancestors. He would call and ask for a ride to the airport to greet a visitor or to go to the newspaper for an interview. One day Suzuki went to Della's house and met her husband, who was afflicted with advanced Parkinson's disease. Suzuki was deeply touched and wondered how she managed to take care of her husband, teach kindergarten, practice zazen, and do so much for him.

"Are there real bodhisattvas on earth?" Bill McNeil once asked Suzuki.

"Yes," he answered, "Della."

One day Della took him to Sears, where he bought a dozen potted plants and a three-foot potted tree. He put the tree in the main entryway and the plants on a table at the top of the stairs, where everyone passed on their way to and from the zendo.

The temple now had a brighter, cared-for look. The cleaning, decorating, and rearranging that Suzuki started the day he arrived had made the place much more inviting. His own room was brighter too, thanks to a window, installed as a gift from the temple's board. The Saturday work period also made a big difference. Even a few people could get a lot done in an hour cleaning the zendo, halls and stairway, bathrooms, steps, and the sidewalk out front.

KATO ASSISTED with Sunday service and visited once or twice during the week. A cantankerous old caretaker took care of maintenance, changing lightbulbs and fixing leaks. Students and congregation women would sometimes bring food over or invite Suzuki to their houses for dinner. Della brought him casseroles and cookies. He often ate lunch and dinner in Japantown, but mainly he cooked for himself and whomever dropped by. Della's favorite was his ginger tofu.

Although students and congregation members helped in their spare time, Suzuki expressed frustration at all he had to do. He told Kato he wished his wife, Mitsu, could join him. He'd always had women to help him run a temple. He wrote asking Mitsu to come, but she refused, saying she was needed at the two kindergartens and would wait for him to return to Japan when his three-year stint in America was up. Mitsu was no longer ill. A doctor had finally diagnosed her with thyroiditis, and a simple operation had corrected her problem, but she was still angry at her husband for abandoning her when she was sick.

Chapter Eleven

Bowing

1960

When there is freedom from self, you have absolute freedom.

BILL KWONG was a mailman who lived in San Francisco with his wife, Laura. They were both second-generation Chinese-Americans who were part of the Beat scene. They had one child, and Laura was pregnant with another. Bill and Laura had gone to Sokoji in Tobase's time to hear a lecture that was translated by a distinguished-looking gentleman. They didn't get much out of it and figured you had to hear it in the original.

One day while delivering mail, Kwong saw a front-page story on Sokoji in the *Nichibei Times,* a newspaper for Japanese-Americans printed in both Japanese and English. It was about the new priest there, Reverend Suzuki, who had some zazen students and a pet bird. One student, a young artist named Bill McNeil, had confronted Suzuki in his office one day, asking why, if he believed in absolute freedom, he kept a bird in a cage. Suzuki had walked right over to the cage, opened the little door, and let the bird fly out. It was a tradition in China and Japan to let birds go at temples as a symbol of liberation. Ironically, birds were sold in front of temples for that purpose. But this was a spontaneous act. Kwong thought he should check this guy out – he must be a great Zen master.

When Bill Kwong walked up to the second floor of Sokoji, went into the zendo, and saw the black zafus all lined up straight and neat like soldiers in a row, nothing there spoke to him and his values. The altar was stacked with oranges in front of the Buddha statue. The room smelled of incense and was filled with paraphernalia – bells, drum, gong, flowers, high red-lacquered seat, black-lacquered memorial plaques with the names of the deceased in gold Chinese characters. It was too much like an old Chinese temple, full of superstition, empty ceremonies, prayers for money and ancestors. "This really is for the birds," thought Kwong, as he chuckled with derision. This didn't look like freedom to him. Freedom was his goatee, his black shirt, dirty jeans, and black boots – freedom from bourgeois grooming and grey flannel suits.

The door to the office opened. A little man in robes came into the room, ignoring Kwong, and started fixing the flowers on the altar. Kwong snickered. "How square," he thought.

Walking up Pine Street toward Van Ness Avenue, Kwong passed a store called the Bazaar which was offering a free poster, a photo of the Kamakura Buddha seated in meditation. He took it home, tacked it to the wall, and told Laura his disappointing experience at Sokoji. He liked Alan Watts's inspiring talks on the radio, but all this guy Suzuki seemed to have was a hall for ceremonies and meditation. Kwong was not into that old stuff. He was into liberation and seeing that *this* was it, as Watts said. *That* wasn't it. Kwong was listening to the hippest people, and nobody was talking about meditation. But he kept looking at that buddha on the wall. Then he met Bill McNeil at the Art Institute and was taken with McNeil's confident energy. McNeil talked about sitting zazen with Suzuki as if it were pretty cool. Kwong went home and the buddha on the wall was still looking at him, so he decided to go back to Sokoji and try zazen.

He arrived in the early morning darkness and followed McNeil into the shrine room. Kwong sat down like the others, watching for cues. Nobody told him what to do. After the service McNeil asked him to have some tea in the kitchen, where he introduced him to Suzuki. Suzuki stared at Kwong's face for what seemed like a long time before saying hello. What a curious person, Kwong thought. Suzuki made tea as the temple cat walked back and forth against his ankles. Della asked Kwong how he had heard about Sensei. He mentioned the newspaper article and asked if the bird was still in the building or had flown off. Everyone looked down. Had he said something wrong?

"The cat," Suzuki said softly.

"The cat?" Kwong asked, looking at the cat curled up now on Della's lap.

McNeil leaned over to Kwong and said, "The cat ate the bird."

"Sensei felt so bad about it," said Della with sympathy in her voice.

Suzuki said nothing. They drank their tea.

KWONG STARTED going to Sokoji regularly. He and Laura were used to doing everything together. The first time she came to Sokoji she was dizzy with pain after not moving the entire zazen period. Her husband had told her this was the rule. Then she stood up too quickly and fainted to the floor. At breakfast she broke a raw egg over her dress, because she thought it was hard boiled, not being familiar with the Japanese custom of mixing a raw egg with hot rice for breakfast.

Laura was trying to be a good Zen student and a good mother. On most days she was busy taking care of their boys, a toddler and a baby, but she'd bring them along on Sundays. Sometimes she'd find friends to help, so she could go to zazen and Wednesday evening lectures. One day in a lecture she heard Suzuki say, "Your practice can be at home." Laura talked to Suzuki about it later and told him she was feeling guilty about not taking care of her children well enough. "You don't have to come here just because your husband does," he said. From that point on Laura stopped feeling like her husband's shadow and devoted herself to finding Buddha at home.

Bill Kwong's life reversed direction. For one thing, his apartment lost a heavy layer of dust, mainly as a result of Suzuki's visiting for dinner one evening. Suzuki hadn't been inside long before his robes started to acquire dust and cat hair. So instead of sitting and talking, he started cleaning up. Bill and Laura joined him. Dinner had to wait.

One day Suzuki talked to the students about the importance of coming to the zendo clean and neatly dressed. Kwong started to wear freshly laundered clothes and shaved his goatee. But he didn't feel criticized by his new teacher. On the contrary, he felt Suzuki was the first person ever who accepted him unconditionally. He was willing to sit zazen day after day without moving his aching legs, at an hour when he used to be just going to bed. He was willing to change his life, because he felt that Suzuki had total confidence in him – more than he had in himself. Rather than being required to have faith in Suzuki, he found Suzuki demonstrating faith in him. This encouraged Kwong to follow Suzuki down a path, even though he couldn't see where it was leading.

*The most important point is to accept yourself
and stand on your two feet.*

THE MORNING zazen began with a greeting. People would come into the zendo and sit on their zafus facing the wall – men on the right side and women on the left, beneath the arched windows. Suzuki would walk to the altar, offer incense, and bow down on his bowing cloth. Then he would walk around the room bent in a bow, holding his teacher's staff. As he passed behind people they would put their hands together in gassho. If a person was new and didn't know about it, he'd lean over and whisper "Greeting." It was the traditional morning greeting, done in training temples in Japan.

The morning schedule concluded with a standing bow to Suzuki as each person left the zendo following service. It was a little ritual that gave a moment of private contact with every person who came, every day. He would stand inside the door to his office, and as people filed out they would stop and bow with him. It was never perfunctory. He gave his full attention to each bow, to each person. Some felt that Suzuki was looking straight through them. The bow at the door was a farewell, a greeting, a meeting. It was an intimate affair, new each day.

"Suzuki-sensei always is encouraging us and thanking us," said Jean Ross. "When I stand across from him and bow, I am reminded he is totally on the level, without a speck of pretension."

A member of the congregation who was a florist would sometimes leave flower arrangements in Suzuki's office. One day he dropped by during zazen and left a magnificent arrangement of cymbidium orchids with hundreds of blossoms. As each person filed by that day, there was Suzuki among the flowers.

Curiously, people would follow this practice of bowing with Suzuki whether he was there or not. The old caretaker would often sit on the couch reading a Japanese newspaper and smoking a cigarette. Every now and then when Suzuki wasn't there, someone who had been sitting in the zendo for the first time would bow on the way out like the others, and would leave thinking that the old man in baggy pants and suspenders, who'd been sitting on the couch and ignoring them, was the Zen master.

We put more emphasis on a physical point rather than on an intellectual one.

PHILIP WILSON was an artist. He was also a tough guy and a teddy bear with a thick neck and massive thighs, who had been feared as a right tackle for the offense of the Stanford University football team. No one wanted to be on the other side of him on the playing field, where he was truly a man possessed. He also had a delicate side, which came out when he picked up a brush. Philip had transcendent experiences both playing football and painting, but it was modeling for other artists that first gave him the calm, subtle state of mind that led to his interest in meditation. Everyone in life drawing class at the San Francisco Art Institute wanted to draw his big, muscular body. It exploded with energy, and when he modeled, he found his energy becoming focused in stillness rather than in the fierceness of combat sport. He felt at home in that state of mind. It wasn't fixed, it flowed, and it was devoid of the complications of social life.

Early one Sunday morning while walking in Chinatown, Philip met an old drunk with a crazy eye. He took him to an AA meeting and then decided on a whim to go to a lecture at the Zen temple. Philip hadn't been to Sokoji before, but he'd heard about it from students at the Art Institute. He and his newfound buddy missed the lecture for the zazen students, arriving in time for Suzuki's talk to the congregation. Unfamiliar non-Japanese were usually asked to leave before this talk, but no one said a word to Philip the gladiator and the smelly bum.

The tiny man on the platform looked to Philip like a samurai. He was golden. He started talking in Japanese and smiling. As Philip stared at him, he entered a time-free zone. (This was not a new experience for Philip. He had been involved in early LSD experimentation with Ken Kesey.)

Afterward, he turned to his companion and said, "I don't know why, but I sure like this guy. I'm not going to say anything to him, though. He's too important to talk to." Suddenly Suzuki was in front of them saying hello. The old guy said, "Oh, I think your lecture was wonderful. I liked everything about it."

Philip said nothing. Suzuki said nothing. The old guy asked Suzuki for some money. Suzuki laughed as if he'd been told a good joke and said, "No. You'd just go buy alcohol with it."

THE NEXT day Philip phoned Sokoji. Suzuki answered, and Philip's words got all tangled up. Finally Suzuki said, "Please come." Philip went over prepared to ask a lot of questions, but as soon as he saw Suzuki, he was tongue-tied again. Suzuki said, "Zazen?" "Yes," Philip managed to say. "Oh, please come," replied Suzuki.

For the next two months Philip sat at the temple, but Suzuki didn't talk to him, give him any instruction, hit him with the stick, or adjust his posture. At the door after the morning service, bowing to each student who walked out, Suzuki would only look to the side when Philip stood before him.

One morning Betty said to Philip, "Ah, you're still here." It was common for people to try zazen for a while and then quit. But each person who stayed added something, figured out something about how to be there, what the possibilities were for working with Suzuki or working on themselves within Suzuki's sphere. Philip wasn't sure if he'd ever be capable of doing zazen correctly. Still, he was drawn there, and the idea of not going back didn't occur to him.

Philip went to his first Wednesday evening lecture thinking that finally he'd find out what it was all about. But it was so complicated. Or was it so simple? He couldn't get a grip on it. Suzuki's accent was hard to understand, and there was all the new terminology to deal with. His metaphors were puzzling. Philip would get the gist of a story but then had no idea what it applied to. Suzuki was smiling all the time, very confident. "Do you understand?" he would ask. And Philip was unable to say no, he was so amazed by the beauty and confusion and perfection of the story.

Philip went back again and again, trying to understand. He was sure he couldn't fool this man. Like an opposing left guard on the field, Suzuki demanded absolute honesty. Suzuki wasn't treating him like somebody who had failed a test – more like somebody who wasn't in the room. What did this behavior mean? Go away? No, the door was open to anyone. Maybe this was an initiation.

He couldn't figure out this beautiful swordless samurai, so he gave up. But he didn't leave. He began to watch, rather than analyze, everything Suzuki did. He thought, maybe I can understand his stories by the way he picks up his stick. He watched how Suzuki walked, with no part rushing ahead of the others or lagging behind, how he sat down with his whole body, how he picked up a teacup with both hands and held it like a baby bird. He watched and imitated. Then one day Philip bowed at the office door after zazen and Suzuki didn't turn away, but looked squarely at him. Philip had found a way to work with his new teacher.

If something is learned just by your thinking mind, it tends to be very superficial. When a mother bird teaches a baby bird how to fly, the mother tries like a baby. She can fly very well, but she imitates the baby. The mother bird becomes like a baby bird and does something that it is possible for a baby bird to do, so the baby bird will study how to fly. That is also practice.

We should practice with a beginner's real innocence, devoid of ideas of good or bad, gain or loss.

"SOMEONE GAVE me a nice *manju*, my favorite Japanese confection." It was the beginning of Suzuki's talk to the congregation one Sunday morning. Five-year-old Kazumi Kato perked up at the subject of the lecture. "It was so good. I like sweet things too much, but I thought, this too is the taste of Buddha. And Buddha's teaching is like candy. So I ate it slowly and fully appreciated it. You may think that Buddha's teaching is something very grave. But it is also candy."

Kato liked Suzuki's low-key, warm talks to the Japanese congregation even though they were delivered very slowly and a bit simply for a priest and scholar such as he. The zazen group was composed of intellectuals, and Suzuki gave more sophisticated talks to them. He appeared comfortable in both roles.

A lot of the older members of the congregation resented the

growing presence of the non-Japanese in their temple. The young ones especially were so awkward and talkative, frequently disheveled and dirty, and often unintentionally disrespectful. And they were always talking about zazen, which was not a toy but a serious practice for monks in monasteries. Did they think they could sit on those cushions and understand Buddhism, which the Japanese had nurtured for one and a half millennia?

Kato understood the resentment. The middle-aged Western women students of Suzuki got along fairly well with the congregation, especially with some of the younger Japanese-American women, but there would always be a gap. These Japanese-Americans had been rounded up and put in camps during the war. They were Americans too, who had worked hard in a new country, but they were still looked down upon as inferiors. They had farmed and built new lives, bought land, and saved money so their children's lives would be easier. They had lost almost everything because of the color of their skin and the country they'd come from. After the war they had scrubbed the floors of the whites for a dollar and a half an hour; women earned even less. Many members were still laborers.

IN 1952 when discrimination was still strong, Kato had arrived in the Bay Area. When he and his wife were married, they couldn't find an apartment in Berkeley near the university. Doors would be slammed in their faces. "We don't rent to Japs!" they'd hear again and again. They had to take a place surrounded by winos and hookers in downtown Oakland. The discrimination wasn't nearly as bad now, fifteen years after the war, but deep resentments lingered on both sides.

Like Suzuki, Kato hoped that if the zazen students joined the congregation's holiday feasts and the promenades around Japantown on Buddha's birthday, the two groups would get to know and understand each other better. Kato and Hagiwara knew these seekers could see beyond the war and stereotypes. Suzuki thought the children might solve these problems in the future. The McNeil children were spending time with the Japanese-American children in the Sunday school.

Soon after he arrived, Suzuki had asked Emi Kato to teach Sunday school. She noticed the way Suzuki played with the children, treating them with great affection and respect, and how all the children loved him. Kazumi always wanted to bring Suzuki a gift because, as Emi said, he had such a warm personality. One day in February when the Bay Area had a freak snowfall, Kazumi made a snowball and put it in a box. She and her mother took a bus to Sokoji, and she gave the box to Suzuki. He opened it excitedly. Of course, the snow had melted. As she cried and tried to explain, Suzuki just said, "My, what a beautiful snowball." He gave her a piece of chocolate, and everything was all right.

Instead of criticizing, find out how to help.

WHENEVER THE Katos would invite Suzuki over to dinner, after a while he'd say that he'd better get back. He didn't want to miss meeting a possible new student or someone with a question. The office and kitchen continued to be the principal places where Suzuki met socially with the congregation and students. But he was careful not to get involved in the sort of socializing he had done in his last years in Japan, when it had become a diversion from his unsatisfying temple responsibilities. He wouldn't play go anymore. He had walked over to the Go Club on the other side of the building one day, reached for the doorknob, paused, then backed away and went home.

If he dropped by Sokoji, Kato knew there would always be food in the refrigerator, often cantaloupe and honeydew melons, his favorites. He and some of the other Japanese-Americans and students were often broke, and Suzuki didn't seem to mind the freeloading. Kato admired the indiscriminate way Suzuki accepted people – even the disturbed wanderers who showed up with interminable questions.

One day a young woman came by whose mother had just died, and Suzuki asked her to help him cook lunch. He spent the whole morning with her in the kitchen, not saying anything, just naturally assuming the role of mother and being with her in her grief.

Kato always remarked how nothing ever bothered Suzuki, but there were exceptions. Tobase's nephew used to come to Sokoji frequently to raid the kitchen, smoke, and chat in Japanese. As is common with people living abroad, he complained about his new country. Suzuki didn't like to hear petty complaints. One day in the office with Suzuki, Kato, and their good friend and temple elder George Hagiwara, the young Tobase was sitting on the couch going on about all the things that irritated him about America. Suddenly Suzuki leaped up from his chair and slapped Tobase's face five times, rapid-fire. Kato and Hagiwara were astounded. "There – that's what you get!" he said, "and if you complain more you'll get more!" Tobase was humiliated. He left and stopped coming. Two weeks later Suzuki called him up. "Hey, Tobase-san, why don't you come over? We have too much food here, and we miss you." So he started coming again.

The forms change, but not just to new forms that people are comfortable with. Dogen said that the best teaching makes people feel like something is being forced on them.

SHUNRYU SUZUKI's zendo continued to take form. The upstairs pews were getting broken up from being moved back and forth every week between the zendo and the balcony. Betty came up with some money to buy twenty folding chairs, and the congregation's budget covered the cost for more, so the pews were hauled down to the auditorium for good.

Suzuki had expected some trouble getting Western students to sit on zafus, rather than in chairs, but even those who had difficulty, like Jean, usually didn't ask to sit in chairs. A few had to use chairs because of special problems or advanced age. Suzuki was careful not to make those who used chairs feel second-class. Asked the difference between sitting on the floor and in a chair, he said, "The only difference is the legs."

One day after service Suzuki announced that he was adding another period of zazen – at 5:30 PM so people could come after work. It was forty minutes long like the morning period, and was followed by a briefer service in which the *Heart Sutra* was recited once between two sets of three full bows. Some people came in the morning, some in the evening, and some joined Suzuki for both. Immediately the practice at Sokoji shifted into a rhythm that seemed to enclose the whole day.

IN FEBRUARY of 1960 Suzuki and his students had a three-day sesshin, the first such extended zazen retreat he had held in America. He never had a sitting group get that far in Japan. People came prepared to sit from early morning till six in the evening, Saturday through Monday. It was a monumental step for the small group and for each individual. They started sitting an hour earlier than usual. There were two periods of zazen in a row with a walking period called kinhin in between. Suzuki demonstrated, walking slowly with hands held together at the solar plexus. Aside from meals and an afternoon lecture, the day was a continuous cycle of zazen and kinhin.

Six months later Suzuki conducted the first weeklong sesshin. Eight people attended most of it. On weekday mornings people stayed as long as they could, went off to work, came back after work, and sat until nine at night. On Saturday they sat all day.

The feeling was strict. Suzuki growled at people if they moved. Jean's temper got the best of her. Suzuki had told her to use more pillows if she got uncomfortable, but sitting there hour after hour, nothing worked. Finally she stood up and said, "These things aren't doing a damned bit of good!" She exhaled angrily and then sat back down. After a few moments Suzuki got up and brought her another pillow.

During sesshin, everyone would have a private interview with Suzuki called *dokusan*. He gave dokusan in the congregation's office at the bottom of the stairs. When it was Betty's turn for dokusan, she sat zazen in the hall until she heard Suzuki's handbell ringing to announce that it was her turn. She fluffed her cushion, bowed, and slowly walked into the office. There Suzuki sat on a zafu facing an empty zafu a few feet in front of him. Behind him was a little altar that had been set up for the dokusan, with a candle that provided most of the light in the room. Following the procedure Suzuki had taught them, Betty bowed upon entering the room and did three full bows before Suzuki. Then she sat on the cushion facing him. They sat there breathing together for a moment. It was terribly intimate. At first she was uncomfortable, feeling in awe of Suzuki, within his undeniable presence. Then she sank into it and relaxed. She asked him a question about a problem she was having in zazen, and he answered her softly. When Suzuki was satisfied with the exchange he rang his bell, Betty bowed and departed, and the next person entered.

People were not encouraged to talk about what happened to them in dokusan. It was private. Betty felt that the less formal exchanges she had with Suzuki were often just as memorable. One day in the hallway as she put on her coat to go home, she said to him, "The more I try to control my breath the worse it gets. It gets too fast, or too slow. I become preoccupied with trying to make it right."

"Oh, just sit," he casually answered, knocking her thoughts away.

IN LATER years, the hours of sesshin were longer and the schedule more demanding, but for some this was the most powerful event of their lives. In the prolonged stillness the students noticed their chattering minds grow calm, their sense of identity shift and expand.

At this first sesshin Bill was the cook (as he would continue to be for years on Saturday mornings and during sesshins). Betty helped him prepare breakfast and was surprised to find that all he planned to serve was leftover rice crusts from the previous day with hot water. The sesshin participants came into the kitchen and sat in chairs at the long wooden table. As Betty poured hot water over her rice crusts, she was overcome with a feeling of gratitude, and tears flowed down her cheeks. She realized she could trust the universe to fill her every need.

On the last day of sesshin, Suzuki told his students in lecture that the more they practiced the more they would refine themselves. Every now and then, within a life of daily sitting, it was good to sit all day or all week, to push oneself a little harder. That would help to make their zazen "more beautiful." "But don't be in any hurry," he said. "It takes a long time to master zazen."

During these sesshins Suzuki was particularly demanding of Bill McNeil and Bob Hense, his first two American students, who still wanted to go to Japan to experience the source.

Bowing is a very important practice for diminishing our arrogance and egotism. It is not to demonstrate complete surrender to Buddha, but to help get rid of our own selfishness.

THE PEOPLE coming to Suzuki weren't seeking devotional religion. They might become devoted to Suzuki, but they still asked more questions every day than he'd been asked in thirty years as a priest in Japan. They passionately wanted to understand Buddhism, Zen, themselves, life, death, enlightenment, truth. They wanted to know the meaning of everything. Suzuki was not quick to define things. "If I give you an answer, you'll think you understand," he said more than once. Why were four-and-nine days taken off? "It's a mystery," Suzuki answered. What is the meaning of the sutra? "Love." Why do we use that particular hand position in zazen? "It's a secret." Why do you shave your head? "It's the ultimate in hairstyling." At times of his own choosing, Suzuki would give reasons and meanings – but they tended to change each time he answered. He wanted people to learn things for themselves in their own time.

THEN THERE was the matter of prostrations, or full bows. Many students weren't prepared to bow down to the floor without asking why. Some complained it was too Japanese and, like begging, not appropriate for American Zen. Suzuki had tried takuhatsu in Japantown, but had given it up.

Suzuki told them how his masters had taught bowing as a central practice of Zen. It was Buddhist, not Japanese. The Japanese secular bow is from the waist, with the head lowered. Buddhist bows are either the gassho with palms together, or full bows which begin with a gassho and end with knees, head, elbows, and hands on the floor. Morning service began and ended with three full bows. Suzuki explained that when the forehead goes down, the extended palms are raised three times to lift the feet of Buddha. "Bowing is second only to zazen," he said before the morning service one day. "It is Buddha bowing to Buddha. If you cannot bow to Buddha, you cannot be Buddha. It is arrogance. So from now on we will start the morning service with nine bows instead of three. In Japan three is enough, but here in America we are so stubborn, it is better to do nine bows."

There were some groans.

"Don't complain," he said. "You want more practice than Japanese want anyway. It may be hard for you to understand why it is so important, but you will come to understand by bowing. Bowing is a very good practice, and after sitting we feel very good when we bow."

Life is like stepping onto a boat that is about to sail out to sea and sink.

LATE IN 1960 Bill McNeil and Bob Hense flew to Japan. Bill Kwong had become quite close to McNeil and was sorry to see his friend go. It made him sad to think of the Sokoji zendo without him. He stood by as Suzuki saw his first students off. It should have been a joyous occasion, but something didn't feel right to Kwong. Suzuki seemed awfully serious. McNeil, always so positive, did not look happy. His wife and children, who were staying behind, were sad to see him go. Hense was especially nervous. Kwong didn't know why, but they seemed like condemned men on their way to the gallows. Maybe they were realizing what they'd gotten themselves into.

It was a loss to the zendo. McNeil had been the live wire of the group, the charismatic artist-philosopher. He had spread the word about zazen from North Beach to the East-West House. He had rallied the troops in the zendo when no one knew what they were doing or why. He had helped to bring Suzuki's group together for a year and a half. And now he was gone. He and Hense had gone off to the source and to the unknown. There had been no farewell party. It was almost a secret.

Suzuki didn't want others to know about their departure, because people had such an unrealistic idea about Zen training in Japan. Many students wanted to go, but Suzuki was not eager for them to do so until they were ready. He did want to exchange students with Japan, but in the fullness of time. He always said something like, "Maybe better to study here first." Since McNeil and Hense had come to Sokoji on their way to Japan, and since their enthusiasm had been sustained, Suzuki had arranged for them to go to his temple and from there to Rinso-in's head temple, Sekiun-in, where there was a teacher who could train them. Suzuki had no idea how it would go, and he knew his students had no idea what they were getting into, but he yielded to their wishes and sent them off with some hope.

Suzuki was alone in the kitchen cleaning teacups. Downstairs on the stage of the auditorium a few young Japanese-American musicians were rehearsing, as they did late every Wednesday night. It was raining, and the falling drops lent a background to the drums, guitars, and horns. Tomorrow there would be zazen, service, cleaning, laundry, shopping, a memorial service, visitors in the afternoon. The music echoed through the halls and floor. Soon he would go downstairs, lock up, take a bath, then climb up the steps to sleep alone in his small niche in that big, empty building.

Things weren't working out well at all for his students in Japan. Lou McNeil had talked to her husband, and Suzuki had received a letter from his son, Hoitsu, who was now a monk at Eiheiji. Hoitsu had met McNeil and Hense when they arrived and had spent time with them at Rinso-in helping them get ready to go to Sekiun-in. There they had their heads shaved and received robes and precepts in Japanese. The abbot, acting for Suzuki, ordained them as monks, and they thus became, in Suzuki's eyes, his first Western disciples. They lasted only about a month at Sekiun-in, and had finally been expelled from the temple.

Americans, Suzuki was learning, were quick to commit but undependable on the follow-through. They had wanted so badly to get ordained and go to Japan, but they had no idea what it entailed. McNeil had gotten interested in the walking practice of Buddhists on Mt. Hiei. Now he and Hense were living in Kyoto, teaching English and studying Rinzai Zen at Ruth Fuller Sasaki's temple in the Daitokuji temple complex. They seemed to be doing a lot of running around. It turned out that one reason they had to leave Sekiun-in was that they were involved in sexual escapades – with other men. McNeil said he had to get out of there, because he was seeing ghosts in the temple.

The band in the basement started to play a familiar melody, one of Suzuki's favorites and one of Japan's most cherished: "Sakura," cherry blossoms. It was a favorite of Mitsu's too – a sweet, sad, simple yet elegant tune. They were playing it over and over. What was Mitsu doing now so far away in Japan? She too would be sleeping alone at the kindergarten. She was still angry at him for not post-poning his trip to America, leaving her there to die.

Every week when the boys' band played this song, he thought of Mitsu. Rain blew against the windowpanes. Suzuki sat in a hard wooden chair in the kitchen, looking into the darkness toward the balcony over the auditorium, tears running down his cheeks.

Chapter Twelve

Sangha

1961–1962

*If you want to study, it is necessary to have a strong,
constant, way-seeking mind.*

BILL MCNEIL had helped the original group coalesce, had
energized them, set an example, then left for the promised land.
But now he was lost, having run into a wall in his attempt to find
the true way in the land of Zen. Bob Hense too had had a horrible
experience with Japanese Zen. After being thrown out of Sekiun-in
with McNeil, he found he didn't get along with Ruth Fuller Sasaki
in Kyoto either. She was too domineering for him.

They had gone to Japan seeking the true way. They had in mind
the satori stories from Paul Reps's *Zen Flesh, Zen Bones,* and the ideal
settings presented by D. T. Suzuki. What they had encountered
was more like an obstacle course: an impenetrable language barrier, endless reprimands that they couldn't understand, no way to
read the ritual chants, hours of painful sitting on the shins, almost
no emphasis on zazen, nothing at all that was relevant or nourish-

ing. The host temple was utterly unprepared to adapt to foreigners, and these foreigners weren't willing to make the considerable effort necessary to continue under those circumstances.

It was March of 1961, and McNeil and Hense were back in San Francisco. McNeil was making an art film. He didn't come around to sit anymore, didn't want to be a monk or study Zen. He said he had discovered his true identity as an artist and homosexual. "I don't want any part of Japanese Zen," he would say. He would still drop by Sokoji occasionally to say hello to Suzuki, and now and then they would bump into each other in Japantown. Sometimes Suzuki would bring a student along and visit McNeil and his Japanese lover at their apartment.

Hense resumed sitting at Sokoji. He realized that it was the only place in the world where he wanted to study Zen, and Suzuki was the only Zen priest he wanted to study with. But he was sad, like an injured soldier home from war. He never wore his robes. Most people didn't even know that he and McNeil had been ordained.

There were a dozen or so regulars at Sokoji, and they sat in order of seniority. Hense was now in the front seat on the men's side, with Bill Kwong and Philip Wilson. Della, Betty, and Jean were still the three loyal ladies in the first seats on their side.

Then, in late spring of 1961, two newcomers came to Sokoji who would alter the character of Suzuki's group and the course of his life. The first of these was an Englishman in his mid-twenties named Grahame Petchey.

ALAN WATTS was giving one of his freewheeling talks at the Berkeley Buddhist Church on a Tuesday evening in May, piecing together Zen, Taoism, psychoanalysis, and Christian mysticism into a fascinating mosaic. Attending the lecture were Watts and Suzuki's colleague Wako Kato, a man named Iru Price, and a formally dressed young couple, Grahame and Pauline Petchey. Over refreshments, Price presented his card, listing numerous positions and ordinations with Buddhist groups in Malaysia, Thailand, Japan, and America.

The Petcheys had recently arrived from Europe. Grahame had already secured a job as a chemist and was looking forward to finding a Zen master and a sangha, a community of practicing Buddhists, in the Bay Area. Price told him he had to meet Suzuki-sensei at once. Kato pulled out a business card and wrote Suzuki's name and address on the back.

Grahame had grown up in England. His father had been in the Palace Guards, the elite corps that protects the royal family, surrounding them with solemn ceremony. From an early age Grahame had wanted to know what life was all about, a query that gave impetus to his religious quest. Grahame called it his nagging question. He first sought an answer from the Church of England. When that didn't satisfy him, he entered a Roman Catholic Carmelite monastery as a layman. There he found monks working on their own nagging questions with an admirable humility, but he left because he couldn't share their beliefs. He went to Rome to get closer to the source, but found only superficiality and hypocrisy.

In Rome he met Pauline, a young French artist who told exciting stories of her family helping downed fliers during the war. Pauline's mother was a U.S. citizen and a Theosophist. In her Paris library Grahame discovered Hinduism, Buddhism, and zazen, the meditation of Zen monks. Pauline had met D. T. Suzuki and Krishnamurti as a teenager. Before long Grahame and Pauline were married and on their way to San Francisco, carrying a large Buddha statue her mother had given them. Grahame's focus from the first had been on trying to figure out what monks did rather than what they were thinking. He tried to do zazen in a chair for a month on the freighter that brought them through the Panama Canal to northern California in early May of 1961. Only a week after arriving, he was on his way to meet the man he hoped would be a master of zazen.

GRAHAME CALLED to make an appointment, and Suzuki suggested he come to zazen at six in the evening. Grahame came at the appointed time, went upstairs and was chagrined to see on a posted schedule that evening zazen began at five-thirty. He abhorred arriving late for his first visit to the temple, his upbringing cried out against it, but the master himself had given him the wrong time – an awkward situation.

The door to the office was open, so he went in to wait. Sitting by himself in a chair, between the streetside din and the office silence, he listened intently to the sounds emanating from the adjacent room – heavy breathing, after a while soft footsteps, and then wham! wham! How surprising! Someone must have dropped something. Then he heard it again. What was going on? Next came bells, chanting, and thumping. He straightened his tie and pulled at his pressed white cuffs.

Finally the door to the zendo opened and Shunryu Suzuki entered. Grahame stood up but Suzuki paid him no mind. He stood by the door and bowed to each of his students as they exited. Grahame was shocked at their appearance. Rather than the uniform cotton robes of the Carmelites, or the suits, starched collars, and dresses of the London Buddhists, the outfits of the ten or so meditators who slowly filed out, stopping briefly to bow with Suzuki, were blue jeans and sweatshirts. But Suzuki looked right, in his beautiful brown robes. He had a wise face that radiated kindness as well as strictness.

After everyone else had gone, Suzuki sat down with Grahame, served him tea, and talked to him for half an hour. Suzuki asked if he knew how to sit zazen. Grahame said he had tried it in a chair, to which Suzuki responded that it would be better on the tatami. Could he do it? Grahame said he didn't know, but he'd try. That first day he made it through thirty minutes sitting cross-legged, upright, and still as a palace guard. He had never sat that long at one time before. Christmas Humphreys of the London Buddhists warned that it was dangerous to do more than ten minutes of meditation without adequate training or experienced guidance.

"You take the sitting position very well," Suzuki told him. "You have no problem." That pleased Grahame. Then Suzuki asked, "Can you come back at 5:45 tomorrow morning?"

"I'm a married man," Grahame responded with shock. Married

Earliest existing photo of Shunryu Suzuki, age 14, at upper elementary school graduation in Mori, c. 1918.

Shunryu, age 25, in the Komazawa University senior yearbook, March 1930.

Shunryu at Eiheiji in monk's pilgrimage gear, c. 1930.

Miss Nona Ransom (Suzuki's English teacher at Komazawa University), in Tientsin, China, c. 1932.

At Zoun-in, c. 1930.
(Left to right) *Shunryu's father Butsumon Sogaku, Shunryu* (squatting), *Hino-san (Tori's husband), Shunryu's sister Tori Hino and baby, temple caretaker, Shunryu's mother, Yone.*

At Zoun-in, c. 1935. (Left to right) *Haruko Shima (Shunryu's half-brother Yoshinami's wife) and baby; Shunryu's wife, Chie; Shunryu's mother, Yone* (squatting)*; Shunryu; Shunryu's sister Aiko Uchiyama and baby.*

Shunryu Suzuki's master,
Gyokujun So-on Suzuki,
age 53, c. 1930.

Shunryu Suzuki's teacher, Ian Kishizawa (in white robe), age 85, c. 1950.

*Shunryu carrying the stick (kyosaku) at Rinso-in during the Pacific war,
while prep school students informally called the High Grass Mountain Group
(Takakusayamakai) sit zazen, c. 1945.*

Rinso-in temple bells on their way to being melted down to make ship propellers.
(Right bottom) *Shunryu and Chie Suzuki (1945).*

Shunryu with young women's study group, c. 1947.

The back pond at Rinso-in, 1996. (Photograph by Bill Schwob.)

Chie Suzuki, c. 1950.

Chie's mother,
Kinu Muramatsu Obaa-san, c. 1966.

Shunryu with temple member—workers at Rinso-in, c. 1955.

Shunryu's family at Haneda Airport, May 21, 1959. (Left to right) *His daughter Yasuko Oishi and her husband, Iwao Oishi; his sons Otohiro and Hoitsu; Shunryu; his wife Mitsu Suzuki; and Mitsu's daughter Harumi Matsuno.*

Shunryu Suzuki at gate waving goodbye.

Shunryu Suzuki carrying the stick in a posed picture in the Sokoji zendo (normally women sat on other side). (Left to right) Jean Ross, Betty Warren, Connie Luick, Della Goertz, Bill Kwong, Grahame Petchey, Paul Anderson, Bob Hense (c. 1961).

Sokoji, Soto Zen Mission, 1881 Bush Street, San Francisco, c. 1965.

Procession through San Francisco's Japantown during Shunryu Suzuki's Mountain Seat Ceremony, officially becoming the abbot of Sokoji, May 20, 1962. (Left to right) Unknown, Taizan Maezumi, Shunryu Suzuki, Wako Kato, Reirin Yamada.

After Shunryu Suzuki's Mountain Seat Ceremony, members of both Japanese congregation, Zen Center, and guests in front of Sokoji.

Shunryu and Mitsu Suzuki at the San Francisco airport on their way to Japan, April 10, 1963. Others: (left to right) *Virginia and Richard Baker (holding Sally), Betty Warren, Connie Luick, Mike and Trudy Dixon, Della Goertz, Gilles Guay, Pauline Petchey (holding David).*

(Left to right) *Shunryu Suzuki, Hoitsu Suzuki, unknown, Grahame Petchey, Pauline Petchey, Philip Wilson, Claude Dalenberg. Rinso-in, October 1966.* (Photograph by Fumiyo Yanagita.)

Sotan Tatsugami, Grahame Petchey, and Philip Wilson at Eiheiji monastery. Fukui, Japan, 1964. (Photograph by Genjiro Yagi.)

Shunryu Suzuki and Richard Baker at Tassajara.
(Above, photograph by Tim Buckley, 1968; below, 1967)

The City Center of the San Francisco Zen Center at 300 Page, c. 1969.
(Photograph by Robert Boni.)

Shunryu Suzuki at Tassajara with Dan Welch and Peter Schneider, c. 1968.
(Photograph by Tim Buckley.)

Suzuki-roshi lecturing in the zendo at Tassajara in the summer of 1967.
In T-shirt to the left of Suzuki's shoulder is David Chadwick.
(Photograph by Minoru Aoki.)

Tassajara, Zen Mountain Center, first practice period work-time photo.
Summer 1967. (Photograph by Minoru Aoki.)

Shunryu Suzuki at the City Center, c. 1970.

Shunryu and Mitsu Suzuki (Okusan) at a Tassajara wedding reception, 1970.
(Photograph by Alan Marlowe.)

At Richard Baker's Mountain Seat Ceremony, November 21, 1971, thirteen days before Suzuki's death. (Left to right) *His eldest son, Hoitsu; Shunryu Suzuki; his wife, Mitsu; and Dainin Katagiri.* (Photograph by Robert Boni.)

A view of the Santa Lucia Mountains as seen from the ridge on the road to Tassajara. (Photograph by Robert Boni.)

and employed. He couldn't imagine getting up to go to a temple that early with a day's work ahead. While he pondered, Suzuki offered him more tea. Somehow Grahame picked up on the Japanese custom of offering more tea when it's time to leave. He begged off, and said goodbye.

Despite his initial reaction, Grahame decided to come back the next morning. The zazen as Suzuki had explained it made total sense to him. All he had to do was face the wall and follow his breath – no faith, nothing to hold on to, just the nagging question to solve for himself under the guidance of this marvelous, dignified little man.

He went home that first evening filled with an overwhelming joy and told Pauline of his good fortune. He dedicated his whole life to zazen on the spot. Grahame went every morning, every evening, every Sunday, to every lecture. He never stopped. And he asked no questions. To Suzuki he was like a good Japanese student. He liked the way Grahame would brush his feet off in the aisle before he swung around on his zafu to sit facing the wall.

Buddha was great because people were great. When people are not ready, there will be no Buddha. I don't expect every one of you to be a great teacher, but we must have eyes to see that which is good and that which is not so good. This kind of mind will be acquired by practice.

THE SECOND propitious arrival of 1961 was a dynamic twenty-five-year-old East Coast transplant named Richard Baker. His studies of Western and Eastern philosophy, art, and poetry at Harvard, in Greenwich Village, and in North Beach had brought him into contact with extraordinary minds, but he had yet to meet an exemplar he could respect and trust. That all changed the evening he went with a friend to Fields Metaphysical Bookstore on Polk Street in San Francisco. Richard and his friend had just come from a Japanese restaurant and were on their way to a samurai movie. Clowning around in the store, Richard swung an air sword and emitted a loud shout, imitating a samurai. George Fields laughed and told him he should go to Sokoji for the lecture by Shunryu Suzuki.

"You should meet Suzuki-sensei," Fields said. "He is a Zen master of the other kind of Zen. He's a wonderful person." By "the other kind of Zen," Fields meant Soto as opposed to Rinzai, which until then had been the focus of almost all the writing in English.

Sitting in a metal folding chair in Sokoji's zendo, Richard was transfixed by Suzuki. It was as if one of the great Chinese masters from the books he'd read had come alive. It wasn't so much what Suzuki said as the unity of his speech and being. Here was a man of deep thought in the classical sense, who knew that thought had its limits and strove for a goal beyond thought.

Later Richard attended a seminar held by Alan Watts and Charlotte Selver, a German woman who taught sensory awareness. Richard already knew Watts and was especially delighted to meet Selver. When Selver left town, he sought out Suzuki again. Though Richard had been to a couple of Suzuki's lectures, he realized for the first time that there was some sort of community around Suzuki. He was definitely interested in this master but thought he himself wasn't up to the meditation.

Later, as he thumbed through a book by D. T. Suzuki (who almost never mentioned zazen), a sentence reached out and grabbed Richard. "To think you are not good enough to practice zazen is a form of vanity." He decided to start going to zazen immediately "in order to stop the wandering of my mind."

Richard Baker's mother wrote poetry and his father was a professor who had taught at Harvard and later at the University of Pittsburgh while Richard went to high school. They were not wealthy but spent each summer at his maternal grandmother's home in Maine, Richard's birthplace, where he felt his roots were. He was always a loner and a reader; at Harvard he was called "The Outsider" and "El Darko." During his fourth year at college he attended lectures by the theologian Paul Tillich, the orientalist John K. Fairbank, and the former ambassador to Japan Edwin O. Reischauer. Despite the impressive qualifications of his teachers, Richard felt dissatisfied with what he was learning. He dropped out shortly before graduation to live in New York City until he was twenty-four. Then he went west on a bus to San Francisco in the fall of 1960 with thirty-five dollars in his pocket. On the first day he found poet Lawrence Ferlinghetti's City Lights bookstore and was soon immersed in the literary and artistic circles of North Beach. He moved into an apartment, got a job with a book distributor, and kept looking for something. He fantasized about meeting a Zen master in neighboring Chinatown. Instead, nine months later, he met a Japanese one.

As soon as Richard started to sit regularly he recognized in Grahame Petchey someone who exemplified the excellence a student could demand of himself. Grahame thought they could, in their own way, be like Suzuki, could know what he knew, and could become Zen masters. The way Grahame applied himself, one hundred percent, was just what Richard believed in.

The two became close friends right away. Richard and Grahame were both tall, thin, well-educated, and serious, but there were differences. Grahame had a much easier time with the physical demands of zazen. He could sit up straight in full lotus for the whole forty-minute zazen period without moving. It was actually even longer than that, because one had to be sitting before the period started. Zazen was painful and uncomfortable for Richard. For a long time he couldn't sit even in half lotus. He called his posture "half lily" – perched on several cushions with more cushions under his knees. He had to move at times, but he set goals for himself, such as not moving until Suzuki had finished going around with the stick, halfway through the period.

Grahame brought his life to zazen, single-mindedly focusing on practice in the zendo. Richard brought zazen to his life, making the world his monastery. He watched his breath while driving, concentrated on his feet while walking, and read Buddhist books voraciously. Suzuki said that Grahame concentrated on the posture and Richard on the idea of Zen.

Not long after he came to Zen Center, Richard met Virginia

Brackett, a student at the Art Institute. In May 1962 Suzuki married them. The Bakers and the Petcheys were close, and their lives had many parallels, the Petcheys tending to be a step ahead. They both drove Volkswagens, went to samurai movies, had tatami in their apartments, and soon were having babies.

One day Grahame and Richard were in the backseat of a car, with Suzuki riding in front. Richard leaned forward and asked, "Suzuki-sensei, do you think we can understand Buddhism?"

"Yes, if you practice. If you know how to practice," Suzuki replied, turning around and looking Richard in the eyes.

At that moment Richard knew he would practice Zen his whole life.

If you want to practice zazen, it is necessary to have good friends. Then naturally you will have good practice.

SUZUKI'S DAUGHTER, Yasuko, and her younger brother, Hoitsu, watched the *Montana Maru* slowly pull out of Yokohama harbor. On board were Mitsu and Otohiro, off to America. Otohiro cried hard and waved goodbye from the deck.

George Hagiwara, Suzuki's good friend in the Sokoji congregation, had set the move in motion late in 1960. Hagiwara was visiting relatives in Japan, and, at Suzuki's urging, he made a special trip to Yaizu to implore Mitsu to go to America. He told her that Suzuki wanted to stay longer than originally planned. So many people were coming to study with him that he felt he couldn't accomplish his mission in just three years. He needed her help.

Kinu Obaa-san also urged Mitsu to go, saying that Shunryu had been living abroad for two years alone, managing everything by himself. It was important work, and she wanted him to succeed. Mitsu succumbed to the pressure, swallowed her pride, and agreed to go.

Obaa-san insisted that Suzuki's youngest son go too. Otohiro was seventeen, almost through high school, and she couldn't be responsible for him anymore. Knowing that he might not be back for a long time, Otohiro visited his sister Omi at the mental institution to say goodbye. She had been there for six years; it would probably be her permanent home. He had come only a few times through the years, and she was happy to see him. She had gained a lot of weight.

Once Mitsu had agreed to go, Suzuki wrote to her, "I've bought you a bed with the very best mattress. Also I got you an American ironing board and fancy new iron. They stand up here to do their ironing. These are the only things I have bought you. It's not much, I know. But I am eagerly awaiting your arrival with Otohiro, whom I also miss very much."

ON JUNE 14, 1961, Mitsu and Otohiro were met by Suzuki and a small entourage from the congregation at Pier 41 in San Francisco. Like Suzuki when he'd first arrived, Mitsu and Otohiro were shocked at the austerity of their living quarters. The rooms were clean, but there was only space enough to sleep. Otohiro slept in the attic chamber across the landing from his parents' room. Suzuki had squeezed Mitsu's new bed next to his own. Later she confided to a student that he did not invite her to his bed for six months. She felt that this was because he had been so affected by the attentions of other women.

It wasn't just the urgings of Obaa-san and Hagiwara that had changed Mitsu's mind. In his recent letters Suzuki had told her how kindly some of the women students were treating him. He hinted that advances had been made, though not from his close women students. It would be easier to resist them if she were there, he wrote. One woman had hidden in the building and approached him after he'd locked up. She wouldn't leave, and he finally had to call a senior student to come help him.

There was a very helpful woman named Alice who sometimes cooked for Suzuki and urged him to try a health food diet that included carrot juice. She noticed that his teeth were bad, took up a collection, and took him to a dentist to get a set of false teeth. She did his laundry and bought him some long johns. He liked them and would continue to wear them to bed and even under his robes when it was cold. She didn't go to zazen much but became a fixture in the kitchen, drinking tea with Suzuki and his students and saying, "Please, Sensei, tell me about Zen. I'm really trying hard to understand." As soon as Mitsu arrived, Alice disappeared and went to India to look for another guru.

THE CONGREGATION and the zazen students welcomed the new Suzukis. They brought gifts and showed them around town. A Sokoji couple, the Katsuyamas, invited them to dinner on a Tuesday night, and soon it became an established custom. Suzuki took his wife and son to Mimatsu, a cheap, old-fashioned Japanese restaurant with high wooden booths, where he frequently went. Three members of the Sokoji congregation owned it. He showed them Honami's fine handicraft store and a Japanese confectionery, where they ate green manju sweets and drank tea. George Hagiwara took them all to the Japanese Tea Garden. It was almost as if Mitsu and Otohiro had gone to another Japanese city.

Otohiro was painfully shy and felt lost. He dreaded finishing high school in America and begged not to be made to go. Maybe he could get a job, he said. He had never done well in school in Japan, and he didn't know any English. His father said he would learn. The worst part was that he had to be a junior again. Suzuki organized a group for older teenage boys, both Japanese and Japanese-Americans, not just temple members. About twenty-five of them met once a week. Otohiro made some friends. After a few months he moved into a small apartment across the street that Sokoji maintained for guests.

If you live together, there is not much need to speak to each other. You will understand.

Mitsu and Shunryu had never lived together before, but they quickly adapted to life together. Her responsibility, as she saw it, was to take care of her husband first, then the members, the zazen students, and the building. She was as industrious as he was. On her first morning, after breakfast, she made pickles while her husband melted down old candles into new ones. She cooked, cleaned, did laundry, received visitors, and met with the women's group. Beyond the call of duty she sat zazen with her husband's students, taking the front seat next to the kitchen door on the women's side. She enlivened Sokoji; there was a lot more talk with her around. And she was no pushover for Suzuki. They were old friends, and he was used to relating to her on a fairly equal basis, considering the traditional culture they came from. Sometimes students would hear them get into squabbles – a new side to their master!

Mitsu took to her new life at Sokoji with admirable ease. She said it was just like her job in Japan, where there had always been people visiting and hanging out at the school, except now there were Caucasians as well as Japanese. She started to pick up English right away – just enough. With her outgoing personality it was probably easier for her to move into the role of temple wife in San Francisco than it would have been in Japan.

Everybody took to calling Mitsu *Okusan,* which means "Mrs." – a traditional address for the wife of the house. A lot of people thought it was her name. Okusan was friendly with the zazen students and especially got along with Betty, Della, and Jean. But she objected to the fact that many of the younger ones were often unkempt and had dirty feet.

"Don't complain," Suzuki told her. "They are good Zen students and you should respect them. In fact, you should wash their feet."

Okusan took him seriously and started to put out carefully folded damp towels at the doorway to the zendo. She would show the students how to wipe their feet before they stepped on the tatami.

"Clean feet, clean feet," she would say in her sweet, musical voice.

The students accepted her right away, and feet were cleaner.

More and more we created a feeling of sangha.

AT A SATURDAY afternoon meeting in the spring of 1961 Shunryu Suzuki suggested that his zazen students form a nonprofit corporation so the contributions some of them were making could be deducted from their income tax. Suzuki was meticulous about not using Sokoji's funds for personal use, and he was likewise careful not to confuse the finances of the two congregations. He insisted, for instance, that the zazen students pay rent to the Japanese congregation for their use of the zendo. He felt uncomfortable taking money personally and wanted there to be a treasurer to handle it. After two years of practicing together, it was time to have an organization.

Bishop Reirin Yamada, the new abbot of Zenshuji in L.A. and now the titular head of Soto Zen in America, agreed that the group should incorporate and suggested a Japanese name. Hense said that a Japanese name would not sit well with English-speaking students and suggested the name Zen Center. Everyone liked it. They tossed the name around – a center for Zen, Zen in the center, center yourself on Zen.

In August 1961 Bob Hense was elected the first president, and he started to work on getting Zen Center incorporated. One Saturday he came to Sokoji for a meeting, leaving all the paperwork in his briefcase on a table in the downstairs office. A boy passing by walked in the open door, grabbed the briefcase, and ran off toward Fillmore Street. Hense couldn't catch him. There were no copies of the papers.

All the while Hense was going through intense difficulties, questioning whether he should continue practicing at Sokoji. He poured his heart out to Philip Wilson one day at Philip's apartment.

He said that Suzuki wanted him to be a priest, but that he couldn't give up his architecture practice and his lay life. He said the East couldn't meet the West, that Jung was as close as they could get. "I can't do it anymore," he said. A few days later Hense had a mental breakdown and had to be hospitalized. It was a crisis for the group as well as for him.

A meeting was held, and Grahame Petchey was elected president, even though he'd been there for only two months. Jean Ross, the most outspoken of the old-timers and the obvious choice to succeed Hense, was planning to leave at some point for Japan to study Zen. She nominated Grahame. He proved to be as efficient and thorough as expected. Six weeks later he submitted incorporation papers to the California secretary of state.

Some people felt uncomfortable with the new institutional status. Philip said they should just sit and not worry about the details; if they lost Sokoji they could sit in a garage. Suzuki wanted to have an established group that did business in a conventional manner. The religion was unconventional enough. He saw practical benefits in a clearly defined organization, and he didn't share his young students' anti-establishment attitudes. Healthy institutions were part of a strong society, he believed, and there was no need to fear that the group would lose its character. He said there would be problems no matter what they did, and that if they concentrated on zazen, on confidence in their buddha nature, they would be all right.

Not that Suzuki himself was a good fiscal manager. Soon after Mitsu arrived, the treasurer of the congregation told her that her husband hadn't been cashing his paychecks. First the treasurer had to explain what checks were; there was no such thing in Japan. She caught on quickly. After some searching, Okusan found the checks when they fell out of a book in the office. From then on they went to her. What had he been living on, she wondered?

Another example of her husband's impracticality led Okusan to insist that she do the grocery shopping. He would sometimes drop by the market on his way home to purchase vegetables, especially his favorite, sweet potatoes. The problem was that he would choose the oldest, most wilted and damaged vegetables. She would ask how in the world he could pay money for such produce. He'd say he felt sorry for them. She had even found him on the street picking up Chinese cabbage that had fallen off of the delivery truck – echoes of his father.

With Okusan there, time with Suzuki became more precious. He wasn't as available as before to go out to movies and dinner, although the pleasant morning teatime continued after service, and people still dropped by to say hello or ask questions. Even though Okusan was friendly and enjoyed being with the students, she was always encouraging her husband to go back to Japan. She thought he was too weak and prone to illness to stay.

Suzuki would make his students nervous when he'd mention the possibility of going back. His three-year term would be up the following spring. People felt it was wonderful being with him, but there was a tinge of fear, because they didn't know when it would end. There was a shared enthusiasm to enjoy it while it lasted, make the most of it, learn what could be learned. Amidst the insecurity, there was a sense of certainty that what they were doing together was deeply meaningful and beneficial.

EVERY ONCE in a while Shunryu Suzuki would do something extreme to dislodge his students from ruts they were in, to knock them off their self-satisfied perches, out of their dreamy lives, and back into the arena of insecurity, where they could rededicate themselves to what he called "beginner's practice." One morning, in the midst of the collective and individual harmony that had accrued from their efforts in zazen and practice, when the confidence level was at its zenith, Suzuki made his morning greeting, walking in gassho around the room behind his students seated on their zafus. He bowed at the altar and assumed his position on the platform facing the room, just as he did every day. In the middle of the period he got up, straightened a few postures, and hit sleepy Bill Kwong on the shoulders, twice each – just as he did every day. He went back to his seat and resumed sitting. Then all of a sudden, from Suzuki's small frame roared out the guttural sound of an angry lion.

"You think you're sitting zazen! You're not sitting zazen! You're wasting your time!" He hopped off his cushion and flew down the aisles, whacking each person four times, twice on each shoulder, quick as lightning, his robes flying back, creating a tornado in the zendo. Then he was back in his seat in silence, the room of stunned sitters electrified.

As each bowed to Suzuki at the door on their way out after service, they were a little less sure of themselves. He looked at them squarely but without a hint of anger, as if everything were normal. Complacency and pride lay shattered on the floor. Using the stick like this is a traditional practice of Japanese Zen called *rensaku*. Suzuki would do it from time to time, often without saying a word.

I think our teaching is very good – very, very good. But if we become too arrogant and believe in ourselves too much, we will be lost. There will be no teaching at all, no Buddhism at all. So when we find the joy of our life in our composure and when we don't know what it is, when we don't understand anything, then our mind is very great, very wide. Then our mind is open to everything. To come to this point, we should be relieved of the arrogance of too much belief in ourselves, and of the kind of selfish, immature, childish mind that is always expecting something. Our mind should be big enough to know, before we know something. We should be grateful before we have something. Without anything, we should be very happy. Before we attain enlightenment, we should be happy to practice our way – or else, we cannot attain anything in its true sense.

*F*irst thought, best thought.

HENSE WAS never the same after his nervous breakdown. One day he dropped by Sokoji and bid his teacher of two-and-a-half years farewell. He was moving to Chicago to work for an architecture firm. Suzuki shared Hense's sense of failure, but, knowing there was nothing he could say to keep him, he let Hense go as gracefully as he'd welcomed him the first day.

Hense had suggested developing a mailing list. Some students wanted to have a way to get the word out that Suzuki was teaching Zen at Sokoji. Thus the idea of a newsletter was born. Philip Wilson and his petite scholar wife, J.J., drafted the first one, but wondered what to call it. Zen Center Newsletter? Various names were suggested.

"I'll name it," said Suzuki, and he went upstairs. Twenty minutes later he came down with a piece of paper. The words "Wind Bell" were written on it with a brush in black sumi ink, beside a drawing of the same. Below the drawing was his translation of Dogen's poem "Wind Bell."

Philip and J.J. tried to run off the newsletter on the mimeograph machine, but the results were too faint. Suzuki joined them in his work pants and undershirt. He used the ink much more liberally. He was excited; these would be his group's first printed words. He made a mess, spilling the ink on himself and the floor. Soon his arms and torso were covered in purple, and he proudly held the first dripping copy.

"I guess I was being too cautious," said J.J., as they cleaned everything up.

THE NEXT day was Saturday, December 2, 1961. People stood around reading the newly printed and smudged *Wind Bells* or tucking them into their pockets. Some took a bunch to post on bulletin boards of colleges and coffeehouses. "What the devil do we need a newspaper for?" Grahame wanted to know. Richard shrugged "Those people interested in Zen Buddhism may be glad to know that there is a Zen Center in San Francisco which, for nearly two and a half years, has been under the guidance of Roshi Shunryu Suzuki," read Grahame.

The honorific title "roshi" came from Richard's friend, Don Allen, one of the foremost editors of the Beat poets, who had become the chairman of the new Zen Center board. He'd been to Japan and said that was what they called Zen masters there.

THE SECOND *Wind Bell,* in January 1962, reported on a visit by Philip Kapleau to Sokoji. He had given a talk on an old Japanese master named Bassui. Afterward he met with students and talked about his nine years of study in Japan with Harada-roshi and Harada's heir, Yasutani-roshi, renegade Soto teachers who were using koans like Rinzai teachers. Kapleau's wife joined him in answering questions. In Japan they had sat many sesshins, practicing arduous zazen all night long in the cold and the heat, concentrating on koans and pushing themselves with fervor toward attaining *kensho* – an enlightenment experience. Harada had died, but Yasutani was still going strong. Suzuki sat listening among his spellbound students. It sounded so different from studying with him; some wanted to go right away to Japan. Maybe they could get enlightened working with Yasutani. Suzuki's way seemed so slow.

At the following Saturday lecture Suzuki emphasized the difference in the two traditional Zen approaches. "Our way is to practice one step at a time, one breath at a time, with no gaining idea."

FOR THE next year there would be a *Wind Bell* every month, each one a little longer than the last. Thus the record of Suzuki's talks began. He was getting more comfortable with his English, and he had people who were qualified to make his teaching available in print.

Richard and some other students were always writing down my lectures and asking me many questions about them. What I said with my broken English was very different from what I had in my mind, so I had to write down something. In the Wind Bell *they didn't get the original talk, but my broken English corrected by someone else, like Richard.*

Richard Baker would go through his notes from Suzuki's lectures, come up with crystallizations of the teaching, go over the text with Suzuki, and submit it to Grahame for publication in *Wind Bell.*

If you think, "I practice zazen," that is a misunderstanding. Buddha practices zazen, not you. If you think, "I practice zazen," there will be many troubles. If you think, "Buddha practices zazen," there will not be trouble. Whether or not your zazen is painful or full of erroneous ideas, it is still Buddha's activity. There is no way to escape from Buddha's activity. Thus you must accept yourself and devote yourself to yourself, or to Buddha, or to zazen. When you become yourself, zazen becomes zazen, and Zen becomes Zen.

Like the birds I came,
No road under my feet.
A golden-chained gate unlocks itself.

SHUNRYU SUZUKI was all decked out in red robes with a yellow brocade okesa and pointy hat. In his hand he carried a white ox-hair whisk. He recited his poem at the door of Sokoji and ceremoniously entered Sokoji as if for the first time. It was May 20, 1962, three days before his third year was up. He wasn't going back to Japan as planned. He was being installed as the abbot of Sokoji in a Mountain Seat Ceremony.

In the downstairs auditorium several hundred older Japanese-Americans in suits and ties and Sunday best, not just temple members but guests from the whole Japanese-American community, sat waiting for him to enter. Scattered among them, tending to take seats in the back, were sixty or so mainly younger Americans in various styles of dress. Amidst the ring of high and low bells and the boom of a drum, struck by Richard Baker in the balcony, Suzuki proceeded upstairs to the zendo and kitchen altars to offer incense and recite poems. Soon the chime of bells approached and a procession of guest priests, congregation officers, and children from both groups with flowers in their hands entered the auditorium. Following them Suzuki glided up the aisle as smoothly as a bride and stepped up to an ornate altar put together for the occasion. He offered a stick of incense and recited another poem. Next to him stood Bishop Yamada from L.A., who was officiating.

> *After I lift this one piece of incense, it is still there.*
> *Although it is still there it is hard to lift.*
> *Now I offer it to Buddha and burn it with no hand,*
> *Repaying the benevolence of this temple's founder,*
> *Successive ancestors and my master Gyokujun*
>
> So-on Daiosho [great priest]

Suzuki then ascended to the Mountain Seat, sitting in a lacquered chair on a platform beside the altar. Finally he was the abbot of Sokoji and had officially received the temple seal. It was his third such installation, after Zoun-in and Rinso-in. He had made another three-year commitment. People weren't happy about this back in Yaizu. They didn't understand why he hadn't returned. If they had seen his ragtag Western students at the reception, they might have wondered why he'd waste his time on them. But these students would be there for zazen the next morning and the morning after that.

You are like loaves of bread cooking in the oven.

SUZUKI STILL had no particular plan, but he had high hopes for planting dharma seeds in America and for developing a mutually beneficial exchange with Japan. In March 1962 there had been a farewell party for Jean Ross, before she left for Japan. Jean was his second student to go to Eiheiji – the first being Nona Ransom. Jean had had her mind set on going to what she called "the source" for quite some time. He knew she would be challenging for Eiheiji, so set in its ways. The experience with McNeil and Hense had made Suzuki more cautious, but he had confidence that Jean would do better than they had. She wasn't naively idealistic. She had a pragmatic doggedness, and Suzuki was convinced that her conservative, sincere style would put her hosts more at ease. She was still coming to Sokoji only three days a week, but she had persevered through a number of weekend sesshins and passed the initiation of the weeklong sesshin in August 1961. That type of tenacity can't be faked.

In May, *Wind Bell* printed Jean's first letter from Eiheiji. She was working and practicing with the monks. She had her own room and was getting up at 3:00 AM to be out of the washroom before they came in at 3:30. She was not complaining about the hours of chanting every day and climbing ninety-five steps daily to Dogen's memorial hall. She was withstanding the culture shock and making friends despite the language barrier.

"These priests from the country are *men,* not saints. Their faces express a high degree of individualism tempered by much discipline," she wrote. And later, more poignantly: "As for me, I stood on the Eiheiji earth, and for the first time I felt planted in earth. I began to recognize buddha nature not only in man but in all forms of life. Such expansion eased the pressure of adjustment."

The practice of zazen is not for gaining a mystical something.
Zazen is for allowing a clear mind – as clear as a bright autumn sky.

IN AUGUST 1962 Suzuki and his students had their third annual weeklong sesshin. This one started earlier in the day, ended later, and was the first one to go morning to night for a full seven days. Suzuki had invited Bishop Yamada to lead it, and he came up from L.A. for the last five days. Yamada gave lectures on the great Indian sage Nagarjuna and the semi-legendary Bodhidharma and conducted dokusan, private interviews. Suzuki rang the bells, made sure everything went smoothly, and sat every period, encouraging his students with his steadfastness. The students endured pain in their legs and backs, boredom and restlessness. Thirty people sat at least some of the sesshin and over half as many stayed for the whole thing.

Pauline Petchey had never had anything important to talk to Suzuki about in dokusan. She would ask him theoretical questions like, if a tree falls in the forest and no one hears it, does it make a sound? "It doesn't matter," he'd answered.

Pauline sat the sesshin. Her legs were killing her. It was tough being the wife of the guy who was setting the standard. Grahame never moved, even in the extra-long periods that Suzuki would throw in unexpectedly. Pauline, on the other hand, was just trying to get through the day without screaming. She sat in the middle of the room and so had an aisle in front of her rather than the wall. During a moment of particular difficulty she saw Suzuki step in front of her. Something about his feet struck her. She watched them intently as he walked slowly by. Then a calm came over her, and the pain separated from her; it didn't matter anymore. Her chattering mind dropped away. Standing for kinhin, she looked around the room as if seeing her fellow students for the first time and realized how trapped they all were in petty social games. She felt love for everyone in the room. She looked at Suzuki and saw him connected with them in this trouble-free space, not in the realm of their delusion.

Soon afterward she saw him in dokusan. After bowing three times to the floor, she sat on the cushion facing him. After a moment of following breaths together, she told him about her experience, which she was sure signaled permanent enlightenment. "Very nice," he said. "You've reached deep zazen."

ON THE last day of the sesshin, at a lay ordination, students who had practiced with Suzuki for over one year received precepts and a Buddhist name. Yamada had brought fifteen rakusus, which turned out to be the perfect number. One by one, in order of their arrival at Sokoji, people came forward to receive their cloth rakusus and lineage papers – the names of the ancestors dating back to Buddha written on rice paper, folded, and placed in a rice-paper envelope with calligraphy by Suzuki on the front. Betty and Della were the first in line (Jean was in Japan). Grahame and Richard were last, having arrived just over a year before.

It was a happy day for Suzuki, another small step in his effort to establish Buddhism as he knew it in the West. The ceremony was conducted in Japanese, which the students didn't understand, but Suzuki told them they were "making the vow to keep the enlightened life." He explained the meaning of their new Buddhist names. Della would still be called Della, but she was also now Zendotei Jundaishi, a rather long name composed of characters that he said meant, "Zen way, faith, refined naturalness." Before the ordination Della told Suzuki that she had not rejected her Lutheran upbringing. "I guess I'm going to be a Christian Buddhist," she said. "That's all right," Suzuki answered.

Suzuki took the backseat, as he had with Kishizawa at ordinations at his temple in Yaizu. He deferred to the older Yamada because it was proper; he was the bishop. In this way word would get back to Japan that there were some serious students in America. He appreciated the support he got from Yamada, obligatory but still helpful. It was good for his students to see and hear another priest. "I am very grateful we have instruction from various teachers," he said. "We need more teachers."

While the sesshin was in progress a letter had arrived from the secretary of state: Zen Center's nonprofit status was official. They had raised almost five thousand dollars that year and had been able to save over five hundred, which would go into a building fund. The ordination and incorporation were important to Suzuki, but he made clear what was essential for his teaching to take hold.

Unless you know how to practice zazen, no one can help you. Heavy rain may wash away the small seed when it has not taken root. You should not be like a sesame with no roots, or your practice will be washed away. But if you have a really good root, the heavy rain will help you a lot.

Some people felt like Philip, who asked why they needed any organization or any ordination ceremony. "It's just like the Catholic Church," he said. Little did he realize how close he was to the truth. Soto Zen was full of hierarchy and ceremony in Japan; but considering the autonomy of individual temples and priests, and the growing role of the membership in making decisions, maybe the Baptist Church would have provided a better analogy.

Suzuki had to show them how these things were done in Japan, he said, because that's what he knew. He had to establish Zen Center in a way that he was comfortable with. Being impatient would not work. Someday they would have their own Buddhist forms. "Transmitting Buddhism to America isn't so simple. You can have your own way someday, but first learn mine. And don't be in too big a hurry. It's not like passing a football."

Chapter Thirteen

Journeys

1 9 6 3 – 1 9 6 4

*I have studied many things in America that I could not study
in Japan, and I think that you will study many things from us
that you could not study in America. In this way our effort will
bring some result, if we keep our straightforward way in practice.*

APRIL 1963. Suzuki returned to Japan for three months,
leaving the Sunday temple duties, including lectures, in Kato's
charge. It had been almost four years since he'd gone to America.
Back in Japan his children could immediately tell that a change had
come over their father. He was much more relaxed and amiable.
They liked the effect that America had had on him. Hoitsu came to
visit from Eiheiji, where he'd been for a couple of years. He found
his room all cleaned and organized. "Who did this?" he asked. "I
did," his father replied. Before he would have scolded Hoitsu and
made him clean it up himself.

YASUKO WAS running the two kindergartens, and many of the old
teachers were happy to see her father come back to visit the schools

he'd cared for like a mother bird. He visited Omi at the mental hospital. He saw his old friend Gido at Soto headquarters, talked to him about sending American students to Eiheiji, and inquired about priests who might come to America to help out. He met with some of his old High Grass Mountain Group students from wartime, and he told them what sincere, dedicated students he had in America. He said there were students who would jump off a cliff if he told them to, though they would ask why on the way down. Suzuki said he was finding English to be an easier language for teaching, more direct than Japanese, though it lacked the subtle emotional distinctions. Sometimes during his sermons to the Japanese congregation in the States, he said, he wished he could speak in English to get something across.

He told temple members about his work in America, but for the most part they couldn't understand why he wasn't coming back to stay. Amano understood. "Kozo Kato was right," he said. "You're going to turn into American soil."

JEAN ROSS came to Rinso-in, bringing her priest's robes. Takashina-roshi, the abbot of Eiheiji whom Suzuki had helped when he was abbot of Kasuisai, had ordained her, not as his own disciple but as Suzuki's. He performed the ceremony so she could sit in the zendo with the other monks. Jean said it seemed that they regarded it as a rite that turned her into a man.

As a woman she still hadn't been allowed to practice fully with the monks, but that probably would have been too trying for all concerned anyway. She had had to stick up for her rights – refusing, for instance, to shave her head. But she was a steady, clear-eyed woman who gained the respect of the monks.

Jean had warm relationships with her Japanese teachers. "In fact, I feel they know me better than my friends and even my family in the States, because there is such vital life at Eiheiji."

She'd been at Sojiji as well and had lived at the venerable Fujimoto Rindo's temple, studying zazen with him. Fujimoto was the teacher of Suzuki's friend Elsie Mitchell, who founded the Cambridge Buddhist Society. Fujimoto and Mitchell had translated and published a small book of his, *The Way of Zazen,* which was the only book on Soto Zen available at the time in America other than Masunaga's *Soto Approach to Zen.* Everyone at Zen Center had read it. Suzuki visited with Fujimoto on that trip as well; he was one of the few people Suzuki corresponded with.

While sitting zazen with Fujimoto, Jean had an experience in which she lost the distinction between herself and everything else. She was so overwhelmed she couldn't speak. After a couple of days Fujimoto had her write a report on what she was experiencing in her zazen. "Thank you for showing me your buddha nature," he said to her in farewell.

Jean and Suzuki talked about the monks she'd met who might be suitable to come to America. Her teacher at Eiheiji, Tatsugami-roshi, was open to Westerners, and there was Dainin Katagiri in the international division of Soto headquarters who'd been helpful to her. He spoke some English and was interested in going to the States. On July 3, 1963, Suzuki and Jean flew back to San Francisco, and on the sixth there was a party to celebrate their return.

When small mind finds its correct place in big mind, there is peace.

TEN YEARS after the end of the Korean War, it looked as if America was getting involved in another conflict in Southeast Asia. Suzuki had not reneged on his commitment to peace, but he had seldom spoken about it in America. There was not much need to: his students and the community around Zen Center were generally pacifists well aware of the global situation – especially Richard Baker, who was doing graduate work in Asian studies at UC Berkeley. But one particular event in 1963 deeply moved Suzuki and his students.

In July of 1963 Quang Duc, a Vietnamese Buddhist, burned himself to death to protest the escalating war there. His death brought to light the horrors of the conflict in Vietnam. On July 28 there was a memorial service for Quang Duc at Sokoji. The *Wind Bell* reported: "A Vietnamese student addressed the congregation. A letter from Zen Center members is being sent urging the United States government to take action in preventing further persecution of Buddhists in South Vietnam." No one could forget the image of the monk sitting zazen, burning, falling over, and then righting himself while in flames to sit straight, then falling a final time.

In October Rosen Takashina, abbot of Eiheiji, came to San Francisco as part of a worldwide tour for peace. He slept in Otohiro's apartment on Miss Ransom's silk futon, which Suzuki had brought with him from Japan. At Sokoji Takashina-roshi conducted a service for world peace. Suzuki was happy to see that world peace was now part of Soto Zen's agenda. But it would have been even better, he said, if they had not supported the militarists so enthusiastically in the thirties and forties.

Suzuki was pleased as well to have students who were supporters of world peace, but he wished they got along better with the Japanese congregation and in some cases with each other. Two of his most earnest students, Bill Kwong and Richard Baker, had had a falling out while he'd been in Japan. Bill couldn't deal with the conflict and stopped coming. He'd moved to Mill Valley and sat there in the mornings; once Suzuki was back, Bill started coming on Saturdays and for sesshins.

There is a limit to physical pain, but there is no limit to mental pain.

AUGUST ROLLED around and with it the seven-day sesshin. Sitting zazen all day was a test of endurance for anyone, and there was the added difficulty of uncertainty. Suzuki would on occasion stretch the length of the periods during sesshin. Zazen was regularly forty minutes from bell to bell; kinhin, slow-paced walking zazen between sitting periods, was ten minutes. Suzuki had begun the sesshin by turning the early morning zazen-kinhin-zazen into a ninety-minute period of sitting without moving. Some people went with it: following the breath, counting the breath, letting go, not fighting. Others were in anguish.

Suzuki told his students during sesshin lectures not to expect the bell – just sit. During a sesshin people would invariably experience pain, mainly in their legs; some felt aches in their backs. An extra-long period would be extra painful. An important aspect of the training of almost all Japanese Zen Buddhists is learning to sit calmly with physical pain. "You must welcome the pain," said Suzuki. "Go with it. It is your teacher."

Many students would tell him in dokusan about experiences with pain – of going beyond the physical pain, of it still being there but it no longer hurting, of it becoming like an electrical charge or even a blissful feeling. They realized what they had thought of as physical pain was actually mental pain; or they gave up, and their physical and mental pain simultaneously dropped away. Some people would get used to their leg pain by the fourth day. Suzuki said his hardest day was always the third, and he reminded his students that he too experienced pain in zazen.

ON AN UNUSUALLY warm day during the August sesshin, Suzuki hit the bell to begin afternoon zazen – twenty people sitting up straight, breathing in, breathing out. He got up and walked around with the stick, gently pushed in a few sagging backs to straighten them, hit a few shoulders with his stick in the prescribed manner (resting it first on one shoulder and waiting for them to gassho). He returned the stick to its resting place next to his zafu, and then, instead of sitting back down, he walked out of the zendo into his office. At about ten minutes after the period should have ended, he walked softly back into the zendo. Everyone clearly heard each footstep, and most found it hard not to look forward to his hitting the bell to end the period. But his footsteps went toward the entry-way to the hall. He went out. He was heard going down the stairs. The front door opened and closed. People sat and sat and sat. On

Bush Street the traffic went uphill in waves with the timed lights, the clock in the office struck the hour, the caretaker went around the balcony into the kitchen, and water ran in the sink. They sat. Grahame worried that Suzuki had forgotten them. Others worried that their legs were going to fall off.

An hour later Suzuki's soft, regular steps came back up the stairs. People felt they were about to die. Most had had to move one or more times. Some were breathing hard. He entered the room. He was shuffling the papers that the schedule was printed on. He was checking the schedule. Surely very soon he'd hit the bell and the period would be over. Then, in one of the most disappointing moments of Zen Center history, Suzuki walked back out the door and up to his room. Finally he came back down, rattled more papers, sat on his zafu, and after what seemed like another forever, at last picked up the striker and rang the small bronze bell. Everyone burst out laughing in relief. It had been two and a half hours. There were muffled groans as people stretched their legs out and rubbed them.

That is what my teacher did with me. Maybe sometimes I forgot, but I didn't feel so bad [laughing]. I'd look at the clock and think, oh, it's been too long, but one more hour doesn't matter.

*A*s long as you seek for something, you will get
the shadow of reality and not reality itself.

ONE EVENING in August of 1963, Shunryu Suzuki ordained Grahame Petchey as a priest. It was Suzuki's first such ordination in America, his second priest ordination ever – the first being his son Hoitsu. He gave Grahame the Buddhist name Tokujun, meaning "full of virtue." Grahame would leave for Japan on the fourteenth of September to go to Eiheiji for the fall practice period; he had to be ordained in order to sit, eat, and sleep with the monks.

At ten in the evening Grahame kneeled before Suzuki on the altar in the dimly lit zendo. Only his wife, Pauline, and Okusan were there to observe. It didn't take long. Grahame didn't even know what was happening. Suzuki didn't explain anything. Grahame didn't receive robes or get his head shaved – Suzuki just waved a razor over his head and chanted in Japanese. To Pauline it seemed like a covert operation. There was no announcement, and she knew why. Others had been asking to be ordained or sent to Eiheiji – students impatient to wear robes or go to exotic places. Grahame was devoted to Suzuki and to Buddhism and was being sent over to get a taste of the practice there for the good of the group. He was being cultivated to be a teacher for the future of Suzuki's lineage.

THERE WAS a going-away party for Grahame and Kato on the ninth of September. Grahame was going for three months, but Kato and his family were moving to L.A. He would be helping Bishop Yamada part-time at Zenshuji in L.A.'s Japantown. Yamada had asked him repeatedly, saying he needed Kato's help in translating, because he couldn't speak English. Kato had quit his teaching position at UC Berkeley and had accepted another job as a professor at Cal State. During his eleven years in the Bay Area, he had seen Zen in America and Sokoji go through a dramatic transition; indeed, he'd been an active part of it. Suzuki thanked him for all he'd done for both the congregation and the students. "He opened all the doors for me when I came to this country and introduced me to so many people. I don't know what would have happened without Dr. Kato," he said. "Maybe I would still be sitting here by myself."

PAULINE ALWAYS had the feeling around Suzuki that everything was all right. But at the airport seeing Grahame off, she suddenly became apprehensive. Grahame was going into the unknown without any special preparation or instruction, and Suzuki didn't show the slightest concern.

A month passed, and from Grahame's letters it seemed as if the only useful preparation would have been to be born in a Japanese temple. Unknown to Grahame, Pauline had been visiting with Suzuki regularly to read him letters Grahame wrote at Eiheiji. Pictures of her husband without any hair on his head were unsettling, but more worrisome was the tough time he was having. Hoitsu had been doing his best to take care of Grahame – he'd met him at the Fukui station near Eiheiji and had taken him to the shop to get his robes. He'd watched over him in the grueling initiatory tangaryo – sitting all day for a week with breaks only after meals. Grahame had no trouble with tangaryo. Sitting would not be his problem at Eiheiji.

Like Jean, Grahame immediately warmed to the burly and friendly Tatsugami, the head of monk's training in the zendo. But Hoitsu and Tatsugami weren't able to give him enough support to counteract everything else. He felt as if he'd been thrown back several centuries. More demands were being made of him than of Jean, who had her own room and who, as a woman in her late forties, had been given more leeway.

Grahame wrote that there wasn't enough food and there was no time to eat – he couldn't keep up with their speed. They did everything so fast. The monks ate and slept in the zendo on the same spot where they sat zazen. At six feet four inches, Grahame was too long to fit on the six-foot tatami he slept on. His head extended onto the sacrosanct meal board. And this, the monks told him, was improper. He asked if he should cut off his feet.

Grahame was going through the same sort of disillusion at Eiheiji that he had in Rome. The junior monks kept cans of meat. Almost everyone smoked strong Peace cigarettes during breaks. Many monks seemed to him arrogant, thoughtless, and hypocritical. There were many ceremonies and duties and little emphasis on zazen, which had been the heart of Suzuki's teaching. One monk was seriously out to get him for a silly slip of the tongue. He'd suffered malnutrition and been in the hospital twice. He missed his family, and the language barrier was daunting. It seemed like boot camp – not spiritual practice, just a lot of physical difficulty. All in all he was just trying to hold on to his sanity.

Suzuki suggested to Pauline that she write her husband that the cold, hunger, and despair he was experiencing were normal for a novice priest in training. As in the zendo, Suzuki's attitude was sympathetic but tough. Suzuki wrote Grahame letters of encouragement as well. On October 22, 1963, he wrote:

My dear Tokujun,

    I am very sorry to hear you are not well. But it is not a matter to worry about, because many who enter Eiheiji monastery become sick and go to the hospital in Fukui, and after they come back they are better. Actually, three months aren't long enough, for the first month will be wasted. Please fix your mind as if you are staying there for ten years and you will get accustomed to the monastic life. But the difference between your way of life and the Japanese way of life is so great that it may be difficult to adjust yourself to it.

    Please relax and do as much as you can. Even if you come back without doing sesshin, I think you will have had many valuable experiences which you otherwise could not have had. First of all, the sincerity that you had when you determined to go to Eiheiji is the most admirable thing. And I am very pleased with the understanding and help of your wife Pauline in letting you go and study.

    I wrote to Rev. Sato, Kanin-sama [the director], to give you good advice, so please ask him what you should do when you have some difficulty. He is the kindest and the most considerate person.

    To study Buddhism is our whole life work. Don't be concerned too much with what you acquire now. No one knows if it is good or bad. I think you will learn what is most important for you.

    Your wife is not discouraged at all.

           Sincerely Yours,

           Rev. Shunryu Suzuki

P.S. If there is something you want to ask my boy to do for you, please ask him.

Suzuki wondered whether Grahame would be able to make it through the arduous weeklong Eiheiji December sesshin, but that was what Grahame could do best, because there is no substantial cultural bias in the sitting. He sat in full lotus every period without moving; it was for him a wonderful experience that balanced his overall disillusionment with the place and tempered his sense of failure. His letter about the sesshin had assured Pauline and Suzuki that at last Grahame had made his peace with Eiheiji.

Grahame returned to San Francisco in mid-December. Suzuki appeared shocked to hear about his negative experiences there. He told Grahame to continue practicing like a layman and not to wear his robes to the zendo except for sesshin. After all, he would be returning to his regular job as a chemist. Grahame knew that Suzuki was hesitant to let Zen Center move toward the excessive ritualism and formality that he'd experienced at Eiheiji. More than ever, he was appreciative of his teacher's simplicity and gentleness. Suzuki said he wanted Grahame and Jean to give lectures on Wednesday evenings about their experiences of studying Zen in Japan. "Not the negative experiences," he said, "just the good ones." He never liked complaining and didn't want to discourage his students.

Suzuki was a little harder on Grahame now that he was a novice priest. One Saturday morning Grahame arrived late for the beginning of a day-and-a-half sesshin. After breakfast Suzuki took him to task in his office saying, "Priests don't arrive late! You're no priest! You have no right to wear that okesa!" Grahame was mortified and started to take off his okesa. "What are you doing?" said Suzuki. "No one has the right to tell you to take off the okesa."

*There may be thousands of koans for us, and just to sit
includes them all. This is the direct way to enlightenment,
liberation, renunciation, nirvana, or whatever you say.*

SUZUKI HAD on his rimless glasses and had been reading and making notes for hours. (He kept them tied to him so he wouldn't lose them.)

"Hojo-san," Okusan said, "why do you work so hard preparing for lecture? It's raining, and the last night it rained only two people came. I hope that ten come tonight."

"One or ten, there's no difference!" he barked at her.

"Very well, I won't worry about it anymore."

FOR A COUPLE of years Suzuki had been giving lectures on the *Blue Cliff Record,* one of the principal collections of Zen koans, associated with the Rinzai sect. These talks, generally on Wednesdays, were more difficult for some students to follow than his more informal Sunday lectures. There were a hundred cases in the *Blue Cliff Record,* and one by one he was getting through them. The *Wind Bell* published excerpts from some of those lectures, and Suzuki added his own written comments:

SUBJECT NO. 46 FROM THE BLUE CLIFF RECORD
Commentary by Rev. Shunryu Suzuki, Master, Zen Center

Attention! Kyosei asked a monk, "What is the sound outside the door?" The monk said, "It is the sound of raindrops." Kyosei said, "All sentient beings are deluded by the idea of self and by the idea of the world as subjective or objective."

Commentary: Kyosei has seen through the monk, who thinks he is not caught by the "objective" sound of raindrops in his subjective world.

The monk said, "How about yourself?" Kyosei said, "I am almost not deluded by myself."

Commentary: Kyosei is just listening to the sound of raindrops. There is nothing but raindrops.

The monk said, "What do you mean you are almost not deluded by yourself?" The monk cannot understand why Kyosei doesn't say definitely that he is not deluded by himself and that he hears the raindrops clearly in his mind.

Kyosei said, "Even though it is not difficult to be free from the objective world, it is difficult to express reality fully on each occasion."

[Then in Suzuki's own hand:]

Give the monk 30 blows..!

It is.

! ! Difficult. To. Express. Reality. Fully. On. Each.
Occasion. ////////

Settle the self on the self.

DAININ KATAGIRI zoomed up the street to Sokoji on the back of a motor scooter, the tail and sleeves of his work robes flying in the air. He held on tightly and grinned in the wind. Suzuki finally had an assistant – the Eiheiji-trained priest that Jean Ross had found to be so eager to come to the U.S. Now there was a new shiny-headed, olive-skinned, black-and-brown-robed, friendly, industrious dharma-heir of Buddha serving the zazen students and the congregation.

Katagiri had originally been brought by Bishop Yamada to help out at Zenshuji in L.A. Yamada had wanted Katagiri to help him with his Japanese monk's training program and with English-speaking members and guests. Zenshuji was a lot bigger and richer than Sokoji, and Yamada had several priests to help him, including Mae-

zumi and Kato part-time. In L.A. Katagiri occasionally stayed with
the Katos. He liked them but couldn't stand the scene at the temple.
To him it was even more old-fashioned and confining than in Japan.
He had no contact with Westerners or anyone he could share his
practice with, so he had more or less run away to San Francisco,
where he stayed at Iru Price's eclectic Buddhist center. After a week
Price took him to see Suzuki, who arranged with Bishop Yamada
to have Katagiri officially transferred to Sokoji. That's how Suzuki
finally got an assistant priest.

KATAGIRI WAS given a desk in the first-floor office and asked to help
with fund-raising for the congregation's new temple, to be acquired
in the distant future. Immediately popular with the Japanese-
Americans, he liked the relaxed informality of their group. But like
Suzuki, he was most interested in the zazen group. He immediately got involved with the project to refurbish the zendo and
enlarge the sitting area on the balcony, used on a daily basis for late-
comers and during sesshin for overflow. Many students were helping out in their spare time. Philip sanded the floor; Betty and Della
painted the walls. Katagiri joined in enthusiastically and at times a
bit clumsily. He was so relieved to be there with Suzuki and his
eager students.

Katagiri missed his wife and son, who were back in Japan, but he
wasn't lonely. The first friend he made was one of Suzuki's oldest
students, a fellow named Paul Alexander, who lived with his mother
a few blocks away. Paul invited Katagiri to live at his place free for as
long as he wanted. Normally quiet and shy, Paul found he could
open up to Katagiri. Katagiri learned how Paul had come to San
Francisco in 1960 looking for a Zen master and a Zen temple, and
how he had walked around town for six months looking but never
asking, until one day he chanced to walk by Sokoji. Now Paul was
restoring the historic organ at the back of the stage as a gift to the
congregation, so they could sell it. Every morning he would drive
Katagiri in on his motor scooter after they'd had breakfast. After a
month with Paul, Katagiri moved into a small room next to Oto-

hiro across the street from the temple. Otohiro was at City College; he and Katagiri commiserated with each other about the difficulties of living in a society where they had to depend on their English.

Katagiri didn't have to worry about food. He received many dinner invitations and was always welcome at Sokoji for meals. The Petcheys started looking after him right away. Pauline's mother, who had moved in with her and Grahame, gave him a Kannon statue. The Hagiwaras gave him some furniture. Iru Price dropped by to see how he was doing. "What a relief to be in San Francisco and on Bush Street!" he said. "Everyone here is so kind."

As for Suzuki, right away he saw that Katagiri was a sincere monk and treated him with utmost respect. Mainly that meant Suzuki gave him a lot of responsibility and left him alone. They didn't talk much but shared a culture and an encyclopedia of nonverbal training.

Students called their new priest Reverend Katagiri or Katagiri-sensei. He was enthusiastic about everything he did: sweeping, cleaning, walking to the store. And he had a warm innocent smile for all – unless he was in the zendo. Then his face took on a determined seriousness, almost a scowl.

KATAGIRI'S FAMILY had belonged to a different sect of Buddhism, Jodo Shin, but he'd been attracted to Soto Zen and zazen because of experiences he'd had during the war, including abdominal surgery without anesthetic, and a general loss of meaning in his life following Japan's surrender. He'd turned to Zen much as the students at Zen Center: because he was suffering and wanted to find some peace, and to understand himself and all existence better.

After the war he met his master, got ordained, went to Eiheiji, and had an awakening experience in tangaryo, which whetted his appetite for more zazen. At Eiheiji he had served and been inspired by Hashimoto-roshi, famous for his monastic discipline. Katagiri had a tiny temple on the coast near Eiheiji which had been his master's, but he spent most of his time at headquarters or at Eiheiji, dealing with Westerners or guests.

KATAGIRI FIT right in at Zen Center. Along with his priestly duties for the congregation, he eagerly sat every period of zazen and
helped Suzuki with services, sesshins, carrying the stick, and giving
zazen instruction. Suzuki knew he was one in a thousand. How
many Soto priests would live in statusless poverty in this foreign
country and put their life energy into sitting quietly, doing nothing,
and sweeping a dusty old building? Katagiri had been a bit of a mis-
fit in Japan and had wanted to go abroad for a long time, to Brazil or
the U.S., to teach Zen. He'd come to America at thirty-six, not knowing what was going to happen with his life. Like Suzuki, he wanted
to practice and teach Dogen's way.

One day Katagiri lit a cigarette in the office. Suzuki went to a
window and opened it. Katagiri put out his cigarette and soon afterward quit smoking – an agonizing experience for him. This was
Suzuki's place, and Katagiri followed his lead.

KATAGIRI KNEW some English, but the onslaught of questions
and stories from the students at Sokoji was putting him through
an intensive course. He was twenty years younger than Suzuki
and more accessible. He studied English at a little school in Pacific
Heights where Suzuki still went occasionally. Pauline and others
tutored him on the side.

In early Indian Buddhism public speaking had been dubbed one
of the Five Fears. One day Suzuki casually mentioned that he'd like
Katagiri to give the talk the following Wednesday evening – in
English. Suzuki learned quickly and seemed to do everything well
(in contrast to the youthful Crooked Cucumber). Katagiri was the
opposite. He labored over every new task and learned at a snail's
pace. He was enthusiastic and tried hard, but nothing was easy –
especially English. He worked night and day in a pitiable state of
dread, preparing for his first talk. On that Wednesday night Suzuki
further terrified him by showing up with Okusan to hear him.
Suzuki introduced him, since some people only came to lectures
and didn't know who he was.

Katagiri threw himself into the talk with fervor, using his own translations of Dogen's unique Zen phrasing. He went on for thirty minutes. Everyone sat alert, listening. Then he and Suzuki walked out of the room together. At last Suzuki really had his helper. Katagiri had no idea how much his arrival meant to Suzuki or what would be in store for him. An exciting time lay ahead: lots of learning, work, struggle, change, and many lectures. The first was out of the way, and there would be another in a few weeks.

Drinking tea afterward, students thanked him for his talk and praised his English. He modestly deflected the praise. He didn't realize that no one had understood anything he'd said.

Human nature encourages our practice and our practice will help our full expression of human nature. So helping each other, encouraging each other, our practice will go on and on.

UPHILL AND around the corner from Sokoji was the BCA, Buddhist Churches of America, headquarters for Jodo Shin Buddhism in the United States. BCA had a much larger and wealthier congregation than Sokoji. Suzuki had come to be close with their chief priest, Bishop Hanayama, and his wife, who was Okusan's tea ceremony teacher. She was also a judge for the granting of recognition to calligraphy instructors in Japan. In keeping with the Japanese cultural admonition to study for life, Suzuki became her student. One afternoon early in 1964, following his calligraphy class, Suzuki dropped by the temple's Buddhist bookstore, perhaps the only bookstore in America specializing in Buddhist books, in both Japanese and English. Behind the counter was a twenty-three-year-old Jodo Shin priest, Koshin Ogui. Suzuki stayed and talked for a while.

Ogui was discouraged. He'd been in America since late 1962, when he arrived from Kyoto to serve with the BCA. First he went to L.A. to perform memorial services and funerals for Japanese-

Americans, but he had argued with the head priest and had gotten so depressed he'd run away. The bishop in San Francisco took him in and gave him a job running the bookstore. Ogui felt he couldn't really be a Buddhist minister, because he didn't understand Buddhism well enough and couldn't answer people's questions. He felt ensnared in tradition and ritual. But he didn't tell Suzuki about his problems, except to say he couldn't learn English. When Caucasians came into the store he was unable to communicate adequately with them. He wanted to go back to Japan. Suzuki sensed Ogui's inner frustrations and loss of confidence.

"Come sit zazen with me," he said. "It might help you."

Jodo Shin priests don't practice zazen. It's antithetical to their way, which emphasizes the futility of personal effort. Jodo Shin is called "other power" in contrast to Zen's "self power." Their central practice is to invoke the name of Amida Buddha, chanting with the understanding that they are fundamentally already saved. Suzuki liked Jodo Shin and sometimes mentioned it in lectures.

Ogui saw a genuinely sympathetic person in Suzuki. It wasn't such a big leap for him to cross the usually solid barrier that separates the sects in Japan. His father's best friend had been a Rinzai Zen priest; they'd gone begging together in their village, and he'd sent his son to live for periods in his friend's temple. Ogui talked to the bishop, who gave him the green light to practice zazen with Suzuki.

Before long Ogui was a frequent addition to the Sokoji zendo as well as to the kitchen, where he often joined Suzuki and Okusan for afternoon tea breaks or dinner. He became friends with Katagiri as well as with Della and other students. He was impressed with the quality and variety of people who came to Zen Center to sit zazen. Before meeting Suzuki his life had been so dismal, and now there was some joy in it. "So many funny things happen around here," he told Katagiri.

One time a young woman came to the zendo wearing a dress made from a tennis court net with a mesh of two-inch squares. It was put together very carefully and fit her quite well; the only problem was, she was still basically naked. She went in well before the period started; Suzuki, Katagiri, and Ogui stood at the office door and peeked at her sitting so seriously and so exposed on a zafu.

Suzuki asked Katagiri, "What should we do?"

Katagiri scratched his head and said, "Ah, I don't know."

Suzuki looked at Ogui and said, "You should go talk to her."

So Ogui went in and told her that the teacher would like for her to "wear more clothes in consideration of other people who come to sit zazen."

"But this is my best dress," she said dejectedly.

"Please go put on another one and come back," Ogui told her.

After she left they could no longer contain themselves and laughed themselves silly.

The more we attempt to manage religious activity,
the more we lose our fundamental way.

ONE SATURDAY after the cleaning period, Philip and Grahame were standing together in the center of the zendo. Suzuki walked up and stood between Philip – playful and eager – and Grahame – prim and upright, looking like he was born to wear the robes. Suzuki pointed to Grahame and said, "You're all priest," and with his other hand pointed to Philip and said, "And you're all pig." Then he reversed the direction his hands were pointing, and his two devotees stood there with dazed grins, like they'd just been whacked.

Philip asked Suzuki why Japanese make their teacups so thin and delicate that they break easily. Suzuki said, "It's not that they're too delicate, but that you don't know how to handle them. You must adjust yourself to the environment and not vice versa." Pauline, who had noticed him often making this point, called it the gentle way.

THERE WAS a going-away party for Okusan and Philip in late March of 1964. They were off to Japan, she to visit for a few months, and he to Eiheiji for a year. Suzuki was sending his bull into the china shop. But first he had to be a monk. You can't practice in the zendo at Eiheiji if you're not a monk. Philip and his wife, J.J., sat in Suzuki's office.

"You wait here. I'll go do the ceremony," he said, and with that he went alone into the zendo.

They could hear him walking over to the altar, hitting bells, and chanting. He came back, pulled up a few strands of Philip's hair and, making the fingers of his other hand into a V, he pretended to cut the lock of hair with scissors. He turned back to his desk, reached into a bag, pulled out a handful of candy, and let it all fall onto the desk before them. Then they drank tea and celebrated Philip's new status.

As THE DAY of Philip's departure drew near, he noticed that Suzuki was not his usual radiant self, but was distraught.

Suzuki gave Philip an old brown bag and said, "Here are some old robes of mine I don't need anymore. Take them back to Rinso-in for me."

"Are you okay, Reverend Suzuki?" Philip asked.

"Ah, ah," he sighed in anguish, "my daughter Omi . . . she has killed herself."

Suzuki's son Hoitsu had telephoned from Rinso-in. At Eiheiji, Hoitsu had gotten word from his sister Yasuko to come home right away. His sister Omi, Suzuki's third child – the sensitive, artistic one who had not recovered from her mother's murder – had hanged herself in the mental institution where she had been living for nine years. Suzuki did not go to Japan, there was no ceremony or memorial plaque placed on the altar at Sokoji, and it was not until many months later that he told Otohiro that his sister had died.

The word "disciplined" is not an appropriate word for our practice. Practice is something that is done with big mind.

"I TRY AND try, and nothing seems to be happening," Grahame told Suzuki in his office. "What is the meaning of all this?"

"The clear mind will rise eventually," Suzuki answered and would say no more. Grahame was grateful for even that much. Usually Suzuki just told him, "I don't know." No magic or great moments where the master tweaked your nose and all became clear.

It was spring of 1965. He'd been with Suzuki for four years. About the only time he'd ever missed a zazen period was when his son was born. He felt he'd been really going for it. His whole life was focused around zazen, but he didn't seem to be getting anywhere. The lectures on Buddhist teachings and koans were interesting, but what really kept him going were the simpler things that Suzuki said, like, "Give it two years, it takes that long just to get used to the posture of zazen." What Grahame had heard above all was: don't worry about anything else – just sit, sit, sit, sit, sit. Okay, he'd been sitting for four years. And now he couldn't stop the questions from coming.

"Even though I practice like this, I still don't seem to deepen my understanding of life. I just can't grasp what it's about." He bugged his teacher over and over until one day Suzuki responded.

"You know, I can't answer your questions," he said. "Very few people can. I'm just a little person in terms of understanding Zen. In Japan I only know six who really truly understand the Zen way."

"Only six out of thousands and thousands of priests?"

"Only six in Soto and maybe six in Rinzai. Maybe twelve in the whole of Japan. Not so good, is it? Zen is not in a very healthy state. There's not so much interest. When I left I had only one old man sitting with me. You should go there and look up these teachers. They have a much bigger understanding than I do. If you really want to know the meaning of Buddhism, you have to go and study with one of these people."

Go back to Japan? Horrors. Grahame had barely survived last time, and that was only for three months. But he also wanted to expunge the sense of failure that lingered from that visit. It was true he knew more now than he had then. He'd studied some Japanese, and he'd be better prepared.

At least if I went back now, I'd have a buddy, Grahame thought. Grahame and Philip got along despite their striking differences. They'd gone camping and to samurai movies many times.

SUZUKI ASKED Grahame about Katagiri. Should he stay or go? It was time for a decision. If he were to stay, his family should come over. The Japanese congregation was so poor. Would Zen Center be willing to make a commitment to him? Grahame thought so.

Suzuki asked Pauline what she thought about the idea of Grahame going to Japan for a year. She said they had two children, and she wasn't to be left behind; that might be the way they do things in Japan, but there was no way she would let Grahame go without his family. In no time it was agreed that they'd all go to Japan, Grahame to Eiheiji, and Pauline, the children, and her mother to Kyoto. She'd lived in Paris and Rome and wanted to live in Japan's equivalent of those great cities.

"So we'll all go to Japan," Grahame said.

"All right then," Suzuki said, "Katagiri stays in America."

At that moment it was as if several pieces were sewn together in the fabric that Suzuki was slowly making, stitch by stitch. It was a gamble, an act of faith, that Grahame would get a feeling for the background of his teacher's teaching and pick up some aspects of Zen and Japanese culture that would benefit him and the West. Zen Center needed experienced priests, and Suzuki would temporarily transplant the straightest tree in his orchard, in hopes that he would come back stronger and more fruitful.

Before Grahame left, Suzuki gave him the names of six venerable old Zen priests to look up in Japan. Fujimoto was on the list, as were Katagiri's second teacher, Hashimoto, the widely revered "homeless" Kodo Sawaki at Antaiji in Kyoto, and the abbot of

Dogen's original temple near Kyoto in Uji. They were all priests in the Nishiari Bokusan/Oka Sotan lineage.

On August 9, Nagasaki Day, 1965, Grahame and Pauline arrived in Tokyo with their children. As they walked through the brightly lit Ginza shopping district, Grahame exclaimed to Pauline, "What have we done!"

When you say "Wait a moment," you are bound by your own karma; when you say "Yes I will," you are free.

OGUI, THE Jodo Shin priest, had continued to sit zazen at Sokoji and developed a unique relationship with Suzuki. They were like buddies, and Ogui saw a side of Suzuki not often exposed to the congregation members, who were older and fairly proper, or to the Zen students, with whom Suzuki maintained some formal reserve. If a samurai movie was being shown in Sokoji's auditorium, Suzuki might ask Ogui to watch with him from the balcony. Sometimes they'd get to laughing so loud that Okusan would come out and tell them to be quiet so the paying moviegoers below could hear.

Ogui noticed the eccentric way that Suzuki would relate to possessions. Suzuki had almost nothing of his own and seemed to want almost nothing. He said that everything he had was borrowed from the world for as long as he needed it, even his glasses, which he was grateful to be able to use for a while for his "tired old eyes." Sometimes he'd play with ownership. A student asked Suzuki what was the right thing to do with a twenty-dollar bill she'd found on the sidewalk. "Here, I'll take it," said Suzuki, and picked it out of her hand. On occasion he would sneak food offerings from the altar and give them to Ogui. One time Okusan caught him slipping a large bottle of soy sauce to Ogui. She demanded he return it, at least until the Obon festival was over, or else the donors would notice and feel slighted. It was not yet his to take.

Okusan said her husband had no greed except for fine old pottery, and Ogui could attest to that. Mrs. Sekino invited the Suzukis and Ogui to dinner. At one point when Mrs. Sekino and Okusan went into the kitchen, Suzuki reached into his sleeve and took out an incense burner. It was Korean, ceramic, with a translucent, pale green celadon glaze. He placed it on the bookshelf. Questioned by Ogui, he explained, "It was so beautiful I had to borrow it. I've enjoyed it enough, so it's time to return it."

Ogui also became good friends with Katagiri, and the three priests would often go to Japanese-American community events together. Katagiri's wife, Tomoe-san, had finally come over with their little boy, Yasuhiko, and they were poor as temple mice. Unmarried Ogui earned more than married Katagiri and more than Suzuki, too. He liked to rib them about it. On Memorial Day there was a memorial service for all Bay Area Japanese-Americans at the cemetery in Colma, south of San Francisco. Afterward Ogui was talking with Katagiri about how well Jodo Shin takes care of its ministers financially. Katagiri joked, "Ah, I should have become a Jodo Shin minister," and Ogui said, "I should have been a Zen priest from the beginning." Then Ogui turned to Suzuki, standing nearby, and asked, "Can I become a Zen priest?"

Suzuki shook his head and said, "That's very difficult."

Then Ogui said, "Katagiri-san would like to be a Jodo Shin minister."

"That is also very difficult."

"Then maybe we shouldn't be ministers at all."

"That is also very difficult," Suzuki said, and the three of them broke into laughter.

OGUI STILL got depressed at the sorry state of his English and was always thinking of going back to Japan. Why stay in America, he thought, if I can't communicate with Americans? Suzuki was aware of this, and one day made a special point to suggest that Ogui come to that night's talk. Expecting it to be mostly over his head, Ogui sat in back.

Suzuki came out from his office, there was a chant, and then he bowed and said, "Good evening." Well, I understood that much, Ogui thought, and waited attentively for more. Suzuki didn't say anything at first but started walking in front of people, back and forth, slowly and steadily. Then he started speaking softly, as if to himself, in Japanese. He was warming up, saying something like, "What can I say? What can I say?" Ogui watched intently. Suzuki sighed and looked at his audience. "Today – today wa ja na, today wa ja na" (Today is . . . today is . . .). My gosh, he's speaking a mixture of English and Japanese together, Ogui thought. "Today izu yappari today" (Today is absolutely today). He walked around some more. "Today izu natto yesterday" (Today is not yesterday). Then again he slowly walked from side to side and said, "Today is not tomorrow." Stopping in front of a young long-haired man in one of the front seats, he grabbed his shoulders and shook him, saying, "Today is just today! Do you understand?" Suzuki let go of the man, smiled warmly and said, "Today is absolutely today. Not yesterday and not tomorrow." He surveyed the audience for a moment and said, "That's all."

Ogui couldn't even stand up with the others. He felt that Suzuki's lecture had been just for him. What have I been frustrated about? he thought. Because I don't have a large enough English vocabulary? Because I lack confidence? Because I don't know much about Buddhism? "Today is absolutely today. Today is not yesterday. Today is not tomorrow." Only a few words. I have studied English through middle school, high school, and college – I know more vocabulary than that. Ogui realized that he was discouraged not because he lacked understanding of the dharma or because of English vocabulary, but because something was lacking in his mind. He was lacking in *hara* – in being centered and courageous. Ogui's frustrated life spun around, and he resolved to remain in America and figure out how to teach Americans about Buddhism. An enormous gratitude swelled within him. He got up and walked home to his apartment, feeling a sense of purpose, yet light and carefree.

Chapter Fourteen

Taking Root

1965–1966

*E*stablishing Buddhism in a new country is like holding
a plant to a stone and waiting for it to take root.

AT 3:45 ON a summer morning in 1965, a grey Volkswagen bug sat running beneath the streetlight in front of Sokoji.
When Shunryu Suzuki appeared on the sidewalk, Toni Johansen
got out of the car to open the door for him. They were on their way
to the Los Altos zendo.

For over a year Suzuki had been making periodic visits to three
satellite zendos – Mill Valley over the Golden Gate Bridge to the
north, Berkeley across the Bay Bridge to the east, and especially Los
Altos, south on the peninsula. Like many a Japanese temple priest,
Suzuki had a regular circuit-riding schedule. In Japan his visits to
homes and other temples had usually been for memorial services
and ceremonies. That was true also in America, when he went to
Japanese homes, but more often, when he rode up Bush Street, he
was going to sit zazen and give lectures.

Arriving in Los Altos just before 5:00 AM, Toni and Suzuki walked into a comfortable suburban living room lined with people sitting silently on cushions facing the walls. The home was owned by Marian Derby, a middle-aged woman who lived there with her four teenage daughters. Marian had started sitting in February of 1965 with Suzuki's Peninsula Group in Redwood City. Before long, both the morning and evening meetings were being held in her spacious living room in Los Altos. In the summer of 1966 her garage was converted into a zendo with seventeen seats. Marian named it Haiku Zendo, after the seventeen-syllable haiku poem.

The Los Altos zendo had a mature membership. Among the regulars were a number of housewives, a few artists and students, a retired ship's captain, and an IBM employee. The atmosphere at Marian's was like Sokoji in the early sixties, with eager students remaining after the morning schedule for a leisurely breakfast and discussion.

ONE DAY after lecture a student sitting on a zafu on the carpet asked, "What is hell?"

"Hell is having to read aloud in English," Suzuki answered. After the laughter subsided, the student persevered, and Suzuki said, "Hell is not punishment, it's training."

On another occasion, over coffee, a woman said it was difficult to mix Zen with being a housewife. She felt she was trying to climb a ladder, but for every step up she'd go down two. "Forget the ladder," Suzuki told her. "In Zen everything is right here on the ground."

TONI JOHANSEN had looked hard for a teacher who would understand the eternal present she'd experienced during an LSD trip. She didn't want to take any more LSD but was looking for a natural way to awaken her potential. None of the priests and ministers she went to got it. Each time she'd try something new, she'd conclude, "Not this." A Sunday school teacher told her about Suzuki. She went, saw a dozen people sitting rigidly facing the wall, and thought, "Not this," but she stayed for zazen. Suzuki entered, and she sensed him behind her when he walked around giving the greeting bow. She didn't know who he was or what was happening, but there was something. After the sitting she looked at him and thought, "Oh, I think so." Just looking into his eyes and having him look directly at her, she thought, "This person knows more about what I want to know than anyone I've ever met. He totally understands what I want to understand."

Toni's husband, Tony, also got involved with Haiku Zendo. Before long they moved to San Francisco but returned frequently to Los Altos as Suzuki's chauffeurs. After a couple of years of study Toni still trusted Suzuki completely and felt his acceptance and trust of her. She even told him once on the way to Los Altos that she had such tremendous feelings of love for him, and that it confused her.

"Don't worry," he said. "You can let yourself have all the feelings you have for your teacher. That's good. I have enough discipline for both of us."

She wrote about that in her journal, which Suzuki would read every week and comment on. Often there were questions about what was called "family practice." That week Suzuki wrote in her journal, "No one knows what is wrong love and what is true love. Have faith in me and yourself and let's have dinner together all four of us. But wait – I must first ask my tigress!" (Okusan was born in the year of the tiger. "He's a dragon," she would say. "When we fight, he's up in the clouds while I'm growling on the ground.")

Emptiness is the garden where you can't see anything.
It is the mother of all.

ONCE TONI and Tony took the Suzukis to Yosemite – one of the Suzukis' rare vacations. Suzuki stood up through the sunroof of the Volkswagen as they drove toward the mountains, his sleeves fluttering in the wind. They visited the great waterfall, Yosemite Falls. Standing below it, Suzuki jumped from rock to rock, and then all of a sudden he was atop a huge boulder. No one knew how he'd gotten there. It had frightened Okusan. On the following Thursday morning at the Los Altos zendo, he talked about his experience at Yosemite.

At the highest waterfall I saw the water coming down like a curtain thrown from the top of the mountain. It doesn't come down swiftly, as I expected; it comes slowly. And it comes down in groups. I thought it might be a very hard experience for each drop of water to come down such a high mountain from top to bottom. I thought our life is maybe like this. We have many hard experiences in our life. But at the same time, I thought, the water is not originally separated. It is one whole water. So we say, "From emptiness everything comes out." One whole body of water, or one whole mind, is emptiness. When we reach this understanding we find true meaning to our life. When we reach this understanding, we can see the beauty of the flower – the beauty of human life. Before we realize this fact, all we see is just delusion.

Suzuki had never lived anywhere without gardens until he came to America and moved into Sokoji. He became starved for greenery. But with the advent of the outlying zendos, he was regularly visiting neighborhoods with trees and yards. He would visit students' homes – especially in Los Altos – and sometimes he'd surprise his hosts by going straight to weeding their flower beds or even playfully rolling on the lawn or zipping up a tree. The first time he walked into one woman's backyard in Los Altos, he went right to the rope swing, stepped on a rock, and swung out, his robes streaming behind him.

If you want to study Buddhism, you have to clear your mind.
You should not have any prejudice. You should forget all you
have learned before.

BY 1966 Shunryu Suzuki had played an important role in the lives of hundreds of people, some who passed through briefly, others who became committed students, and everything in between. A few long-term students seemed candidates to eventually become teachers in their own right, continuing Suzuki's lineage in America. Of these, Richard Baker was foremost. In 1966 Richard had been around for five years, and his devotion to Suzuki and to penetrating into the heart of his teaching had not diminished. Suzuki was giving him more and more recognition and permission to help determine the future of the group. Richard was president of Zen Center and editor of *Wind Bell,* and he was keeping an eye out for a site outside the city to develop a retreat center for more concentrated study. With Grahame and Philip both in Japan, Richard sat on the front cushion on the men's side in the zendo, and Suzuki wouldn't let anyone sit in his place if he wasn't there.

Richard accompanied Suzuki to L.A. for a meeting of Soto Zen priests. On the way home he asked, "Suzuki-roshi, many people in Los Angeles asked me if I was your disciple. May I say I am your disciple?"

"Yes, you can say you are my disciple."

NOTHING THAT happened between teacher and disciple, verbal or nonverbal, was too small for Richard to notice – or for Suzuki to notice. One day in the zendo Richard straightened a picture on the wall before he sat down. During zazen Suzuki got up, walked to the picture, returned it to its crooked position, and went back to his seat.

Back in 1963, just before Suzuki's Mountain Seat Ceremony, Richard had had a terrible bicycle accident in which his forearms were severely injured. Both arms were in casts. He had been asked to play the large standing drum at the ceremony and had been practicing for weeks. He continued to practice after the accident, with considerable effort. The most difficult parts were the roll-downs. But Richard was absolutely determined that he was going to hit the drum during this ceremony, no matter how much it hurt or how impossible it seemed. He continued to practice in great pain, and when the day of the ceremony came, he did it, and he did it well. Suzuki was proud of him for making such an effort.

A year or so later, for no reason that he knew, Richard experienced great mental difficulty. It got to the point where he considered committing himself to an institution. One night he was in such anguish he ended up standing on the street outside Sokoji at midnight. He considered waking Suzuki and asking him for help, but he decided against it and finally went home. Not long after that, when it was his turn to bow to Suzuki after zazen one day, he saw, on a zafu by the door, the very drumsticks he had made such an effort with at Suzuki's Mountain Seat Ceremony. They were normally stored with the drum outside the zendo, so they were conspicuously out of place. Richard bowed to Suzuki and moved on, deeply touched and encouraged. During the next few weeks his mind cleared up; the storm had passed.

Richard persevered. "Suzuki's responses to my questions were various, sometimes brushing me off, sometimes definitely and clearly answering. It was a study in how to ask questions. I often couldn't look to his responses as answers in the usual sense, so I accepted them as foils, mirrors, changes in energy, or sometimes as hints. Sometimes he'd answer with his body. If I asked him about breathing, he might change the way he breathed."

"Do you think I should go to Japan to study and practice? Do you think I should get to know Japanese monastic life?" Richard asked.

"Dick, there is no place to go," Suzuki said.

"Is there something you would like me to do?"

"There is nothing to do. You can do anything you want. Just be yourself."

CLAUDE DALENBERG was a quiet, serious man with a dislike of religious pomp and ceremony, true to his Dutch Reform roots. He had been pursuing Buddhist studies since 1949 after hearing a talk in Chicago by Alan Watts. Claude had come to San Francisco in the early fifties. At the American Academy of Asian Studies, he met D. T. Suzuki, Wako Kato, Gary Snyder, and a whole raft of Asian scholars, poets, and philosophers of the Beat generation. The character Bud Diefendorf in Jack Kerouac's *Dharma Bums* was based on Claude. In L.A. he had studied with Nyogen Senzaki, the iconoclast Rinzai priest, and had been in the study group at Sokoji with Tobase years before Suzuki had arrived. "Back then," he said, "sitting ten minutes of zazen was as challenging as climbing a huge mountain, because as far as we were concerned, zazen was completely unknown territory. Now, for new people, it's as easy as falling off a log."

During Suzuki's first few years in America, Claude was in Kyoto. On his return Claude was attracted to the Quaker-like simplicity of Suzuki's Zen Center and immediately became his student and trusted advisor. Claude was almost thirty, knew something of investment and management, and had been a founder of the East-West House back in the fifties. Suzuki regarded him as practical and mature and talked to him about ideas for the future, particularly about developing the community of Zen practitioners, the *sangha,* possibly getting a house near Sokoji where some of them could live together. It was an idea Suzuki had considered on and off since the first year he was in America. Suzuki also talked to Claude about his wish to create a strong program of study, and about his plans for a seminary.

Claude appreciated the Japanese congregation, thought there was a good deal that could be learned from them in terms of Buddhism, and had sympathy with Suzuki's desire to keep some connection between the two congregations, even though they were not in harmony. The Japanese-American congregation was planning to build a new temple around the corner that would be just theirs. Suzuki thought that when they moved out, Sokoji might be remodeled to serve the needs of American Buddhism. It could include a Buddhist seminary and living quarters. He could take care of both if he could get another priest from Japan. Maybe with a little separation the two groups could coexist more easily.

IN A WEEKLY study group at Sokoji Claude noticed Suzuki's emphasis on understanding Buddhism within one's own background and culture. One evening the topic was a book about the meeting of East and West. Suzuki sat with his hands behind his head, as usual listening and not saying anything. The direction of the discussion was to compare the attributes of East and West, and the West was losing.

One person said, "The East is nondualistic and aims to be in harmony with nature, while the West is dualistic and materialistic and aims to conquer and use nature."

"Yes," said another. "The East is intuitive and integrative, while the West is rational and separative."

As conversation continued in this vein, Suzuki spoke up, obviously upset. "If you want to be a good Buddhist," he said, "first you're going to have to learn how to be a good Christian." Then he got up and walked out.

MEL WEITSMAN had been a regular at Sokoji since Philip Wilson had told him about Suzuki in 1964. Mel was an artist and a flutist in his mid-thirties who drove a cab to get by. He had a soft, easygoing way and was well liked.

The first time he went to sit at Sokoji, Mel couldn't believe he'd sat through the whole forty-minute period. He practically went into shock when, after kinhin, he saw everyone sit down on their zafus again for more. Then during that period, Suzuki came up behind him and put Mel's hands into the zazen mudra. He straightened his back and showed him where on the wall to cast his eyes. As Suzuki walked back to the altar, Mel's life took a different course.

It's been said, in Zen parlance, that your first enlightenment experience is when you decide to practice. It's the first turning. "This is
it," Mel thought.

A woman told Suzuki she'd heard others saying that he could
read their minds. When asked if this was true, he answered, "No!"
In the next few lectures he denied having such abilities. Mel said if
you looked for miracles or extraordinary powers you'd miss the
man. "Sensei's magic is the ordinary," he said.

One day Suzuki, Katagiri, Mel, Claude, and a student named
Silas Hoadley were looking at an apartment across the street from
Sokoji. Silas had just moved into a room in the apartment, and
there were food and dishes in the kitchen. They decided to eat
breakfast there. There was no furniture, so Suzuki spread a newspaper on the floor like a tablecloth. Cups and bowls were set out,
and soon they were eating and drinking tea. Mel ate silently with
the others, impressed that his teacher had just turned an empty
room into a dining room with only a newspaper.

Mel watched Suzuki closely and found that he taught as much
with his body as with his words. Suzuki's body reminded Mel of
Gandhi's, agile and light. He taught by example how to stand, walk,
breathe, and sit in a chair. Suzuki's rhythm and movement deeply
impressed Mel the musician. "He had the feeling of being completely within the activity of the moment. Approaching a chair, he
wouldn't just carelessly sit down – he'd really make contact with it.
He harmonized and merged with whatever he met. He was at ease
because he wasn't off balance. So he walked in a very relaxed way,
and when he sat down he would remain in balance. He was never in
a hurry, even though things had to be done. He always took the
time to do everything. That's being in time. The way he sat down
was being in time."

SILAS HOADLEY, a Yale graduate from a quaint Connecticut town,
had been experimenting with peyote in an early Haight-Ashbury
commune called the Spaceship. He also ran his own import-export
business and traveled occasionally to Asia on business trips. He

went with a friend to Sokoji on April Fool's Day in 1964. Before meeting Suzuki, he said, he hadn't considered that there might be something to Buddhism beyond the words and ideas, which were plentiful in his circles. As soon as he met Suzuki, that changed. He felt that Suzuki was in touch with a truth that was bigger than the truth Silas had been basing his life on. It was the physicality that attracted him. In his studies of psychology and philosophy he'd never run into anyone who said that it all starts with the body – being aware of the body and the breath. Silas was already a disciplined and serious person, and he had no particular difficulty making the shift to sitting zazen once or twice a day at Sokoji.

MORE AND more people were showing up at Sokoji who had prior experience with Zen practice. One such person was Bob Halpern, an intense young man with thick brown hair reaching down to his shoulders. Bob sat facing Suzuki in his office, cluttered with knick-knacks, books, stones, and plants. A large, old-fashioned clock on a shelf chimed the hour. Suzuki patted the bronze heads on a statue of three monkeys. Their hands were covering their eyes, ears, and mouth. "They are my favorites," he said, imitating each monkey as he chuckled and recited, "see no evil, hear no evil, speak no evil." Then he added, "What can I do for you?"

Bob said that he had sat for a year with the Rinzai teacher Joshu Sasaki-roshi in L.A. He had just completed a sesshin in Mill Valley with Yasutani-roshi, at which Maezumi-sensei translated. Yasutani was the Soto priest who used koans in the Rinzai fashion and who emphasized pushing oneself hard in sesshin to have an awakening experience, whether concentrating on a koan or just sitting zazen. Yasutani was giving sesshins on the West Coast and had attracted a following, partly due to the success of Philip Kapleau's new book, *The Three Pillars of Zen,* which told a great deal about zazen, koan work, and Yasutani's brand of Zen. People at the sesshin had mentioned Suzuki, so Bob dropped by Sokoji. "What sort of practice do you have here?" he asked, self-consciously feeling the need to say something.

Suzuki explained the schedule at Sokoji – daily sitting, a weekend sesshin every other month, and the seven-day sesshin in August. He told Bob that some students, especially Richard Baker, were interested in finding a practice place in the countryside. "I think everything is just fine in the city the way it is going. People are practicing pretty well here, but if that is their wish, I'll do it. They want it to be a place for men and women to practice together," Suzuki told him. "We don't do it that way in Japan, but this is America."

Bob eyed Suzuki while he talked. He seemed to be the opposite of Yasutani, who was fierce and yelled a lot during sesshin. Suzuki was younger but seemed sedate, ordinary, even frail in comparison. He didn't have a gruff samurai-type voice, but was gentle and soft-spoken. He leaned back in the office chair, hands clasped behind his head and legs crossed like a woman. Bob thought he was a very nice man but didn't think he could be a real Zen teacher.

LATER, IN L.A. for a meeting of Japanese Soto priests in America, Suzuki accepted a dinner invitation from Maezumi. Bob was there. He had sold his business, the Satori Bookshop on Sunset Strip, and was living with Maezumi and helping him establish a new center in his living room. Bob sat bolt upright and kept quiet, trying to make a good impression. Maezumi served a dish with rice, meat, and vegetables, and Bob was careful not to take any meat. He was a fanatic vegetarian and thought of it as an important part of Buddhism, both in terms of not killing animals and for encouraging a peaceful state of mind. Suzuki was running into this sort of thinking more and more.

"Oh, you don't eat meat?" said Suzuki to him.

"Sometimes I eat meat," said Bob.

"Sometimes I eat rice," said Suzuki.

This seemingly inconsequential exchange ate away at Bob. Suzuki had immediately seen his point of greatest attachment and poked him there. It would not be the last time.

In the evanescence of life we can find the joy of eternal life.

GRAHAME PETCHEY and his family had been in Japan for almost a year. He'd stuck it out at Eiheiji again and had done better this time, though he was out a lot with severe back problems caused by trying to lift a large steamer trunk during the move. He eventually found a practice more to his liking at Antaiji, a small training temple in Kyoto founded by Oka Sotan early in the century. It became the temple of Oka's disciple, "Homeless" Kodo Sawaki, the venerable old monk whose practice included a great deal of zazen, little ceremony, no stick, and a level of criticism of Soto Zen that made Suzuki's concerns seem minor. When Sawaki had been offered the abbotship of Eiheiji, he replied that not even a dog would take it. Sawaki was one of the six masters whom Suzuki had suggested to Grahame, to help him solve his nagging question.

Grahame had tried to find all six masters. Two were dead, and the others were either too old or too sick to take on students (including Fujimoto, the closest among them to Suzuki). Grahame felt honored to meet old Kodo Sawaki on his death bed at Antaiji.

Grahame started to sit at Antaiji with Sawaki's disciple, Uchiyama-roshi, whom he liked very much. At Antaiji there was more zazen and much less structure than at other Zen temples that offered regular zazen. He settled right in, living with his family and going to the temple regularly. Suzuki's list of six masters had worked after all. Finally Grahame had found a teacher and a practice in Japan that worked for him.

When Sawaki died in December 1965 at the age of eighty-five, Grahame joined the forty-nine-day memorial sesshin in his honor. Sesshins usually last a maximum of seven days, but Grahame sat at Antaiji for forty-nine days, from before sunrise till after sunset, in honor of this great sitter.

Several doctors had told Grahame to remain prone as much as possible due to his slipped disk. Surgery was being considered. But, wearing a corset, he started the sesshin. When it was time for kinhin, he stood and walked in slow, precise steps with the others.

Contrary to what the doctors had told him, during the sesshin his spine corrected itself and the pain disappeared. His mind gradually became calm and clear. Sitting day after day, Grahame forgot about cultural differences, language barriers, doubts, and above all, his nagging question. He gave himself completely to zazen. His senses opened wide. He could hear insects walking on the floor. His experience continued through the weeks and expanded. It was simply beautiful, the culmination of his Zen travels, the unraveling of his anxiety. He was filled with gratitude for his years with Suzuki and for having found Antaiji.

*In a busy country like America there must be some time to
spare for zazen. We should have more composure in our life,
and we should respect our traditions, both Buddhist and Christian.*

IF YOU GO south from San Francisco to Monterey County on the coast of California and take the Carmel Valley Road toward Arroyo Seco, midway along this winding drive through rolling hills, crooked oaks, and pastures, you'll come to a grade where ranches meet. Here the surrounding trees are full of mistletoe and Spanish moss, and there's a road with a sign that says "Tassajara." After a few miles the road turns to dirt and twists into wooded mountainsides, ascending to five thousand feet at Chew's Ridge before going back down to fifteen hundred. At the end of this fifteen-mile dirt road lies Tassajara Springs.

Known for a thousand or more years to the local Esselen Indians for the healing properties of the water, the hot sulfur springs were discovered by explorers in the mid-nineteenth century. With the help of Chinese laborers a narrow road to the springs was, with great difficulty, carved out of the steep, mountainous terrain. Ever since the 1860s Tassajara had been the most remote and pristine resort in Monterey County.

*The other day (April 7), I went to Tassajara Hot Springs near Monterey to
see the land for our new retreat. It is an incredibly good place for our
monastery, if we buy the hot springs too. I have written to Katsuzen-san
[Philip] about it as well.*

From a letter from Suzuki to Grahame Petchey.

After years of patiently following leads to potential spots for a
rural retreat, Shunryu Suzuki had found what he wanted – Tassajara. The right place had come along at a time when there was
enough maturity in his group to warrant the move and enough curiosity and open-mindedness in America to support, in this way, a
teaching that challenged many commonly held assumptions about
space, time, being, life, and death.

Different people had mentioned this old resort to Suzuki and
Richard a few times through the years. San Francisco historian
Margot Patterson Doss told Suzuki it was the only place he should
consider for a retreat. Grahame and Philip stumbled on it in 1961
while camping. At Grahame's suggestion, Richard and Virginia
Baker camped in the same area. They likewise came upon the little
cluster of faded white wooden cabins and some sturdy structures
of wood and stone, a large swimming pool, and hot springs with
large plunges and a steam room. Richard was dazzled. But the time
wasn't right till the spring of 1966, when Richard took Suzuki there.

Tassajara is nestled in the Los Padres National Forest inland from
Big Sur, four to five hours' drive south of San Francisco. On the way
to see it for the first time, Suzuki started thinking that it was too far.
He had imagined a place closer – in the Santa Cruz Mountains perhaps. But after passing through breathtaking views on the hour-
long drive over the precipitous dirt road and arriving at Tassajara,
he fell in love with it immediately. Tassajara is exceedingly isolated
and incomparably beautiful, a narrow creek-lined valley cut
through a rough, wooded wilderness, with a waterfall visible from
a ridge.

They left in mid-afternoon. When they got to the ridge where
the road levels out, Suzuki said to Richard, "Stop the car here." He

got out and jumped and danced in the roadway. "It's great! Like China!" he said. Then he went dancing down the road – excited, buoyant, swinging his body – with Richard driving slowly behind. Seeing Suzuki's unbounded joy made it clear to Richard that they were going to do whatever was necessary to purchase this land.

Two couples, the Becks and the Roscoes, owned Tassajara. Bob and Anna Beck were in the process of buying the Roscoes' share and weren't willing to part with Tassajara yet. Bob Beck showed Richard a 180-acre parcel of undeveloped land nearby called the Horse Pasture, which he would sell to the Zen Center for a retreat. Suzuki hiked in to the Horse Pasture with Richard. It was beautiful, but it was Tassajara that caught his fancy. Suzuki agreed to the plan to try to buy the Horse Pasture, while keeping an eye on Tassajara for the future.

PEOPLE WENT into action, overnight creating a fund-raising drive for $150,000, spearheaded by Richard. The entire Zen Center budget for the previous year in the city had been just eight thousand dollars. Richard quit his job putting on conferences at UC Berkeley. Suzuki was astounded at his commitment to getting this land and his obvious skill at going about it, but he wondered if it could really be done. Zen Center had never before asked for anything from people beyond its membership. Everyone got enthused and did what they could to help. The Kwongs held a fund-raising party; a benefit art sale was planned.

Richard knew many people outside Zen Center, and he knew how to spark their interest. He went into overdrive to give Suzuki a secluded, natural setting to establish his way. A brochure was developed, and more benefits were planned. Among those who lent their enthusiastic support early on were a number of philosophers and writers who knew Buddhism well, including Alan Watts, Gary Snyder, Huston Smith, Nancy Wilson Ross, Paul Weinpaul, Allen Ginsberg, Joseph Campbell, and Michael Murphy from nearby Esalen Institute.

WITH RICHARD around so much, the scene at Sokoji was markedly more lively. A lot of people had fun working with him, especially some of the newer students, who didn't see him as a peer. But his closeness to Suzuki as a student and his dominance in the fund-raising and planning for Tassajara tended to overshadow other people and created some resentment and jealousy among the older students.

Richard was not apologetic. He even gave the impression at times that he thought he was the only student who was actually practicing, the only one who'd really made Suzuki's teaching work in San Francisco. He saw others relating to Suzuki on a business level, on a clubby level, and on a love-of-Roshi level, but he always maintained that, except for Grahame, people weren't really willing to break through their attachments to establish a fundamentally engaged level of practice. It was infuriating to others to hear Richard say things like this, but Suzuki would not contradict him. This did not mean that Suzuki was giving his support solely to Richard – no one had that feeling – but that he trusted where Richard was taking the group as a leader. Above all he saw that Richard was committed to creating opportunities for others to practice with him and his sangha.

Among his closest and most senior students, there were others whom Suzuki saw as having the commitment, potential, and inclination to develop into teachers. Of these the most prominent were Grahame and Philip in Japan, Bill Kwong in Mill Valley, and Jean Ross. Then there were Mel Weitsman (whom Suzuki had asked to take over the Berkeley zendo), Claude, Silas, and Marian of the Los Altos zendo.

Okusan had other ideas. Suzuki was planning to go to Japan to turn over his temple to his son, but she wanted him to stay there and retire. He'd accomplished what he'd come to do in America, she said, and he wasn't healthy enough to do more. He had a persistent cough and was subject to catching the flu. If he wanted to live long, he should rest. He ignored her. To Suzuki it was all just beginning.

"These sincere Americans have made up my mind," he told his friend Reverend Ogui. "I will stay in America for them. For them I will become American soil."

*T*rue *religion cannot be obtained by seeking for some good; that is the way to attain something in a material sense. The way to work on spiritual things is quite different. Even to talk about spiritual things is not actually spiritual but a kind of substitute.*

SHUNRYU SUZUKI walked up the steps beneath the giant cryptomeria through the entrance gate at Eiheiji. Beside him towered Grahame with shaved head and black robes. They were staying in the director's quarters as honored guests. To Grahame, who had attempted three painful practice periods there as a novice monk, visiting was a pleasant alternative. He watched a new American student chanting sutras while painfully sitting in seiza in the massive Dharma Hall and sympathized with his plight.

They visited with Tatsugami, the *ino*, in charge of ceremony and much of the monks' training. Once he had been the sumo champ of the monastery. He was Suzuki's age, sixty-two that year, 1966. Suzuki thanked him for being so good to Jean, Grahame, and Philip while they were there. Tatsugami was polite and interested in what Suzuki was doing in America, but Grahame also knew that Tatsugami regarded Suzuki as an inferior, a temple priest not qualified to start a monastery.

Next they met with the abbot and head of the whole Soto sect, the elderly Kumazawa-roshi. They quietly sipped the highest-quality green tea from fine old cups. Kumazawa asked if Grahame had a temple to go back to in America. Suzuki gave him the fundraising brochure. "A Zen Mountain Center," it said on the cover. It unfolded into poster size and was half filled with beautiful photographs of the Horse Pasture and surrounding views – boulders amidst live oak, mountains in the clouds, a stone-bordered creek pool in shade.

"How about the name Zenshinji?" (Zen heart/mind temple), Suzuki asked. He hinted that it would be helpful if a sincere young priest could come over to help out.

Grahame couldn't tell if Kumazawa had answered Suzuki's questions directly or not. He'd mainly made guttural sounds, but Grahame felt they'd been well received considering their lowly status. Suzuki seemed satisfied.

GRAHAME AND Suzuki stood on the platform of the Fukui train station. There had been a festive dinner with sake and laughter, and the two had missed the last train out. The next one was at 5:30 AM. Suzuki sat down, slid a newspaper inside his robe over his belly for warmth, and dozed. Grahame walked around in the cold.

A drunken man waiting for the last train in the other direction got irritated with Grahame's pacing and told him to stop and sit down. He got madder and madder at Grahame, a unique sight in his robes. Rambling in phrases that began with "We Japanese," he started lunging at Grahame with karate chops. Grahame might have had to defend himself if some men had not arrived and restrained the attacker. Fortunately the drunk's train came soon. Suzuki and Grahame were once again alone and cold. Suzuki had just sat through the whole altercation, letting Grahame deal with it by himself.

GRAHAME AND Pauline were amazed at the fund-raising brochure Suzuki had shown them: such a giant step in growth and so much money needed, such a professional and formal look, with impressive quotes and dazzling descriptions. And it was going out to twenty thousand people! Zen Center had never mailed anything out to more than a few hundred. Could Richard really pull this off? What a gamble Suzuki was taking. If it failed, he would be humiliated in the eyes of his colleagues in Japan. What faith in his students he was demonstrating!

Suzuki was trying to gather support in his homeland for the monastery in America. He had in mind to bring over some "good priests" who might lead the training for a year or a practice period. He considered Uchiyama, whom Grahame was studying with, and Niwa, Noiri, and Yokoi – all Kishizawa's heirs. But there was not much appreciation there for what he was trying to accomplish, and he couldn't get any experienced priests to commit to coming. He and his ambitious plans were puzzling. "In terms of Japan, he's just a typical country priest," Yokoi said when asked what he thought after Suzuki had visited him at Komazawa.

It was October of 1966. Suzuki had been in Japan since August 25. Okusan had stayed in America to help Katagiri tend to Sokoji. Along with Suzuki at Rinso-in were the Petcheys, Philip, who'd been at Eiheiji, and Claude, who'd flown over at Suzuki's request. He introduced them to his family, friends, colleagues, temple members, and old students from the High Grass Mountain Group as they dropped by to visit.

Philip had just finished nine months at Eiheiji. His direct, emotional style had made him popular. It was hard to imagine bulky, thick-fingered Philip in Japan, much less at Eiheiji. He had endured an enormous amount of pain, especially from long periods of sitting seiza on his shins. Everything at Eiheiji was done in seiza except for physical labor, sleep, and zazen. He had survived the tangaryo, sitting from the predawn hours till nine at night. He said they made him do two weeks of it because he could only sit in half-lotus. Philip did fine at Eiheiji, relatively speaking, because he was who he was – difficult, but not arrogant, and lovable. He took Suzuki's advice to adjust himself to his surroundings. Tatsugami had been so mad at Philip for leaving Eiheiji that he wouldn't come out of his room to say goodbye. "Stay at least one year," he said.

In Japan people are raised sitting seiza. Philip contended that it molded their tendons and bones. He'd sit two hours at a stretch in Tatsugami's chanting classes till his legs were on fire. On his first day there they made him sit like that for eleven hours in an office, the most painful experience of his life – worse than football. But he was equal to their initiations.

Now he was at Rinso-in, up to his thick thighs in the scummy water of the back pond, resetting a heavy moss-covered stone that Suzuki was sliding into place with the help of a pole. In 1963 Suzuki had sent Philip to study with a Japanese gardener of bonsai and stone in Hayward, California. He had gone almost every day for six months to work with him. Now, for the first time, he was working with Suzuki.

Philip asked Suzuki, "Am I really a monk?" The monks at Eiheiji had questioned him about his ordination and said that it wasn't real, because he hadn't gone through the proper ceremony. He hadn't done any takuhatsu, monk's begging. He hadn't had any hair shaved or received robes till he arrived in Japan.

"If you don't believe I'm a monk, don't let me in," Philip had told the dubious monks. They let him in but continued to tell him that if it wasn't done according to proper form, it didn't count. He said, "Take it up with Reverend Suzuki."

"So, am I a monk or not a monk?"

"Things go the way the mind goes," Suzuki told him. "If you think you're a monk, you're a monk. If you don't think so, you're not a monk."

In a free moment Suzuki called Philip to his room to show him a traditional way to fold his robes. He laid them out and, using two pieces of parallel bamboo, folded them back and forth like dough into a perfect square.

Philip remembered the old robes Suzuki had sent with him to return to Rinso-in. On the boat he kept them by his third-class bunk, where he slept with poor Japanese-Brazilian farmers. He entered customs with the brown bag in one hand and a small suitcase in the other. The customs official was curious about the bag. "Oh, it's just some old robes that Reverend Suzuki gave me."

Among the robes the customs official found what turned out to be a five-hundred-year-old Bodhidharma statue.

"How did you get this?" he said with suspicion.

"I don't know."

"What are you going to do with it?"

"Take it to Rinso-in. I think that's where it belongs."

Little by little Suzuki was returning Buddhist objects he had brought from Rinso-in to America. He had just borrowed them till he had something to replace them with. It was a secret.

CLAUDE AND Pauline watched as Grahame and Philip, bald-headed and black-robed, walked carefully along the edge of a rice paddy in their straw sandals. They were following Suzuki to a home to do another memorial service. The high formalism of the occasion challenged Claude's religious tastes.

"Yes," Pauline agreed with Claude, "Buddhism in Japan is a lot more complicated than the pared-down version we get from Suzuki-sensei in America." She'd been there a year and had seen a lot of this. "Here there are hungry ghosts, spirits in the trees, and fifteen hundred years of custom winding around it all."

Suzuki's students also met his old friends – godfather Amano, Seison Suzuki, the potter, and those in his High Grass Mountain Group who had survived. Claude was surprised there weren't any priest disciples – only Hoitsu, his son. There was a constant stream of visitors, but they were colleagues, friends, teachers from the kindergartens he'd started, lay students, members, villagers.

EVERY DAY Suzuki and his disciples were outside Rinso-in, sweeping, pulling weeds, cleaning windows. Villagers came to look and help out. They were getting the temple ready for the big ceremonies to come – Suzuki's stepping down and his son's stepping up to the abbotship of Rinso-in. Hoitsu joined them, as well as his older sister, Yasuko, who worked inside cleaning and preparing meals with Kinu Obaa-san, her maternal grandmother, still the matriarch of the temple. Obaa-san sat at the heated *kotatsu*, her legs under the table's blanket, mostly observing, sometimes making remarks. Occasionally she pulled out her thin porcelain pipe and smoked a pinch of tobacco.

After all the preparation, there was a horrendous typhoon. It blew tiles off the temple roof, sent a large branch crashing through a wall, and left the place a mess again. Grahame had been knocked cold when the wind smashed him into a doorway as he tried to help. With Rinso-in's extensive support group, they all put the temple back together in time for the big ceremony.

THE PETCHEYS bid farewell to Suzuki and his family outside the entryway of Rinso-in. They were on their way to England so Grahame's parents could meet their grandchildren. To Grahame there was something disturbing about the parting with Suzuki. He'd been so vague, saying nothing about the future. Why didn't he set a date for Grahame to return or offer him some role in the new monastery?

In Kamakura, Grahame and Pauline visited Philip Kapleau, who had been studying for years with Yasutani. Kapleau was furious with them for having been in Japan a year without looking him up. Wasting their time! He told them that none of the Soto teachers were enlightened – not Suzuki, not Uchiyama, nor anyone at Ei-heiji, and that they should have studied with his teacher. "I'm very happy to have studied with such unenlightened teachers," Grahame told him. It was a disappointment to have that sort of exchange with Kapleau after the wonderful time they'd had four years before, when the Kapleaus had visited Zen Center.

The Petcheys sailed off to Russia to take the Trans-Siberian Railway to Europe with nothing warm to wear – in fact, with nothing to wear but what they had on. All their bags had been lost in transit to the docks in Yokohama. Pauline had gone shopping and bought the kids some silly Mickey Mouse blue jeans and warm Donald Duck boots. She was wearing a summer dress and Grahame a suit. That's what they wore all the way to Moscow, wrapping themselves with newspapers to keep warm. Luckily Grahame had all the money and papers with him in a valise. Not long after they were out to sea, some Russian women pressed vegetarian Grahame to eat borscht and sausage. He was entering into new worlds, and was ready for the change. Japanese Buddhism was so exhausting.

OCTOBER 23. Shunryu Suzuki walked among the tall cedars in his formal pilgrimage gear – black robes, round bamboo hat, with white cotton gaiters covering his lower legs and forearms. It was a good day for Suzuki's farewell, for him to retire from the duty of being abbot in the Stepping Down Ceremony, and for Hoitsu to take on his father's role in the Mountain Seat Ceremony.

Claude noticed that they had to recruit a relative to be the head monk for the ceremony. He wondered why were there no real students or monks who could fulfill this role. What sort of Zen master had no disciples? More and more it seemed as if Suzuki was just an ordinary Soto Zen priest. There must be fifteen thousand of them. How do you learn about Buddhism, he wondered? Do you find the best master, or is the best master the priest who's nearby? And which was Suzuki?

There was another image-shattering formality. Not only had Suzuki passed Rinso-in to Hoitsu on this trip, but he had also given Shoko Okamoto dharma transmission. Shoko had not studied with Suzuki, but was the disciple and son of his old dharma brother Kendo Okamoto. This was done in accordance with an old agreement between Suzuki and Kendo Okamoto. These two monks who had never studied with him were his only dharma heirs in Japan.

"Don't you have any monk students who studied with you?" Claude asked him later. "No, I never had any disciples in Japan," Suzuki said.

"THERE ARE those who think my father is not so great," Hoitsu said, irritated at the adoration of Suzuki's Western followers. "He should have stayed until he passed the temple on to me. Some see him as a deserter. If he had stayed, I would have been able to study with him." Suzuki thought that other masters would make better teachers for his son, but he had asked Hoitsu to consider coming to America to help him out. In deference to his father, Hoitsu had tried to prepare: he had stopped studying the martial art of kendo, which he loved, to be tutored in English, which he hated. It was so painful that his father had agreed in correspondence to let him give up and go back to kendo. Hoitsu also didn't want to further antagonize the

Rinso-in members by leaving them, as his father had done. And Hoitsu wasn't attracted to the whole American thing. If his father hadn't given up his temple, he told Philip, he could still be at Eiheiji.

It amazed Philip that Eiheiji wasn't difficult for Hoitsu; and Hoitsu didn't even like zazen. He was there three years, in charge of the Joyoden, Dogen's memorial hall. Now he had to run Rinso-in, get married, have a family, and look after all the members and branch-temples – and along with the responsibilities came the inescapable temple politics.

How could he get married with a kitchen like that, he asked his father. It was so small, with a wood-burning hearth-type stove – too much work, nothing modern. Suzuki said a priest shouldn't seek for some glamorous woman who needed expensive things. No wife would have him with that kitchen, Hoitsu replied. Suzuki asked Godfather Amano and some other wealthy members to help get the kitchen remodeled so his son could establish a family, and it was soon done.

IT WAS TIME for Suzuki to return to America. He had done what he'd come to do. Before leaving Rinso-in, he ordained Claude as a priest in another of his mysteriously abbreviated ceremonies and asked him to stay at Rinso-in as a first step in turning it into a temple where Westerners and Japanese could practice together. He also talked to Philip about going to the East Coast to assist a zazen group in Vermont that he had close ties to.

He visited his family's ashes sites behind the temples at both Rinso-in and Zoun-in. He cleaned up the grave and offered incense to his master, Gyokujun So-on, to his father, Butsumon Sogaku, to his mother, Yone, to his second wife, Chie, to So-on's lover, Yoshi, and with great sadness to his daughter Omi, who had hung herself two years before. Suzuki was not proud of himself as a family man. On this trip he had brought to these departed loved ones his greatest offering and only atonement – Western disciples and the hope for his dharma seeds to be spread and to cross-pollinate the Buddha's way between the two cultures he lived and breathed.

*Usually we think our mind is working very well when we attach
to or concentrate on something. But actually we are already making
a big mistake because we misunderstand our mind as something
which is continuous. Our mind is not continuous at all. It is more
than continuous or discontinuous.*

WHEN SUZUKI returned to San Francisco in November 1966, he found it had changed considerably. A veritable cultural explosion was occurring. There were more long-haired young people than before; the *San Francisco Chronicle* columnist Herb Caen had dubbed them "hippies." The publicity from the fund-raising drive had brought more people to zazen, many wearing beads and colorful loose clothing.

I was one of the newcomers, a scruffy, talkative twenty-one-year-old from Texas. After dropping out of college in 1964, I spent the spring and summer involved with civil rights and left-wing student groups in Mississippi and the Midwest. After that I lived in Mexico for a year. In the winter of 1966 I came to San Francisco. For months I wandered around getting high on marijuana and enjoying the carnival-like atmosphere of the hippie scene. A few times I took LSD and meditated in silence, with a friend acting as guide. As a result of these experiences I decided to leave the drugs behind, find a guru, and learn to meditate. The first time I went to the Zen Center, Suzuki was in Japan. I felt comfortable with Katagiri and the people who sat there. Despite having been told very little about zazen and Zen, and with no particular encouragement from anyone, I nevertheless resolved to come every morning for both zazen periods and every afternoon for one year.

Then one day Suzuki was back. Our first encounter was when I bowed to him after zazen. I could barely see him through the million thoughts that raced through my mind. A moment later I was in the hall putting on my sandals. I could see Suzuki in his office, behind the crowd of people on their way out. Still my mind was bubbling. He turned, caught my eye, and smiled, and for the tiniest increment of time everything stopped, and I saw him. Later Silas introduced us; my mind was racing again, and I don't remember anything about it, but I still hold a snapshot in my memory of that first moment of direct contact with the man who had just become my teacher. More than anything, it was in small, seemingly insignificant, nonverbal exchanges that Suzuki established contact with students and guided us along our invisible paths. We were almost entirely on our own.

WHEN SUZUKI returned from Japan, almost everyone was addressing him as Suzuki-roshi. Alan Watts had sent a donation for the purchase of the Horse Pasture and included a letter suggesting that it was time to stop calling Suzuki "reverend." Watts said it was not an appropriate title, and they were using it incorrectly anyway. He advised against calling him "sensei" as well. They should say "Suzuki-roshi" and use "sensei" for assistants like Katagiri.

Richard and some of the others had been calling him "roshi" for years, but the community had not made up its mind how to address Suzuki till then. In the *Wind Bells* of the time one could find references to Shunryu Suzuki, Rev. or Reverend Suzuki, Suzuki Sensei, Sensei, Roshi Shunryu Suzuki, Suzuki-roshi, Master Suzuki, and Master of Sokoji.

Watts's suggestion came from his familiarity with Rinzai Zen, in which the title "roshi" really does mean something close to "Zen master." In Soto Zen, "roshi" is used as a term of respect by priests to address older priests.

Suzuki asked why people were calling him roshi. When they told him about Alan Watts's letter, he became convulsed with laughter. His older students talked to him about it in a meeting. He protested but, after discussing it with Katagiri, finally gave in, and from then on he was Suzuki-roshi.

RESPONSE TO the brochure had been enormous. Money poured in from all over the country. As Suzuki had hoped, at the last moment the Becks agreed to sell Tassajara Springs, for twice the price of the undeveloped Horse Pasture, three hundred thousand dollars. The board quickly authorized Richard to put the twenty-two thousand dollars that had been raised for the Horse Pasture toward purchasing Tassajara, which was ready to move into. The first payment was made in December. But now there was another payment of twice that amount due in a few months. A second brochure was sent to eighty thousand people. A few months earlier, Zen Center had been known only to a small, esoteric group of Buddhists, scholars, and artists. Now, for better or for worse, it was on the map.

So many people had helped. There were a number of benefits and a "zenefit," where the Grateful Dead, Big Brother and the Holding Company, and Quicksilver Messenger Service played at Chet Helm's Avalon Ballroom. Ali Akbar Khan gave a concert. Charlotte Selver and Charles Brooks offered a body/mind awareness workshop. Alan Watts gave a talk. Gary Snyder and many other poets, artists, and musicians donated time, readings, performances, and works. Suzuki showed up at the zenefit and waved to the crowd, who cheered him.

Many people were giving all their spare time to fund-raising, helping out in the office, going down to Tassajara to get it ready. Silas Hoadley, Zen Center's treasurer, raised money and negotiated no-interest loans to help the group cope with the enormous increase in expenses. Wanting Zen Center to be as solvent as possible, he had strongly supported the idea that they continue to run Tassajara as a summer resort. Plans were made for a guest season and a summer practice period. There were reservations to be taken, food to be purchased, students to be signed up.

Suzuki was amazed at all the checks that arrived in the mail, at the full zendo, the overflow of people sitting in the balcony, and the swelling attendance for his lectures. Richard was taking Suzuki to the East Coast to give talks, to visit Zen groups and friends like Elsie Mitchell of the Cambridge Buddhist Society, and to meet potential donors. Suzuki expressed concern for Richard's health. How could he keep it up? But Richard was fine, feeling his oats.

Amidst all this activity Suzuki still focused on being at zazen and keeping the temple clean, never losing sight of the purpose for the whole exciting venture. Spending a whole afternoon on a cushion at the low table in his office, Suzuki drew a sumi circle for the cover of the second brochure, drawing one incomplete circular stroke after another till he got the one he wanted.

SEEING THE endless work that had to be done, Suzuki realized he needed the help of his senior disciples. Jean was already around. Claude came back from Rinso-in, and Philip would not go assist the Vermont group. He also wrote to Grahame in England praising him for his accomplishments in Japan, mentioning how highly he'd been spoken of at Eiheiji and Antaiji. Now Suzuki wanted him back.

"When I returned I found San Francisco quite a different place, more active than before. It is so nice and warm here. Please tell your mother-in-law to come back here." He asked Grahame to write to the monk Kobun Chino in Japan to make sure he was coming over to help, as they had discussed. "I think we should concentrate on this project right now, because we have announced it all over America and Japan. In England some people know about it already too. Especially if we fail, Japanese people will not trust us anymore. So for me now the Tassajara Project is a matter of vital concern. I want you to come back to San Francisco as soon as possible."

Suzuki further appealed to Grahame by writing out a quote from the first brochure, turning its intent toward Grahame:

The establishment of a Zen monastery in the wilderness area near Carmel Valley is an important event in the history of religion in America. You are urged to join this oldest of ventures – the establishment of a community for the cultivation of the spirit. Only your support will make it possible.

Paul Lee, Professor of Philosophy, University of California, Santa Cruz

Grahame couldn't come back right away. He had taken a year's lease on an apartment and had a job. Why hadn't Suzuki asked him when they were in Japan? He could have arranged for a one-month visit to England. Grahame now had a zendo, where people came and sat with him. A disciple of Soen Nakagawa was helping him. So he'd have to be there at least a year. Suzuki was disappointed. He wrote again to Grahame: "Please send my best regards to your wife and children and mother-in-law. Pauline's drawing of the rock garden at Rinso-in is so real to me that I hang it in my bedroom." He sent the name and address of an old friend to look up, "my old teacher of English when I was at Komazawa University, Miss Nona Ransom."

Chapter Fifteen

Tassajara

1967–1968

The goal of Buddhism is to bring about right human life, not to have the teaching, or teacher, or sentient beings, or Buddhism, or Buddha. But if you think that without any training you can have that kind of life, that is a big mistake.

THE OPENING ceremony for Tassajara as Zenshinji, Zen Mountain Center, was held on a sizzling July 3, 1967. Over 150 people attended the opening ceremony, including members of the Sokoji congregation, old students and friends of Suzuki's, and a smiling old priest called Bishop Sumi, who in 1965 had replaced Yamada at Zenshuji in L.A. Wako Kato also came up from L.A., as did Maezumi. Kato was amazed at the beauty of the place and the large number of students. A few already had simple grey robes, and some of the men had shaved their heads, following the example of their teacher.

Although in Japan it might have gone on for days, the California ceremony lasted just over an hour. It was a day of great joy, high expectations, and collective gratitude. It was certainly a big day for Suzuki – a milestone in his life.

Kobun Chino had arrived from Japan to be a priest for the Los Altos zendo; but for the foreseeable future he would be needed at Tassajara. He was friendly, spoke English well if slowly, and was cherubic. He knew the details of Eiheiji life and ceremony and would be the students' Zen friend and Suzuki's technical advisor. Zen Center had no formal affiliation with Soto Zen in Japan, and no one from Soto headquarters was there to officially recognize the opening of this pioneering Buddhist monastery in the Western Hemisphere. But they had sent Kobun with the generous gifts of a *taiko,* a huge standing drum, and some other necessary ceremonial instruments: a wide bowl bell, and a mokugyo, giant and hollow, made from one piece of wood, with dragons carved on the side. It was hit with a padded mallet to keep rhythm during chanting. Mokugyo means "wooden fish," but it looked more like a snail.

THE NIGHT before, Richard Baker had been ordained as a priest in a full ceremony. For the first time, Suzuki did a priest ordination that wasn't private and extremely brief. Richard looked awkward in his heavy black robes, sweating before his family, his fellow students, and a crowd of close associates. Suzuki was standing before him, chanting, ceremoniously sprinkling water on him with a fern. Suzuki gave Richard the Buddhist name Zentatsu Myoyu (Penetrating Zen, Mysteriously Dissolving). He was also installed as head monk of the Tassajara practice period, which would begin in this season of blazing sun. Normally there would be some years before a newly ordained priest became head monk, but Suzuki considered that Richard had done the work between the two initiation ceremonies already. Suzuki was also ignoring seniority in choosing his first head monk. Jean, Philip, and Claude were at the ceremony, and all three had been ordained as priests years before Richard.

Richard was a busy man with a lot of work ahead of him. He was still the president of Zen Center and editor of *Wind Bell,* and now the head monk, too. To many of those who had been practicing zazen every morning and evening as they got the place into shape, Richard had seemed like a busy outsider who didn't fit in. Those who had been around long enough to have some perspective appreciated what he was doing and knew he was making a sort of sacrifice so others could have this opportunity. But more than half of the students at Tassajara were rather new. Time slowed down and the whole world tended to shrink to the size of that valley after you had been there for a while.

On the day of the opening it all came together. Suzuki gave a talk in which he made clear how much they all owed to Richard. "I am so grateful to Zentatsu Richard Baker for all he's done to establish Buddhism in America." After that, Richard moved from behind the scenes of Tassajara to the forefront, not only as organizer but also as primary disciple.

RICHARD AND Suzuki had been going over every aspect of student life at Tassajara. Richard always spoke his mind with Suzuki and had a great deal of influence in deciding what sort of place it was going to be. Suzuki respected his opinion and his insight and often seemed to defer to him. He conferred with others, of course, like Claude, Silas, Bill, Jean, and Mel. But while many people had been working hard to make this day a reality, Richard's role in establishing Tassajara was close to that of cofounder. He was defining Zen Center and Tassajara, but he ran everything through Suzuki. They had become a team.

Before anyone had gone down to Tassajara, Suzuki and Richard had considered the prospect of having a monastery with men and women living and practicing together. There had been some talk of having separate practice periods for men and women, but it never got very far. Many of Suzuki's students were couples who both practiced, and some of his strongest students were women. Richard said he wanted his wife and daughter to be able to spend time with him there, at least in the summer. He also thought it would be harder to raise money to buy Tassajara if it wasn't coed. Suzuki had no experience with women in a monastic setting, but he was willing to try. "No women, no Tassajara," Richard summed it up, and Suzuki threw out a twenty-five-hundred-year-old tradition.

Suzuki had wanted to have a tangaryo that was five to seven days long, but Richard thought that three days of constant sitting would be enough of an initiation for the eighty or so students who were signed up. Some had never even sat zazen before. Suzuki deferred. He had doubts about doing the chants in English, but Richard urged that they start chanting something in English right away. They agreed that the long meal chant would be translated and chanted in English during lunch, which, like most meals during the practice period, would be eaten in the zendo while sitting on zafus – an extension of zazen.

IN RICHARD's ordination ceremony, Suzuki gave him the precepts, the Buddhist ethical guidelines. Suzuki read them and Richard agreed to follow them. He wouldn't kill, steal, misuse the senses, elevate himself above others, slander the teachings, and so forth. Suzuki had talked about precepts a little in lectures, but on that day he gave them in public for the first time since the lay ordination of fifteen people in 1962. Precepts had always seemed like something far off: strictures that Indian and Chinese monks were involved with. As in the lay ordination of 1962, the ceremony was to be in Japanese. Richard asked if it should be translated, and said he didn't want make promises that would be impossible to live up to.

"Just say yes," Suzuki told him.

The most important point is to follow the schedule and to do things together.

IN THE COOL dark of early morning, at 4:30 AM, a student offered incense, took the handbell from the altar of the Tassajara stone zendo, and ran around the cabins ringing the wake-up bell. Glass kerosene lamps were lit in rooms, and students washed their faces, brushed their teeth, and donned robes or loose clothing. In front of the zendo hung a thick board with Chinese characters on it. A woman in a grey robe picked up a mallet and hit the board, called the *han,* one strike per minute. Its sound pierced the whole valley, calling all to the zendo for morning zazen. Students walked silently with their hands held together just below the chest, a position called *shashu,* used for zendo activities.

Fifteen minutes later, when Shunryu Suzuki walked in, students were to be on their zafus, with a few in chairs, seated erect, chins in, eyes half-open. Suzuki offered incense and sat on his zafu, tucking his robes under his crossed legs, then swung left to right in diminishing arcs until he was still. Suzuki and Kobun sat facing out; everyone else sat facing the century-old walls built of mountain stone. The large new drum at the back of the zendo was hit in tandem with the new hanging bell outside, creating deep, rich sounds. After ten minutes there was only the sound of Tassajara creek, an occasional pot banging in the kitchen, someone clearing their throat. Now they were all in harmony – Suzuki, Richard, Philip, Bill, Silas, a number of older students, and many new ones: following their breaths, counting their breaths, just sitting, looking, with no props and no beliefs, some sleepy, some with chattering minds, some with legs already aching. No hurry. Sit zazen, and compulsive thinking and dominating emotions will be eroded, as a mountain is smoothed over in time by wind and rain.

After forty minutes a small bell rang and there followed ten minutes of kinhin. Suzuki walked around observing and correcting, spacing people evenly apart, showing with his fist between their ankles how far apart the feet should be.

The morning schedule continued with another zazen period, then morning service as at Sokoji, beginning with nine full bows and featuring the *Heart Sutra* recited three times in the old Sino-Japanese. Anyone who had been around knew the *Heart Sutra.* With the punctuating bells and the rhythmic thump of the mokugyo, it got the blood going, bringing everyone together in a choral, multi-tonal, quasimusical experience of dynamic harmony and energy.

EVERYTHING AT Tassajara was unusual compared to any other version of American life, but the most exotic part of the schedule for a newcomer was the oryoki style of eating. Oryoki are cloth-wrapped eating bowls. The Soto Zen way of using them is a simple yet elegant ceremony that includes chanting, unwrapping and setting out bowls and utensils, eating, and cleaning up – all without leaving your zafu. The oryoki meal at Tassajara was a type of active, concentrated zazen that took almost an hour, less than half of which was spent actually eating. Clackers were hit signaling servers to enter, bow, and ladle out food from large pots. At the end of the meal, servers brought hot water; the bowls were washed and wiped clean. Wash water was collected in buckets and later poured on the garden. Bowls were wrapped, and after the final chant, the students fluffed their cushions and stood. Everyone bowed with Suzuki at each of three rings of a small bell. Then he walked out, followed by Kobun and Richard. Another bell was hit, and people walked slowly in shashu to greet the light of day after three hours in the zendo.

A short break after the meal was followed by a study period, then morning work, which ended in sweltering heat. By eleven o'clock they were back in the zendo for a sauna-like zazen, a brief service, and lunch. An afternoon work period was broken by a tea break, blessed bath time, evening service, dinner, and two hours of zazen or a lecture in the evening. At the end of the day most students fell asleep as soon as they lay down – at about 9:30. Up to seven hours of the day would have been spent in the zendo. Four-and-nine days were almost days off; then there were only two zazen periods, one in the morning and one in the evening. Between breakfast and dinner people could sleep, hike, do laundry, read, or talk.

This was the Tassajara schedule, the heart of Tassajara life. It was formidable, and no one could do it without earnest intent. Some men who had been in the army likened it to boot camp, without the harshness. But a slight person could practice this discipline as well as a strong one. Suzuki did it all, morning to night, day after day, setting the tone and the pace, unhurried, at home, just being himself.

Through the years the schedule would be the first teacher that new students would have at Tassajara. "Just follow the schedule," they'd be told when they arrived. That would be enough. People who didn't necessarily get along nevertheless supported each other and respected each other for continuing with the schedule, day in day out. It was climbing a mountain, trekking through a jungle, crossing a desert. It was waiting patiently like a hunter, not moving for hours. It was sitting with pain or with subtle feelings of deep pleasure. Bubbling up from people's minds came anxiety, confusion, fear, joy, giggling. In time, moments of clarity and satisfaction started to appear in the hearts and minds of Suzuki's diverse students as they followed the schedule together, taking the first step in establishing Dogen's way in the California wilderness.

Just to be there in the corner of the garden is enough.

AUGUST AT Tassajara was dry and hot. The clean air carried the smells of sun-baked sycamore leaves and fresh bread from the ovens in the kitchen. Tassajara Creek was low but still gurgling, a host to dragonflies, turtles, and tiny flies called no-see-ums that buzz around the eyes at dusk. At eleven in the morning Suzuki was in his baggy black monk's work clothes, using an iron bar to shift a big stone with Philip.

All around him Tassajara was finding its rhythm. The generator purred, and a table saw whined at the shop. The beat-up 1953 Chevy pickup bounced on the bumpy road to Grasshopper Flats to get some two-by-fours, kitchen workers chopped vegetables and kneaded bread, the person in charge of the zendo for the day filled lamps with kerosene and trimmed the wicks. Students in jeans or black robes walked past the cabins on the dusty road and glanced at Suzuki making his new garden. It had been a long time since he'd had a garden to work in.

Undistracted, sweating, ignoring flies, Suzuki worked quietly, steadily, and with obvious satisfaction. Whatever he did, he did it completely, with his whole body and mind. Once he said, "A tiger catches a mouse with all its strength." There was nothing Suzuki liked more than working in his garden at Tassajara, just quietly moving in the midst of his students, close to the earth and what grows out of it.

I think most of us study Buddhism like something already given to us. We think what we should do is preserve the Buddha's teaching, like putting food in the refrigerator. We think that to study Buddhism is to take the food out of the refrigerator. Whenever you want it, it is already there. Instead, Zen students should be interested in how to produce food from the field, from the garden, should put the emphasis on the ground. If you look at the empty garden you won't see anything, but if you take care of the seed it will come up. The joy of Buddhism is the joy of taking care of the garden.

LOUISE PRYOR was Suzuki's first personal attendant. Having no predecessor to learn from, she had to figure out for herself what the job was all about. She liked the way he set up his cabin, simply and with muted colors. Everything had a place. Things were beautifully spaced. Nothing was new or specially purchased for the cabin. On the first morning of her new position, Suzuki washed his feet on the doorstep after working in the garden. Louise, who was standing just inside the door, handed him a towel. She then reached down and pinched one of his toes. He smiled and said, "That is one of the powers of Buddha."

"What?"

"To see what someone needs and give it to them."

Another time Louise said to him, "I compare myself to other students and feel inadequate. I haven't read anything about Buddhism."

"Oh! That's the best way to come to practice," Suzuki answered.

LOUISE LOVED to walk him to the baths. He was never in a hurry. When he met people along the way, he'd stop and bow, looking directly in their faces. Louise saw how his face would change to reflect the person he met. Sometimes he would stand on the arched bridge over the stream, looking down for a long, long time.

She'd seen him in vulnerable situations. Once, as she drove him into Tassajara from San Francisco, he asked her to pull over. He got out to take a leak off the side of the road. Louise called out that maybe he shouldn't have had that second cup of coffee at the Thunderbird, the bookstore cafe in Carmel Valley. As she stretched her legs beside the car, she heard a sound like a small rock tumbling down the steep incline past manzanita, madrone, and oak. "Oh!" Suzuki called. "My teef!" Louise went over and discovered that his false teeth had fallen out. He looked pathetic and comical, like a skid-row bum. Suzuki scooted down the bank, getting his robes all dirty. They looked and looked but couldn't find the teeth. At Tassajara he had her drive straight to his cabin and refused to see anyone till another set of teeth arrived from San Francisco.

Our rules are based on a warm, kind mind.
It is not so important to follow the rules literally.

BEFORE TASSAJARA, rules didn't seem so important. One might think about how the precepts applied to one's everyday life in the city, but the main thing people did together was zazen, and Suzuki always emphasized that zazen included all the precepts. If he pushed your back in with his stick when you were slumping, you'd no more argue with him than with your tennis coach about the proper grip on the racket. But outside the Tassajara zendo lurked trouble, especially now that men and women were living and working together closely in a monastic situation. The rules took on more gravity. Within the context of that demanding life, however,

Suzuki's way was easygoing; he liked to keep rules to a minimum and would suggest new ones only as problems occurred.

IN APRIL of 1967, before the official opening, a crew was preparing Tassajara for the first practice period, and Suzuki came down from San Francisco for a week to join his young, hard-working students. He followed the schedule, sitting zazen early, doing physical labor during the days – stonework, sweeping, and cleaning. In the evenings he'd lecture, and there would be questions. A lot of the discussion had to do with the demands of the new round-the-clock communal situation.

Bob Halpern's hand shot up at the end of Suzuki's first lecture. Bob had been coming up from L.A. to the August sesshins at Sokoji for a couple of years, and now he was at Tassajara. Bob was always trying to be a model student, fanatically attempting to do everything right, and tripping over himself in the process. Suzuki had a soft spot for him because of his enthusiasm and mischievousness.

Bob asked if it might not be good for Tassajara to have more rules, like monasteries in Japan. For instance, people were using the baths outside the scheduled time, and there was a lot of talking going on there. Like an amoeba dividing, the room polarized. There were serious nods and exasperated exhalations.

"Yes, rules are important," Suzuki said. "And if there are rules you should just follow them. But if there is no rule you don't necessarily have to make one." He paused. "Hmmm . . . yes . . . rules . . . good . . . we need some rules." Then he looked around with a twinkle in his eye and fixed on the corner of the room. "Ah, see that broom over there? It's standing on its bristles. That's not so good for the broom. The bristles will bend, and it won't work so well or last so long. It's better to rest the broom on the handle. There – that's a good rule."

I was there that evening, and I've always thought of this as the first rule of Tassajara.

THE NEXT evening during his lecture Suzuki talked about the baths. He said he appreciated people's youthful sense of freedom and was glad to see how comfortable they were with each other in the baths. On the other hand, he said that in a Zen monastery the baths are one of the three silent places, along with the zendo and the toilet. The atmosphere of the baths should be more like that of the zendo than the courtyard, where we say hi to each other and drink tea and coffee. In a monastery, he said, the baths are second only to the zendo as a place for zazen, and it would be best to reduce the distractions there by being silent and having men and women bathe separately. At the time there was mixed nude bathing, which nearly everyone thought was natural and good. He was cutting it off. There are two plunges, large tubs, he pointed out, so we can keep the same schedule and have the men on one side and the women on the other.

There were a lot of questions after the lecture. Don't Japanese families bathe together in community spas? Doesn't this support guilt-ridden American Puritanism? Suzuki said that men and women rarely bathe together in Japan, and that Japanese are very modest about their bodies. He sighed, adding that they were not Japanese, so that was no argument one way or another. "Anyway, this is the best way for us – it has nothing to do with Japan or America or good and bad. It will just be our rule and we should do it."

Most people accepted what he said, but some argued further. Two couples who had been at Tassajara before Zen Center bought it, and who had been told they could stay, left partially because of the new bath rules.

A couple of days later the guys were quietly soaking in the men's plunge after a hard day's work when tiny, naked, practically hairless Suzuki slowly entered the deep, hot sulfur water, holding a washcloth-size towel over his genitals, as they do in Japan, a practice no one else copied. Bob was there, audibly taking deep breaths, keeping an obvious silence, staring straight ahead, showing his teacher he was doing meditation in the baths as he was supposed to. Suzuki sidled up to him nonchalantly and said, "Oh, the water's very hot. How hot do you think it is?" Bob didn't know what to do.

If we feel too close, it doesn't make any sense, we cannot help each other. So we need some distance. The rules will give some distance between teacher and disciple. Because of the distance, the student may have some freedom in his activity, and the teacher will find out how to help him. When you play a game, if you are too close, you cannot play. Only when you have some distance between you can you play something.

Suzuki told an old Chinese folk tale about the difference between heaven and hell. In hell everyone has very short arms. They sit around tables full of sumptuous food, trying to eat with very long chopsticks, but they can't get the food in their mouths because the chopsticks are too long and their arms too short. They try in agony to feed themselves, to no avail. In heaven everyone also has short arms, but everyone is feeding each other across the table and having a lovely time.

He said the beings in hell are driven by greed and selfishness, always wanting more, just repeating their bad habits in confusion. So how do creatures of habit come to act naturally, like the beings in that Chinese heaven, when they're so lost to begin with? First he said, "We must establish our practice in our delusion." The way to do this is to have some rules, which we receive from those who have gone before us and whom we respect. He likened it to putting a snake in a bamboo tube. He'd had plenty of such straightening out in his life from childhood on, more difficulty and effort than his students could imagine.

What I want to talk about now is how to orient your mind in practice. For the beginner it is inevitable that there will be hard discipline, the observation of some rules. Rigid rules are not our point. But if you want to acquire vital freedom, it is necessary to have some strength, some discipline, in order to be free from one-sided dualistic ideas. So our training begins in the realm of duality or rules: what we should or should not do.

As always, his students would ask why. Suzuki said in Japan no one would even think of asking why. He admired the sincerity and honesty of his students but cautioned that it would be hard to establish a practice if they had to think about things so much. He said he wasn't asking anything unreasonable and that most questions would answer themselves in time. Philip told them of a saying at Eiheiji: "Don't say no for the first five years." Suzuki often said, "Just do it!"

WITH RULES, sometimes Suzuki would emphasize kindness and sometimes he would emphasize strictness.

When we practice our way, we should forget everything and try to find ourself in our everyday life. That is why we must be strict, we must have strict rules. Our human nature is very sneaky. Without some strict way we will go this way and that way.

The countercultural credo of the times was "Do your own thing," and vague yet passionately held ideas of love and freedom were in the air. Many of Suzuki's students had ridden the waves of hippiedom into the Zen Center, rejecting to various degrees the mores of middle America. Others had resisted the authority of government in civil disobedience or had broken the law by taking psychedelics. They had thrown off some of the shackles of their society and were looking for liberation. They were a striking mix of individualists and eccentrics who would never have ended up together, following that disciplined life, if not for Suzuki. Now they were getting up in the dark, practicing zazen in full or half lotus, chanting together in an ancient, unfamiliar language, wearing robes, eating in silence, working hard, and making every attempt to follow a life far more structured than the ones they'd rejected.

These kinds of rules are necessary, because before you start practice or realize the necessity of a religious life, before you adore something holy, you are bound in the realm of necessity, controlled completely by your sur-

roundings. When you see something beautiful, you will stay there as long as possible. When you are tired of it, you will go to another place. You may think that is freedom, but it is not freedom, it's being enslaved by your surroundings, that is all. Not at all free! That kind of life is just material and superficial.

Some people took to discipline easier than others, and some worried more about their fellow students' adherence to the rules than about their own. Some wanted less structure, and some wanted more; frequently those who wanted more had the hardest time keeping to it. A woman who had lived in a hippie commune for a year called this tug-of-war the Nazis versus the Gypsies, but of course there were more shades of grey than that. It all worked because Suzuki was there to moderate, point the way, and knock people off the position they were attached to. The path he indicated was often not in the direction that was expected. And before long he'd be there pointing in another direction that wasn't expected. He often stressed that what's important is to follow the spirit of the rules, not the letter of the law. He said that fundamentally people knew what they were doing, and their development was up to them.

Within the rules, you should try to break one. You should do something like that, on and off. Then you will know what is wrong with you.

There was a morning tea called *chosan,* held in Suzuki-roshi's cabin after breakfast and before work period, in which Suzuki would meet with his senior disciples and the officers of the monastery. They would start by prostrating together before his altar. Then the students would bow to Suzuki and he to them, everyone saying good morning. They sat in seiza on the tatami in silence while Suzuki's attendant made tea. After sipping and munching for a while, Suzuki would say something. He would comment on the quality of the morning chanting or the change of season, and when he was finished, others were free to speak. Then the everyday workings of the monastery would be discussed – meals, changes in the schedule, an upcoming ceremony, or a special problem that had arisen. It might be mentioned that someone had left Tassajara without permission, or Suzuki might clarify some temple etiquette, like a fine point on how to enter the zendo. For the officers it was the high point of the day, because they got to be with Suzuki for thirty minutes in a fairly intimate setting.

As head of the dining room during summer guest season, I generally attended the morning tea. One morning I woke up late. I'd missed zazen, service, and breakfast, looked terrible, and reeked of alcohol, having stayed up the previous night with some guests. This was not the first time I'd slept in. At tea, one of the officers looked at me, fuming. As soon as Suzuki had made his remarks and there was an opening, the officer spoke up loudly.

"Suzuki-roshi, what do you think of a student who flagrantly violates the rules of the monastery?" It was obvious whom he was talking about.

Suzuki took a sip of his tea and said, "Mmmmm." He frequently made a sound like that to give some space. Then he said, "Everyone is doing their best. This practice is not so easy."

"Yes, but, Roshi, *flagrant*. Breaking rules all the time so that everyone can see."

"Better that we see it than that they hide it."

"Yes, but shouldn't he follow the rules?"

"Of course, but you can break the rules sometimes and still follow the spirit of the rules."

The others were listening attentively. I kept my eyes down, and my occasional winces must have seemed more the result of my headache than what anyone was saying. The poor fellow wasn't getting what he wanted, but he tried again. "Yes, but, Roshi, can't you keep the rules and the spirit too?"

"Of course," said Suzuki brightly. "That's the best way."

Don't kill" is a dead precept.
"Excuse me" is an actual working precept.

SUZUKI WAS lecturing on the precepts. When he got to the third one, he said:

Do not commit adultery [laughing]. That means attachment, you know, extreme attachment. This precept emphasizes especially our attachment to some particular thing. But it does not mean not to attach to the other sex [laughing more].

Generally sex was not as big a deal in students' lives as it had been before they'd gotten involved with Zen. Suzuki's tactic was to focus on the practice, the Tassajara schedule. That didn't leave much time or energy for anything else. Almost everyone was so exhausted from following the schedule that they'd go to sleep before the fire watch went around with the good-night clackers at ten. But there would often be one or two people up late reading, sneaking into the baths, stealing food from the kitchen, or slipping into someone else's sleeping bag.

THERE WAS more interest in the topic of sex in the city. One student had been involved in a free love scene before coming to the Zen Center. After some time at Zen Center he decided to become celibate and shaved his head. "Is it necessary to have sex in order to have a complete understanding?" he asked Suzuki.

"Maybe you shouldn't have too much sex," Suzuki said and paused. "But maybe you shouldn't have too little either," he added, to howls of laughter.

ON ANOTHER day a student asked: "Roshi, I have a lot of sexual desire. When I sit I just get more. I'm trying to concentrate on my practice, so I'm thinking of becoming celibate. Should I try to limit myself in this way?"

"Sex is like brushing your teeth," Suzuki answered. "It's a good thing to do, but not so good to do it all day long."

A GIRL WEARING many strings of beads raised her hand when Suzuki asked for questions. "Suzuki-roshi, what is sex?"

"Once you say sex, everything is sex."

WITH HIS students Suzuki mainly avoided the subject, feeling there were cultural differences he just didn't understand. Sometimes he'd back off when familiar monastic forms ran headlong into sixties sexuality.

"Since you're going to be ordained, it would be better if you didn't have a girlfriend for five years," Suzuki said to me in his cabin at Tassajara.

"Oh gosh, Roshi, I don't think I can do that. I have a girlfriend here now! Didn't you know that?"

"Don't tell me," he said, averting his eyes.

How do you like zazen? How do you like brown rice?
I think this is a better question. Zazen is too much. Brown rice,
I think, is just right. But actually, there is not much difference.

AS IS COMMON in communal situations, there was often wrangling at Tassajara over food. There were raw-food proponents and eat-anything proponents, but the most fanatic were those expounding the glories of brown rice. They were influenced by the macrobiotic diet, a Japanese vegetarian movement that associated itself with Zen. It was often called the Zen macrobiotic diet. Some people came to Zen Center with the idea that eating brown rice and soybean products was integral to Zen. Others insisted there was no connection at all.

Suzuki would neither accept nor reject macrobiotics. "There is some overlap," he said once when pressed to reject it. But, in general, he had a distaste for food fanaticism. "We eat what we're served." The macrobiotic movement was reminiscent of the Brown Rice Movement in Japan during the war, zealously promoted by his old friends Kozo Kato and his wife. A good deal of brown rice was eaten at Tassajara, and Suzuki did want Tassajara's diet to be based on grains and not served in some fancy way – but he didn't want ideology served as food.

Suzuki did have trouble with the Tassajara dietary regimen, though. He got thinner at Tassajara, and some said it was because the diet was hard on him. He'd eaten white rice all his life and had trouble chewing the brown rice and a lot of the other food because of his false teeth. Ed Brown was head of the kitchen, and when there was a dish that Suzuki couldn't eat Ed would serve him something else. But he just wanted to eat the same as others. One day Suzuki broke a tooth, and he was put on a diet of soft food. "You have no idea how humiliating it is to be served mashed bananas," he told Ed.

ED HAD WORKED in the Tassajara kitchen during the previous summer, before Zen Center had purchased the resort, and had learned a lot from the chefs – especially how to make the great bread that would become the acclaimed staple for Tassajara lunches. Ed conferred with Suzuki regularly about food and factions, emotions and Zen practice.

One day Ed came to Suzuki distraught and told him he was being besieged by people with strong ideas about how he should cook – no salt, more salt; no sugar, more sugar; no dairy, more cheese. Some people were accusing him of poisoning them if he didn't accommodate their preferences. Suzuki told Ed he was the head cook and he should decide. Pressed for further advice, Suzuki told him, "When you wash the rice, wash the rice; when you cut the carrots, cut the carrots; when you stir the soup, stir the soup."

SUZUKI WAS primarily vegetarian, and he insisted that student food at Tassajara not include meat or fish, but he did not advocate strict adherence to any food regimen outside the monastery. His wife frequently served him small amounts of meat and fish at Sokoji. Even though the food at Tassajara was vegetarian, Suzuki would remind his students that in order to live we had to kill, and that we shouldn't feel morally superior because we didn't eat meat. "You have to kill vegetables, too," he said. Sometimes he'd use a meal to make a point that Buddhism wasn't the captive of any trips, especially food trips.

Suzuki had again crushed a finger while resetting stones, this time at the base of a wall at Tassajara. It swelled up and turned purple. Bob Halpern drove him into Carmel, making a special effort to sit up straight and not to talk for the first few miles, but then he started asking Suzuki about Buddhism and vegetarianism. Suzuki promptly went to sleep.

The finger wasn't broken. The doctor drilled into the nail to relieve the pressure, wrapped it up, and told him to keep it high.

Walking past the Carmel boutiques, Suzuki said to Bob, "Let's eat, I'm hungry." Bob started looking for a restaurant where they could get a vegetarian meal. "Let's eat here," said Suzuki, going into a little hamburger joint while Bob mumbled, "But, but . . ."

Bob studied the menu with horror.

"You haven't had any meat in a long time, have you?" Suzuki said to him.

"No, Roshi, not in two years. No animal food. No dairy or eggs."

"That's very good," Suzuki said, as the waitress walked up. "You order first."

"I'll take a grilled cheese sandwich." It was the best he could do with that menu.

"Hamburger please," said Suzuki, "with double meat."

Their food arrived and they each took a bite. "How is it?" asked Suzuki.

"Not bad."

"I don't like mine," Suzuki said, "let's trade." With that he picked up Bob's sandwich and replaced it with the double-meat hamburger. "Um good. This is good. I like grilled cheese."

*O*ur practice will not take you away to somewhere better. Just stay here and follow the schedule with others, not trying to be too good or to understand Buddhism too well. The most important point is not to go on any trips. Don't go on any trips.

PAUL DISCOE, Tassajara's master builder, was moving a cabin. It was one of those occasional projects that turned the monastery upside down; people were excited, immersed in the action. The study period was canceled. Lunch was informal so people didn't have to change into robes. Suzuki energetically threw himself into the project. There were trucks, jacks, chains, rope, pulleys, boards, and a two-wheel trailer. It took a lot of hands and backs to get the job done, and there was an enjoyable drama to the proceedings.

At the height of the energy, sweat, and excitement, Suzuki and Bob were watching the cabin slowly creak over the bridge. No one was enjoying it more than Suzuki. He turned to Bob. "I love work trips," he said, wiping his brow. "I hate food trips, but I love work trips."

"SHE IS TOO serious," Suzuki whispered to me, discreetly pointing to another student. We stood at the base of the grand old oak tree by the central sandstone steps. I didn't know what to make of it. I wanted to think that he was talking to me about her, but I had the uneasy feeling that he was talking to me about me. I saw myself as sort of a cutup who should probably be more serious, so why was he saying that?

Suzuki frequently used an indirect approach. In lecture he said that if he scolded you in front of others, not to feel too bad, because it might be intended for someone else who isn't ready to hear it. "If I hit you with the stick, it's because I trust you, because you're a good student. Sometimes it's for you, sometimes it's for the person next to you."

I went to Suzuki's cabin unannounced after dinner one night and was invited in. Never known for moderation, I was, at this time in my life, alternating between periods of austerity and indulgence. I felt guilty. I told him I couldn't stop snacking in the kitchen. Sometimes I'd sneak into the kitchen at night, eat leftover guest desserts, and drink their half-and-half.

Suzuki reached under his desk conspiratorially. "Here, have some jelly beans," he said.

Suzuki had great respect for the difficulty of changing one's course, for the tenacity of habit, the addictiveness of thoughts and beliefs, the power of delusion. He was always teaching the importance of developing good habits so as not to become lost and confused, the importance of not wanting too much – this was called following the precepts. "Make your best effort," he said. But still he cautioned not to try too hard, saying that we would naturally follow the precepts if we just relaxed within our practice.

In zazen it was the same. Try hard, but don't try too hard. Thoughts were easier to deal with than emotions, but the approach was the same. "In zazen leave your front door and your back door open. Let thoughts come and go. Just don't serve them tea."

ONE DAY Suzuki asked me to bring him some wheelbarrow loads of dirt, so I hauled one after another from way down the road past the baths. We made a little mountain with it in his garden, working quietly, as was the rule. While we were working I asked him a question about Zen. He didn't say a thing, just kept on working. Later, when the bell rang to end work and begin bath time, he offered me some tea. While we were drinking it outside his cabin he said, "You know, I don't want to teach anything so much. I'd rather not even give lectures. I'd just like to sit zazen with everyone, take a bath, eat simple food, and work. That should be enough."

Maybe I am a very smoky kerosene lamp [kerosene lamps were used to light the zendo]. When I start to talk about something, it is already a smoky kerosene lamp. As long as I must give a lecture, I have to explain in terms of right and wrong: "This is right practice, that is wrong, this is how to practice zazen." It is like giving you a recipe. It doesn't work. You cannot eat a recipe.

*A*s Dogen says, people like what is not true
and they don't like what is true.

ONLY THE first practice period was in the summer. After that Tassajara settled into the traditional pattern of having two ninety-day practice periods a year, one that started in early fall and one that started in winter. Philip was the head monk for the second practice period, which began in February 1968. Suzuki had a terrible flu that winter and spent a lot of time at Sokoji in bed. One day in late April, Suzuki joined his students on a walk to the Horse Pasture for a picnic. He danced while I sang a song I'd written called "I Wanna Be a Bodhisattva Baby." It was an especially enjoyable day. During his evening lecture, however, the mood changed.

There was a student who had a rather extreme reaction to the rigors of life there. He warded off the cold with a down jacket under his robe, and woolen socks and mittens, and he kept a huge stash of candy bars in his room to tide him over between meals. After Suzuki's lecture this student asked about austerity. Buddhism is the middle way, so aren't we off course if we're too hard on ourselves? Do we have to do all this Japanese stuff? Shouldn't we get more sleep?

"When you're tired, your ego is tired," Suzuki said. He agreed people shouldn't be too hard on themselves, but that Zen is hard and ignorance is deep. The bundled-up fellow kept questioning Suzuki's responses until he fumed. Then he exploded – at everyone.

"Spineless! You are spineless! All of you are spineless! You only want a sweet pill! You never want the bitter pill! Spineless!"

He stormed down to the zendo floor and began hitting the student with his short teacher's staff while shouting more. His stick couldn't penetrate the buoyant down, which made sounds like a pillow, and that made him madder. Then he went around and hit everybody two times on each shoulder. Back on his cushion he continued speaking with intense emotion.

"You say you want the truth. None of you want the truth! If I told you the truth I'd be left sitting here alone listening to the sounds of your cars driving up the road!"

Then Suzuki softened. He sat silently for a moment and sighed. "I understand you. You think that pain is bad, that suffering is bad. You think that our way is to go beyond suffering, but there is no end to suffering. When I was young I felt very bad for all the suffering that people have. But now I don't feel so bad. Now I see suffering as inescapable. Now I see that suffering is beautiful. You must suffer more."

It was a difficult point to understand and a terribly depressing ending to a lovely day. After trying long and hard, the students were being told that they refused to accept the teaching. The next morning after breakfast Suzuki spoke meekly, apologizing for having lost his temper. But he didn't take back what he had said.

In Japan, a teacher doesn't like for other teachers, especially from other sects, to come speak in his temple. He doesn't want to confuse his students and is jealous. I was the same. But this is America, so we are learning a new way.

IN THE LITTLE world of American Zen there was a big event that summer of 1968. An entourage of senior Zen teachers came to Tassajara. This gathering of priests with strikingly different styles benefited from the fresh smell of the wilderness and the magic of Tassajara. Students were excited to learn suddenly that Soen Nakagawa-roshi and Yasutani-roshi were among eight teachers coming to visit. Nakagawa was the priest who, while visiting Suzuki at Sokoji in 1959, had dramatically torn up the non-Zen sutra book. They brought some of the ashes of Nyogen Senzaki, who had died in L.A. in 1958, to be scattered at Tassajara.

All eight teachers used koans with their students and were critical of Suzuki's less aggressive style of Soto Zen, calling it sleepy and unproductive. But it was an ecumenical three days, a time to recognize Nyogen Senzaki as a primary ancestor of American Buddhism, and an initiation for Suzuki's baby monastery. Nakagawa's disciple, Eido Shimano of the New York Zen Studies Society, generously called Tassajara the hara, the center of gravity, of Zen Buddhism in America.

A number of students at Tassajara were former or even present students of one or more of the visiting teachers. Yasutani had been coming from Japan and conducting sesshins in America for six years. He was a dynamo who used the stick freely and often yelled exhortations such as, "What are you wasting your time for? Die! Die! Don't leave this zendo without having died!"

Suzuki led his guests from the baths to the steam room and then into a warm pool behind the little rock dam in the creek. They met in the fireplace room, talked and did calligraphy, exchanging their creations.

There were talks in the zendo. The wall-to-wall raised platform at the end of the zendo was crowded with the visiting priests, along with Suzuki, Kobun, and Richard. Yasutani, old, hollow-eyed and bent, spoke with vigor, scolding Soto Zen for abandoning koan practice and saying that the Japanese temple system was a weight hanging around Zen's neck. Only a return to the ancient Chinese basics would save Zen, he declared. That was one thing they all agreed on.

Nakagawa gave a dynamic lecture, strutting back and forth across the altar platform. The talks went on and on, but no one minded – it was such a treat. There were questions and answers. I asked what was the best way to establish Buddhism in America, and everyone had an answer: Yasutani, Nakagawa (both translated by Maezumi), Shimano, and then it was Suzuki's turn. "I have nothing to say," he said, getting up and going out the side door. Everyone roared in delight, and it was over.

In a talk that night Suzuki said Yasutani and Nakagawa had come to Tassajara and painted in the pupils of the eyes of the dragon that he had been drawing for years. "There's a lot for me to learn from them. Before, when I heard the word Rinzai, I always felt a little uncomfortable. It was because I felt a separateness. Now when I hear it I feel complete." (Yasutani was Soto but he used koans, like the Rinzai.)

In a ceremony with all students present, Suzuki received a portion of Senzaki's ashes from Nakagawa and placed them on the Tassajara altar. The only rain of the summer fell that morning, and a double rainbow met people as they walked out of the zendo into the early morning light. Two weeks later Suzuki, Kobun, and some students went up to the ridge and cast Senzaki's ashes to the wind.

On the last morning of the teachers' visit, everyone sat zazen. Bob was carrying the stick and sporting a down-turned samurai scowl to let his old teachers, Maezumi and Yasutani, know that he hadn't gotten soft, and that Soto Zen wasn't sleepy. He stopped before a dozing student, placed the wide stick on her shoulder, and gave her a whack on each side. They bowed together and he went on. Walking slowly down the maroon linoleum aisle, he lifted his gaze to see in the kerosene lamplight the historic cast of dharma transmitters on the platform: Suzuki, Yasutani, Nakagawa, Shimano, Maezumi, Aitken (from Hawaii), Richard, Kobun. Every one of them was nodding, sound asleep.

Chapter Sixteen

The City

1 9 6 8 – 1 9 6 9

If you want to be a circle, you must first be a square.

BACK IN San Francisco things were humming. Suzuki's students were an active presence at Sokoji all the time, in the zendo, kitchen, and office. Yvonne Rand, Zen Center's full-time secretary, shared an office with Katagiri. Yvonne was a Stanford graduate. She had met Virginia Baker at a weaving class a couple of years earlier and had become fast friends with the Bakers. Before working for Zen Center, she had taught math at a private school. She was married, had two children, loved plants and animals, had a natural tendency to help people, and at thirty years old was efficient and sharp. She was one of those people who Suzuki said were older students the day they arrived. Once she met Suzuki, Yvonne was happy to handle Zen Center's secretarial tasks for a pittance, just to be around him. It was an exciting time to be there, at the birth of a monastery. Yvonne became a board member virtually overnight too.

Richard would come into the office, joke around, get an update from Yvonne, and then be off to Tassajara. Claude was managing five rented apartments across the street, where zazen students lived and ate communally. Newcomers, mainly in their twenties, were finding their way up the Sokoji steps to learn about Zen. With all this activity, the rift between Suzuki's zazen students and the overwhelmed Japanese-American congregation widened.

Your life in the hippie age is very different. I think it is very Buddhist-like. Maybe that is why you like Buddhism. But if you become a Buddhist, your life will change more – you will become a super-hippie, not a usual one. Your lifestyle looks Buddhist, but that is not enough. When you have a strict practice that doesn't ignore the weak points of your practice, then eventually you will have good practice. More and more you will understand what Zen masters have said, and you will appreciate their lives.

There were plenty of hippies and young people of various descriptions appearing in the San Francisco streets and the Sokoji zendo. Life at Zen Center was too formal and disciplined for most of them. Doctrinal disputes were common. The air was full of ideas about what was spiritual or what was Zen. The word had a glamour to it and tended to be used freely, as in, "That's very Zen." People were making Zen into whatever they wanted. A psychedelic periodical called the *San Francisco Oracle* had reprinted the Zen Center's *Heart Sutra* chant card with an overlay of a naked woman lying across it. Zen seemed to be the coolest thing going. Zen Center often acted as an antidote to that assumption – with the silence, stillness, and alertness of zazen, the almost military crispness of the group sutra chanting, the disciplined atmosphere in the clean building, and the subdued dress and short hair of the older students.

"Man, you guys are uptight," said a long-haired, colorfully dressed young college dropout smelling of patchouli oil. "The real Zen's on the street, dancing and getting high. Anyway, your teacher can't be enlightened. He shaves his head, which means that he had to have the idea, 'I'm going to shave my head,' which means his mind wasn't in the clear light."

One student had spearheaded a drive to start a zendo in the Haight-Ashbury. He'd shown Katagiri a proposed space in the Straight Theater. Katagiri was used to hippies, but this was right in the middle of their scene. He told Suzuki that he didn't think the sort of discipline that was needed to study Zen could be sustained there.

Students had been talking to Katagiri and Suzuki about psychedelics since 1965. Of the two, Suzuki took it more seriously. Many students who'd come to him in the past few years credited psychedelics with awakening their interest in Buddhism. He was aware that Richard Baker had organized the first major LSD conference in the U.S. at the University of California extension in San Francisco. The student who was promoting the idea of the Haight-Ashbury zendo urged Suzuki to try LSD, and finally Suzuki took a capsule of the not-yet-illegal substance from him. A week later he decided to flush it down the toilet. A reporter for the biggest underground newspaper in the area interviewed Suzuki at Tassajara; after five minutes of talking about LSD, he gave up trying to find out what Suzuki's position was. He said that the best he could come up with was that Suzuki didn't seem to think it was relevant to anything.

A Stanford professor told Suzuki that many college students were smoking marijuana all the time and taking LSD. Maybe it was good in some ways for them to experiment, but it was interfering with their studies. What did Suzuki do about this problem? "Oh, nothing," said Suzuki. "I just teach them how to sit zazen, and they forget about those things pretty soon."

Suzuki would occasionally mention that he did not want people to come to the temple while high. At the wedding of a couple who were involved in the psychedelic scene, he said, "Our way is not to seek some deep experience. We accept ourselves just as we are. We do not take drugs. It is superficial." On the whole, though, he seemed quite unconcerned about drugs and alcohol. He saw more pernicious attachments among his students. When he spoke on the precept forbidding consumption or distribution of alcohol or intoxicants he sometimes gave it a surprising interpretation. "This means don't sell Buddhism," or, "This means don't try to give people some medicine, don't boast about the superior teaching of Buddhism. Not only liquor but also spiritual teaching is intoxicating."

ALLEN GINSBERG had come to be recognized as the poet laureate of the Beat and a hero of the hippie movement. He had met Suzuki a few times in the early days at the Academy and around Japantown, then later at a major Berkeley poetry conference that Richard had organized. In 1963 Ginsberg took an extensive trip to Asia, during which he investigated Hinduism and Buddhism. In Kyoto he visited Ruth Fuller Sasaki's temple and sat zazen with his old buddy Gary Snyder for six weeks at Oda-roshi's temple in the Daitokuji complex. He was delighted with this first experience of zazen and a little miffed at Snyder for not introducing him and Kerouac to zazen years before, when they visited Snyder's Horse Pasture Hermitage in Marin County, one of the first zendos in the West. Upon his return to America, Ginsberg meditated at Sokoji a few times in the fall of 1963. It was a little restrictive for him; he liked to hit cymbals and spontaneously chant and sing Hindu songs during his meditation, but he was always appreciative of Zen Center practice and from time to time he recommended that people go there.

On January 14, 1967, Ginsberg and Suzuki met again. Some students had brought Suzuki to the Human-Be-In in Golden Gate Park, where tens of thousands of hippies, fellow travelers, and the curious gathered to celebrate, dance, get high, and enjoy the sunshine. As usual, Okusan had tried to stop him, saying he should rest, but it was a free Saturday afternoon and some students were begging him to go, so he did. Suzuki was welcomed on the platform, where he sat with Ginsberg, Timothy Leary, Gary Snyder, and the poet Michael McClure, among others. A young woman handed him a god's eye, a multicolored, hexagonal religious symbol on a stick, allegedly American Indian in origin. After a while he passed it on, and someone else gave him a flower. He sat there with the flower and enjoyed the flower children, the music, and the idealistic speeches. He was there when Owsley, the manufacturer of Clear Light Acid, parachuted in. After a while Suzuki excused himself and was taken home. Gary Snyder told Ginsberg it was significant that he'd come, a recognition that there was more to the aspirations of youth than hedonism and foolishness.

In the spring of 1968 Ginsberg returned to Sokoji to ask for permission to use Suzuki's translation of the *Heart Sutra,* which he wished to sing in public. "I've looked at all the translations," Ginsberg said, "and am most intrigued with yours. It's so succinct." He called the style "telegraphese." Suzuki hadn't even thought of it as a translation. Ginsberg showed him the sutra card that the zazen students used at Sokoji to chant the sutra in Sino-Japanese. There were the romanized syllables, the Chinese characters, and the basic meanings of the terms in English below that. Suzuki had never intended the English to be chanted. Ginsberg had memorized it and created a melody. He sang his version to Suzuki and asked if it would be all right for him to perform it in public. "Sure," said Suzuki enthusiastically. "Please do. You have the right spirit."

AN ENTHUSIASTIC new arrival told Suzuki-roshi he wanted to move into the temple to be closer to him. "That would be good," Suzuki said, "but it would make the other students jealous. So why don't you come to the temple before morning zazen and we'll clean together?"

The next morning he joined Suzuki at 4:15, and they cleaned the zendo and halls and bathrooms till 4:45, when people began to arrive for zazen. They vacuumed, mopped, and dusted.

One morning as they were cleaning Suzuki excused himself. Suddenly there came a sound of knocking and then a voice calling in Japanese. Suzuki was in the bathroom by his office, brushing what teeth he had left. He went out to the stairway to see what the racket was. He and the student tried to locate the source of the ever-increasing pounding and yelling. Suzuki opened the door to the basement.

There was Okusan, full of fury, screaming at him. She'd been locked in all night. The women's club had met the night before, and they had gone around and locked up too thoroughly before they left. She'd been taking a bath, while Suzuki was upstairs reading. Finally he'd gone to sleep not noticing that she wasn't back. He even got up in the middle of the night to pee as always, not noticing that she wasn't in her bed and her sandals weren't at the door. She yelled at him machine-gun fashion.

Suzuki realized what had happened and began to laugh. He laughed so hard that foam from the toothpaste ran down from his mouth onto his kimono. The new student got out of there.

The world of thinking is that of our ordinary dualistic mind. The world of pure consciousness or awareness is that of buddha-mind. Phenomena in the world of thinking are constantly being named or labeled by our minds. The world of awareness does not label or name, it only reflects. The world of pure consciousness thus includes the opposites in the world of thinking.

ALAN WATTS, Richard De Martino, and Eric Fromm, among others, had written about Zen and psychoanalysis. Some psychologists and psychiatrists had taken an interest in zazen and other forms of meditation. Would it help their patients? What did it do? How could it help them learn about consciousness? Dr. Joe Kamiya of the Langley Porter Institute was doing tests on meditators. Some of the students at Zen Center had gone to get hooked up to his electroencephalograph to see how their brain waves changed when they meditated. A number of students had prolonged states of alpha with some theta waves, which were correlated with calm states of mind. Richard Baker and his friend Mike

Murphy from Esalen Institute produced theta waves for longer periods, characteristic of the meditation of yogis and Zen masters. Suzuki and Katagiri were wired up as well. Both of them fell asleep immediately.

Suzuki respected some aspects of Western psychology and psychotherapy based on what he'd heard from analysts he'd met, but he didn't claim to understand it and didn't compare it to Zen. He made it clear that Buddhism was not a method of self-improvement, but he did speak about body, mind, and will, revealing his own brand of Buddhist psychology and analysis.

The way to study Zen is to be always aware of yourself, to be careful, to be sincere with yourself. Awareness means that when reading, including Zen materials, your mind should not get caught by any idea. It should remain open. Similarly with sights and sounds: don't allow your mind's self-awareness to get lost or absorbed. In other words, always remain conscious of what you are doing, of what is going on.

A psychiatrist and researcher named Arthur Deikman had had a life-changing experience in the early fifties when he began to meditate on his own every day in the woods. That led to years of clinical experiments involving meditation. He had been amazed at the results; many subjects (all were college students) experienced a striking change of consciousness after only fifteen minutes of sitting and staring at a blue vase. What would happen to people who did this all their lives? Wanting to find a qualified meditation teacher, he came to San Francisco to meet with Shunryu Suzuki, whose name had been suggested by colleagues on the East Coast.

Deikman brought a tape recorder, but Suzuki declined to let him use it. He told Suzuki about his research and said he wanted to understand consciousness better. Suzuki told him he should go sit a sesshin with Yasutani in L.A. Not knowing what a sesshin was, Deikman went and returned some weeks later. He didn't know if Suzuki had sent him because the dates just happened to be right or out of a mischievous desire to test him or throw him to the lions.

He'd had amazing experiences of altered states. At one point his head had seemed to disappear. At night he'd been awakened by what he thought was someone smashing blocks together, only to find that it was the person in the next sleeping bag softly smacking his lips during sleep. While impressed with what happened working with Yasutani on koans, Deikman continued to seek out Suzuki. "Where he is is where I want to be," he told his wife, Etta, "in that place of sanity." They went to Tassajara for the summer. They worried that their very active younger daughter wouldn't fit in, but there was no problem. They even took her to Suzuki's lectures, and Etta marveled at how her child would calm down and fall asleep.

Sometimes in a lecture Suzuki would say something that seemed to speak directly to Deikman's conundrums, but more important to Deikman than Suzuki's words was his attitude, his perspective on the world, his transparency.

From what he'd seen and heard at Zen Center, Deikman knew that Suzuki wouldn't be excited by any special states of mind that came up during his zazen. After a lecture, a student just back from a private thirty-day sesshin had asked Suzuki how to maintain the state of mind he'd attained.

"Concentrate on your breathing, and it will go away," Suzuki said.

In another lecture Suzuki said, "If you're dissatisfied with your zazen, it shows you have a gaining idea." The next time he talked to Suzuki, Deikman just told him there seemed to be more clarity, vividness, and intrinsic value in his experience – nothing he could define, but he felt he'd had a glimpse of Zen. "That might be the case," Suzuki said. But in time Deikman got discouraged. He experienced these higher states, but they just passed. What was the use?

Suzuki laughed and said, "That's right, no use. All these states come and go, but if you continue, you find there's something underneath."

"You can't have it, because in the act of having it, it's gone," said Deikman.

"Yes, that's right," Suzuki answered.

Deikman continued to come to the West Coast to see Suzuki. As with most people, the reason he came was not the reason he stayed. He remembered what Suzuki said to him when he first came to learn more about consciousness: "I don't know anything about consciousness. I just try to teach my students how to hear the birds sing."

The true experience of Zen is not some ecstasy or some mysterious state of mind, but it is a deep joy that is even more than joy. You may have this true experience through some change in your mental state. But a change of mental state is not, strictly speaking, enlightenment. Enlightenment is more than that. That comes with it, but it is more than that. What we experience is joy or mysterious experience, but something follows. That something which follows, besides this experience, is true enlightenment. So we should not suppose that enlightenment will always be experienced in terms of consciousness.

There will always be war, but we must always work to oppose it.

ONE DAY in late summer of 1968, Suzuki-roshi and I sat eating hot dogs in front of the student union at the University of California at Berkeley. Before us a colorful street scene unfolded – students of every race, jocks and hippies, professors, businessmen and -women, and singing, dancing Hare Krishna devotees, with backpacks and briefcases, suits and sarongs, long hair abounding. Suzuki was comfortable amidst the ragged, revolutionary youth, and they responded well to him. In his brown robes with drooping sleeves he was immediately identifiable as an ally, not part of the establishment, and people passing him would smile, nod, or sometimes bow.

Earlier that day, I had driven Suzuki in predawn darkness to the

Berkeley zendo so he could join the morning schedule and give a talk. Mel Weitsman now lived there and was in charge. We sat around talking till midmorning when, at Suzuki's request, I had taken him to Telegraph Avenue to visit the bookstores and walk around.

People were handing out leaflets promoting Scientology and opposing the war in Vietnam. From the distance the echoes of an amplified voice approached, blasting out a message from loudspeakers mounted on a van's roof. They were calling for the overthrow of the "racist, imperialist, war-mongering United States government, by any means necessary."

"What do you think of that, Roshi?" I said. "Most people aren't even paying attention to it. Quite a country you've come to, huh?"

Suzuki kept chewing noncommittally.

I told Suzuki how almost every guy I knew had avoided the draft, some by pretending to be homosexual or crazy. Many of Suzuki's own students, including Richard and myself, had used their wiles to escape the draft.

"Roshi, I heard that you opposed the war when you were in Japan. Is that true?" I asked him.

"Yes, in a way, but there was not much I could do. We tried to look at the root cause."

"Did many priests do that?"

"No, not till after the war. Then they all did."

"What was it like then?"

"Japan was under the spell of some strange idea. There was a lot of confusion."

"How did you get away with it? How come you weren't arrested?"

"I didn't oppose the government. I just expressed ideas – like if there were peace, that the country and also the government would be stronger. And I encouraged others to think about careless assumptions."

"I heard you printed things."

"Yes, before the war – but if you saw what I wrote, you wouldn't understand. Not so direct. It was different from your situation here." He sighed. "It would be very hard to explain. You would have to know so much background."

A NUMBER of Zen students had applied for status as conscientious objectors to military service. Some were doing alternative service in the fire department at Tassajara. As a result, two FBI agents showed up at Sokoji one day and interviewed Suzuki. He didn't speak about war and peace in the clear-cut terms that they were used to hearing from Quakers and other pacifist Christians, but he did say that Buddhism sought accommodation rather than conflict, was fundamentally pacifist, and that it was better for monks not to become soldiers.

Ironically, in Japan Buddhism had never been pacifist, and all Buddhists supported the government's wars. When they asked what he thought about the Vietnam War, he startled them by saying offhandedly, "Oh yes, I have a son in Vietnam. He's a barber and a mechanic in the U.S. Army. He enlisted. My wife's worried about him, but I think he needed to get out and do something." He showed them a letter he'd just received from Otohiro. The agents finally gave up trying to understand his position. Zen Center continued to provide support for and be host to conscientious objectors.

SUZUKI WAS impossible to pin down on most issues and wouldn't support his students' positions if they were simplistic and one-sided, especially if they carelessly threw Buddhism into the mix. He encouraged people to take responsibility for their own actions and not use good deeds as an excuse to avoid facing themselves, or as a substitute for practice. Suzuki didn't like hearing the name of Buddhism hastily invoked for noble purposes any more than he liked Buddhist teachings to be twisted to serve greed, hate, and delusion, as had happened in Japan during his lifetime. If students were clear about their motives, he would be supportive.

"Roshi, can't I consider my practice to be helping people?" said a woman student after a lecture. "There are so many people who need help, and there is so much to be done. I don't have much time left over to sit zazen or go to Tassajara."

"It is very difficult to help people," Suzuki answered. "You may think you're helping them and end up hurting them."

HE WAS interested in establishing a way of life that created peace, working on the root cause of war rather than railing against the symptoms. Talking about karma, he said:

You may foolishly try to ignore karma, but this will never work, and if you fight it too much, you will invite destruction that is worse than war. We are actually creating war through our everyday activities. You talk about peace in some angry mood, when actually you are creating war with that angry mood. Ughhh! That is war! We should know. We should open our dharma eyes, and together we should help each other forever.

In the early fifties Suzuki had told his young neighbor Yamamura that he longed to go to America to teach about peace and internationalism. But his American students were already politically conscious, some of them active, and he was clearly sympathetic with the peace movement.

In 1960 Suzuki had enthusiastically supported the decision of a student named Barton Stone to join a yearlong peace march from San Francisco to Moscow. In 1964, in response to a letter from Barton, Suzuki visited him twice in prison, where he was serving a year for trying to obstruct nuclear testing in the Pacific. Later, when Barton got out of jail and visited Suzuki at Sokoji, Okusan showed him a newspaper clipping from Japan with a photo of her husband marching with other Buddhist priests. There were banners and a large crowd. She said it was a march against nuclear testing in the Pacific.

Suzuki joined Richard Baker and some other Zen students for a large demonstration in the fall of 1968, walking up Market Street in peaceful opposition to the war. His decision to go may have been influenced by an emotional exchange he had had with students a few hours earlier.

SUZUKI WAS back in town from Tassajara. People in the city missed him, and attendance was high for his Saturday lecture at Sokoji. A young man named John Steiner, who had studied with Suzuki for two years, was among those who sat near the front on goza mats. John had been involved in some of the original protests against the war at UC Berkeley two years earlier and, like a number of people at the lecture, was planning to attend the protest march that day. Minds buzzed with thoughts of life and death, peace and horror, helplessness and hope.

After his talk, Suzuki asked if there were any questions.

A woman said, "What is war?"

Suzuki pointed to the goza mats. They are about three by six feet, big enough for two cushions. He said that sometimes there are ripples on the rows of straw, and people put their hands down to push the ripples out after they sit down. This works okay on the sides, but when there's a ripple between two people, it won't smooth out; it just moves toward the other person. Without noticing it, people sometimes push these ripples back and forth toward each other. "That is the cause of war. Karma starts with small things, then it accelerates. You should know how to deal with those small difficulties."

A fellow in the back spoke up with irritation in his voice. "How come we're meeting here when there's a war going on out there?"

Suzuki didn't understand him. John repeated the young man's question more slowly and clearly: "He said, 'Roshi, how come we're meeting here when there's a war going on out there?'" Suzuki smiled. John smiled.

Then, as fast as a cat leaping on its prey, Suzuki jumped off the altar platform and was behind John with the stick on his shoulder, loudly saying, "Gassho!" He started hitting him over and over shouting, "You fools! You fools! You're wasting your time!" He continued to hit him until John fell forward on the floor. "Dreamer! Dreamer! What are you dreaming about?"

He got back on the platform and faced the totally stunned audience, most of whom had never heard him raise his voice. The normally tannish skin of his face was white, as he said unconvincingly in a barely audible voice, "I'm not angry." He caught his breath and continued. "How can you expect to do anything in the world when you can't even tie your own shoes?"

After the lecture everyone was fairly quiet. Bob Halpern came up to John and said, "Roshi told you to gassho. You didn't gassho when he hit you."

Being hit with the stick isn't a punishment; it's a particular form of communication, and part of the formality is to bow when one receives the stick. To gassho shows respect, expresses the unity of shoulder, stick, and hand, and puts the person in the best position to receive the stick. John had been so shocked he hadn't done his part in this exchange, even though Suzuki had yelled at him to gassho.

John went to Suzuki in his office to apologize for not gasshoing. Suzuki in return apologized to John very sweetly for being so fierce. John had not expected anything from Suzuki. He saw what had happened only in terms of his teacher trying to enlighten him.

"The reason I got so . . ." Suzuki said, his sentence trailing off, "is that I was reminded of what I went through in Japan during the war. It brought up that old frustration." John saw in his teacher's eyes a glint of pain. Then Suzuki put his hand on John's shoulder, an unusual gesture for him. The wide sleeves of Suzuki's robe exposed loose skin hanging down from his thin arm. John was struck with Suzuki's age and fragility and could feel his teacher's compassion and suffering.

*The teaching given by Shakyamuni Buddha during his lifetime
was accommodated to each disciple's particular temperament, and
to each occasion's particular circumstances. For each case there should
be a special remedy. According to circumstances, there should even be
teachings other than those which were given by Buddha. In light
of this, how is it possible to interpret and pass down an essential
teaching that can be applied to every possible occasion and individual
temperament?*

FOR THE first six years Suzuki was in America, he and his main students resisted the idea of recording his lectures; what he said was for the moment and for the people at hand. He wasn't codifying his teaching but working with people day by day, situation after situation. Nevertheless, in 1965, when she was a new student, Marian Derby started recording lectures in Los Altos on her reel-to-reel tape recorder with Suzuki's permission. Also with his permission she transcribed them and made the transcripts available. Soon after that they started doing the same in San Francisco.

IN THE SUMMER of 1966 Marian's parents came to visit. They wanted to check out this Zen teacher, to see who Marian had brought into her home and into the lives of their grandchildren. They met Suzuki and were delighted with him. Marian's father drove him back to San Francisco to get to know him better. He asked Suzuki what his personal ambition in life was, and Suzuki said, "I'd like to write a book." When her father passed this on, Marian took it seriously and asked Suzuki if she could put a book together from his morning talks. He was enthusiastic. So every Thursday morning after the group left, she'd read to him from her edited transcripts. Marian loved the way Suzuki would sit with folded legs on her sofa in front of the crackling fireplace, his robes tucked under his legs, the aroma of coffee and cinnamon rolls still in the air.

The purpose of studying Buddhism is not to study Buddhism but to study ourselves. That is why we have teaching. But the teaching is not ourselves. It is some explanation of ourselves. To study the teaching is to know yourselves. That is why we do not ever attach to the teaching, or to the teacher. The moment you meet a teacher you should leave the teacher, and you should be independent. You want a teacher so that you can be independent. So you study yourselves. You have the teacher for yourselves, not for the teacher.

"Did I say that?" he'd often comment.

MARIAN TOLD Suzuki that Richard was opposed to the idea of her doing the book. He thought she was too new a student. Suzuki suggested she pass the manuscript on to Richard so he could edit it. In March of 1967 Marian gave the completed manuscript to Richard, which she had titled *Beginner's Mind*. Much to Marian's frustration, it took him months to get around to looking at it. When he did read it the following fall, he agreed it was good material for a book – after more work. Marian let go of the project. Richard found himself too busy to take it on, so he offered it to a student named Peter Schneider, who had editing experience. Peter turned down the task, since he was fully occupied as director of Tassajara.

In the spring of 1968 Richard turned the manuscript over to his good friend Trudy Dixon, who, like Richard, had edited Suzuki's lectures for *Wind Bell*. Trudy took on the task even though she had two small children, had undergone surgery for breast cancer, and was in poor health. She threw herself completely into it, listening to the original tapes, painstakingly working on the material word by word, thought by thought, organizing it and conferring often with Richard and occasionally with Suzuki directly.

AROUND THIS time a Zen student came up to Richard on Bush Street and said he'd heard that Richard was going to Japan. That's how Richard learned of Suzuki's next plan for him. He went right in to Sokoji and asked Suzuki about it. Suzuki had a number of reasons for sending him. He said he wanted Richard to experience Zen practice in a Japanese setting and to get a taste of Japanese culture. He wanted him to go to Eiheiji, study with various good teachers, learn tea ceremony, and go to Noh plays. Suzuki didn't make it public at the time, but he considered this a necessary part of Richard's preparation to someday succeed him as a teacher and maybe even as the abbot of the Zen Center.

Suzuki also said he wanted to dislodge Richard from his excessive responsibilities and give other students a chance to run things. Richard was so dominant and his mind worked so fast that it was hard for others to develop leadership skills in his presence. Some people, like Silas, would get a chance to do things without so much conflict and competition with Richard. In addition, Suzuki did not hide another reason: "I can't control him," he said, "so I'm going to give him a big problem. I'm going to throw him in the ocean." The most astonishing purpose that Suzuki had in sending Richard to Japan was to reform Japanese Buddhism, one of his lifelong goals. He wanted to bust up the fossilization of Zen in his homeland with influence from novice American Buddhists, who would bring a fresh approach. As usual, he never fully explained his vision or how he saw this sea change in ancient institutions coming about.

Hundreds of people came to Richard's going-away party. Lou Harrison's Chinese music ensemble played, followed by Mel Weitsman's recorder trio, and then there was dancing to a rhythm-and-blues band. Richard and Virginia stood for a while talking to Suzuki and Okusan. After clowning around, pretending to dance like the students, the Suzukis went home early.

Many of those present owed a lot to Richard: he'd gotten them into Tassajara or out of the draft, helped foreign students stay in the country, helped people get jobs, and when it was really important arranged for Suzuki to see them right away. He'd been everywhere at once, and now he was going away. People wondered what Zen Center would be like without him.

On October 23, 1968, Richard sailed for Japan with his wife, Virginia, and daughter, Sally. He took with him the completed manuscript for *Zen Mind, Beginner's Mind,* which he had further edited and gone over with Suzuki. He was going to seek a publisher in Japan, and he wrote the introduction onboard as the ship headed toward the land of his teacher.

TRUDY DIXON had been doing graduate studies in philosophy at UC Berkeley, specializing in Heidegger and Wittgenstein, when her husband, Mike, first took her to Sokoji in 1962 to hear Suzuki lecture. Mike was a student at the San Francisco Art Institute. They arrived late and stood in the back of the zendo. Suzuki embarked on an unusual line of thought that evening. He compared the practice of Zen with the study of philosophy – expressing one's truth with one's whole body and mind instead of thinking and being curious about the meaning of life. He said he'd had a good friend in Japan who was a philosopher. Ultimately his intellectual pursuits didn't satisfy him, and he killed himself. At exactly that point in the lecture, Suzuki looked intently at Trudy. She backed up a few steps. Trudy could not get that experience out of her mind. She and Mike continued coming to lectures and soon decided to start practicing with Suzuki. They became close disciples.

In *Zen Mind, Beginner's Mind,* Trudy put her whole being into expressing the essence of Suzuki's teaching. After she passed the manuscript on to Richard, she concentrated on taking care of herself at her home in Mill Valley and dealing with her approaching death. She remained cheerful on the outside, but her mind was possessed by fear, which she revealed to her analyst. After an operation her lungs filled with liquid, and she couldn't breathe. She struggled for breath with all the energy she could find until she went beyond thoughts, words, and fear into what she called breath-struggle samadhi. After five difficult days of recovery Mike brought Suzuki and Okusan to visit her. She said the sight of them was like seeing the sun rise for the first time.

She went to Tassajara and fasted. There she had a powerful, joyous experience that included life and death, health and illness, fear and courage. She said she finally stopped fighting and was "accommodating the enemy," as Suzuki had described it. On the verge of death Trudy had been reborn. Her analyst said that at her next visit she seemed like a new person, a fearless and radiant woman. To her husband, caretakers, and friends she became an inspiration. "My self, my body," she wrote, "is dissolved in phenomena like a sky's rainbow caught in a child's soap bubble."

One day after zazen at Bill Kwong's Mill Valley zendo, Betty Warren visited Trudy. She arrived wishing there was something she could do. Trudy burned away Betty's pity with one phrase, referring to her illness as "this blessed cancer."

On Mondays Suzuki visited Trudy at her home after giving a talk to Bill's zazen group. One day after such a visit he returned to the car with Bob Halpern. Suzuki's eyes were wet. "Now there's a real Zen master," he said of Trudy, as he sank into his seat.

On July 1 Trudy's brother drove her to Tassajara. They shared a cup of clear creek water with Suzuki, slept outside in the moonlight, and returned the next day to the hospital. A couple of days later she came back to Tassajara and practiced prone zazen in the zendo with Suzuki and the students. On the eighth she and her teacher returned to San Francisco.

On July 9, 1969, Mike called Suzuki at Sokoji and told him that Trudy had just died in the hospital – too quickly for Suzuki to have gotten there. Suzuki fell apart crying on the phone, which disturbed Mike – he thought of Suzuki as imperturbable. Suzuki came to the hospital and was composed by then.

At her funeral two days later Suzuki was uncharacteristically emotional. He cried and said, "I never thought I'd have a disciple this great. Maybe I never will again." As is customary, the funeral included an ordination in which Suzuki-roshi gave his deceased student the precepts. Then he delivered a eulogy.

Go, my disciple. You have completed your practice for this life and acquired a genuine warm heart, a pure and undefiled buddha mind, and joined our sangha. All that you have done in this life and in your past lives became meaningful in the light of the buddha mind, which was found so clearly within yourself, as your own. Because of your complete practice, your mind has transcended far beyond your physical sickness, and it has taken full care of your sickness like a nurse.

A person of joyful mind is contented with his lot. Even in adversity he will see bright light. He finds the Buddha's place in different circumstances, easy and difficult. He feels pleasure even in painful conditions, and rejoices. For us, for all who have this joy of buddha mind, the world of birth and death is the world of nirvana.

The compassionate mind is the affectionate mind of parents. Parents always think of the growth and welfare of their children, to the neglect of their own circumstances. Our scriptures say, "Buddha mind is the mind of great compassion."

The magnanimous mind is as big as a mountain and as wide as an ocean. A person of magnanimous mind is impartial. He walks the middle way. He is never attached to any side of the extreme aspect of things. The magnanimous mind works justly and impartially.

Now you have acquired the buddha mind and become a real disciple of the Buddha. At this point, however, I express my true power. . . .

Then Suzuki let out a long, mighty roar of grief that echoed through the cavernous auditorium.

When you try to do something, you lose it, because you are concentrated on one out of one thousand hands. You lose 999 hands. Before you try, you have it.

ABRUPTLY, A demand had come from Sokoji's board of directors in the spring of 1969: choose us or them. Suzuki had hoped the two groups would grow together and learn to coexist in harmony, but the divide between them had only grown deeper. Students were no longer invited to the congregation's festive events, except for a few old timers like Claude, Betty, and Della. Suzuki still thought rapprochement was possible, but the board was firm. They no longer wanted a priest with divided loyalties.

They wanted Suzuki to stay, but even more they wanted a priest who was theirs. Their new temple wouldn't be built for years – and they did not wish to rent the zendo to Zen Center anymore. There were too many students; Zen Center had become too big and busy and was completely overshadowing the Japanese congregation. While some of the congregation members respected the students' sincerity, many didn't feel at home in their own temple. The old caretaker, who never had a smile for anyone, and whom some students were afraid of, was the most outspoken supporter of the students. Suzuki's close friend George Hagiwara, now president of the congregation, was supportive of Suzuki as well, but he knew it was a lost cause.

Suzuki said, "Eighty percent of the problem is long hair and unusual clothing." The younger Japanese members were more understanding, but the elders ran Sokoji. He said that the Issei, the first-generation Japanese-Americans, had a Meiji Buddhist approach. They admired the progress of the West, yet clung to a type of Shinto nationalistic Buddhism focused on making offerings to the spirits of ancestors. Suzuki said he came to America to bring "the pure way of Zen Buddhism."

Rumi Kawashiri, whose family belonged to Sokoji, wrote a college paper called "Sokoji and Zen Center" that year. Suzuki told her that he taught his Zen Center students the fundamentals of Buddhism, while his intent with the congregation was to point out the folly of their "mixed-up understanding and strong attachment to their own views and way of life." That didn't increase his popularity. He was harder on them than he had been on his congregation back at Rinso-in. Suzuki further said that the best hope for the congregation was "in the Sunday school and with the young in general." The youth liked him, but they were not enthusiastic about Zen. As in Japan, they thought Zen was for old folks and ancestors. He wouldn't give up on pure Zen, so the congregation gave up on him.

At the board meeting Suzuki didn't say anything in his own defense.

One relatively new member, a man who didn't often come to the temple, expressed an interest in being president of the Japanese congregation. Suzuki thought the man was getting in over his head and encouraged him to reconsider. The man responded by spearheading the move to oust Suzuki, bringing things to a head. Suzuki gave up, saying that maybe it was better to defer to those who wished him to leave. He confided to his disciple Peter Schneider that he had finally been given an excuse to quit.

Katagiri offered to stay on, but he was told that if he planned to continue working with the Zen students, the congregation didn't want him, so he resigned with Suzuki. Okusan was distraught, but George Hagiwara told her it was all for the best and not to worry.

ONE EVENING after zazen, Bob made up some reason to stay and talk with Suzuki. Suzuki served Bob tea, confiding that he was having a hard time writing to his old supporter Gido at headquarters, the man who'd sent him over and one of the few who he felt understood what he was doing. He wanted to send a letter of resignation and didn't know what to say.

Bob suggested that Suzuki call him on the phone right then. It was a novel idea to Suzuki. He reached Gido, talked to him for a few minutes, and got his blessing. Afterward he got out some special manju and gave Bob all he wanted.

We should follow the original way of Zen, which goes beyond Tassajara practice or city practice.

AT A GENERAL meeting of the membership, it was de-cided that Zen Center would look for its own place, with all the problems that would entail. Suzuki asked Claude and Silas to look for a residential building for the Zen Center since they both dealt in the worlds of business and property. Suzuki would soon retire from his position at Sokoji to concentrate on working with his stu-dents and disciples. Eventually Claude and Silas found such a place.

At the corner of Page and Laguna Streets in San Francisco's West-ern Addition stood a handsome, three-story, redbrick building. It had been a Jewish women's residence called Emmanuel. In the summer of 1969 it was for sale. Claude, Silas, and Suzuki walked up the steps and between two columns to a solid, double front door with upper panes of thick, translucent glass. An older woman in-vited them in. The entryway had a high ceiling and opened into a wide hall with benches. A chandelier and sconces were unlit, but in-direct light entered through the windows from a courtyard garden. To the left of the entryway were offices, and to the right was a large room lined with arched double windows. The building was mag-nificent, spacious, sturdy.

"Let's get it," Suzuki said, and he started looking around.

The next time they went to the building on Page Street, fifty other students joined them to view their prospective home. They all walked the twelve blocks together. It was perfect, ready to go without any remodeling. There was a large dining room and a vast meeting room in the basement that could be used as a zendo right away. Everyone was impressed with the quality of the details – the built-in wooden cabinets and trim, the ironwork, and the view from the walkway on the roof. This gracious building had been designed by Julia Morgan, the architect of Hearst Castle and many other ac-claimed buildings in California.

Marian Derby and Chester Carlson, a founder of Xerox and the single largest donor toward the purchase of Tassajara, provided the down payment, and the Bank of Tokyo offered generous financing. Starting with the first month, all payments were met by modest resident rents and members' dues.

ON NOVEMBER 15, 1969, students helped Suzuki and Okusan carry their few possessions to the waiting cars, and they said good-bye to the home they'd lived in, he for ten and a half years. An official stepping-down ceremony would take place later, but on this day he offered incense at Sokoji's altars, bowed to the building from the sidewalk, and rode away. Okusan was sobbing, feeling rejected. They had tried so hard to take good care of Sokoji and the congregation.

The Page Street building had residential space for up to seventy-five people, large communal bathrooms, and a second-floor suite that was perfect for the Suzukis, with three rooms and a bath. Most of the students who had been living in the apartments across the street from Sokoji moved in. At last Suzuki had the residential center in San Francisco that he'd been talking about since he came. There was a lot left to do – tatamis and bells to buy, altars to build, walls to paint (especially the zendo walls, which had a candy-cane motif). Hagiwara personally provided ceremonial equipment for the buddha hall.

At five PM Suzuki walked slowly down the wide central stairway, followed by a student carrying a burning stick of incense held high. After offering incense at simple altars in the kitchen, the buddha hall, and the basement zendo, Suzuki and his students sat zazen together. Not one period had been missed in the transition. First things first.

We say our practice is the ornament of Buddha. Even though students don't know what Buddhism is, if they come to some beautiful buddha hall then they will naturally have some feeling. But essentially, for Zen Buddhists, the real ornaments of the buddha hall are the people who practice there. Each one of us is, should be, a beautiful flower. And each of us should be Buddha leading people in our practice.

IN JANUARY 1970, the new zendo was officially opened and named the Mahabodhisattva Zendo. On the main floor, near the front door, the white-walled, arch-windowed buddha hall contained a fine maple altar built by a student. The room was covered with tatami, except for an aisle of the original reddish tile around the edge. Over a hundred students now resided in the neighborhood of Page and Laguna, and people drove in from around the Bay Area for zazen and visits. There were four zazen periods a day, three services, two meals in the dining room. Everyone participated in meal preparation, dishwashing, and building cleanup. They had a library, a laundry room, and a shop. Claude said he was almost embarrassed to be in such comfortable surroundings.

The old students should lead the new students so they can practice our way more easily, but without telling them this way or that way, you should do this or you shouldn't do that. And our daily life in this building – extended from our zazen practice – should include a good relationship with our neighbors. Someone may have a beautiful nose, but it should not be fixed upside down.

To practice being good neighbors, sangha members swept the sidewalks daily and planted trees. As on Bush Street, students were asked not to jaywalk. A neighborhood association had formed, and Suzuki suggested that only one or two members of Zen Center join it and mainly listen at the meetings.

The students, many of them idealistic, college-educated, young liberal do-gooders, now found themselves learning how to live in a predominantly black neighborhood, on the edge of one of the most dangerous areas in San Francisco. Japantown had also been near the Fillmore, but it was safer and had provided a type of invisible support. In this new neighborhood there were muggings, even murders. Catty-corner from the new building was a grocery store that sold canned goods, cigarettes, and liquor. The Chinese proprietor had died in a robbery there, and his wife had shot and killed two robbers since then, one of them soon after the Zen Center moved into the neighborhood.

The Zen practice at Page Street had nothing to offer the poor, disenfranchised neighbors – no money, no self-defense, no visible power. It was hard to figure out how to be helpful. Some neighbors complained that these newcomers made it harder to park. They were being called rich, self-involved hippies who didn't care about the problems of the local poor.

The sangha quickly learned that the doors to the building had to be locked. Neighborhood children figured out right away that the Zennies were suckers. They would roam the building at will. Things were stolen. One day three tough black teenagers came in the open door and were having fun being sassy to a few students who were trying to be good, nondiscriminating liberals. Suzuki approached in his robes, carrying his short teacher's stick.

"Hey, the man in the robes. You know karate? You fight?" one of the teenagers demanded. Suzuki's eyes lit up and he walked right up to them – short, unthreatening, yet full of spunk. "What's the stick for?" the biggest one asked.

"To hit you with," said Suzuki, and whacked him on the shoulder. Then he escorted the boys to the front door, while they laughed and sparred with him.

*M*y original motivation in coming here was not only
to propagate Zen in America, but also to revitalize Zen
in Japan. They are sleeping.

PETER SCHNEIDER and Suzuki were hunched over a couple of sheets of paper. "Shunryu Suzuki, Curriculum Vitae" was written in large letters at the top of the first. With Kobun's help Suzuki had reluctantly prepared a chronicle of his externally significant achievements for Peter, whom he had also reluctantly allowed to interview him about his past. Peter, Zen Center's historian, had been editing *Wind Bell* and was considering doing a book on Suzuki someday.

The curriculum vitae was a pretty dry document. There was a line or two each for public schools, Komazawa University, Eiheiji and Sojiji monasteries. It listed his years at Zoun-in and Rinso-in and positions he'd held at various other temples, and it mentioned the certificate he'd received – to teach ethics and English. It was all new to Peter, who was asking Suzuki various questions. Suzuki was not very interested. His mind wandered, he was not always articulate, and he made little mistakes with dates and details.

Peter kept trying to figure out when his teacher had become a Zen master. Ten times during the interview he asked. Suzuki would point to the résumé and say, "Here, no maybe there," or he'd get back to the previous topic. Any priest in Japan who had completed his training would be considered a master to his disciples. There was no word in Japanese that corresponded to the way "Zen master" was used in America. In Japan the title "roshi" was a formality, but good teachers were known by reputation or personal experience.

SUZUKI'S OMISSIONS in recalling his life were notable. He hardly mentioned his family. He talked about how his second and third marriages were opposed by some Rinso-in members, referring to them as his first and second marriages. He never wanted to talk about his past unless he thought it would help in some way. It was unimportant, private, and sometimes embarrassing.

What Suzuki enjoyed talking about most was Nona Ransom. When Peter asked about her, Suzuki started laughing and said, "I must tell you about Miss Ransom. She was my old, old girlfriend." He said she gave him the confidence to teach Westerners. She had died, and he was sad about it. He regretted that for the past few years he hadn't answered her letters.

I thought it might be all right not to write her, but that was my mistake. She passed away last year. I trusted her very much and she trusted me so much, so I thought whether I wrote to her or not didn't make much difference. But now I don't know. As long as she was alive it seemed all right. Now I regret a little not writing to her.

After Suzuki had talked a good deal about his struggle to become abbot of Rinso-in, Peter asked about the use of the material.

PETER: Do you think it would be interesting, Roshi, for the students to know all this, or is it best to keep your biography very simple?

SUZUKI: Maybe so. It doesn't make much sense though. I'm afraid if they don't understand what was going on in the background, it will just confuse them.

PETER: I'm trying to decide how much should be included from your history. It's interesting to your students, but also maybe . . .

SUZUKI: No! Maybe interesting for someone who is *not* a student. Because of these kinds of experiences I decided to come to America. There's nothing interesting in all this. This is just a record, just confusion. My life in Japan was spent fighting, in struggle. Fortunately I knew how to handle the problems most of the time, but fighting just made for more difficulties. I was a very impatient and angry person, and I always started fights because of my impatience. Once I started to fight, I had to become very patient or else I'd lose that fight and it would be endless. I always won the struggles, but that is not the best way. It is better to surrender. [pause] If I had known the truth about American life earlier, it would have been *sayonara* to Japan a long time ago. Like this, you know [waving goodbye].

In answering a question about patience, Suzuki got a little impatient and expressed his frustration with the whole point of looking at his past.

SUZUKI: It's a big job talking about all this. I'm not interested. I have no accurate record of my life, and I don't want any.

PETER: Is there any meaning at all in having something about you in the *Wind Bell*?

SUZUKI: This sort of thing?

PETER: Some sort of history, some biography, not too elaborate, but something. Not a book though. Maybe about four or five pages? Is that a mistake?

SUZUKI: Four or five!

PETER: How much do you think? One? Half a page? A paragraph? One sentence? What about your biography saying only, "I do not think much of this sort of thing and have not kept any records." End of biography. How do you feel about this?

SUZUKI: I didn't get answers to these kinds of questions from my teacher. I don't have much interest in it either. If my life is seen in this way, everything will be lost.

Chapter Seventeen

One and Many

1 9 6 9 – 1 9 7 0

One purpose of our practice is to enjoy our old age. But we can't fool ourselves. Only sincere practice will work.

ONE DAY at Tassajara in late April of 1969, after the spring practice period was over and just before the guest season was to begin, Shunryu Suzuki walked downstream with some students to eat bag lunches and enjoy the water in the hot afternoon. Tassajara Creek was fairly high, and they had to cross it in one place over a fallen sycamore trunk. They hopped on stones across the little stream feeding into the creek at the base of the trail to the Horse Pasture. Then they came to a waterworn granite passage called the Narrows. There they sat on stream-polished ledges near the gushing water and ate their cheese sandwiches, cookies, and apples, reaching down to get handfuls of the creek water.

Once the guest season started, the smooth, sloping rock sides and pools would usually be adorned with a half-dozen naked bodies. There was a rule against skinny-dipping at the Narrows, which most students ignored unless in larger mixed groups. That day everyone had on swimsuits or shorts. After eating, everyone but Suzuki jumped in the cold mountain water. He watched them freely sliding over the waterfall into the deep pool. Dan Welch went down the wet sloping face next to the waterfall in full lotus and others followed. Suzuki saw some good places to sit on the opposite bank in the direct sun and decided to go there via the deep pool where his students were enjoying themselves. He entered the water. The current was fast. It carried him into the whirlpool bowl and quickly down the falls into the deep water. Then he kept going down – straight down. He couldn't swim.

He reached his arms out but no one noticed or thought anything of it as he went under. He thought to walk out but couldn't touch bottom. He found himself at the clear bottom with the crayfish and trout. He looked up at the legs moving in the water. They were too far away to grab. He became frightened and started to take in water.

Up top someone asked, "Where's Roshi?"

They quickly fished Suzuki out, coughing up water and gasping.

Suzuki recovered and walked back upstream the mile to Tassajara. In his lecture that evening he mentioned what had happened and said that not being able to breathe had shown him how deeply he was attached to life and air. It had made him realize how poor his practice and understanding were. He had to be more sincere and diligent in his efforts to concentrate on "the great matter."

A FEW WEEKS after he almost drowned, on his sixty-fifth birthday in a lecture at Sokoji, Suzuki appealed to his students to join him in a rededication to sincere practice. He said he was on one hand happy to be getting older, but on the other hand regretful of the shortcomings of his past practice. Maybe it would be better for everyone, he said, if he went off to seek the truth. He had mentioned at times, almost wistfully, that he'd like to go to India, Thailand, and Burma – wherever he heard there was someone who could give him instruction.

He said that he felt a great responsibility as a teacher and was always thinking about what to do with so many students. While in bed recovering from a cold, he had thought about these things and decided, "It might be better for us to concentrate on a simpler practice. I think the most simple practice is counting the breath."

Whatever their problems in zazen – pain, confusion, sleepiness, frightening or seductive images – the students were to join Suzuki in counting their exhalations from one to ten, over and over. "We're not advanced enough students for koans or *shikantaza* [Dogen's term for just sitting]. We need more of a beginner's practice." And he admonished, "If you count your breathing, you will easily notice when you are not taking care of your everyday life. I have many difficulties in my practice, so I think you too will find it very difficult to sit in good zazen."

*E*nlightenment *is not a complete remedy.*

OKUSAN CAME down to Tassajara from San Francisco. She stayed in a one-room cabin with tatami and shoji screens next to her husband's. There she practiced tea ceremony. Suzuki talked about her in a lecture. He said she was always trying to teach him not to be so introverted and thoughtless with her. He used the American phrase, "Can't live with her, can't live without her."

During the spring practice period Suzuki had declared in a lecture that Okusan had experienced some sort of breakthrough. Some students took this to mean that she'd attained permanent, perfect, cosmic consciousness, and others thought it meant she'd had an epiphany.

"Really," he said, "she got enlightened. I never thought it would happen," and he kept laughing and explaining. He said that her enlightenment came about because she couldn't find a priest to do a funeral for a member of the Sokoji congregation. Suzuki was always having to leave Tassajara to do funerals; many members wanted him for their funeral even if another priest was available.

This is the most important thing that Zen priests do, as far as Japanese laypeople are concerned.

On his way from Tassajara to Sokoji, Suzuki asked the student driving him, Jane Runk, to make numerous stops. She didn't know he had to do a funeral and he had forgotten all about it. They went to the beach, to shops, and had an unusually carefree time. Meanwhile, Okusan was frantically searching for another priest. Katagiri was at Los Altos. Kobun was in Japan. Her sense of responsibility was so strong that she practically had a nervous breakdown. Then she realized that the world would keep turning if there were no priest. In an instant she gave up, let it go, decided just to do her best. Bang. Something happened.

SUZUKI KNEW that when he talked too much about enlightenment, people tended to get fixed ideas about what the word meant, and got obsessed with it as a goal. Students would sometimes talk about it, but there was no agreed-upon definition. Most thought of Suzuki as enlightened, but he wouldn't say he was. If asked, he would usually deny it. But whatever he had, his students wanted to have too; whatever he knew, they wanted to know. Some, like Claude, said Suzuki wasn't enlightened and had clearly said so through the years. Mike Dixon said he obviously was, pointing out that in earlier years Suzuki would occasionally start a story by locating it, for instance, after his second enlightenment experience. But mostly such talk was avoided. Suzuki did not promote enlightenment as a final resting place.

Some students didn't think they were going to get enlightened with Suzuki, or felt they couldn't have enough contact with him, and went on to study with other teachers: Yasutani, Nakagawa, the Rinzai master Sasaki in L.A., Maezumi in L.A., Kapleau in Rochester, Aitken in Hawaii. All those teachers used koans as well as zazen, saw students frequently for private interviews, and were clearly encouraging people to have kensho, or enlightenment experiences. Often people wouldn't get to see Suzuki for dokusan more than once in a year. At Yasutani's sesshins there would be public recognition of students who attained kensho. Zen Center seemed to be short on enlightenment, indeed, a little sleepy compared to the other teachers with their vigorous styles.

Suzuki didn't talk about enlightenment as something that could be controlled. He said that most priests weren't enlightened and some laypeople were. He spoke of a farmer near Rinso-in who was enlightened, even though he'd never been a practicing Buddhist. Of his students he once said that maybe only one in ten would get enlightened, but that it wasn't really necessary; to do the practice was itself enlightenment, even if people didn't realize it. Things did happen to his students, though.

KEN SAWYER, a carpenter from Canada, had been at Zen Center for a couple of years. During a sesshin in San Francisco, while sitting in afternoon zazen, he dissolved into an amazing spaciousness. He kept it to himself at the time, but later told Suzuki of his experience in dokusan at Tassajara.

"Yes, you could call that enlightenment," Suzuki said. They sat there for a moment in Suzuki's cabin, facing each other. "And how's your work coming?"

Later that summer at Tassajara Ken was carrying incense for Suzuki on the way to zazen. Suzuki crossed the bridge, and Ken followed with the green incense held high, trailing a pleasant thin wisp of smoke behind him. Suzuki went to the edge of the bridge and stood looking at the creek below. Periodically the echoing sound of the mallet on the wooden board would pierce the air – the third and final round. While Suzuki looked down at the creek, Ken saw him disappear, blending totally with the water, wood, and air. A moment later they were walking down the dirt and cobble path and toward the zendo. Ken didn't know what had happened, or if it had happened to him, to Suzuki, or both. But he had learned one thing: Suzuki's way was not to latch on to the highs but to accept every moment of life as it comes, step after step. So he walked on and made nothing of it.

If you are enlightened, the whole universe tells the truth to the whole universe.

If your practice doesn't include every one of us, it is not true practice.

BOMBERS WERE pounding Hanoi. Four students at Kent State had died protesting Nixon's invasion of Cambodia. The first nuclear-tipped MIRVs were placed in underground silos. It was the year of the first Earth Day. Reagan was running for his second term as governor of California, and Salvador Allende was running for president of Chile. Alexander Solzhenitsyn won the Nobel Prize for literature. *Patton* won the Oscar for best film. Bertrand Russell died.

At Tassajara in May of 1970, all this news seemed remote. Tatsugami-roshi, who had kept Jean, Grahame, and Philip under his wing at Eiheiji, had come to lead the spring practice period at Tassajara. He was back in Japan for the summer but was scheduled to return to lead the fall practice period. While Tatsugami was at Tassajara, Suzuki had been concentrating on Page Street, but now he was back in his briar patch. Now the last of the winter's heavy snowfall was melting away on the ridge.

In the year when the Pope declared priestly celibacy to be a fundamental teaching of the Roman Catholic Church, Suzuki acknowledged the success of women and men practicing together at Tassajara. Most students were single, but there were some married couples, a few unmarried couples, and lots of children. Buddhism had hardly ever seen anything like it. The disparate group of former students of Asian culture, longhairs, and individualistic seekers who had gathered around Suzuki had managed to get along and get on with the practice and study of Zen with far greater cooperation than had seemed possible at the outset.

Suzuki was no longer calling Tassajara a "baby monastery." From May first till after Labor Day weekend in September, Tassajara's tradition of welcoming guests continued; the guests were enthusiastic about the quiet and efficient way the place was run and were full of praise for the food. There had been less meat and fish served each summer, and now the fare was totally vegetarian, due to Tatsugami's insistence that it was improper to serve meat or fish in a Buddhist monastery. He said that the guests would understand. He was right – the food just got better. Tatsugami, as well as Katagiri, had told the men who weren't monks not to shave their heads but just to cut it short. As a result they looked a little more normal to the guests.

Because Tatsugami had spent so much time teaching chanting and ceremony, there was a great deal of catch-up work to do on the buildings during that guest season. While most students took care of the guests, a crew of carpenters was finishing the ambitious stone-and-beam kitchen and the adjoining entryway and library. Suzuki's cabin was moved to make way for the stone foundation for a new, more substantial cabin for the abbot. The crew had to interrupt their work briefly when they discovered that Suzuki and Mel, exhausted from moving stones, were taking a catnap on the cabin floor when it started to move.

That summer a segment of a film on gurus called *Sunseed* was shot at Tassajara, and Suzuki played with a yo-yo for the camera. Charlotte Selver and Charles Brooks held another Sensory Awareness workshop in the dining room. A psychotherapist and naturalist named Sterling Bunnell gave a talk about the geological history of the land, and said that Tassajara was a meeting place of three major California ecological zones. Robert Bly read his poetry.

SUZUKI FREQUENTLY gave lectures in the evening. Eager students on cushions squeezed up front on the tatami and on the time-darkened linoleum aisles. There was a brief chant at the prompt of a small bell, then a pause that would magnify the sounds of the creek, frogs, crickets, and guests walking by on the road.

He was lecturing on the *Sandokai* (Unity of One and Many), a thousand-year-old Zen poem that Tatsugami had included in the morning service. In this and other ways Suzuki was giving his blessing to the new forms that Tatsugami had instituted, and giving them more life and relevance as well. He had attended years of lectures by Kishizawa on the *Sandokai*; now he was undertaking to shed some light on that scripture. (He would use the phrases "things-as-they-are" or "things-as-it-is," depending on whether he was speaking from the viewpoint of multiplicity or oneness, form or emptiness.)

Usually, even though we say "to observe things-as-they-are," or more accurately "as-it-is," actually we are not observing things-as-they-are, because we think, "Here is my friend; there is the mountain; there is the moon." That is a dualistic way of observing things, not actually the Buddhist way. We find the mountain, or San Francisco, or the moon, within ourselves right here. That is our understanding, the so-called big mind.

Suzuki explained how the *Sandokai* was written in China to clarify then-current misunderstandings and to elevate the dialogue among bickering factions. There was a parallel at Tassajara, in that Suzuki and Tatsugami had quite different approaches, and there had to be room in students' minds to include them both.

I STUDIED THE *Sandokai* with Suzuki that summer and prepared the blackboard for him every day, writing out the Chinese characters from the ancient poem so he could point to them as he lectured. One day I told him that I'd often stay up all night studying, sometimes even going to bed when the wake-up bell came around and not getting up till after breakfast. It was the complete opposite of the way he had told us to follow the schedule and to do each thing at its proper time with everyone else. He nodded his head and held his curved teaching stick. "Keep it up," he said. "Everyone will think you're crazy, but keep it up. It's pretty good."

DIANNE GOLDSCHLAG worked in the dining room and was a favorite with the guests because of her warm, outgoing personality. She was from an old-fashioned Jewish section of the Bronx. An adventurous, free-spirited child of the sixties, she'd been arrested protesting the Vietnam War and had hitchhiked around the Middle

East, fibbing about her Jewish heritage in Arab countries. She first came to Tassajara in 1968. She and her close friend Margaret were not textbook Zen students. They followed the schedule pretty closely and worked as hard as anyone else, but they were always getting into mischief and breaking the serious quiet with giggles and singing. Once during dokusan with Suzuki, Dianne reached into the sleeve of her robe and brought out a drawing of a fantasy creature with three legs and stars for eyes. They crouched over the picture, talking about it like two little children. Sometimes he'd call Dianne and Margaret into his cabin and give them candy, saying, "You don't need candy, you need salt. I should be giving you salt. I'm not a good teacher for you. I treat you too much like grand-daughters, not like students."

Once, taking a walk by the creek with a group of students, Suzuki came upon Dianne and Margaret skinny-dipping. Dianne called out that the day was so hot and the creek looked so cool that they just had to jump in. Suzuki shook his finger at them and said, "Remember, you're two fishes, not one."

Later that day, about to leave for San Francisco, Suzuki was in his cabin talking over last-minute details with two officers when there was a knock on the door. It was Dianne. She said she and Margaret had found a beautiful rock and put it in his changing room at the baths. She wanted him to see it and say whether he liked it or not before he left. The two officers, visibly upset, said there was no time for that now. Suzuki told them to wait at the gate, and off he went with Dianne to see the rock. She had worked with him in his garden and had a good feel for stones. The rock she had placed in the corner of the narrow room was tall and squarish with white ripples of quartz. Suzuki said, "Ohhhh," inspected it closely, and asked if he could keep it. They walked together to the gate where a number of students were waiting to see him off. Margaret came running up to say goodbye. "Remember – you're two fishes, not one," he said, getting into the car.

When you become a stone, that is our zazen practice.

As usual, Suzuki-roshi spent a lot of time working with plants and stones in his garden that summer. During his life he'd come to understand a good deal about stones – their balance points and breaking points. He said that some stones were alive and others were dead. One day Suzuki and his attendant, Alan Marlowe, were trying to rotate a large stone in Suzuki's garden. Alan was six-four and muscular, but the two of them could not move the stone, even with the help of a long steel bar. Finally Suzuki told Alan to go to the baths, the customary end to everyone's workday. Alan went and was surprised half an hour later to find that the rock was reset. He called out at Suzuki's cabin door, opening it when there was no answer. Inside he found Suzuki asleep. There was vomit around the edge of the toilet. Alan cleaned it off and left. Suzuki stayed in bed for three days.

Another student, Steve Tipton, was trying to do the hardest job imaginable in the summer heat. There was only one appropriate spot for a septic tank for the new toilets near the baths, and in that spot the Tassajara soil held an enormous granite boulder. There was no room for a crew, so Steve was working by himself. Every day after his bath, Suzuki would stop to check on his progress. Steve had dug a three-foot-wide, six-foot-deep trench around the seven-foot boulder. He was trying to break it up by drilling, placing spikes in the holes, and then driving them in with a sledgehammer. After a week he had broken off only a few shards.

Finally Suzuki said, "Are you trying to break up that rock?"

"I'm trying to," Steve answered. "You got any ideas?"

Suzuki motioned for Steve to get off as he tied back his robe sleeves and leaped to the top of the boulder. He carefully looked at the rock, patted it, and chuckled. He called Steve back and pointed to the surface: "Here and here and here." Steve drilled and drove in spikes where Suzuki had indicated, and the stone broke into pieces that could easily be winched out.

That summer was a high point in Suzuki's life – a hard-working, early-rising season of energy and harmony. Tassajara was good, the city was good. Suzuki seemed healthy and strong, and his dream was tangibly unfolding before him.

The secret of Soto Zen is just two words: not always so.

"Not always so" was never far away in Shunryu Suzuki's teaching. He prefaced much of what he said with the word "maybe," and yet he did not seem at all unsure of himself. When he said this sort of thing, it seemed to come from a deeply rooted strength. He did speak of the absolute, but in enigmatic terms. "There is nothing absolute for us, but when nothing is absolute, that is absolute."

He talked about the Buddha's teaching as something fluid and living. "To accord with circumstances, the teaching should have an infinite number of forms."

He talked about enlightenment, but said, "Enlightenment is not any particular stage that you attain."

Not always so. In Japanese it's two words, three words in English. This is the secret of our teaching. If you understand things in this way, without being caught by words or rules, without too much of a preconceived idea, then you can actually do something, and in doing something, you can apply this teaching which has been handed down from the ancient masters. When you apply it, it will help.

It couldn't be grasped. It was a paradox, he said, that could only be understood through sincere practice and zazen. The point of his talks wasn't to tell the truth as he saw it, but to free minds from obstacles so they might include contradictions.

Suzuki thought it was a frequent weakness of Buddhist teachers to cling to a fixed understanding; it was not a weakness of Dogen.

Usually a Zen master will give you: "Practice zazen so that you will attain enlightenment. If you attain enlightenment, you will be detached from everything and you will see 'things as it is.'" But our way is not always so. What the Zen master says is of course true. But what Dogen-zenji told us was how to adjust the flame of our lamp back and forth. The point of Dogen's zazen is to live each moment in total combustion, like a kerosene lamp or a candle.

"Buddhism is a two-edged sword," Suzuki said, pretending to swing a sword, turning his wrist, a mischievous smile on his face. "Back and forth, back and forth. Sometimes I strike you with this side and sometimes with that." He often spoke of the dual nature of reality, but what the two sides were was not so easy to understand. It wasn't just oneness and duality, but "the duality of oneness and the oneness of duality." He said one couldn't speak the whole truth, that there was always another side created by whatever was said, and if his students didn't get it on their own, they'd get it by the sword that cuts away the side they're attached to.

We should understand everything both ways, not just from one standpoint. We call someone who understands things from just one side a tambankan. *This means a "man who carries a board on his shoulder." Because he carries a big board on his shoulder, he cannot see the other side.*

Often he said, "Just keep sitting." Very often. Sitting would loosen the grip of what seemed to be reality. But then the idea of sitting or zazen might grip the sitter. Zazen was the first thing he taught, but if it became something too special he'd pull out the rug. Someone would ask for more periods of zazen, and he'd say the schedule was fine as it was. Someone would speak of pain in their legs, and he'd say sit more.

EVEN "NOT always so" was not always so. It wasn't offered as a formula to cling to.

"There is no question," a student said, "because there is no answer. Whatever you say will not always be so. So I will just sit."

Suzuki shook his head.

"No?" the student said. "But you said . . ."

"When I said it, it was true. When you said it, it was false."

IF THERE IS always another side in Suzuki's teaching, what's the other side of "not always so"? To look for that, you must take the board off your shoulder.

Almost all people are carrying a big board, so they cannot see the other side. They think they are just the ordinary mind, but if they take the board off they will understand, "Oh, I am Buddha, too. How can I be both Buddha and ordinary mind? It is amazing!" That is enlightenment.

Suzuki talked about the first principle and the second principle from his early days in San Francisco. He said the first principle had many names: buddha nature, emptiness, reality, truth, the Tao, the absolute, God. The second principle is what is said about the first and the way to realize it – rules, teaching, morality, forms. All those things change according to the person, time, and place – and they are not always so. Suzuki said that talking about Buddhism was not truth, but mercy, skillful means, encouragement. "There is no particular teaching or way, but the buddha-nature of all is the same, what we find is the same."

THE FIRST principle is not something that Buddha or other people came up with. Suzuki spoke about Buddha's sermons in the woods, where he "proclaimed the first principle, the Royal Law." And he added, "If you think what Buddha proclaimed is the Royal Law, that is not right. The Royal Law was already there before he was on the pulpit."

Suzuki taught that Buddhism is not the first principle, but is a way to know and express the first principle. Buddha's teaching can only be thought of as the first principle in "its pure and formless form."

If you have a preconceived idea of the first principle, that idea is topsy-turvy, and as long as you seek a first principle that is something to be applied in one way to every occasion, you will have topsy-turvy ideas. Such ideas are not necessary. Buddha's great light shines forth from everything, each moment.

Suzuki-roshi always made clear that the first principle is beyond discrimination or knowing in the ordinary sense, in the way that relative truth is known.

Bodhidharma said, "I don't know." "I don't know" is the first principle. Do you understand? The first principle cannot be known in terms of good or bad, right or wrong, because it is both right and wrong.

Once Suzuki divided up the zendo: those on the right were to ask questions about the first principle and those on the left about the second. If someone asked about the wrong principle, they'd have to move to the other side of the zendo. Nobody actually changed sides, though they had a good time trying to present their understanding of the first principle. In the end it seemed like there was nothing at all to say.

Sometimes I'm the teacher and you're the student, and sometimes you're the teacher and I'm the student.

A VOICE called from outside Suzuki's door in polished Japanese, "Ojama shimasu" (Excuse me for bothering you). Suzuki opened the door and sighed a delighted "ahhhh." Finally his old student Grahame Petchey had made it to Tassajara. Grahame entered the cabin and they talked as Suzuki poured hot water from a thermos into a teapot. Grahame congratulated Suzuki on the marvel of his American monastery and on the wonderful new building in San Francisco.

It was June of 1970, and they hadn't met since the fall of 1966 at Rinso-in, before the Petcheys went to England. Grahame's life had continued to take its own course. He and Pauline had gone back to Japan after a year. In 1967 Suzuki had again tried to get him to come back to Zen Center, but again he was too late. Grahame had written back saying he'd come if Suzuki wanted him to break a two-year contract with a firm that had hired him to start an English-language school in Japan. The last correspondence Grahame received from Suzuki in England was a telegram that simply said, "I agree with your plan to go to Japan."

Grahame had been living in Tokyo and running the school for over two years. He continued to have a relationship with Uchiyama in Kyoto, but his life was now that of a businessman. That night in the zendo Grahame gave a talk about the old days at Sokoji and studying Zen in Japan. Only a few of the oldest students had ever met him. To the rest it was a treat to see and hear the almost legendary first Westerner whom Suzuki had personally ordained, the one who first incorporated Zen Center, Richard's old dharma brother. People wondered why he'd stayed away and if there was a chance he would return.

The next day Grahame and Suzuki talked about Miss Ransom. In 1967 Grahame had looked her up in England at Suzuki's suggestion, and he'd taken to visiting her every week or so. Pauline and the children also met her. Pauline said Miss Ransom reminded her of Katharine Hepburn – tall, thin, and elegant, with shoulder-length hair. She liked the way Miss Ransom teased Grahame for being so well-dressed and proper in his black suit – she said he looked like a Mormon missionary, except for his shaved head. Ransom had been amazed to see the fund-raising brochures for Tassajara and to hear about what her old English student had done. "That little monk has gone off and opened a monastery in the West?" she said to Grahame. "I just can't believe it." Often when Grahame visited, he would hear new stories about her times with that little monk in the late twenties. She told him about the Buddha statue and how that experience had led her to respect Buddhism. The statue had been damaged and was no more.

In his letters to Suzuki, Grahame sent word of Miss Ransom, his zendo, and his family. In the fall of 1967, Suzuki had planned to visit the Petcheys and Miss Ransom in England after a trip to the East Coast, but he got too busy with Tassajara and canceled at the last minute. It was a disappointment to all of them. Miss Ransom wrote to her former houseboy, translator, and mentor of Buddhism. Suzuki replied through Zen Center's secretary, Yvonne. Ransom was outraged by this, and Grahame sympathized. She sent an angry letter back telling Suzuki to write to her himself; she didn't care how bad his English or his handwriting was. He could put it on a postcard, but he must never write to her again through a secretary! Suzuki stopped answering her letters. It upset Miss Ransom a great deal and Grahame as well.

In her old age she had become a more devout Quaker and regularly went to meetings at the local Friends' Hall. She was known in England not for her experiences in Japan but for her relationship with the last emperor of China, Pu Yi, and his wife, Wan Jung. She had been interviewed on the BBC about Pu Yi and Wan Jung, and there had been some newspaper articles about her. In 1969, her eighty-second year, she passed away of emphysema, going peacefully while holding on to a photograph of the young empress.

Grahame had brought some things that Miss Ransom wanted passed on to Suzuki. There was some sixteen-millimeter motion picture footage that she took of him in the garden of Zoun-in in 1930, and a dark brown cup made from a special clay found in her native Somerset. With the cup was a card sending her greetings and asking him to please write. Suzuki put the card to his forehead and placed it carefully on the low table. He picked up the cup with two hands and examined it carefully, as is done in tea ceremony.

"Please explain something to me," Grahame said earnestly. "Miss Ransom told me so much about the two of you, how close you were, and she always spoke of you with such affection. How could you have written to her through a secretary and then stopped writing her altogether? How could you not respond to her letters? By British standards, that was very rude, especially to a lady of her age and class. I cannot understand it."

"The reason I didn't respond," Suzuki replied, "was that she asked me questions about our past and wanted to check on dates. I was afraid she wanted to write a book about the period of her life when I knew her."

Grahame was flabbergasted. She had never even written a book about her experiences in China!

Grahame said he had agreed to do some work and excused himself. He put on work clothes and joined a crew digging a ditch. Suzuki's attendant came to Grahame after about thirty minutes and said Suzuki would like to see him again. Grahame said that he had agreed to do this work and would continue to work. They never discussed Miss Ransom again.

We get no letters from the world of emptiness, but when you see the plant flower, when you hear the sound of bamboo hit by the small stone, that is a letter from the world of emptiness.

A SHIPMENT arrived at Page Street one morning in the summer of 1970: several boxes of *Zen Mind, Beginner's Mind* by Shunryu Suzuki. It was the second book to come out of Zen Center, after Ed Brown's wildly popular *Tassajara Bread Book*. Students stood around the front hall picking up copies. On the grey dust jacket in black and white was calligraphy done by Suzuki in his cabin at Tassajara using a yucca leaf for a brush. It was the Japanese characters *nyorai*, or *tathagata* in Sanskrit, "thus come," one of the ten traditional names for Buddha. Between the red-lettered title and author's name was the subtitle, *Informal talks on Zen meditation and practice*. It was a thin hardcover, only 134 pages, with short chapters. Each chapter started with a quote from the text. The prologue, titled "Beginner's Mind," carried the quote: "In the beginner's mind there are many possibilities, but in the expert's there are few."

There wasn't much thought about the impact the book might have on the Buddhist world or any other world. It was nice to have a little book of Roshi's lectures that could be sent to friends and family. The *Wind Bell* usually carried only one lecture, and was published infrequently.

Suzuki and Okusan came downstairs and joined the handful of students. He looked at the book with comic amazement. Okusan was irritated at the picture on the back cover, a black-and-white close-up of Suzuki's head and shoulders, a picture taken at Tassajara shortly before he shaved his head and face (done once every five days, on four-and-nine days, in a Zen monastery). He wore his stark black Japanese work clothes, his ever-changing face settled into a penetrating, clear gaze, a pleasant hint of a smile, those black eyes with crow's-feet like bookends, the slightly raised eyebrow adding a suggestion.

"In Japan we would never do this," she said. "Why not a nice formal picture of Hojo-san in his best robes?" People teased her, and she gave up.

Someone showed Suzuki the two textless pages in the center of the book, empty except for a small fly on the right side, drawn by his old student Mike Dixon. People left him alone as he looked at the book, which reflected his teaching through the work of Marian Derby, Richard Baker, and Trudy Dixon.

After a moment he moved up next to me and chuckled. "Good book," he said, thumping the cover with an index finger. "I didn't write it, but it looks like a good book."

Later he said, "I read *Zen Mind, Beginner's Mind* to see what the understanding of my disciples is."

Buddhism is transmitted from warm hand to warm hand.

"I HAVE SOME good news for you," Suzuki said, slapping his thighs. It was the fall of 1969, before the move to Page Street. Bob Halpern and I had gone over to Sokoji in the afternoon, and

Suzuki had welcomed us into the office. He'd been in bed with a flu, and his students hadn't seen him for a long time. Suzuki continued. "I'm going to Japan to give Richard transmission."

Suzuki looked as pleased as he could be. We froze, shocked. "Suzuki-roshi," Bob said after a thoughtful pause, "if you give Richard Baker transmission, everyone is going to think you've gone crazy."

"Oh, no no no," Suzuki said, unfazed. "This is good. You should be happy. Now, when he returns from Japan, you'll have an American teacher."

An American teacher? We didn't want an American teacher. We wanted a Japanese teacher, mainly Suzuki. The Japanese priests seemed to know what they were doing, were comfortable in their roles, and looked the way Zen priests were supposed to look. The peccadilloes and shortcomings of Americans were so easy to see. Bob and I both liked Richard, thought he had great energy and kept things lively, and we completely trusted Suzuki's judgment. But Bob knew this would be a tough adjustment to make and was warning Suzuki about what to expect. Bob knew the pulse of the place.

Later that day I ran into Kobun on the street and told him. Kobun recoiled with his hands held in front of him, like an actor in a horror movie, "No! no! Not Richard! It is a mistake! Maybe Philip! Maybe Philip!"

Bob and I were at his communal apartment across the street from Sokoji. Dianne dropped by and we told her about Suzuki's intention to give Richard transmission. "How could that be?" she gasped. "Richard's so arrogant and uptight. He seems to me to be the least spiritual of Suzuki's students."

"You know who thinks Richard will make a good Zen master?" Bob said.

Dianne looked at him. "No. Who on earth?"

"Suzuki-roshi."

TRANSMISSION IS the final stage of ordination, in which a priest receives the master's blessing to be an independent teacher in the

lineage started by Shakyamuni Buddha. Richard called it the passing on of signless states of mind. At that time no one at Zen Center
knew of any Westerner who had received transmission in the Japanese Zen tradition. There were no examples to observe first hand,
so Suzuki's students tended to see transmission in idealistic terms,
as they'd read about it in Buddhist books, where it was referred to
as "mind-to-mind transmission." Nobody paid much attention to
Claude, who said it was the equivalent of getting a teacher's certificate. Suzuki had said in lectures, "Transmission is nothing special,"
or "Actually, there is nothing to transmit." As always, he spent more
time knocking away his students' assumptions than creating definitions for them to cling to. But regardless of the contradictory things
he'd said about transmission through the years, Suzuki had also
talked about his way as "transmission Zen" since he arrived, and he
insisted on the importance of the master-disciple relationship.

*My lecture for tonight will be very short, especially after having a good din-
ner of noodles, which were very long. Our transmission should be a very
long, long one. And our transmission is a special noodle. Dogen-zenji says,
"When you realize buddha nature, you are the teacher." You are the
teacher of your master too, and you will be even the teacher of Shakyamuni Buddha.*

Transmission might be "nothing special," but to Suzuki it was
indispensable, the living heart of his practice, passing on Buddha's
way. He said he was always looking for successors who would share
his responsibility.

While I was driving Suzuki to Tassajara he told me of his plans
to send students out to teach. "You can go to Texas and others will
go to the East Coast, Portland, all over America, even beyond America." I told him I had no interest in going to Texas to start a group. I
felt completely unworthy and couldn't imagine I ever would be
qualified to do that. I wondered if many students were ready for
that. Suzuki said it would take time, but at some point, like baby
birds, we'd just be kicked out of the nest and be teachers whether
we were ready or not. Surprised, I was quiet for a minute. Then I

asked, "You mean your disciples will get transmission before they completely understand your teaching?" "Yes," he said.

"Well, tell me, Roshi," I went on, "have you ever had a student who completely understood your teaching?"

"Yes."

"How many?"

"One."

"Man or woman?"

"A man."

"Was he American?"

"No."

"Japanese?"

"Yes."

"What happened to him?"

"He died." After that, as usual, Suzuki fell asleep.

AMERICAN STUDENTS had always treated Japanese priests with the yellow and brown robes of transmission as if they were semi-celestial beings. It irritated Richard when, as soon as Kobun arrived, Suzuki's students treated him with immense respect and asked him questions about the dharma. Richard would point out that many of Suzuki's students had been studying longer than Kobun.

From Richard's ordination in 1967 to the fall of 1970, Suzuki had ordained nine students as priests. Mel Weitsman, the head of the Berkeley Zen Center, was ordained in 1969. Bill Kwong and Silas Hoadley received their robes early in 1970. Silas had given up his importing business and was involved full-time with Zen Center. Peter Schneider and Dan Welch took their vows together in 1970; Paul Discoe the builder and Reb Anderson came later that year. Reb was the newest of the bunch, exceedingly concentrated and devoted to Suzuki. Suzuki had also ordained a young couple early in 1970, before they went to Japan to study in monasteries – Ron and Joyce Browning. And on New Year's Day of 1971 he was going to ordain a longtime IBM employee named Les Kaye at the Los Altos zendo.

BOB AND I were among a half dozen others with whom Suzuki had been discussing priests' ordination. One day at the City Center he called Bob and me to his tatami room and told us that he wanted to ordain us together. It was a little hard to imagine. Neither of us had been very successful in learning to control our desires. We were definitely among the loose cannons that Suzuki kept on deck. We considered many of his other lay students to be much better examples to new students and deeper rudders for the community. But we didn't protest. We sat up straight and serious. I just nodded quietly, thinking that if I said anything he would realize his mistake. (He used to say, "I think you're all enlightened until you open your mouth.")

"Do you think we should sit extra zazen at night in order to deepen our zazen?" Bob asked.

"The most important point for both of you," Suzuki said, "is not to sit more but to develop patience. I had the same problem." Then he said, laughing, "To develop patience you need patience." He raised his left eyebrow and softly said, "The main thing is not to fight." Then he called in Okusan, and they measured us for robes, while laughing and teasing us.

BY NOW THE six original priests ordained before Richard were gone or on the periphery of Zen Center. Very few people had heard of Bill McNeil or Bob Hense, whom Suzuki considered his first two ordained disciples. Jean Ross was living in Carmel; a small sitting group met in her apartment. (These first three were ordained as Suzuki's disciples in Japan by other priests.) Grahame Petchey was still in Japan and seemed to have drifted away. Philip Wilson had moved north to Santa Rosa with his wife in 1969 before the move to Page Street. He wasn't comfortable with all the new people and hierarchy, and there didn't seem to be any role for him. Claude Dalenberg was involved in the practice at the City Center, but he too wasn't happy with the new, bigger Zen Center. He remembered the days when Suzuki talked about getting a large house where ten or so of them could live communally – like the East-West House.

Claude felt that Suzuki had reneged on a commitment to support a basically lay practice at Zen Center.

BY THE SUMMER of 1970, six priests had been head monks at Tassajara: Richard, Philip, Claude, Jean, Silas, and Mel. Soon Peter, Bill, and Dan would follow. The presence of more and more American priests at Tassajara and at the City Center made a great difference in the atmosphere. Students were considering whether they wanted to receive ordination as priests – mainly those who'd come since Tassajara started. Most of the old-timers who were still around were satisfied with the lay practice they'd developed.

Lay practice and lay ordination had not been neglected. In late August of 1970, thirty-six students took the precepts in the first lay ordination since 1962. Suzuki said he waited that long because he'd been discouraged by the number of people who had quit after ordination. A couple of students had even given back their rakusus. Suzuki felt confident in the commitment of the 1970 ordination group. They'd all been with him at least three years.

Suzuki and his sangha were discovering and redefining for themselves what it meant to be a lay Buddhist or a priest in America. They were figuring out what it meant by living with it, learning from their elders, and giving it whatever meaning was in their hearts. They hardly knew what terms to use. "Monk" was too austere, and "priest" seemed too advanced. Both were used at times, but perhaps "priest" was more suitable for someone who had received transmission or at least had gone through the head monk initiation. It was suggested that the new ordainees be called novices, but it didn't catch on.

Suzuki emphasized that being a priest was in no way superior to being a layperson. It was just a different role. And what was the difference between these so-called priests and the laypeople? All the priests except Jean were married or dating. Suzuki had asked Mel not to have any girlfriends for a year, but at the end of the year he told Mel casually he knew he'd failed. At Tassajara and in the city nearly everyone, priest and lay, got up early, sat zazen, recited sutras, studied Buddhist texts, and worked hard living semi-monastic lives. In the city, people were more free, however, to have private lives and go out together. Many were involved intimately. Some had outside jobs. In several lectures Suzuki had said, "We are neither priest nor lay, but something in between." Something new was being created at Zen Center. He was willing to let it take its course.

One day Mel asked Suzuki, "What does it mean to be a priest?"

"I don't know," Suzuki answered. Mel would have to find out for himself.

For almost a year Suzuki had been informing people of his decision to give Richard transmission in Japan, and little by little he got their feedback, much of it negative. He asked Silas what he thought, and Silas said that maybe Richard was too smart for the community. "Maybe the rest of you aren't smart enough," Suzuki answered. At a meeting at Tassajara, he finally said that the community was going to have to trust him on this one.

"OKAY, ROSHI, then what does transmission mean?" I asked Suzuki in his office at Sokoji on that day in 1969 when he had told Bob and me of his plan. "Does it mean that Richard Baker is perfectly enlightened, and that his mind is the same as the mind of Buddha? Is his understanding complete?"

"Oh, no no no," Suzuki said. "Don't make too much of it. It means he has a good understanding. A good understanding and a complete commitment."

Zen practice is to get to our True Mind, the mind not accessible to thinking. This mind cannot be consciously known by ordinary efforts. An unusual effort is necessary. This effort is zazen.

SUZUKI LEFT for Japan in August 1970, planning to stay for four months. Aside from performing Richard's transmission ceremony and visiting with family and old friends, he wanted to look for places where he could send students.

Okusan convinced him to leave a month early so he could join her and some friends from the Sokoji congregation for a pottery tour on the southern island of Kyushu. She had to beg him repeatedly to go to Kyushu and not to bring any disciples with him. She knew it would be the only real vacation of their lives. Just before they were to leave, he got ill and asked her to go without him. She pleaded, saying he wouldn't have to do anything but rest. And so they went.

In old-fashioned Japanese style, Okusan carried his and her luggage, and he carried only a handkerchief. In the hot muggy early autumn they went from town to town and kiln to kiln. He kept up as well as he could. In the evenings she massaged him and applied acupuncture. He got worse; the second week of the tour she stayed with him at hotels while the others were out sightseeing. After the tour, back at Rinso-in, he finally recovered.

GRAHAME CAME to visit his old teacher at Rinso-in, and Suzuki talked with him about the problem of finding a place to send his students in Japan. Noiri's health wasn't good enough to permit him to take on more students. After visiting some other training temples, Suzuki had concluded that they were not suitable for his students. Eiheiji was clearly too big and weighed down by elaborate traditions. Richard was there and couldn't stand it. He said it was a total waste of his time – a magnificent place, but not for foreigners to study Zen. It was more of a seminary for Japanese priests to learn priestcraft. In Kyoto, Richard practiced a year at Antaiji, then sat at Daitokuji with a Rinzai teacher. Suzuki wasn't entirely pleased with this choice and didn't want to send people to study koans, but he let Richard decide for himself.

"You clearly need to see Antaiji," Grahame told Suzuki. The zazen-only approach appealed to Grahame, and so did the abbot, Uchiyama. He didn't try to accommodate the hierarchy as Suzuki did, and he scoffed at the state of Zen in Japan. Grahame had been displeased with the growing formality he'd experienced during his visit to Tassajara and hoped that a little of Antaiji's way would rub off on Suzuki, bringing him back to the approach they'd had in San Francisco in the early days.

They went to Kyoto and met Uchiyama. In the afternoon Suzuki gave a brief talk in Japanese to Uchiyama's Japanese zazen students. In the evening he met with Uchiyama's Western students, and there was a lively, three-hour question-and-answer session. Some of the Japanese students who went to the English discussion as well said it was only then, when they heard Suzuki speak in English, that they realized why he had so many students. In Japanese he just bored them.

AT RINSO-IN Richard Baker sat on tatami in a room in the far wing off the main hall. With a brush he was carefully copying the characters for the names of Suzuki's lineage. It was a part of his transmission, a private ceremony between the two of them that would take weeks. Suzuki was on the other side of the main hall meeting old friends and members of the temple congregation. There was almost always someone dropping by. Richard had left Eiheiji before the end of the practice period. He was completely fed up with the hollowness of the practice, which was, for the most part, aimed at getting a temple license. He detested the show of practice put on daily for hundreds of visiting lay Buddhists and bus-loads of tourists. As had happened with Grahame, there was even a particular monk who was out to get Richard. Suzuki tried to get him to complete the practice period. He asked Grahame what to do, and Grahame told him to insist that Richard stay, even though he himself had experienced enormous difficulty at Eiheiji and understood Richard's feelings. Richard was adamant. Suzuki gave in. It was a big embarrassment to Suzuki, but he cared more about Richard than about Eiheiji, and accepted his decision.

At Rinso-in Richard got frustrated because Suzuki just kept meeting with people and ignoring him, leaving him by himself in the back wing. Finally Richard went into the family quarters and told Suzuki that if he didn't have any time for him, he'd go back to Kyoto where his wife and daughter were. Suzuki started spending more time with him, Richard stayed, and on Buddha's Enlightenment Day, December 8, 1970, the ceremony of transmission from master to disciple was completed.

BEFORE HEADING back to the States, Suzuki went to headquarters in Tokyo and tried to register Richard and his other priests with the Soto organization. He had tried the same in 1966 and gotten nowhere. Suzuki was too much of a maverick, and his disciples hadn't followed the prescribed path. Japanese monks were routinely registered with pretend ceremonies and qualifications, but there was no leniency for him and his barbarians.

Richard wasn't aware of Suzuki's efforts to register his disciples. He remembered Suzuki saying that Zen Center shouldn't have any official relationship with Japanese Soto Zen, just a friendly one. For instance, after receiving transmission, there is a ceremony in Japan called ten'e, wherein a priest receives recognition of transmission from the Soto school. In this ceremony the priest is "abbot for a day" of both Eiheiji and Sojiji and carries an ox-hair whisk. Suzuki told Richard, "But I think you should go to the White House in Washington, D.C., and wave your whisk there."

While still in Yaizu Suzuki went to see his family doctor. Suzuki said he felt fine, but Dr. Ozawa said his liver was weak.

"See," Okusan said, responding to this news, "you should let Richard take over Zen Center. Stay here. I'll go to San Francisco to get your stuff and come back to take care of you."

"No," he said. "It's time for us to return. I want to celebrate the New Year with my students at Page Street."

Chapter Eighteen

The Driver

1 9 7 1

*How can you practice zazen? Only when you accept yourself
and when you really know you exist here. You cannot escape from
yourself. This is the ultimate fact, that "I am here."*

AFTER RETURNING from Japan, Shunryu Suzuki experienced a period of relatively good health and was enjoying life with
his students at Page Street. He went to zazen, led services, ate frequently with residents and boarders in the dining room, and saw
many students privately for dokusan and tea.

While full of confidence in his sangha and in Richard still back in
Japan, Suzuki was not naive about shortcomings and stumbling
blocks. In lectures he warned about clinging to Buddhism and said
that religion indeed could be an opiate – let it fall away and just be
yourself. He'd been reminded during his 1970 trip to Japan of the
decay inherent in institutions. "Don't give me that old-time religion," he said, and urged his students to be ever vigilant. One danger he saw was "losing oneself in a group." While extolling the

virtues of the sangha, he warned his students not to become like sheep. During Suzuki's recent visit to Kyoto, Uchiyama, like his outspoken master Sawaki, had railed against Japan's "mob psychology" and tendency toward "group paralysis." In a lecture at Page Street, Suzuki spoke in his back-and-forth, contradictory fashion on this subject.

We know how we can develop Dogen's practice in Zen Center. Our practice is individual practice; at the same time it is group practice. It is hermit-like practice, and at the same time, it can be practiced in this modern world. This is the characteristic of Dogen's practice. This is the true meaning of settling oneself on oneself. Even though you are in this modern society, you should not lose your fresh experience moment after moment. We should not be caught. We should know the fresh vitality within ourselves.

The most important thing in our practice is just to follow our schedule and to do things with people. Again, you may say this is group practice, but it is not so. Group practice is quite different; it is a kind of art. In wartime, when we were practicing zazen, some young men who were enthusiastic about Japan's militaristic mood told me that in a sutra it says, "To understand birth and death is the main point of our practice." They said, "Even though I don't know anything about that sutra, I can die easily at the front." That is group practice. Encouraged by trumpets, guns, and war cries, it is quite easy to die. That kind of practice is not our practice. We practice with people, first of all. But the goal is to practice with mountains, trees, and stones – with everything in the world, in the universe – and to find ourselves in this big cosmos, this big world.

Suzuki led the City Center sesshin in February 1971. The buddha hall was packed when he spoke. His lecture on Saturday, February 27, left a number of students with an empty feeling. They would refer to it later as the Driver Lecture.

He started by saying that the reason we practice is to be fully enlightened. The problem is delusion – we don't have the eyes to see clearly. "Naturally you are wondering how to find the truth, and you want to have some clear map of which way to go. That is why you must have a teacher who gives you a map or some instruction on which way to go."

He talked about how to work with a teacher, how not to waste your time or the teacher's time. "When he goes fast, you go fast, and when he goes slow, you go slow. Maybe your teacher will be like your driver." He said that students may ask the driver to stop at a coffee shop, and that's okay, but then they may want to hang out there.

In that way you may lose your driver, because it takes too long. If he is very old, he will die. In that case, in order to arrive at the city, naturally you must find another driver. You have an advantage, because you have already come so far. Ah, but you know, I think you will miss the driver. After he is no more you will miss him a lot. And there you have another advantage. Because you miss him, you will try hard this time not to waste your time. You will not disturb your driver anymore, saying, "Let's stop here!" Especially since you don't know how far it is to the city, this time you naturally will not disturb the driver.

This was an unusual approach for Suzuki to use in a lecture. He was giving advice about how to relate to a teacher, and how to relate to *someone else* as a teacher. He was worried about his dear passengers and the drivers to come. He was worried that his health was failing.

ON MARCH 12 Suzuki flew to Portland to visit a group associated with Zen Center. Okusan worried about his health and asked Reb Anderson to accompany him. Reb had studied with Suzuki since 1968, when he had driven up to the front door of Sokoji in a grey Cadillac hearse to visit his best childhood chum, Bob Halpern. Reb had been a championship heavyweight Golden Gloves boxer and had studied psychology, philosophy, and math at the University of Minnesota. Then he met Suzuki and through steadiness and persistence became a close disciple. He was ordained as a priest just two years later. In this short time Reb had already read more about Buddhism than most students ever would. He was a zealous practitioner who would sometimes sit zazen all night alone. He wanted to be near Suzuki, and since he was so concentrated and consistent in his efforts, he often was.

Suzuki gave a lecture on the evening of the first day in Portland. Late the next morning, as Reb was carrying the stick, he saw Suzuki bent over on his cushion. Reb went up to him, and Suzuki said, "I have a terrible pain." He was immediately taken back to the house where they were staying. The next morning he was still sick and coughing up bitter bile. Suzuki managed to endure the flight back to San Francisco, and Yvonne and Okusan met him with a wheelchair. Though he could hardly walk, he refused it, stubbornly and uncharacteristically saying, "No, I am a Zen master."

Back at Page Street, Reb knew things were really bad when Suzuki took off his robe and just let it drop to the floor, something he had never done in front of Reb, who was always watching and copying his teacher.

For the ride to the hospital Suzuki had to be carried to the car. The doctor quickly discovered it was his gallbladder, and before long he was in surgery.

To understand Buddhism, direct experience, direct practice is necessary. If you want to do it, you have to be very straightforward and open, ready for anything that might happen to you.

IN THE WINTER of 1971 Dianne Goldschlag had been coming home to Page Street and crying almost every afternoon. She was unhappy with her job at an insurance company cafeteria in Chinatown, where she was working to save money to go back to Tassajara. In dokusan Suzuki suggested that when Dianne cleaned the tables she should talk to them as if they were her friends, telling them how much she enjoyed cleaning them and how she hoped they felt better. It did help to talk to each table like that, Dianne found. But she still cried. Her room was over his room. One day she was crying hard in her room just before zazen. In the zendo Suzuki walked around with his stick, and when he came to Dianne he rested it gently on her shoulder but didn't hit her. He just stood there with the stick on her shoulder for a long time.

One day Dianne got off early from her job with only one thing on her mind. She was going to visit Suzuki at Mt. Zion Hospital, where he was recovering from his operation. Okusan had said no students should visit him, but that wasn't fair, thought Dianne. She owed him a visit – and a dime.

The previous summer, Suzuki had visited her in the hospital in Monterey when she had an abscess removed from her fallopian tube. Okusan was with him. After greeting Dianne and telling her to get well right away, Okusan went over to the window to leave her husband and his student alone and also to make sure they didn't visit too long. Dianne didn't say anything; she just looked at him. He leaned over and said, "I'll give you a dime to see your scar."

Now he was in the hospital and she wanted to support him.

When she reached the door of his room, some Japanese people were just leaving. Okusan looked harshly at her.

Suzuki told Okusan, "I want her to come over here by me. You go away."

Dianne went over to Suzuki-roshi's bed and, after inquiring about how he felt, reminded him that he'd seen her scar for a dime. She had a dime and wanted to see his scar. He showed her. It was fresh and red, with the stitches still in it. She asked what medication he was on, and he said none. He tried not to sleep during the day so he could sleep at night, in spite of the pain. She massaged his toes, gave him a poem that her friend Margaret had written for him, and showed him a funny little picture she'd drawn of multicolored fantasy animals. He marveled at her creatures. They were silly together for a while, and then she bowed and left him alone.

The way you study true Zen is not some verbal thing. You should open yourself and give up everything, and whatever comes up through practice, you should try it, whether you think it is good or bad. This is the fundamental attitude toward study. You should be like a child who draws things whether they are good or bad. Sometimes you will do things without much reason. If that is difficult for you, you are not actually ready to practice zazen.

How not to be lost in our problems is our practice.

SUZUKI REMAINED in the hospital for a few weeks after his operation. The doctor had told him that people frequently feel a lot better and regain their former energy after their gallbladders are removed. So the hope was that he might get back the sort of health he had before his debilitating flus of the winters of 1969 and 1970. But while in the hospital he got another blow.

The doctor came to talk to the Suzukis together. A routine biopsy had shown that the gallbladder was cancerous. This surprised the doctor, because gallbladder cancer is very rare. The doctor was confident they'd gotten all the cancer before it spread; the surrounding tissue was pink and healthy looking, so they shouldn't worry too much. Still, it was disturbing news. Suzuki feared he might not live the ten years he'd been hoping for – fearing not for himself but for his students. The cancer was kept a secret. No need to disturb people.

A FEW DAYS later Okusan brought her husband mail and messages. Among the get-well cards and notes was a letter from Katagiri stating his intention to resign soon. This was a completely unexpected blow, and it saddened Suzuki tremendously.

Suzuki was already concerned that Zen Center was getting much too large for him to deal with effectively, even with Katagiri's help.

Katagiri was an essential teacher for the community and had become an increasingly important presence in the seven years he'd been there. Very little was more important to Suzuki than having Katagiri around. But he'd misread him, hadn't given him enough space or appreciation.

Katagiri was at Tassajara translating for and assisting Tatsugami and hating it. To him Tatsugami represented everything he disliked about Zen in Japan. Katagiri saw the old man as imperious, condescending, and caught up in ritual. He wanted to get away from being the perennial second string. He loved and respected Suzuki, but it was a little hard on him to live and work constantly with people who, perhaps blinded by cultural differences, seemed to regard Suzuki as a flawless master. Suzuki had mentioned the idea that he might retire as abbot to work closely with a few people, that Richard would then become abbot, and that Katagiri would be Zen Center's senior dharma teacher. But Katagiri wanted to have his own group.

Suzuki couldn't move out of his bed. He was so helpless, and now with Katagiri's impending resignation he felt even more so. Okusan could see what a disaster it was for him and worried that this news alone would kill him.

Back at Page Street Suzuki did not get back his energy as everyone had hoped. He spent a lot of time in April recuperating in his bed. In May he began to get out. He gave a lecture one evening and went to the dining room for the regular question-and-answer period, told the students he was feeling fine, even opened up his robe and showed them his scar.

SUZUKI'S YOUNGEST son, Otohiro, was back from Vietnam. After a couple of years of depression and recovery, he went to work for Japan Airlines. On Memorial Day he picked up his father and Okusan at Page Street and took them to the annual ceremony at the cemetery at Colma. There Suzuki found Katagiri, and they stood talking at the edge of the crowd. Suzuki asked what his plans were after Zen Center. Katagiri said he didn't have any idea. Suzuki was surprised at this. He and Okusan had assumed that Katagiri had been invited to lead another group. "Please don't leave," he said. Katagiri didn't say anything.

A few days later Katagiri was back at Tassajara, preparing to leave. Suzuki was coming down from the city. Katagiri had asked Suzuki's attendant, Niels Holm, a carpenter and sailor from Denmark, if Suzuki had left the city yet. Niels assured him that he hadn't. He was lying. Suzuki had called and asked Niels to stall Katagiri at Tassajara till he got there. Katagiri didn't want to see Suzuki, because talking to him at Tassajara would be different from talking to him in public at Colma. It would be harder to say no or to say nothing.

All of a sudden there was Suzuki in front of him. Katagiri looked at Niels and realized he'd been betrayed. Niels made tea in Suzuki's tiny cabin, and watched the two teachers act as he'd never seen them act before. They bowed prostrate to each other, sat in seiza, and spoke formal, polite Japanese with ceremonial sincerity, rhythm, and tones. It was quite foreign to Niels, but he could see that Suzuki was asserting his seniority. Katagiri agreed to stay a while longer and attend the upcoming board meeting.

AT THE BOARD meeting there was talk about Tatsugami, who had led the previous three practice periods and had been invited to do the next one. Tatsugami was controversial. Some students had warmed to him, others tolerated him, and a couple of students had left. He had guided Tassajara from a communal to a monastic style as much as he could, on the Eiheiji model.

Tatsugami was treating the place as his own. He still saw Suzuki as a temple priest who didn't have the training to run a monastery. To him Suzuki didn't deserve such authority, but he himself did, having been ino, the priest in charge of monks' behavior and ceremony, for thirteen years at Eiheiji. In a meeting at Eiheiji during the time Richard was a monk there, Tatsugami bragged to his colleagues and assembled monks about his monastery in America. Richard, who had originally invited him to come, let it pass until

Tatsugami had finished. Then he stood up and thanked him for his kindness in being Zen Center's guest teacher.

Suzuki had made it clear to Richard in Japan that he didn't appreciate Richard's having invited Tatsugami to come to Tassajara in the first place; but he didn't complain to other students. Tatsugami definitely had his good points, and Suzuki did keep inviting him back. Tatsugami was like a choreographer who had taught the troupe the basic steps and rules of the song and dance, freeing Suzuki to work further with some students on fine points and essential spirit. Maybe Tatsugami had put a bit too much emphasis on ceremony, but Suzuki said his influence would be good "if you watch Tatsugami-roshi's practice carefully, with your mind open to learn something." It would not be so good "if you see him with your mind based on a gaining idea. Then what you learn is the art of Zen. It is not true Zen."

Suzuki had let Tassajara evolve into something unlike anything that existed in Japan, but Tatsugami didn't necessarily appreciate this vision. It would disturb Dan Welch, who was often translating for him, when Tatsugami would say in an offhand manner that Suzuki's Zen was weak. Suzuki said he only taught what he knew, which was zazen. Similarly Tatsugami taught what he knew, which was Eiheiji's monastic form. But even if Suzuki wasn't completely pleased with Tatsugami's influence, the fox in him didn't mind a bit of confusion and doubt for his students to deal with.

Suzuki clearly wanted Katagiri to stay. At the board meeting that May, the two problems converged. Suzuki used the leverage of the board meeting to ask Katagiri to please stay and help. He was being more verbal and definite than ever before. Katagiri was resisting. Then one by one all the board members, who were also students, told Katagiri what he meant to them, how much they loved him and wanted him to stay as a coteacher with Suzuki. It was heartfelt and tearful.

Then Suzuki played his trump card. He asked Katagiri to lead the fall practice period and said he'd disinvite Tatsugami – a serious slight which would surely end Zen Center's relationship with him.

Katagiri made a countermove, saying, "Okay, I'll do it, but only if you come down to Tassajara and help me." Suzuki agreed, and suddenly Katagiri was back and Tatsugami was gone.

In Japan, Grahame visited Tatsugami. He kept to himself that he didn't like what he'd seen of Tatsugami's influence on Tassajara. Tatsugami told Grahame that he planned to retire at Tassajara and showed him a photograph of the attendant whom he'd ordained at Tassajara – an attractive young woman. It was obvious that they were very close. He said that each trip he brought more of his belongings and left them there. Someday soon he would go and not return, except to occasionally visit his wife and son, to whom he would leave his temple in Japan. But none of that was to happen. Soon Tatsugami would get the letter withdrawing the invitation, which surely would break his tough heart.

When Tatsugami had first arrived in America, Suzuki met him with some students at the airport. As they watched him walk off the plane in his traveling robes, swaggering with confidence, Suzuki said, "I can see how much he's going to suffer here."

Our way is to see what we are doing, moment after moment.

DESPITE THE disastrous problems most of his students had encountered trying to study Zen in Japan, Suzuki continued to explore the possibility. Paul Discoe had gone there with his wife and son and was doing quite well, studying Zen and temple carpentry. Suzuki had ordained another couple before they went to Japan. The wife did fine at a nunnery, but her husband was forceably sedated and shipped out of Eiheiji. A woman from Zen Center had such horrible experiences in Japanese temples that she rejected Buddhism entirely, bought a wig, and moved to L.A.

Suzuki had talked to Reb about going to Japan, and he was studying Japanese in preparation. A student named Angie Runyon was to be ordained in the fall. Suzuki was considering sending her to a women's temple in Japan. Suzuki was talking to Dan Welch about Japan, too. Reb, Angie, and Dan were devoted to Suzuki and did not wish to be with another teacher, especially since it wasn't clear how long Suzuki would be around. But they were prepared to do what their teacher asked.

Other students, including myself, who were less reticent about arguing with Suzuki, had refused to consider going, at least for the time being. Judging from those who'd gone, studying Soto Zen in Japan seemed to be exceedingly difficult. Only the renegades Uchiyama and Yasutani had attracted any following among Westerners. But Suzuki seemed willing to risk losing disciples in order to promote his old idea of exchanging students, of trying to establish this transmission of knowledge and understanding. He seemed to think it was necessary, that there was more to be learned about Zen and Japanese culture than he and his Japanese assistants could teach in America.

Yvonne Rand argued with Suzuki about sending any more women to Japan. Suzuki said he was unsure of himself as a teacher for women priests, and thought a woman teacher would understand them better. Angie, though not arguing with him, said she could not hope to meet anyone who understood her as well as Suzuki. Yvonne told him that Japan was not a good place for women to practice, because they were second-class citizens there. She said to a friend that if he persisted, she would lie down and kick and scream on the tatami in front of him until he changed his mind. In the end, neither Reb nor Angie nor Dan went. But others went later, and in time the exchange did begin to become more fruitful.

EARLIER, LOUISE Pryor had been present when Suzuki, Okusan, and an assistant priest named Ryogen Yoshimura were discussing her husband Dan Welch's future. Dan, a priest who spoke good Japanese from his Rinzai training with Nakagawa, was to go to

Japan to live in a temple for two years. The discussion was proceeding as if she weren't there.

"What about me?" she asked.

Yoshimura explained that Louise couldn't go because she wasn't Japanese and would be a burden on the priest's wife. She should remain in America for a year or two while her husband studied in Japan.

Louise became angry. "All of you think it's better to be a man than a woman, you think it's better to be a priest than a layperson, and you think it's better to be Japanese than American. But I will always be a woman, and I will always be a layperson, and I will always be an American, and here I am."

Everyone was silent. Suzuki turned to her and said, "What you have just expressed is the spirit of the bodhisattva's way."

You cannot judge a teacher by your low standards.

IN EARLY 1970 Shunryu Suzuki had been reading the book *Meditation in Action* by Chogyam Trungpa Rinpoche, a Tibetan teacher who had just arrived in America. Some of Suzuki's students had heard Trungpa speak, had met him, and had talked to Suzuki about him in glowing terms. One evening while sitting with students after dinner at Page Street, out of nowhere Suzuki said, "Someone is coming. After he comes, maybe no one will be left here at Zen Center but me." Then he laughed. Nobody had the faintest idea what he was talking about. He was talking about Trungpa.

Trungpa and Suzuki met at Tassajara in June of 1970, and they immediately made a strong connection. Trungpa, his very young British wife, and a few of his students ate supper late the night they arrived. At the end of the meal, Suzuki came in and sat down across from Trungpa. They looked at each other intently and spoke unhurriedly with long pauses.

Suzuki asked Trungpa to give a talk to the students in the zendo the next night. Trungpa walked in tipsy and sat on the edge of the altar platform with his feet dangling. But he delivered a crystal-clear talk, which some felt had a quality – like Suzuki's talks – of not only being about the dharma but being itself the dharma. After that he asked Trungpa to come to Page Street and lecture when he was in the city, which Trungpa did. Suzuki had no relationship like this with any other teacher. They talked about the loneliness of being a teacher. Trungpa called him his new spiritual father, and Suzuki told him, "You are like my son."

Suzuki's relationship with Trungpa disturbed some people, maybe because Trungpa, in addition to being a brilliant, inspiring speaker and the beloved teacher of many disciples, was also an outrageous alcoholic who slept with some of his female students.

One afternoon in May of 1971, Trungpa dropped by Page Street unannounced. He brought his newborn son to be blessed by Suzuki. Still recovering from his operation, Suzuki nonetheless put on a fancy yellow robe and high hat, quite appropriate for Tibetans, and performed a little ceremony in the buddha hall. Afterward they went to the courtyard for tea.

Later a number of Suzuki's students started studying with Trungpa. Some, including Bob Halpern, went to Boulder, where Trungpa spent most of his time; others stayed at Zen Center and went to Trungpa's San Francisco place when he was in town. Suzuki was comfortable with this and even suggested to some students that they go study with Trungpa. He communicated to Trungpa by letter and through students who went back and forth. Suzuki was interested in Trungpa's ideas of exchanging students, starting a Buddhist university, sharing tapes and transcripts of lectures in their libraries, and founding a center to work with what Trungpa called "mentally extreme" students.

Trungpa's scene was new and exciting. He was younger and more energetic than Suzuki. Suzuki expressed concern that because of his indulgent lifestyle Trungpa wouldn't live long enough to establish his way. As austere as Suzuki's own lifestyle was, and as controversial as Trungpa was, Suzuki did not reject him for his ways but always related to him with love and acceptance. In July 1971 Suzuki mentioned Trungpa in a lecture:

Because emptiness has no limit and no beginning, we can believe in it. Isn't this so? This is very important. I am not fooling you! Okay? If you really understand this, tears will flow. You will really feel happy to be a Buddhist. If you struggle hard enough, you will feel how important this point is. The way you can struggle with this is to be supported by something, something you don't know. As we are human beings, there must be that kind of feeling. You must feel it in this city or building or community. So whatever community it may be, it is necessary for it to have this kind of spiritual support. That is why I respect Trungpa Rinpoche. He is supporting us. You may criticize him because he drinks alcohol like I drink water, but that is a minor problem. He trusts you completely. He knows that if he is always supporting you in a true sense, you will not criticize him, whatever he does. And he doesn't mind whatever you say. That is not the point, you know. This kind of big spirit, without clinging to some special religion or form of practice, is necessary for human beings.

E̲verything you do is right, nothing you do is wrong, yet you must still make ceaseless effort.

IN JUNE 1971, during a sesshin in the city, Suzuki gave public talks for the first time since his gallbladder operation.

In his first talk Suzuki-roshi said, "Our practice is just to sit." He explained that the usual way of doing things is to expect something. From this point of view, if his students kept sitting and applying themselves day after day, their practice as well as their mental and physical health might improve. "But that is not a full understanding of practice. We also do zazen with the understanding that the goal is not there one or two years in the future, but right here." Further in his talk he said that real practice implies more than a scientific search for truth. Without ignoring the objective side of the truth, it has to be subjective as well, Buddha's whole teaching just for you, something you can taste. Not something to believe in but to discover, to experience.

To accept some idea of truth without experiencing it is like a painting of a cake on paper which you cannot eat. There is no taste, and you will give up, because it doesn't mean anything, even though you sit seven days. But our true zazen cannot be like that. If Zen was like that, it would have vanished from this world a long time ago. Zen is still alive because of the other side of the truth.

Only when each one of us feels the truth, appreciates the truth, accepts the truth, and is ready to follow the truth, will it work. When someone puts himself outside of the truth in order to study the truth, he won't know what to do when something happens to him.

Do you know the story of the true dragon? In ancient China, there was a person who liked dragons very much. He talked about dragons to his friends, and he painted dragons, and he bought various kinds of dragon sculptures. Then a dragon said to himself, "If a real dragon like me visited him, he would be very happy." One day the real dragon sneaked into his room. The man didn't know what to do! Whaaaah! He could not run away. He could not even stand up. Whaaaah!

For a long, long time we have been like him. That should not be our attitude. We should not be just a fan of dragons; we should always be the dragon himself. Then we will not be afraid of any dragon.

On the last day of the sesshin Suzuki recalled the time two years before when he had almost drowned at the Narrows of the Tassajara Creek, revealing what a pivotal experience it had been for him.

At that time I realized that we will never have good practice until we become quite serious. Since then my practice has improved a lot. Now I have confidence in my practice. It was a very interesting experience. I was among beautiful girls, and it reminded me of Buddha's overcoming demons. They were not evil demons, they were beautiful girls, but if I am dying, those beautiful girls will not help. Now I am really dying, not because of water, but because of my sickness. So we can sit with demons or with beautiful girls. When I am dying even snakes will not hurt me, they will be happy to be with me, and I will be very happy to be with them. In that situation, everything is with us, and we are happy to be with everything, without being hard or harsh or disturbed. Usually it is difficult to feel that way, because we are always involved in gaining ideas, expecting something in the future. The most important thing is to confront yourself and to be yourself. Then naturally you can see and accept things as they are. You will have perfect wisdom at that time.

Suzuki's offhand comment about dying was disturbing. He seemed to have recovered from his operation and was having a lot of contact with students. But there was still an uneasiness, a fragility in his laughter. During one lecture that June, talking about the decline of Buddhism in Japan, he paused and said with emphasis, "But things, you know, teach best when they're dying."

A *garden is never finished.*

AT TASSAJARA, Okusan and her husband spent an evening writing haiku, a rare moment together. She was staying in the Japanese-style cabin next to his, teaching and doing tea ceremony with students. She had started both haiku and tea ceremony while in the States – both at the prompting of her husband. "They are the only things he ever gave me," she said.

Along the creek
we look for tea-room flowers
dew-moistened trail

Summer 1971, Tassajara: Hojo and I stay in Tassajara during
the month of August. Dharma talk evening after evening.
There's blood and sweat. Hojo and I write haiku together.

from *Temple Dusk* by Mitsu Suzuki

Suzuki was a regular dynamo that summer. He was following
the whole schedule – zazen, service, silent breakfast with oryoki
bowls, seeing students for dokusan, giving lectures almost every
night. He worked in his garden in the mornings and afternoons
with one or two students at a time. He didn't spend much time
preparing for lectures, tending to find what he wanted to say when
he sat down on his cushion. Instead, in the hottest part of the day
after a nap and in the evening after dinner, he wrote with a brush in
sumi ink on the white backing of rakusus for fifty-five students who
were to receive lay ordination in late August in San Francisco. On
each rakusu he wrote the four-stanza robe chant, the date, his
name with red ink seal, and the four-character Buddhist name he'd
chosen for the student. Okusan was trying without much luck to
get him to rest more.

WORKING ALONE, Suzuki leaned into a large stone in his garden,
turning it slightly while his attendant, Niels, stood by the bridge looking down the road past the zendo. Suddenly Niels whistled – the
sign that Okusan was on her way back from the baths. Then Niels
took Suzuki's place wrestling with the stone while Suzuki went to
sit in the shade on the bench by his cabin, taking on the appearance
of a supervisor. She eyed them with suspicion. The next day she
sneaked back before her bath and caught him working with Niels.

"Hojo-san!" she yelled at him in Japanese. "Working out here in
your garden on a hot August day with a shovel taller than you are!
You are cutting your life short!"

"If I don't cut my life short, my students will not grow."

"Then go ahead and cut it short, if that's what you want!" she
scolded, wagging a finger.

"Stop that racket!" he said, returning to his task.

Okusan had reason to be upset. She knew and he knew he had not recovered from his operation. His urine was brown and so was his Japanese underwear. She'd wash it right away so his cabin cleaner, Maggie Kress, would not see it. But she would show Maggie his perspiration-soaked, robelike undershirt, wring it out and say, "Look, he's sweating blood. He must rest more," as if Maggie might be able to control him.

ONCE AT morning tea Suzuki was discussing the menu with senior students. At the request of the head cook, he agreed to demonstrate how he made udon, thick Japanese noodles. Before long he had a whole batch of people mixing rice flour and water and rolling dough while cooling breezes came through the screened windows.

Some people worked the flour into dough on the long sycamore worktable, others kneaded away on bread boards on the tile floor, while Suzuki kept adding more flour. Okusan came into this chaos, and they snapped at each other in Japanese till he pushed her out of the kitchen, laughing and undaunted. More people joined in – some preparing lunch, one making bread for guests, another washing pots in the corner, another passing around cups of tea and coffee. Suzuki kept adding more flour and water to give the new arrivals work to do.

"Who's running Tassajara?" asked one of the officers. "We have a guest season going on."

"You go run it!" laughed Suzuki.

After some hours, as the dough was being rolled out thin and cut into strips, Okusan returned, fuming. Suzuki waved goodbye, all smiles, as she dragged him out the door. What had started as a meal for a dozen older students ended up as dinner for sixty people, with seconds and thirds, two nights in a row.

"WHY DON'T you ever talk to me?" Okusan said one evening, exasperated. "What are you always thinking about?"

"Buddhism in America," he answered.

"Why can't you be like other husbands and tell me you love me?"

He looked at her. "Honey, honey, honey," he said.

"That's already too much," she said and went back to her cabin.

YVONNE CAME to Tassajara to drive Suzuki to a doctor's appointment in San Francisco. Okusan came along. As Yvonne was now president of Zen Center, she mentioned Jean Ross's recent resignation from the board. Zen Center had gotten too big and institutional for Jean, who felt she didn't get enough support for her little Carmel zendo. But the main reason she had quit the board was because Richard, who was living in Japan, still seemed to be running things at Zen Center in absentia. Jean had always admired Richard's energy and intelligence; indeed, it was she who had nominated him for president back in 1965, but everything had gotten to be too much for her. Suzuki nodded, not saying much.

He asked Yvonne how her children were doing. He talked about his family and expressed regret. "My focus was always on being a priest. It might have been better if I'd never gotten married. I have been a very bad family man. A bad father and a bad husband."

"Oh yes, veeeery bad husband," said Okusan. "Gooood priest, but baaaaad husband." She often said that.

PEOPLE WITH children were coming to Tassajara for "family practice." Pauline Petchey spent the summer there with her and Grahame's three children. Beat poet Diane diPrima, an old student of Suzuki's, spent a month with her four children. Toni and Tony Johansen brought their two children and ran a little summer school down in the barn. With Katagiri's help a children's ordination was arranged. Twelve of them sewed their own rakusus with their parents, and Suzuki performed a lay ordination, telling them they were the good children of Buddha.

ALAN WATTS came to Tassajara for the first time that summer with his wife, Jano. He had been a great help to Suzuki from the first, sending him students and introducing him to colleagues in the San Francisco Asian studies scene. Several of Zen Center's major donors at the time of the purchase of Tassajara had come through Watts and his East Coast connections. Though he loved rituals, Watts had scorned discipline, zazen, and the institutions that reminded him of the stuffiness of British boarding schools. He had interpreted Zen to millions and helped to open the minds of a generation, yet Suzuki's simple presence could make him feel off balance.

Watts was a heavy drinker. He had ended a long dry period that summer on the drive down to Tassajara. Suzuki sat with him and Jano that night on the back porch of a century-old stone room overlooking the creek. Niels, attending Suzuki, joined them. Watts, usually so confident, able to improvise lucid spiels on live radio when he couldn't even walk straight to the mike, had lost his cool and was chattering nervously. Suzuki was being terribly quiet, which just made Watts talk more. Jano was being quiet, too. Watts kept getting up to "have some of your marvelous water," and he'd come back smelling more of alcohol each time. Niels, unable to take it any longer, started talking with Watts and kept a running patter going for an hour while Suzuki and Jano sat silently.

The next day, as Niels helped Suzuki in his garden, they could hear Watts on the bridge expounding his understanding of all-that-is to some dazzled guests. He had regained his composure and was standing tall with a toga and a staff. Niels expressed regret at having talked so much the night before, saying he'd been a very bad student.

Suzuki said, "Oh no, you were a very good student last night. Thank you very much."

"Well, we used to think he was profound until we found the real thing," Niels said.

"You completely miss the point about Alan Watts!" Suzuki fumed with a sudden intensity. "You should notice what he has done. He is a great bodhisattva."

ONE DAY while walking in the vegetable garden at Tassajara, Suzuki noticed a student who was sitting on a stone looking at a sunflower growing nearby. He went over and sat by her.

"What are you doing?"

"Meditating with the sunflower," she said. "It rotates with the sun."

Suzuki sat with her for a long time. That night Suzuki referred to his garden visit.

Unless you get through to emptiness, you are not practicing. But if you stick to the idea of emptiness, you are not a Buddhist yet. Someone was sitting in front of a sunflower, watching the sunflower, a cup of sun, and so I tried it too. It was wonderful; I felt the whole universe in the sunflower. That was my experience. Sunflower meditation. A wonderful confidence appeared. You can see the whole universe in a flower. If you say, "Oh this is a sunflower which doesn't really exist" [laughing], that is not our zazen practice.

Y*ou stick to naturalness too much. When you stick to it, it is not natural any more.*

I WAS HAVING tea with Suzuki in his cabin and asked him the meaning of the scroll behind him.

"Stones in the air."

"Stones in the air?"

"Yes. It was given to me by my master Kishizawa-roshi. It means don't create some problems which are extra. Just the problems you already have are enough."

"You mean like you can't ride a horse on a horse?" I asked, referring to another proverb that Suzuki sometimes mentioned, which likened problems to horses. You can ride one horse but you can't ride a horse on a horse. It was a point he made in various ways – that if we don't compound our problems we'll be able to deal with them.

"Yes, same thing," Suzuki answered.

"Oh!" said I, excited. "I understood something!"

Suzuki laughed. "Is that unusual?"

"Yes! I never understand anything."

"What do you not understand?"

"What you talked about last night in lecture – *ri*, the first principle. Every time you talk about that I give up. I think it's impossible for me to understand."

"No, no, no," he said, like a mother consoling a hurt child. "I don't mean to discourage you. You can understand. You can understand completely. It's just that the way you're trying to understand is like going south to get to San Francisco."

SUZUKI LECTURED almost every night at Tassajara that summer, more than he'd ever done before. On August 17, the night before he left, he spoke to his students about something he'd been returning to – the first principle and the second principle.

He warned about confusing the first and second principles. He'd become aware that many people didn't understand what he was saying. The problem was that one couldn't talk about both sides, emptiness and form, at once. He especially emphasized not confusing these two aspects when it came to rules.

There are two completely different viewpoints. One is to say that everyone, everything has buddha nature, nothing is great and nothing is small. When we speak in that way it means we are talking about our original nature, from the standpoint of the first principle. Everything has buddha nature, period. No idea follows. We shouldn't say therefore or but. That is the first principle. The other viewpoint is to put emphasis on rules, on actual practice, on the second principle. Practice is the way to attain direct experience of the first principle. But when we talk about it we cannot say both sides at once.

We always smile. Even though the way that we practice is hard, we know it is the second principle, it is something to help us. Even though your teacher is angry, you do not take it so seriously [laughing]. You know that is the second principle, not the first principle. So when I say something about rules, I say it smiling, so you don't take it so seriously [laughing].

"You talked about the first principle again, but I still don't know what it is," I said to Suzuki.

"I don't know," he said, "*is* the first principle."

There is no special path which is true.

IT HAD BEEN over five years since Shunryu Suzuki had first traveled the winding, dusty road to Tassajara with Richard in April of 1966. In that time he had come to know intimately the stones in the creek and the plants and trees on the hillsides. He had delighted in the natural setting: stopping on the Hogback Trail to gaze across the valley at the waterfall and breathe the clean wilderness air, soaking in the large mineral-water plunge. Suzuki savored the sights, sounds, and smells of his hidden paradise, but he was only there because of the people who had joined him and helped him to establish his way.

Tassajara represented everything he loved: a place to listen to the birds, to move rocks, to sit zazen with his Buddhist friends, and to extend that zazen everywhere endlessly. Tassajara was Suzuki's reward and at the same time his gift. Whenever he arrived or departed, students would stop what they were doing to come stand on the road to bow in gassho as the car pulled up or away, and he would bow with them. At those times it was most obvious how Suzuki's heart was planted there at Tassajara.

MAGGIE WAS packing Suzuki's bags. He was supposed to leave before lunch, but since morning tea all he'd done was work in his garden. Maggie had gone out to question him a few times: Did he want her to pack this or that? Did he want some tea? But he wouldn't answer or even look up. He just kept nudging the stones this way and that and moving a few of the plants. He was getting his garden the way he wanted it and doing so with a sense of finality that had echoed in his lecture the night before. Finally he stopped. He stood looking for a while. At least for now, his work had come to an end.

Yvonne had driven in from the city to pick up the Suzukis. She accompanied Okusan to get her things. Niels and Maggie went with Suzuki into his cabin to do the last bit of packing. Suzuki untied his work clothes and let them drop to the tatami. In the subdued light he stood in the middle of his room in his white underwear, exhausted, almost unable to move. Suddenly he looked sickly and weak, his skin yellow. It seemed to have just happened, as if he'd used himself all up. He could hardly dress himself. He walked slowly with Niels to the baths and then to the zendo to offer incense, something he always did when arriving or departing.

Dan, the director, brought Yvonne's Volvo over the little bridge, and they loaded the back. A dozen students stood around silently. Suzuki came back from the zendo and smiled at them. He looked so weak. Okusan helped him into the back of the car as Dan, his wife, Louise, and Angie Runyon got in. Maggie was standing at the side, crying. He kept bowing, and everyone was bowing back. Faintly he said through the open window that he was sorry to leave and would try to be back soon. People said, "Yes, come back soon." Yvonne drove off with Suzuki still smiling. The Volvo slowly crossed the wooden bridge over the small creek, passed the narrow stretch below the upper garden and above the stone kitchen and zendo, curved up the dirt road past the shop and the screened junkyard, drove under the roof of the gatehouse and up the bumpy road in a cloud of dust, Tassajara disappearing behind.

Chapter Nineteen

Final Season: Autumn

1971

*D*rive *the wave, ride the wave.*

AFTER LEAVING Tassajara that day, Suzuki-roshi asked Yvonne to pull the car over when they reached the ridge. The view of coastal mountains, wide blue sky, and a streak of Pacific Ocean at the horizon was spectacular. Everyone got out and had a picnic. Below them were the rugged watersheds that fed into Tassajara Creek. Suzuki felt better after lunch and a rest. This was the spot where he had done his dance after first seeing Tassajara.

They made another stop at a retreat center near San Juan Bautista, where Soen Nakagawa was in the last hours of a weeklong sesshin. The Tassajara group joined in for the last period of zazen and the closing ceremony. In the retreat center of the mission Nakagawa prepared and served thick green matcha tea to the Tassajara visitors and to some of the sesshin participants. Each bowl of tea was shared by two people, an uncommon style. The first one went to the Suzukis. They drank and admired the bowl made by Naka-gawa from clay in Jerusalem, where he had established a zendo.

THOUGH HE wasn't feeling well the next day, Suzuki gave the Saturday lecture in the city. He spoke of the visit with Nakagawa.

At the end of his sesshin we bowed maybe more than thirty times, calling many buddhas' names. He called some by special names: Sunshine Buddha, Moonlight Buddha, Dead Sea Buddha, and Good Practice Buddha. Many buddhas appeared and bowed and bowed and bowed. That is something beyond our understanding. When he bowed to all those buddhas, the buddhas he bowed to were beyond his own understanding. Again and again he did it.

And he served us matcha from a bowl which he made himself. What he was doing, I don't know, and he didn't know. He looked very happy, but that happiness is very different from the happiness we usual people have. Our practice should go to that level, where there is no human problem, no buddha problem, where there is nothing. To have tea, to have cake, to make a trip from one place to another is his practice. He has no idea of helping people. What he is doing is helping, but he himself has no idea of helping people.

And then Shunryu Suzuki, sipping water from the cup Miss Ransom gave him, concluded his last public lecture by saying:

To solve our human problem doesn't cover all of Buddhist practice, and we don't know how long it takes for us to make the buddha trip. We have many trips: work trips, space trips, the various trips we must have. The buddha trip is a very long trip. This is Buddhism. Thank you very much.

To observe things in a flash – that is nonduality.

SILAS HAD given some lectures that summer at Suzuki's behest. In early September Suzuki asked Silas to come see him. As they talked, seated in the tatami room of Suzuki's apartment, Suzuki fingered his *mala,* a Buddhist rosary. It had large sandalwood beads, each carved into the shape of a skull. Silas looked at the skulls and at Suzuki, and he felt deeply apprehensive.

Suzuki was very ill. His skin was yellow; the doctor said he had hepatitis. Okusan was taking care of him with assistance from Yvonne, who also kept him abreast of Zen Center matters. They were very careful to avoid infection and didn't share any food with him, as had been their habit. Aside from attending an occasional zazen, the last time he'd done anything in public was the lay ordination for fifty-five students at the end of August. He hadn't even been able to attend his own ordination of four new priests in September. Katagiri, now called Katagiri-roshi at Suzuki's request, performed it for him by proxy, having come up from Tassajara where he was leading the practice period. Ed Brown was first in line, then me, then Lew Richmond, who'd been studying with Suzuki since 1967, and Angie Runyon.

Suzuki's absence was conspicuous. It was a somber occasion. Afterward we all went to his apartment to greet him and stood at his bedside. He acted like it was the happiest day of his life. After leaving his room I went up on the roof of the building, walked amidst the potted plants, looked out over San Francisco, and cried.

A YOUNG MONK named Ryuho Yamada arrived from Japan in late September. Over tea, Okusan learned that he knew the healing arts of shiatsu (pressure-point massage) and acupuncture. She asked him to give her a treatment, and he passed the test. He was supposed to have gone straight down to Tassajara, but now he was needed in the city. Every afternoon he worked on Suzuki for a couple of hours.

Ryuho was a thick-spectacled, enthusiastic, naive young monk, and he immediately started gobbling up the strange experience of Zen in America. He knew quite a bit of English and spent a lot of time talking with students.

"Ryuho-san, if you continue to live in America, and you want to be a success in America, you have to be *majime*. If you are not majime you will not be appreciated." Suzuki was sitting up in bed, talking in Japanese to the new monk. Okusan had told him the same thing. "Just be majime and you'll have nothing to worry about."

Majime is usually translated as "serious," but it includes the qualities of sincerity and enthusiasm. In Japan, Ryuho knew he could easily get by as a priest with canned majime; there were centuries of tradition and the cloud of vagueness to hide in. But in America the students were straightforward, and everything was clear. He loved the communal aspects of Zen Center: the natural food, women and men living together on an equal basis. Even Suzuki's wife was willful and would tangle with him. The students saw in Ryuho, as in other Japanese monks, qualities that they admired. A perfect place for Japanese monks, he thought. They can learn from us, and we can learn from them.

Ryuho discovered Suzuki could be short-tempered. Once Ryuho commented on a Buddha statue, casually saying it was just a piece of wood. Suzuki barked at him not to speak so flippantly: until he knew the true meaning of the statue he should shut up. Then as quickly as the anger came, it was gone. Ah, thought Ryuho, he's innocent and honest, like a child.

"SO, YOU'VE come to see our yellow roshi," Yvonne said, and that's how Albert Stunkard learned Suzuki was ill.

"Yellow?" he asked.

"Yes, he has hepatitis."

Dr. Albert Stunkard was chairman of the department of psychiatry at the University of Pennsylvania. In September 1971 he had come out to work at Stanford Hospital for a year, largely because he wanted to be near Suzuki, whom he had studied with in the past. Stunkard, one of the senior Zen practitioners in the States, had started his study when he was a doctor to Japanese prisoners being tried for war crimes in Tokyo in 1946. One of them had told him about D. T. Suzuki. He met the great scholar and subsequently became his student and occasional doctor. Stunkard had studied with Nakagawa, Yasutani, and other teachers as well. He met Shunryu Suzuki for the first time at Sokoji in 1967, and Suzuki embarrassed him by asking him to deliver the lecture for that evening.

Entering Suzuki's bedroom, Stunkard saw that Suzuki was scratching. A chill went down Stunkard's spine. He knew there were two types of jaundice – one infectious (hepatitis), the other obstructive. An obstruction to the outflow of bile causes itching. The most common obstruction is cancer. He felt terrible but didn't say anything at the time. He just asked if he could confer with Suzuki's doctor.

If you were not born in this world, there would be no need to die. To be born in this world is to die, to disappear [laughing].

ON OCTOBER 10, 1971, Shunryu Suzuki called his Bay Area disciples together. They were asked to wear their robes. At ten o'clock they entered the apartment and gathered around his bed, joining his team of caregivers – Ryuho sitting on the floor, Okusan by the door, looking tired, and Yvonne at the bedside fussing with Suzuki over an office cassette recorder. Mel had driven in from Berkeley and Bill from Mill Valley. Also present were Silas, Reb, Lew, and Angie, all of whom lived in the building. Claude came from his home in San Francisco. Everyone was quiet. There was a feeling of tense anticipation.

Suzuki sat up in bed, propped up by pillows. He was frail and thin, and his skin had become a darker yellow, but his spirits were good. He smiled warmly, glad to be with so many of his closest students. He hadn't seen them much in the past six weeks. They returned his smiles and stood in a semicircle around his bed. On Page Street cars passed, and birds chirped in the rubber tree outside the window.

Suzuki cleared his throat and turned on the tape recorder. Then he softly told them what they feared to hear.

As you know, my doctor thought I had hepatitis, but my symptoms didn't change for such a long time, so he thought it might not be hepatitis, maybe cancer. So I went into Mt. Zion Hospital again three days ago and they checked me out – and the doctors discussed my illness. The day before yesterday my doctor came and told me, "You have cancer." And he explained exactly what is happening. So now I am telling you.

Suzuki immediately set about putting people at ease and giving a positive spin to the news. He spoke as if it were no big deal, adding that it was a great relief to find out that he had cancer and not hepatitis, because now he could eat and drink whatever he wanted, and they could share food with him without worrying about contagion.

I myself selfishly feel good, but on the other hand, I am very sorry for you. But I think buddha will take care of everything, so I won't worry too much. How long I'll live I don't know. No one knows actually. I asked the doctor, "Two years?" "At most," he said. I am not so sure about it. So I want you to be prepared. If I live longer, it is better, of course, for me and for you. I think I can live one more year for sure, I feel that way. I don't feel so discouraged or weak. So maybe I want you to allow me to be a lazy monk, that's all. I shall be a very bad example, but [laughing] instead, you should be a good example. Okay? That's all that I want you to do – to prepare. Most things you can decide among yourselves. If necessary, I can join your discussions. Physically, I get tired quite easily. Thank you very much.

Abruptly he turned to Claude, the oldest, whose counsel he had valued since they first met in 1963. "Claude, I want you to stay here, even though I am no more. Okay? Please." Claude, cornered, affirmed that he would. "Thank you," Suzuki said, going on to make a point about their roles as priests and about the priest's responsibility within the larger Buddhist community. "You shouldn't feel you have to do exactly what I did, you know. You are free to develop our way as people want you to do. That is the bodhisattva idea."

He leaned close to the mike when he said this. He was speaking to Richard Baker, for whom the tape was being made. Suzuki's tone of voice said, you should come back now and assume this responsibility. Richard and Suzuki had been corresponding with Yvonne's assistance throughout his stay in Japan. Since the spring there had been discussion of Richard's returning in the fall or winter to assume some of Suzuki's responsibilities. Richard had been resistant to the idea – he didn't feel ready for that. Now Suzuki was twisting his arm.

After some joking with his disciples, Suzuki had the tape rewound and played. At the exchange with Claude he listened carefully, stopped the machine, and acted pleased that Claude was on tape saying he would stay, although his answer was fairly inaudible. Suzuki bowed to his crestfallen disciples and they bowed back, going out with tears in their eyes to share the tragic news with the community.

THE DAY before, when Yvonne had gone to the hospital to pick up Suzuki, she'd found him sitting on the edge of his bed with legs dangling below his hospital gown. Okusan was in the hall saying goodbye to some visitors. The nurse had just brought his lunch, and he patted the bed and motioned to Yvonne to come over. She knew something was up. He slowly mouthed the words, "I have cancer," with a big grin on his face. She was confused because the two things didn't go together – cancer and grinning. As she sat next to him, he pulled over the food tray. "I have cancer. That means we can eat together again." He took a forkful from his plate and fed it to her. Yvonne threw her arms around him and cried.

"This cancer is my friend, and my practice will be to take care of this sickness," he told her.

Dr. Stunkard, who had first realized Suzuki had cancer, talked to him about going to the cutting-edge Stanford cancer unit, but Suzuki decided against it, saying, "This doctor is my doctor, and I have to respect him. It wouldn't be appropriate to see another doctor." Stunkard tried to tell him things were different in America, but Suzuki stood firm. After talking further with his colleagues at Stanford, Stunkard decided that Suzuki had made the right decision. The type of cancer he had was not responsive to treatment, it had spread, and radiation and chemotherapy would just make him sicker.

"You know we often talked about teaching in the past," Suzuki said to Stunkard. "So many of these young people are afraid of dying. I can show them that you don't need to be afraid of dying. It's a wonderful teaching opportunity."

"I wish you were doing some other kind of teaching," Stunkard said.

"Yes, I don't want to die. I don't know what it's going to be like when I die. Nobody knows what that's going to be like. But when I die, I'll still be a buddha. I may be a buddha in agony, or I may be a buddha in bliss, but I'll die knowing that this is how it is."

Wherever you go you will find your teacher, as long as you have the eyes to see and the ears to hear.

Ryuho continued to do shiatsu on Suzuki every day. He concentrated on points in Suzuki's back that corresponded to the liver. He pressed his feet and legs and arms. Suzuki was weak but alert. If Ryuho's mind wandered while working, Suzuki would immediately tell him to concentrate.

Ryuho was intrigued by the people who came to see Suzuki: disciples, students, friends, scholars, artists, teachers, priests, members of the Japanese congregation at Sokoji, other Buddhist teachers. There was Maezumi, the teacher of the L.A. Zen Center, who'd known Suzuki since 1959, and Bishop Sumi from Zenshuji in L.A. Eido Shimano, Nakagawa's disciple and the teacher at the Zen Studies Center in New York, dropped by to pay his respects one day.

Bob Halpern visited. He had been studying with the Tibetan teacher, Trungpa, in Boulder. On Suzuki's bedside table was a large postcard Bob had sent. Instead of a note, he had drawn a picture of Trungpa's altar, which had a Buddha in the center, Trungpa's Tibetan guru on the left, and Suzuki-roshi on the right. Trungpa came a few days later. Suzuki spoke to him optimistically about the future of Buddhism in America. Trungpa sat by Suzuki's bed, holding his hand for over an hour.

Almost every day some old-timer would enter Suzuki's room and stay for half an hour – Betty, Della, Jean, Mike Dixon, and others. Suzuki had asked Philip to come as much as possible, and he would drive in every few days from Santa Rosa. Okusan told Philip that Suzuki said to let him in any time he came. Philip said he'd break down the door if he couldn't get in.

Grahame sent a letter from Tokyo expressing concern and saying that he'd come as soon as he could, in late December, when he would be visiting Pauline and the children in Mill Valley. He was fully involved with the English language school he had started and could not get away until then.

Ryuho stood by and listened as Alan Watts and Jano paid their respects. He couldn't understand what they were saying, but it was a lively meeting, considering Suzuki's condition. Watts was in fine form. Jano teased her husband, and Ryuho worried that Suzuki would die on the spot, he was laughing so hard.

LOUISE BROUGHT her newborn daughter to visit wearing a tiny rakusu, the last that Suzuki had inscribed. The little one's name was Johanna. Suzuki was sitting on a low table in the tatami room. In front of him was his well-worn pocket-sized dictionary, brought from Japan and often carried back and forth between Tassajara and the city. He picked it up and said, "This will live longer than I will."

Suzuki expressed great regret over his cancer. "Before my disciples are ready to come out of the oven, I will be going into it." Louise was surprised at his sadness, because she still had the idea that a Zen teacher wouldn't have that kind of feeling.

SUZUKI TOLD Bill Kwong the opposite, saying: "I've put my cookies in the oven, they've come out fine, and now I'm going to crawl in." He'd say different things at different times, but clearly he was thinking about his disciples and what to do for them before he died.

Richard Baker was coming back. There was going to be a ceremony to make him the new abbot. Page Street and Tassajara were abuzz with talk about it. How could this be? He'd received transmission, but still, how could he take on Suzuki's role? What about Katagiri? What about the other priests? What about Bill Kwong, who'd been with Suzuki almost from the first and who had a zendo in Mill Valley? What about Silas, who was giving lectures, Jean in Carmel Valley, Mel in Berkeley, and other disciples?

Suzuki told Claude that he wanted to give transmission to a number of his disciples before he died. Especially, he emphasized, he must complete Bill Kwong's transmission ceremony. But there were others. He was thinking of giving transmission to six to twelve disciples. He wanted to ask Noiri-roshi to come over from Japan to work with these students for several months in preparation for the ceremony. Claude asked what would be the difference between Richard's transmission and these, and Suzuki said, "They will be the same as Richard's – no difference."

Claude conferred with a few people, and they all agreed that Suzuki was too ill to do this. Okusan was also opposed to her husband's plan. Noiri needed a special diet, and she'd have to take care of them both, which would be too much for her. Suzuki made it clear how much he wanted to do it, but Okusan told him to leave it to Richard, who was coming back and could carry out Suzuki's wishes. She and Claude agreed; and after they told Suzuki how they felt, he gave up and didn't mention it again – not even to Richard.

SUZUKI ASKED Okusan to go back to Japan after he'd passed his authority to Richard in the Mountain Seat Ceremony. He said he wanted to do *saitokudo*, reordination. She knew that he wanted to spend the remaining time with his students and to let them take care of him, to be as close to them as possible. He'd read a book Katagiri had given him by Kodo Sawaki, with an introduction by Katagiri's second teacher, Eko Hashimoto. It stressed that priests should practice celibacy and not live with women. It didn't seem very practical to Okusan.

She said, "I'd comply with your wish if you were getting well, but I couldn't possibly leave you in this condition. Who would cook rice gruel and other Japanese food for you? You need someone who can understand your needs by a single wink."

She wrote to Hoitsu immediately, and he wrote right back, urging her to stay with her husband by all means, or they'd just have to send someone else from the family to take care of him. Hoitsu sent a similar letter to his father. So Suzuki gave up on that idea too. One by one he had to let go of his wishes.

When he had enough energy to walk down the stairs to the basement, Suzuki still went to zazen occasionally. Afterward he couldn't get back up. He wanted to make it on his own but couldn't. Sometimes Reb and Peter would make a chair out of their arms, and he'd sit and enjoy the ride. He made it fun. He was very sweet about such dependence. His life was not in his own hands anymore.

Z̲en is the practice of all existence with everything else – stars, moon, sun, mountains, rivers, animate and inanimate beings. Sometimes the pain in our legs practices zazen. Sometimes our sleepy mind practices zazen on a black cushion, on a chair, or even in bed.

RICHARD BAKER returned with Virginia and Sally. As soon as they arrived, he went to see Suzuki. Soon Suzuki-roshi would pass to him the enormous responsibility of taking care of Zen Center and all the people who came there. He would be the chief priest. "I'm so sorry for what I'm about to do to you," Suzuki said to him, tears filling his eyes.

"How could someone with your intuition choose to marry someone as difficult as me?" Okusan asked.

"Because you are ridiculously honest," he said.

"What should I do when you die?" she asked him.

"Stay here," he said. "Don't go back at all." He said everyone would be happy if she stayed, that her ten years in America would make it hard for her to adjust to Rinso-in. But how could she be helpful at Zen Center? she wanted to know.

"You are fair in your dealings with people. It will work out naturally."

"Should I become a nun?"

"Oh, that would be best."

"I'm too old for that. Maybe I'll be a monk in my next life."

That got him laughing, which started him coughing. Okusan helped him over onto all fours so she could pound his back. He stopped coughing. "You're lucky you have someone to take care of you to the last moment," she said in a teasing voice.

Suzuki raised a hand in a faint gassho. Then he farted loudly. "That's for you," he said.

*N*irvana is seeing one thing through to the end.

Knowing that their father could pass away at any time, Suzuki's daughter Yasuko and son Hoitsu arrived for the first time in the States with godfather Amano, to say their farewells. They were shocked to see him so jaundiced and weak. They stood at his bed saying a few polite phrases, not knowing what to do. But Suzuki was more open and easygoing than in the old days, and before long they were talking comfortably with him and among themselves. Okusan was making noodles in the cramped kitchen. Then Philip, a familiar face, came to visit.

At Page Street, and later at Tassajara, his children witnessed with amazement what Suzuki had accomplished in his twelve years in the States. It was hard for Yasuko and Hoitsu to imagine that their father was a dharma teacher with many disciples, and that a book of his lectures was selling well. They were impressed that everyone called him Roshi and amazed to hear from Americans such enthusiastic praise for his lectures. "Mother always said his problem was that he didn't know how to lecture about Buddhism, that he didn't express himself well enough," Hoitsu said. Their father had hardly ever said anything to them about Buddhism, so they didn't even think of him as someone with a particularly good understanding of it. But the evidence of his effort lay before their eyes.

Yasuko, Hoitsu, and godfather Amano arrived at Tassajara in time to attend Bill Kwong's head monk ceremony, at which Katagiri officiated. One after another the American students put their hands in gassho and asked the head monk questions about dharma and life. Hoitsu couldn't believe what he was seeing and got teary – they were doing the ceremony sincerely, spontaneously, and in good form.

I CAME UP from Tassajara to pay a visit to my dying teacher. Richard answered the door. I'd already spent time with Richard at Tassajara, so we just greeted each other briefly. "Right now is a good time to see Roshi," he told me. Knowing me well, Richard was quite firm about the time limit. "Don't spend any longer than five minutes unless Suzuki-roshi absolutely insists that you stay longer."

"Okay, I promise," I told him.

After I'd put on my robes I went to his room. Okusan led me into the bedroom and directed me to a chair next to his bed. Suzuki looked up and smiled. We bowed. He looked terrible. With some difficulty he pulled himself up and sat on the edge of the bed, close to me. Then he slapped his thighs like he'd do to indicate pleasure. I just sat there moping. "I feel fine," he said. "I don't feel so serious." That was all I needed. "Okay," I said snapping out of it.

He asked me what I was doing at Tassajara, and I said I was the assistant director. He acted impressed. Then he gave me a little advice. He said that, as a priest, I should have two specialties, one primary and one secondary. My first one, he said, should be to take care of guests, something I'd done since Tassajara opened. And the second one could possibly be scholarship. His point wasn't to tell me what to do. He trusted that my seniors at Zen Center and I would work out the details on our own. It didn't matter to him so much what I did, I think, but he knew I needed some wholesome activity to be engaged in through the years that would both express my true nature and keep me out of trouble.

I was touched by his concern. Here he was wasting away, and all his attention was on another, giving me a boost, conspiring with me to the end to have faith in myself.

We talked a while longer and then I said I had to go. "No, no, stay," he said. I remembered what Richard had said, and I also thought Suzuki should lie down and rest, so I stood up and bowed. Then he said, "If you leave I will be unhappy. If you stay I will be happy." "Okay," I said. He asked me if I'd met his family and I said yes, that I'd shown them around Tassajara. So he called them all in and we talked and visited for half an hour. It was lots of fun, and I completely forgot that Suzuki was dying and this was the last time we would meet. I don't even remember saying goodbye to him.

"WITH THESE hands I have done many things in my life," Suzuki told Hoitsu. "I never imagined all the things I would do with these hands in America. Now my work is almost finished. It would be good to go back to Japan and die there."

"Would you like to go back to Japan with me?" Hoitsu asked.

"I will crawl if necessary," his father answered.

Hoitsu was surprised to hear his father say that. Since his third year in America it had seemed that he would never return. Seeing his two eldest children and Amano must have awakened a nostalgia for his homeland. The ceremony was a week off. They could bring Suzuki back with them right after that. Hoitsu talked to Okusan, Yasuko, and Amano; with help from Okusan, he talked to Suzuki's doctor, who said Suzuki could do it. Hoitsu went to tell his father.

"Master, the doctor said you can come back with us."

Suzuki looked up at Hoitsu and laughed. "Isn't it obvious there's no way I could leave here? Can't you people even take a joke?"

"You were just telling us what we wanted to hear," Hoitsu said.

"Yes, of course. I will become American soil."

YASUKO SAW her father in a new light in America. Putting a positive spin on his misfortune, he told her he'd lived longer than he'd expected, that his master So-on had died at the age of fifty-five, he was now sixty-seven. The twelve extra years were his time in America. (Suzuki's chronological accuracy was sometimes off – So-on actually died when he was fifty-seven.) He was thin, soft, and open to her. She'd never felt closer to him and was sorry she'd seen so little of him since he left Japan. She could finally forgive him for the death of her mother and saw his accomplishments in America not only as atonement for but as partially motivated by her death.

She thought of the time in the fifth grade when he'd taken her to Shizuoka City and, embarrassed to be seen with him, she'd walked on the other side of the street. She didn't feel that gap now.

"The bond between children and parents is never lost," he told her.

GODFATHER AMANO felt he had accomplished the purpose of his trip. He had seen Suzuki, his temples, his students. He could see that Suzuki was going to die. "I'd better go back now," he said. He too had cancer and trouble with his bowels; and though he wasn't dying or sick like his old friend, it was difficult for him to stay. But Suzuki wanted him to witness Richard's Mountain Seat Ceremony.

"Father," Suzuki said to him, "there is one more important job I need to do as a monk. Please see it and report it to the membership at Rinso-in. Tell them what I have done since I left them and came here."

"Father, please fulfill Hojo's wishes," said Okusan.

Finally Amano agreed to stay.

IT WAS MORE difficult every day for Suzuki to talk, but he could do it, especially with Okusan, with whom he could communicate with much less effort. "I won't interfere with Zen Center at all once I have handed it over to Richard. It's entirely up to him whether it will be ruined or not," Suzuki said to his wife. He even told her and Richard that he didn't want any more Japanese priests to come to Zen Center as teachers. "From now on, they should come as students."

*The most important point is to continue our way
and to have a good successor.*

ON SUNDAY, November 21, at ten in the morning, the halls and courtyard of Zen Center were filled with people talking softly and waiting. They had come for the Mountain Seat Ceremony in which Richard Baker was to be installed as the chief priest of Zen Center. The foyer and hallway were lined with rows of chairs. The buddha hall, where the ceremony was to take place, was too small for the five hundred guests. Chinese, Tibetan, and Japanese priests of various sects attended with some of their disciples. Many of the key figures in Suzuki's life in America were there: Wako and Emi Kato, Reverend Ogui, George Hagiwara, and many from the Japanese congregation of Sokoji. Bill McNeil stood in a corner in a leather jacket; poets and artists from the old Beat days came in the front door. So many people who had become deeply connected in the past twelve years, so many stories like fibers running among them, so many for whom Suzuki had opened dharma gates or been there with a nudge when their lives turned.

The bell downstairs was being struck every minute, informing the crowd that it was time to settle down. People patiently sat or stood where they were. They could hear a procession moving from Katagiri's apartment up the street, into the building, and to its various altars. The rumble of the deep buddha drum echoed through the halls and the high "ching-chung" of the handheld bells a half note off from each other provided the tune of the moving rite. On the second floor the procession stopped outside Suzuki's room, where Richard offered incense and said: "Although I don't know how I came, through your heart-teaching I am always here."

Katagiri-roshi, Kobun-sensei, and a few of Suzuki's senior monks accompanied Richard down the stairs to the hushed buddha hall. Richard wore a blue and gold robe with bright-colored flying phoenixes, which Suzuki had given him for this day. He carried a ceremonial horsehair whisk.

The assembled crowd was utterly hushed when the spine-chilling sound of intermittent thuds and jangling bells jolted everyone to attention. Suzuki was walking with the staff Alan Watts had given him. Affixed to the top was a bronze headpiece with rings. At his sides were Hoitsu and Okusan. They helped him down the stairs and past those seated and standing along the way, to the double doors of the buddha hall. With each step he struck the floor with his staff, as if continuing to plant the dharma in America. There he was, his reddish-brown okesa draping over a yellow koromo. All eyes were on him. Many people hadn't seen him in his illness, and even to those who had, his appearance was crushing. He was so dark, weak, and shrunken. Yet as he moved into the buddha hall toward the specially built Mountain Seat altar, his enormous effort and dignity shone through.

Reaching the brocade-covered altar, still supported on both sides, he slowly pulled out from the sleeve of his robe a bowing cloth. Gathering his strength, he laid it out properly, bowed down to the floor, and rose, somehow, drawing strength from the depth of his will, calm and powerful, the way frail old Kitano-roshi had risen from his bows at Eiheiji, amazing and inspiring the young Suzuki. Hoitsu helped him to a cushioned ceremonial chair to the right of the altar. He sat and looked with eyes straight ahead yet downcast, as in zazen.

People were just catching their breath when Richard Baker entered. After the *Heart Sutra* was recited, Richard stood before the Mountain Seat altar and said in classical style: "This Mountain Seat, climbed many times before, is the everywhere bodhimandala. With the help of my Master and everyone here, in the ten directions and the three times, I will climb this mind-seal altar. Do not wonder about it at all."

He offered incense to buddhas, bodhisattvas, and ancestors, to Trudy Dixon, Katagiri-roshi, and "to my own subtle and compassionate teacher, Suzuki Shunryu-daiosho," to whom he said, drawing from Suzuki's own Mountain Seat Ceremony at Sokoji in 1963:

This piece of incense
Which I have had for a long long time
I offer with no-hand
To my Master, to my friend, Suzuki Shunryu-daiosho,
The founder of these temples.
There is no measure of what you have done.
Walking with you in Buddha's gentle rain
Our robes are soaked through,
But on the lotus leaves
Not a drop remains.

Richard sat on a red lacquered chair before the altar. Katagiri spoke for Suzuki loud and clear: "Dragons and Elephants! Accept this holder of Buddha's First Seat!"

Then Richard Baker said, in what may be called the first lecture of his abbotship, "There is nothing to be said."

A *mondo* followed, ritualized yet impromptu questions, which

Richard answered quickly and dramatically. Telegrams were read, formal congratulations were made, and the ceremony was over.

Suzuki was helped to face the altar, where he made another slow, painful prostration from which he rose almost by himself. Then he started down the aisle to leave. Halfway to the opened doorway he stopped in the midst of his sangha, disciples, students, former students, admirers, old friends, visiting teachers, and guests. There was utter silence. He looked to the left, then decisively rolled the staff several times between his hands; the rings at the top burst out jangling. He looked to the right and rolled his staff again, and again the rings rang out. It was the sound of an ultimate effort. It was the sound of his love and his freedom.

Tears and sobbing began on all sides. Hearts cracked open. Everything was suspended in his presence, in an immense shared feeling – a car honking on the street, pigeons cooing, the crying in the room, and a deep stillness. Time stopped. A moment that started the day he arrived in America continued as he was helped out of the room, striking his staff to the floor as he went. He left behind him a room full of palms pressed together saying thank you, saying goodbye, saying what could not be said.

AFTER THE ceremony, Suzuki met with his disciples. Twenty or so sat on the tatami in his sitting room. It was done. He'd passed on Zen Center, Page Street, and Tassajara to Zentatsu Richard Baker, who sat next to him a head higher in his fancy robes, his eyes down, the weight of what he'd received all over him. Suzuki turned to him, nodded, and smiled. The room was hushed. In a faint voice Suzuki said thank you to everyone and to Richard and then, nodding toward Katagiri, another breathy thank you "for all you've done, for which I am so grateful." All of a sudden a howl arose. It was Katagiri who crawled toward Suzuki crying out, "Don't die!" Sobbing, he hugged frail Suzuki, who said in a soft rasp, "Daijobu. Daijobu" (It's all right).

KATAGIRI HAD said goodbye to Suzuki and was on his way back to Tassajara for the last few weeks of the practice period. He left in sadness and with some discomfort at his situation. Seven years he'd served Suzuki – hard work, low pay, no time off. Katagiri was dependable and had a seamless constant practice. He'd come to be seen as a coteacher by many. Suzuki and Katagiri had contained their feelings, speaking little through the years. Until the meeting with his disciples following Richard's Mountain Seat Ceremony, Suzuki had never verbally expressed his gratitude.

Suzuki was still troubled by Katagiri's intention to leave. He wanted him to remain a senior dharma teacher for the whole community. "Maybe Katagiri can still help," he said to Okusan as he went to sleep.

Katagiri wasn't the only person he had troubled thoughts about. Unfinished business pressed at Suzuki. Bill. Silas. He wanted to take care of his disciples. Suzuki's style was to let things happen, nudging them, patiently waiting, acting skillfully by not acting rashly. He hadn't known how quickly his illness would overcome him. Some disciples were disturbed. A few had postponed or given up careers to devote themselves to studying with this dying man. Would he leave no final instructions?

So far Suzuki's instructions were not about practical matters but about dying with dignity. It was tragic for his students to see the deteriorating physical condition of their dear teacher, yet at the same time it was marvelous to witness his composure and see how undiminished he was at heart.

IN HIS LAST meeting with Hoitsu before his son returned to Japan, Suzuki implored, "Take care of Bill Kwong for me. Make sure Bill gets transmission – you can do it for me."

Suzuki wanted Hoitsu to be available to help his disciples in whatever way he could, but Hoitsu knew his father didn't want him to interfere with Richard. "Leave Zen Center to Richard," he'd said several times. Hoitsu also knew that leaders need assistance, and his father knew it too. Richard would need help from his elders, like

Katagiri and Claude, and from his peers, like Bill and Silas. Even if he disagreed with them, he should work with and respect them. Suzuki knew there was rivalry but hoped it could move toward cooperation. "It is done," he said to his son. "All I can do now is hope."

With the trust he had in Richard and in others, and considering his patience and acceptance of problems, Suzuki's hope might have included more possibilities than were imagined by his students. If some disciples couldn't work together, maybe they could work separately. If there were sharp difference, maybe time would smooth the edges. Ultimately, if people were sincere, it would be okay. He might have looked at his students through his dying eyes and thought, as when Tatsugami landed, "You have no idea how much you're going to suffer."

AMANO CAME to his bedside to say goodbye. "I've finished all my duties," Suzuki told him. "Please report the details to the members."

"Hai," Amano answered in the affirmative.

Suzuki gave Amano his mala bracelet with the skull-shaped beads. He told Okusan to roll up a scroll for Yasuko and to give Hoitsu the staff with the bronze rings he'd carried in the ceremony. The clanger on top of the staff was the last item he wanted to return to Rinso-in, of those he had borrowed when he'd left in 1959.

"Well, we're leaving now," said Amano.

"Okay. Goodbye, Father. Have a good trip," Suzuki said softly.

Hoitsu couldn't believe how casually the two said farewell, as if it were just another day.

Sitting on the plane before takeoff, Yasuko was crying. She wanted to get off and stay with her father. Hoitsu told her they had to go back now to help Amano explain to people what their father had been doing in America these twelve years, what he had created and was leaving behind. Nobody had really understood why he left. Now Amano, Yasuko, and Hoitsu knew and could tell the others, who should feel some pride in this too.

The ancient bodhisattvas were not afraid of, but found joy in failure, poverty, and death – and in doing small things.

A HOSPITAL bed was put in a second-floor room overlooking the courtyard. There Suzuki could have a sense of the rhythm of the building and some time in the sunlight. The buddha hall was right below; during morning service he'd listen to the sounds of chanting, drums, and bells coming through the window and the open door. Okusan would wash his face, and he'd have a glass of orange juice – that was his service. He was too weak to get out of bed.

Ryuho would get lost looking at Suzuki's face as he gave him shiatsu treatments. It was spacy and changing, he said, and it didn't look Japanese. He could obviously die at any time – Okusan and the doctor said so, too. His skin was dark, almost the color of the brown okesa robe. But to Ryuho the light of his eyes was powerful.

Yvonne was there every day, staying with him while Okusan cooked, did laundry, and cleaned. They took turns caring for him and massaging his back, legs, arms – wherever he'd indicate. Yvonne would be sitting by his bed and a skinny arm would come out from the covers and go into the air. She'd rub it for a while; then he'd pull it back under the covers. Later the other arm would appear. She and Okusan massaged and moved him enough so that he hadn't gotten any bedsores. He never complained and always appreciated the attention he received.

There was a bottle of painkillers on the table. He refused them, as after the gallbladder operation. He had tried them once because his doctor told him to, but he didn't like the state of mind that resulted, so he asked Yvonne to take them away. Still, he told Richard that sometimes he felt like he was being tortured.

One day Suzuki asked Yvonne to come close to him, and when

she did he apologized for not having ordained her as a priest, saying again that he lacked confidence in training women. "I didn't recognize your seriousness to practice," he said.

SUZUKI ASKED Yvonne about Silas and was pained to hear that he had already left to lead sesshins in Portland and Quadra Island near Vancouver. Silas had come to say goodbye, but Suzuki had been sleeping. He sat next to him for a while and then left. Silas did not see eye to eye with Richard and had argued that the membership should have had a chance to approve of Richard as the new abbot. But most people just wanted to do what Suzuki wanted. The board members were all students and couldn't accept Silas's democratic and legal approach. He hadn't seen much of Suzuki since Richard returned. Now Suzuki was thinking about Silas.

WITHIN A WEEK of the ceremony, Suzuki had almost completely stopped talking. Then he stopped eating. His body was soft and weak and thin, the size of an eight-year-old child. It had always had a childlike quality, but with great strength and energy, the power to move large stones. Now it was a dark, dying child's body. Okusan told Ryuho not to bother coming anymore. Either Okusan or Yvonne stayed close by. They still massaged him gently, but to Yvonne it seemed that mainly they were just breathing together. She felt there was almost nothing they needed to do. Just leave him alone, be with him, and respond to his few requests. They wiped his face. When he stopped drinking, they kept his lips and mouth moist with a washcloth.

RICHARD CAME every day. Sometimes he would talk to Suzuki with Okusan's help. She said he could hardly hear now. "Where will I meet you?" Richard asked, standing in gassho at the foot of the bed. Suzuki's hands came out from under the covers in gassho. Then, with index finger extended, he drew a circle in the air, bowed into it, and returned his hands under the covers. Richard bowed in return.

That we are here means we will vanish.

ON THE EVENING of December 3, Suzuki was moved from the hospital bed overlooking the courtyard to his own bed in his apartment. "Tomorrow," he told Okusan in a hoarse whisper, "I must talk to Richard about Silas."

Okusan went into the tatami room and spread out the futon. For the first time she didn't put on her pajamas, but left her clothes on and lay down exhausted to sleep.

Suzuki's son Otohiro had been there for a couple of days and said he would stay till the end, which he knew was near. He slept on Okusan's bed, up against his father's in the small room. At about two in the morning Otohiro shook Okusan awake. "Mother! Mother! Father wants a bath."

"No no no." She went in and told her husband to go back to sleep. He repeated that he wanted a bath. The thought of it made Okusan anxious. He hadn't been in a tub for a long time.

"It's okay," he said.

Otohiro wasn't going to argue. He knew the old man would be stubborn to the end. Okusan went into the bathroom and started to fill the tub. Otohiro carried him into the bathroom slowly and placed him in the tub. Suzuki started gasping for air, breathing fast. "It's all over," he said between short breaths.

"Calm down, calm down," Otohiro spoke soothingly in his ear holding him. "Breathe slowly, breathe slowly." Otohiro breathed loudly and slowly, and his father's breath slowed down till they were both breathing together at the same slow rate.

Suzuki asked for the bar of scented soap that Della had given him. He never used anything scented, but he took it and slowly made a good lather, and they helped him to clean himself thoroughly. Then he took a long, relaxed bath.

Afterward Suzuki lay on the bed and sighed. Slowly and faintly he spoke. "Ahhhh, what a good feeling," he said, with a wisp of pleasure on his face. "Don't wake me in the morning."

"Maybe you're thirsty," said Okusan. "Would you like some orange juice or ice cream?"

"Orange juice." He drank some orange juice, closed his eyes, and went to sleep.

Okusan went back to her futon and Otohiro lay down next to his father in the bed. Before long it was four and he heard the wake-up bell – a handbell run through the halls to get people up for zazen. It was not just any day's zazen, but December 4, the first day of a five-day sesshin that would culminate on Buddha's Enlightenment Day, the eighth of December. Over a hundred people were participating. Otohiro could hear people opening and closing doors carefully, running water in the bathroom across the hall. Then came the sharp sound of the wooden han being hit, indicating that the new abbot, Zentatsu Baker-roshi (as Suzuki said to call him), was on his way to offer incense at various altars. The last altar was the one in the zendo, where he would open the sesshin and begin the first period of zazen.

The sound of a bell could be heard faintly coming from the distant zendo. Otohiro felt his father move slightly. Suzuki's hand reached over and clutched his arm.

"Get Baker," came a thin whisper.

Otohiro jumped out of bed and ran into the tatami room. "Mother! Something's happening with father! He said to get Baker!"

Without a word Okusan leapt up and went quickly down to the zendo.

Richard had just sat down on his cushion and straightened his robes when Okusan opened the side door. Lew was sitting in the space nearest her. "Get Zentatsu!" she whispered urgently.

Richard took long strides to the zendo door and then dashed up the stairway to Suzuki's room. Okusan and Otohiro left Suzuki alone with Richard. He was still conscious, and with the last strength of his life he just barely reached his hand out to his beloved disciple. Half sitting, half kneeling by the bed, Richard held his hand and touched his forehead to Suzuki's. They rested that way for a few moments, then Richard felt the man most dear to him slip away, let go of his life. Slowly, Shunryu Suzuki-roshi faded away – so gently that Richard could not tell when he died; he just knew it had happened.

Richard let go of Suzuki's hand. He waited a moment and felt for a pulse. Then he went outside to Okusan and Otohiro. Richard had his hand on his heart. He spoke in Japanese, his voice cracking, as he told them, "Suzuki-roshi's life has ended."

Epilogue

Student: Roshi, what are you doing here?
Suzuki: Nothing special.

IN THE twenty-seven years since Shunryu Suzuki died, his students and their students have continued the teaching and practice that he brought to America, and his influence has spread in numerous ways. Zen Buddhism is now an established part of American culture. I can buy a zafu at a local store. There's a quote from *Zen Mind, Beginner's Mind* on a carton of soy milk in my refrigerator. Suzuki's legacy can be found in sitting groups, in the homes of Zen practitioners with little or no connection to any group, and in the nonabsolutist, open-minded approach of many Westerners who don't even consider themselves Buddhists. His photo is on altars and bureaus all over America, but there is no cult of Shunryu Suzuki. Rather there is gratitude to this man who added some important threads to the emerging culture – a way of living with humility and dignity in this transient world, with a tolerance for imperfection. He didn't particularly want to be remembered, but the seeds of practice that he planted have taken root and keep encouraging us to find out who we are.

Suzuki-roshi had wanted to start a Buddhist farm, and the year after he died the San Francisco Zen Center acquired one, just north of San Francisco. One day in April of 1995, I sat in the guesthouse of Green Gulch Farm in Marin County with Taizan Maezumi-roshi, founder of the Los Angeles Zen Center. Maezumi didn't tell me any anecdotes or stories about Suzuki, and he resisted historical analysis. What he did say, though, stuck with me. "Nobody can tell you about the past," Maezumi said. "What's important is not what happened or didn't happen back then. What's important is what we have here now – this wonderful farm with the big barn zendo and the conference center where we're all meeting, so many people coming here for lecture and zazen. There's Page Street in the city and Tassajara. So many people sitting zazen all over America, even Europe. When he came, there was none of this. Many priests came before him. Even before this century, all kinds of priests in the Zen tradition came to America. We don't really know why, but until he came, no one started anything that lasted. After him, so much happened. That's what I most appreciate."

In the spring of 1972 Mitsu Suzuki went to Tassajara for her husband's ashes ceremony. She wore his zoris, because he had said he wanted to go back there one more time. Having decided not to return to Japan "until the tears of his students have dried," she stayed, living in the City Center, writing haiku and teaching tea ceremony for twenty-two more years. In the fall of 1993 she returned to live with her daughter in Shizuoka City, not far from Rinso-in.

SHUNRYU SUZUKI is not widely known in Japan or regarded as an important teacher by the Soto school. But he is well remembered and loved by members of the High Grass Mountain Group, a few of whom still keep in touch and sometimes visit Hoitsu Suzuki at Rinso-in. The young men in the group eventually became carpenters, farmers, artists, bureaucrats, politicians, businessmen, and a publisher. Some have passed away. Most are now retired. One of them, Suetsune-san, visited the San Francisco Zen Center while Shunryu Suzuki was still alive. These men were not monks but were the students whom Suzuki remembered most dearly in Japan, especially for the bond they shared during the ordeal of wartime.

Shigeo Kozuki, head of the printing section of the Ministry of Finance, published an article in 1974 in Japan's principal financial newspaper, the *Nikkei*. The article was named "Kokoro no Furusato," literally "heart's hometown." It read, in part: "There was a man who went to San Francisco to open the minds of young Americans, to create a home for their hearts. In America he sat in silence and acted in a natural way that imparted the importance of everyday life. Our Hojo-san was this person. Rinso-in at High Grass Mountain with its lovely camellias was the home of our hearts. There we used to do zazen with him and hear the enchanting sound of young Hojo-san's voice reciting the sutras. He did not preach or tell us what to do, for he was a person of action and living. At the time of great confusion during the war, a silvery light from Hojo-san caught the hearts of the young. He couldn't be satisfied just taking care of the danka of his temple, and so he went to America."

After her husband's death, Mitsu Suzuki wrote to Yasumasa Amada, who sent out her letter with one of his own to the members of the group. Amada said farewell for everyone. "What we would like to say to you, Shunryu-san, is: you were our teacher, our big brother, our friend; you taught us human nature and you taught us compassion. With deepest respect we say to you, Well done, Hojo-san! Well done!"

Notes on the Text
and Pronunciation

THE QUOTES at the beginning of sections and all unascribed quotes are from Shunryu Suzuki and are not chronologically exact. Quotes have been edited without indication of omissions or additions.

Marcrons (long marks over extended vowels in Japanese and Sanskrit words) are not used here except in the glossary. In a few cases the vowel is doubled to indicate pronunciation.

For notes on the text and more material, see http://www.cuke.com (in progress as of January 1999).

Approximate Japanese pronunciation:

a is similar to the *a* in *father*
i is similar to the *ea* in *eat*
u is similar to the *oo* in *look*
e is similar to the *e* in *egg*
o is similar to the *o* in *go* (said quickly)

From *An Introduction to Modern Japanese*
by Osamu and Nobuko Mizutani, Japan Times, Ltd., 1977.

---

*Sumi circle on previous page was drawn by Shunryu Suzuki.

Acknowledgments

THIS BOOK is the result of the kind, attentive, and considerable contributions of many people over the past five and a half years. First I extend my most sincere gratitude to the family of Shunryu Suzuki for their total support and for giving of their time so generously whenever they were asked. Endless thanks to Mitsu Suzuki for numerous interviews with me and others and for personally asking people to help me; to Hoitsu and Chie Suzuki for being gracious hosts at Rinso-in in Yaizu and to Hoitsu Suzuki for arranging interviews and continually helping me in many ways; to Yasuko (Suzuki) Oishi, Tatsusan (RIP) and Aiko (Suzuki) Uchiyama; and in San Francisco to Otohiro and Mitsuyo Suzuki.

I would particularly like to thank my wife, Elin Chadwick, for her unfailing support, long hours of work through the years, and excellent advice; Michael Katz, my agent and friend, who has guided me through this project with utmost patience and skill; Michael Wenger and Bill Redican of the San Francisco Zen Center for all they have done to make this book possible; Bill Schwob for years of help with photography and photos in America and Japan; Liz Tuomi for years of transcribing; and Fred Harriman for so much of his time, skill with Japanese language, and knowledge of Japanese culture and history.

I am also deeply indebted to the following people for all they have done and apologize that there is not space to adequately give them the credit and praise that they deserve. To all of you, and to some whom I have surely neglected, I offer nine bows.

For extensive help with editing: Elin Chadwick, Michael Katz, Jisho Cary Warner, Linda Hess, Holly Hammond, Bill Redican, Carol Williams, and Charlie Conrad of Broadway Books.

For other editing, corrections, and suggestions upon reading the manuscript or parts of it: Richard Baker (especially for his work on editing Suzuki quotes), Ed Brown, Gwen Catterton, Ananda Dalenberg, Arthur Deikman, Mike Dixon, Della Goertz, Daya Goldschlag, Janet Goldstein, Bob Mipham Halpern, Silas Hoadley, Wako Kato, Bill Lane, Taigen Dan Leighton, Koshin Ogui, Grahame Petchey, Pauline Petchey, Louise Pryor, Yvonne Rand, Lew Richmond, Angie Runyon, Peter and Jane Schneider, Albert Stunkard, John Tarrant, Steve Tipton, Betty Warren, Mel Weitsman, Dan Welch, Michael Wenger, Philip Wilson, and Marian Wisberg.

To Yuki Ishimatsu, librarian for Japanese reference services at UC Berkeley, for frequent assistance; Kirk Rhodes for all the help in Yaizu; Harry Ransom Rose for generously answering so many questions about his adoptive mother, Nona Ransom; Grahame Petchey, Hideko Petchey, Mark Petchey, and Pauline Petchey for all sorts of help; Toshikazu Yasui for Japanese weather reports and details on Shoganji; and Elsie Mitchell for letters and more.

For scholarly information and suggestions: Carl Bielefeldt, Jeff Broadbent, Angelika Cedzich, Rick Fields, Wako Kato, Taigen Dan Leighton, Shohaku Okamura and Taiken Yokoyama of the Soto Zen Education Center of North America, Peter Schneider, Frank Joseph Shulman, Kazuaki Tanahashi, Philip Yampolsky (RIP), and Brian Victoria, who commented on the sections about Shunryu Suzuki and Japan's militaristic period, with thanks for his skeptical tolerance of my unscholarly narrative method.

For translation of interviews: Carl and Fumiko Bielefeldt for simultaneous translation on tape and Fred Harriman for written translation of the Schneider interviews and of his own; Kyoko Furuhashi for translating her own interviews and to her and Shizuko Takatsuka for translating my Japan interviews of 1993 and Kaz Tanahashi's interviews with Mitsu Suzuki; Takayo Harriman and Hideko Petchey for additional translation assistance.

For transcribing: Liz Tuomi, Jose Escobar, Layla Bockhorst, Bill Redican, Gary Brandt, and, in years past, Brian Fikes, Katherine Thanas, Barry Eisenberg, Tom Cabarga, and others.

For work on or assistance with audio tapes of Suzuki-roshi lectures and various interviews: Mark Watts, Bill Redican, Jim Wheeler, Peter Schneider, Michael Katz, Tony Johnson, Mike Dixon, Emma Bragdon, Michael Wenger, Howard Hammerman, Dan Gurley, Stan Jacox, and Kenji Muro.

For photos: Bill Schwob for his and Raymond Rimmer's copy photos of archival photos, Pat McFarlin for the front cover photo, Tim Buckley for the back cover photo, Robert Schilling for the author photo. For providing historical photos of Shunryu Suzuki's Japan years: Hoitsu and Otohiro Suzuki, and Harry Ransom Rose. For the American years: San Francisco Zen Center, Crestone Mountain Zen Center, Sokoji Soto Zen Mission of San Francisco, Katrina Boni, Della Goertz, Pauline Petchey, Peter Schneider, and Dan Welch. For other photo help: Richard Baker, Rosalie Curtis, Christina Lehnherr, Ikki Nambara, Susan O'Connell, Bill Redican, Russell Smith, Jeannie Stern, Meiya Susan Wender, Michael Wenger. Special thanks to Robert Boni (RIP). Every effort was made to identify photographers of photo inserts. Thanks to those not identified.

For design of the book: David Bullen. For the dingbat: Frances Thompson. Other graphics help: Mark Wiley and the folks at Spirit Copy Center in Sebastopol.

For various types of assistance or suggestions: Gil Fronsdal, Jane Hirshfield, Shozen Hosokawa, Dan Kaplan, Michele Lesure, Paul Maxwell, Misha Merrill, Jun Mink, Ikki Nambara, Brian Power, Diane Renshaw, Laurie Schley, Akemi Shinomiya, Steve Snyder, Shigematsu Soiku, Reiko Takahashi, Steve Tipton, Brian Unger, Betty Warren, Dan Welch, Celeste West of the San Francisco Zen Center Library, Daphne Woodall, and Shin Yoshifuku.

From Broadway Books: Rebecca Holland, Roberto de Vicq de Cumptich, Ted Sammons, and Rebecca Cole.

Sources

MY OWN memories of Suzuki-roshi's lectures and conversations with him and his other students, family, and acquaintances through the years are essential sources for this book. In addition, I have studied all the surviving transcripts of Suzuki's lectures (almost three hundred), including Marian Derby's original transcript of twenty-one lectures which led to *Zen Mind, Beginner's Mind* (book and tapes, which I did not use as a source for quotes, though I reread and listened to them several times). I found other useful materials in the archives and library of the San Francisco Zen Center, such as board notes, letters, and brochures.

Most useful were the interviews: Peter Schneider's with Shunryu Suzuki in 1969 in English and others with Suzuki's oldest students in that year, and the interviews done by Peter and Jane Schneider and Carl and Fumiko Bielefeldt in 1971 and 1972 in San Francisco and in Yaizu, Japan, with the Suzuki family, Gen'ichi Amano, and Kojun Noiri. Fred Harriman's interviews in Japan in 1995 with Hoitsu Suzuki, Taro Kato, Tsuna Kato, and Kan Kimpara, Kyoko Furuhashi's interviews with Hoitsu Suzuki and Masaji Yamada in 1993, Kaz Tanahashi's interviews with Mitsu Suzuki, and other interviews and records of people's own memories in *Wind Bell* and in the San Francisco Zen Center's archives and other publications.

Aside from the family of Shunryu Suzuki, those whom I interviewed in Japan were Skoko and Mrs. Okamoto of Zoun-in, Kando and Tomiko Sugiyama of Zuioji, Seison Suzuki, Jr., Kumataro and Mrs. Yamada, Masaji Yamada, Shunko Yamaguchi, Masao Yamamura, Kin'ichi Sugizaki, Takei Yuzo of Shoganji, Ryuho Yamada, and Sadayoshi Asaoka, Yasumasa Amada, and Yasuo Suetsune of the Takakusayama-kai (the High Grass Mountain Group).

In the course of writing this book I interviewed and informally talked to about 150 people in America, some of them a number of times for many hours and some of them for a few minutes. The following list includes the names of those people and an equal number who wrote to me, those who had memories printed in *Wind Bell* and the *Chronicles of Haiku Zendo*, some whose stories from before this project I recalled, those whom I have heard speaking at meetings, those whose letters are collected in the San Francisco Zen Center archives, and those whose memories of Shunryu Suzuki came to my attention through someone else. A few of them never met Suzuki but relayed second-hand information on him or background information. Mark Abrams, Robert Aitken, Marc Alexander, Paul Alexander, Donald Allen, Jonathan Altman, Peg Anderson, Reb Anderson, Rusa Chiu Anderson, Frank Anderton, Antoinette Artino, Tony Artino, Tim Aston, Art Atkinson, John Bailes, Peter Bailey (RIP), Richard Baker, Virginia Baker, Marty Balin, David Barrow (RIP), Joshua Bear, Anna Beck, Bob Beck, Lucy Bennett, Bill Benz, Ken Berman, Layna Berman, Craig Boyan, Emma Bragdon, Jeff Broadbent, Anapurna Broffman (Georgianne Coffey), Ed Brown, Tim Buckley, Joanna Bull, Sterling Bunnell, Tim Burkett, Susan Burns, Katy Butler, Del Carlson, Ahdel Chadwick, Susan Chadwick, Kobun Chino, Milton Clapp III, Darlene Cohen, Don Collins, Bill Colvig, Kathy Cook, Peter Coyote, Linda Ruth Cutts, Arthur Dahl, Ananda Dalenberg, Dave Davenport, Gertrude Davenport, Kent Davis, Don deAngelo (Donnie Crockin), Lee deBarros, Arthur Deikman, Etta Deikman, Gene DeSmidt, Peter DiGesu, Lorraine Dieudonne, Paul Discoe, Ruthie Discoe, Mike Dixon, Pam Dixon, Trudy Dixon (RIP), Issan Tommy Dorsey (RIP), Margo Patterson Doss, Jane Dunaway, Jack Elias, Rick Fields, Jacob Fishman, Stephanie Flagg, Tim Ford, June French, Mark Frisch, Robert Front (Roovane Ben Yumin), Jerry Fuller (RIP), Charles Gilman, Allen Ginsberg (RIP), Della Goertz, Herb Gold, Jack Goldberg, Daya (Dianne) Goldschlag, Eva Goldsheid, Richard Gomez,

Edmond Gordillo, Bob Mipham Halpern, Jerry Halpern, Gladys Halprin, Larry Hanson, Lou Harrison, Trudy Hartman, Blanche Hartman, Lou Hartman, Mitzi Hartman, Dave Hazelwood, Roy Henning, Pat Herreshoff, Harriet Hiestand, Barbara Hiestand (RIP), Silas Hoadley, Ned Hoke, Niels Holm, Irene Horowitz, Liz Horowitz, Tony Johansen, Barbara Kaiser, Dahlia Kamesar, Jack Kamesar, Dainin Katagiri (RIP), Tomoe Katagiri, Wako Kato, Les Kaye, Mary Kaye, Fran Keller, Durand Kiefer, Fred Kimball, Richard King, Taiji Kiyokawa, Allen Klein, Howard Klein, Arnie Kotler, Margaret Kress, Rowena Pattee Kryder, Bill Kwong, Laura Kwong, Joanne Kyger, Myo Denis Lahey, Lewis Lancaster, Bill Lane, Paul Lee, Rick Levine, Mark Lewis, Yvonne Lewis, Jim Lewinson, Jed Linde, Maria Linde, Margo Locke, Juan Lopez, Dot Luce, David Lueck, Molly Jones MacGregor, Deborah Madison, Taizan Maezumi (RIP), Andrew Main, Alan Marlowe (RIP), Barrie Mason, Toni (Johansen) McCarty, Willard McCarty, Pat McFarlin, Grace McLeod, Chris Miller, Elsie Mitchell, Russ Mitchell, Reb Monaco, Daigyo Moriyama, Carolyn Morton, Jim Morton, Rick Morton, Kenji Muro, Michael Murphy, Toshiaka Nakahara, John Nelson, Koshin Ogui, Phil Ohlson, Ann Overton, Peter Overton, David Padua, Caroline Page, Charles Page, Susan Page, Loring Palmer, Tony Patchell, Grahame Petchey, Pauline Petchey, Jerome Peterson, Rene Petit, Pat Phelan, Brian Power, Larry Prager, Louise Pryor, Brit Pyland, Mary Quagliata, Yvonne Rand, Norman Randolf, Jerry Ray, Carole Raymond, Richard Raymond, Charles Reeder, Eric Remington, Amy Richmond, Lew Richmond, Doug Roberts, Sue Roberts, Fred Roscoe (RIP), Nancy Roscoe, Harry Ransom Rose, Paul Rosenblum, Jean Ross (RIP), Loly Rosset, Angie Runyon, Sue Satermo, Ed Sattizahn, Elizabeth Sawyer, Ken Sawyer, Jill Schireson, Jane Schneider, Peter Schneider, Kenneth Schnelle, Bob Shuman, Holly Schwarz, Mary Lou Schwarz, Charlotte Selver, Helen Seward, Henry Shafer, Ippo Shaku, Jim Shriner, Noboru Shumizu, Bill Shurtleff, David Silva, Amy Simpson, Bill Smith, Huston Smith, Gary Snyder, Mary Kate Spencer, John Steiner, Brother David Steindl-Rast, Jeanie Stern, Norman Stiegelmeyer, Will Stocker, Barton Stone, Erik Storlie, Steve Stroud, Teah Strozer, Albert Stunkard, Jim Sullivan, Kazuaki Tanahashi, Katherine Thanas, Frances Thompson, Steve Tipton, Al Tribe, Fran Tribe (RIP), Ted Tripp, Elizabeth Tuomi, Helen Tworkov, Edward van Tassel, Jack van Allen, Helen Walker, Betty Warren, Bob Watkins, Sandy Watkins, Judyth Weaver, Steve Weintraub,

Mel Weitsman, Dan Welch, Jack Weller, Bill Wenner, Philip Whalen, Gerald Wheeler, Stan White, Tom Wright, David Whitaker, Wesley Williams, J.J. Wilson, Philip Wilson, Stephen Wiltse, Marian Wisberg (Derby, Mountain), Daphne Woodall, Tom Wright, and Barbara Young.

Throughout the book I have referred to people by their real names. By necessity, many people who were close to Suzuki were left out, and a few people in the book are, to a small extent, composite characters: Gen'ichi Amano (there were actually two godfathers); Yasuo Suetsune (who represents himself and Yasumasa Amada in the High Grass Mountain Group); and, in Part Two, George Hagiwara and Bob Halpern.

Contributions of further memories and stories about Shunryu Suzuki, lost lecture tapes or transcripts, or financial support to help continue the archiving work may be sent to: The Archive Project to Preserve Shunryu Suzuki's Teachings, Zen Center, 300 Page Street, San Francisco, CA 94102.

Bibliography

Anderson, Reb. *Warm Smiles from Cold Mountains: A Collection of Talks on Zen Meditation.* Rodmell Press, 1999.

Baker, Richard. *Original Mind: The Practice of Zen in the West.* Riverhead Books, 1999.

Barry, Ernie. "The Way of the Gateless Gate." *Berkeley Barb,* September 29, 1967.

Behr, Edward. *Hirohito: Behind the Myth.* Villard, 1989.

Brown, Edward Espe. *Tomato Blessings and Radish Teachings.* Riverhead Books, 1997.

Chadwick, David. *Thank You and OK! An American Zen Failure in Japan.* Penguin Arkana, 1994.

Doss, Margot Patterson. *San Francisco at Your Feet.* Grove Press, 1964.

Fields, Rick. *How the Swans Came to the Lake* (third edition, revised and updated). Shambhala, 1992.

Fujimoto, Rindo. *The Way of Zazen.* Cambridge Buddhist Assn. Inc., 1966.

Gaskin, Ina May. *Spiritual Midwifery.* The Book Publishing Co., 1990.

Gaskin, Stephen. *Amazing Dope Tales.* The Book Publishing Co., 1980.

Hiestand, Barbara, editor. *Chronicles of Haiku Zendo.* Haiku Zendo Foundation, 1973.

Jeschke, Matthew Paul. "The Interpretation of Zen in the West." Thesis, Division of Philosophy, Religion, and Psychology, Reed College, May 1995.

Kato, Kozo. *Soufuku (Running and Resting)*. Tomokichisha, 1994.

Kawashiri, Rumi. "Sokoji and Zen Center." Unpublished paper, Department of Anthropology, University of California, Berkeley, June 6, 1969.

Kaye, Les. *Zen at Work*. Crown, 1996.

Kozuki, Shigeo. "Kokoro no Furusato" (Hometown of the Heart), Nikkei, Tokyo, 1994.

Lahey, Denis Myo. "Climbing the Mountain Seat." Unpublished paper, Department of Sociology, University of California, Berkeley, 1972.

Leighton, Taigen Dan. *Bodhisattva Archetypes*. Penguin Arkana, 1998.

Matthiessen, Peter. *Nine-Headed Dragon River*. Shambhala, 1986.

Mitchell, Elsie. *Sun Buddhas, Moon Buddhas*. Weatherhill, 1973.

Mountain, Marian. *The Zen Environment*. William Morrow, 1982.

Needleman, Jacob. *The New Religions*. Doubleday, 1970.

Olson, Philip. *The Discipline of Freedom*. State University of New York Press, 1993.

Power, Brian. *The Puppet Emperor*. Universe Books, 1988.

Reischauer, Edwin O. *Japan Past and Present* (third edition). Knopf, 1964.

Richmond, Lewis. *Work as a Spiritual Practice*. Broadway Books, 1999.

Ross, Nancy Wilson. *Buddhism: A Way of Life and Thought*. Knopf, 1980.

Schneider, David. *Street Zen*. Shambhala, 1993.

Storlie, Erik. *Nothing on My Mind*. Shambhala, 1997.

Storry, Richard. *A History of Modern Japan*. Penguin, 1960.

Suzuki, Mitsu. *Temple Dusk*. Parallax Press, 1992.

Suzuki, Shunryu. *Zen Mind, Beginner's Mind*. Weatherhill, 1970.

Suzuki, Shunryu. *Branching Streams Flow in the Darkness: Lectures on the Sandokai*. University of California Press, Berkeley, 1999.

Tipton, Steve. *Getting Saved from the Sixties*. University of California Press, 1982.

Trungpa, Chogyam. *Born in Tibet* (third edition). Shambhala, 1985.

Trungpa, Chogyam. "Suzuki-roshi: A Recollection of Buddha, Dharma, Sangha." Garuda. Tail of the Tiger and Karma Dzong Communities, Spring 1972.

Tworkov, Helen. *Zen in America*. Kodansha, 1994.

Uchiyama, Kosho. *The Zen Teaching of "Homeless" Kodo,* Kyoto Soto Zen
Center, 1990.

Victoria, Brian. *Zen at War.* Weatherhill, 1997.

Wenger, Michael. *Thirty-three Fingers.* Clear Glass, 1994.

Wind Bell (publication of the San Francisco Zen Center), 1961–1998.

Wise, David Thomas. "Dharma West: A Social-Psychological Inquiry
into Zen in San Francisco." Ph.D. Dissertation, Department of
Sociology, University of California, Berkeley, September 1971.

Glossary

Definitions of Japanese, Sanskrit (Skt), and English words as used in this book.

abbot Used for *jūshoku*, chief priest of a temple or monastery.

Amida Buddhism (Amidism) A devotional form of Buddhism venerating the mythic/cosmic Buddha Amida (Skt: Amitābha). Includes Jōdo and Jōdo Shin Buddhism.

Avalokiteshvara (Skt) The mythic/cosmic *bodhisattva* of compassion who hears the cries of the world. Japanese: Kannon.

Bodhidharma (Skt) A semi-legendary Indian monk who became the first ancestor of Zen in China.

bodhisattva (Skt) Enlightening being, one who vows to awaken to ultimate truth together with all others.

bow Can mean Buddhist *gassho* or prostration, or the Japanese *ojigi*, wherein the head and upper body are tilted forward without the hands joining.

buddha (Skt) An awakened one, referring both to specific historic or mythic persons such as Shakyamuni Buddha and Amida Buddha, and also to ultimate awakened reality and to the possibility of awakening in all beings.

buddha hall *(hondō, hattō)* Central room in a temple where ceremonies and services are held before buddha images.

427

Daikoku-sama named after one of the seven gods of good fortune, women who lived, worked, and loved in Buddhist temples before it was permissible.

daioshō "great priest," an honorific title for priests.

danka The community of lay members/supporters of a temple in Japan.

dharma (Skt) The teaching, also the truth or reality that is taught, and the path to approach that truth.

dharma brothers Disciples of the same teacher.

dharma transmission The authorization to teach passed from teacher to disciple.

Diet The assembly of nationally elected legislators in Japan.

Dōgen, Kigen (Eihei Dōgen, Dōgen-zenji) The founder of Sōtō Zen in Japan in the thirteenth century.

dokusan A formal private practice or dharma-related interview with a teacher who has received dharma transmission.

Eiheiji In Fukui prefecture, one of the two head temples/training monasteries of Sōtō Zen (along with Sōjiji in Yokohama). Founded by Dōgen.

emptiness A technical term denoting the lack of inherent, fixed existence of any entity. Implies interconnectedness, relativity, and the dependent co-arising of all phenomena. Not a thing, rather the nature of all existence. Not nonexistence as opposed to existence. Comes from root meaning "to swell."

four-and-nine-days Traditional days of relaxed schedule in Zen monasteries.

futon Japanese mat-style bed and bedding.

gasshō Buddhist gesture or greeting with the palms placed together.

genkan Entryway.

geta Wooden platform sandals.

go An ancient East Asian board game, the national board game of Japan, played on a grid with black and white disk-shaped "stones." A deceptively simple and intricately subtle game traditionally enjoyed by Zen adepts. The winner of the game is the one who defines and gains the most space.

goza Thin grass mats used for sitting or bowing.

hai Yes.

Haibutsu Kishaku The persecution of Buddhists at the beginning of the Meiji era.

haiku A seventeen-syllable verse form usually emphasizing natural images with seasonal references.

hakama A pleated traditional skirt for men and women. Still used in martial arts.

han (literally, "wood") A wooden plaque struck with a mallet, used to call monks to the zendo and for other ceremonial purposes.

head monk *(shuso)* The training position for a monk who helps lead the teaching during a practice period.

Heart Sutra *(Hannya Shingyō)* The shortest and most widely used of the Prajñā Pāramitā (Perfection of Wisdom) Sutras, especially by Mahayana Buddhists; a concise distillation of the teaching on emptiness.

hibachi A cast-iron or earthen pot containing charcoal used for cooking.

Hōjō-san Title for the head priest of a temple.

ikebana Traditional Japanese flower arranging.

-ji, -in, and -an Suffixes used for the names of temples

jinrikisha A two-wheeled taxi pulled by a person.

Jōdo Shin-shū "The true school of the Pure Land," a faith-oriented sect of Buddhism, the largest in Japan. In the U.S. called the BCA, Buddhist Churches of America.

kanji Chinese characters (ideographs) used in Japanese writing.

kenshō (literally "seeing the nature") A sometimes dramatic experience of insight.

kesa Monk's outer patchwork robe signifying ordination (*okesa,* more respectfully).

kinhin Walking *zazen* or meditation.

kōan (literally, "public case") An exemplary story or dialogue to be used as a meditation object worked on with a teacher.

koromo The long-sleeved monk's robe of Chinese origin worn over the kimono.

kotatsu A low table covered by a blanket, heated from underneath.

kyōsaku The stick used to hit drowsy monks on the shoulder.

lay ordination A formal ceremony for lay people to take the precepts and express their commitment to Buddha's way.

ohaka Graveyard, place where remains, usually ashes, of the dead are interred (informally, *haka*).

ōryōki Monk's stacked and cloth-wrapped eating bowls.

manjū A Japanese confection made from rice flower and bean paste.

matcha Strong, thick, powdered green tea, served in tea ceremony.

Meiji The period of Japanese history from 1868 to 1912.

mochi Sweet glutinous rice cakes, especially popular at New Year.

mokugyō (literally, "wooden fish") A hollow drum carved from one piece of wood and struck with a padded mallet.

monastery Term used for large training temples for monks, nuns, and sometimes lay people.

monk Someone who has received home-leaving ordination and who lives according to monastic discipline and schedule.

Mountain Seat Ceremony *(Shinsanshiki)* A rite in which the abbotship of a temple is passed on to the abbot's successor.

mudra (Skt) A hand position or physical gesture or posture that embodies an aspect of Buddhist teaching.

nirvana (Skt) In early Buddhism, the cessation of all suffering. In Zen, nirvana is understood as ultimately not separate from everyday life and the worldly cycles of suffering.

Obon Japanese summer festival in which the spirits of the departed return.

pachinko An upright form of pinball machine, totally dependent on luck, played in noisy, crowded halls where one can win small prizes.

practice period *(ango,* "dwelling in peace") A time, usually three months, of intensive monastic training under the guidance of a teacher in a temple or monastery.

precepts Ethical guidelines of conduct for expressing buddha mind. They include taking refuge in buddha, dharma, and sangha, and a series of descriptions of awakened ethical conduct that begin with refraining from taking life.

priest Someone who has received home-leaving ordination (monk training), and who performs ceremonial and pastoral functions.

prostration *(raihai)* Full bow with the shins, forehead, hands, and elbows touching the floor.

rakusu Bib-like vestment received in monk or lay ordination.

Rinzai Zen One of the two main sects of Zen, emphasizing vigorous dynamic style and systematic kōan study.

rōshi "Venerable old teacher," respectful title for priest, Zen master.

sama Very polite form of address used after a person's name, more polite than *san.*

samādhi (Skt) A deep meditative state. Many specific samadhis are listed in Buddhist writings.

sangha (Skt) The Buddhist community. Originally the order of monks, later coming to include all practitioners.

satori A sudden flash of deep insight into the nature of reality.

seiza Traditional Japanese kneeling position.

sensei Title used for teachers, doctors, and other respected persons.

sesshin A concentrated *zazen* retreat of one or more days, usually five or seven.

shashu A formal position used in walking meditation, wherein the hands are held together at the solar plexus.

shiatsu Japanese pressure point massage.

shikantaza "Just sitting," *zazen* without a fixed object of concentration, emphasizing upright posture and presence.

Shinto Japan's indigenous spiritual tradition, involving veneration of nature spirits.

shōji Sliding door of wood latticework and translucent rice paper.

Shōwa The period of Japanese history from 1926 to 1989.

shū A religion or a religious sect or school, as in Sōtō-shū.

Shushōgi A compilation of important Sōtō writings put together in the late nineteenth century.

Sōjiji *See* Eiheiji.

Sōtō Zen One of the two main sects of Zen, emphasizing "just sitting" or silent illumination meditation and its application to everyday activity.

stick *See kyōsaku.* Not to be confused with the teacher's stick.

sumi Traditional black ink used in calligraphy and painting.

sūtra (Skt) Discourses of the Buddha, used for old Buddhist scriptures or scriptures to be chanted.

tabi White socks with a separate pocket for the big toe, worn with *zori*, *geta*, or other sandals.

Taishō The period of Japanese history from 1912 to 1926.

Taoism (also Daoism) An ancient Chinese religion/philosophy emphasizing an appreciation of nature and harmonious life.

takuhatsu (literally, "to entrust the bowl") Monk's formal begging.

tatami Japanese rigid straw floor mats approximately two inches thick and three by six feet in area.

tea ceremony *(chanoyu)* A formal, aesthetic method of preparing and serving tea, originating in Japan around the sixteenth century.

teacher's stick *(nyoi)* A short, carved, curved stick carried by teachers in formal situations, often with a tassel.

theosophy A Western spiritual movement founded in the nineteenth century in Europe, highly influenced by Eastern religions.

the ten directions Shorthand for everywhere: north, south, east, west, their midpoints, the zenith and nadir.

the three times Past, present, and future.

tokonoma An alcove in a Japanese room in which may be placed such objects as a calligraphy scroll, a stone, or a flower arrangement.

transmission *See* dharma transmission.

unsui (literally, "cloud and water") A monk, often novice monks.

whisks, horsehair and ox-hair *(hossu)* An emblem of a teacher, traditionally used to whisk away flies.

zafu *Zazen* cushion, usually black and round.

zazen Zen meditation, sitting meditation.

zazenkai In Japan, a regular lay *zazen* group, usually meeting weekly or monthly.

Zen A school of Buddhism originating in China which emphasizes *zazen,* direct insight, and actual experience of Buddhist truth in everyday activity.

zendō A Zen meditation hall, zazen hall. Also used herein for *sodō,* which in Japanese training monasteries is also used for sleeping and eating.

zenji A title meaning Zen master.

zōri Traditional Japanese sandals, thongs.